SOUNDING OUT THE STATE OF INDONESIAN MUSIC

A volume in the series
Cornell Modern Indonesia Project
Edited by Eric Tagliacozzo and Thomas B. Pepinsky

A list of titles in this series is available at cornellpress.cornell.edu.

SOUNDING OUT THE STATE OF INDONESIAN MUSIC

Edited by Andrew McGraw and
Christopher J. Miller

SOUTHEAST ASIA PROGRAM PUBLICATIONS

AN IMPRINT OF CORNELL UNIVERSITY PRESS

Ithaca and London

First published 2022 by Cornell University Press

Library of Congress Cataloging-in-Publication Data
Names: McGraw, Andrew Clay, editor. | Miller, Christopher J., 1969– editor.
Title: Sounding out the state of Indonesian music / edited by Andrew McGraw
    and Christopher J. Miller.
Description: Ithaca : Cornell University Press, 2022. | Series: Cornell
    modern Indonesia project | Includes bibliographical references and
    index.
Identifiers: LCCN 2021053928 (print) | LCCN 2021053929 (ebook) |
    ISBN 9781501765216 (hardcover) | ISBN 9781501765223 (paperback) |
    ISBN 9781501765230 (pdf) | ISBN 9781501765247 (epub)
Subjects: LCSH: Music—Indonesia—History and criticism. | Music—Social
    aspects—Indonesia. | Musical groups—Indonesia. | Performing
    arts—Indonesia.
Classification: LCC ML345.I5 S68 2022 (print) | LCC ML345.I5 (ebook) |
    DDC 780.9598—dc23
LC record available at https://lccn.loc.gov/2021053928
LC ebook record available at https://lccn.loc.gov/2021053929

Contents

Acknowledgments

This book springs from the fourth state-of-the-field conference of the Cornell Modern Indonesia Project, held March 29–31, 2018. We are indebted to Eric Tagliacozzo, the project's current director, for roping us into its latest endeavor. The conference would not have been possible without the extensive assistance of the Southeast Asia Program and its staff, particularly Thamora Fishel, James Nagy, and the indefatigable Divya Sriram. We are also grateful for financial support from the Department of Music, the Cornell Council for the Arts, the Comparative Muslim Societies Program, the American Institute for Indonesian Studies, the Cornell Indonesian Association, the Consulate General of the Republic of Indonesia in New York, and especially the Mario Einaudi Center for International Studies. Thanks to Ellen Avril and the Herbert F. Johnson Museum of Art for sponsoring the residency of Jompet Kuswidananto. Thanks to the Fulbright Foundation for supporting Danis Sugiyanto's participation and to their staff at its AMINEF offices in Jakarta, especially Alan Feinstein, for their crucial support for intellectual and artistic exchange between Indonesia and the United States. Thanks to SEAP Publications, and especially Sarah Grossman, for shepherding us through the publication process. Chris Miller would like to thank Marty Hatch and Kaja McGowan for their unwavering support. Most of all, we wish to thank the participants in the conference and the contributors to this volume for their creativity, intellect, and dedication to Indonesian music—and also for their patience.

Technical Notes

Language and Names

Non-English terms are set consistently in italics unless they are commonly used in English contexts. In most cases the original language is Indonesian. For chapters in which non-English text comes mostly from a regional language such as Balinese, Javanese, Minangkabau, or Sundanese, the language is identified in the notes for that chapter, and the abbreviation "I" is used to indicate Indonesian text or an English translation from Indonesian. For other cases, the language is indicated in full when it is not otherwise identified, or clear from the context or source, and when it is not a musical or other specialized and culture-specific term.

As in Indonesian languages, where nouns have no distinct plural form, number should be inferred from context.

Honorifics and terms of address, such as "I" and "Ni," "Bapak" and "Ibu," "Pak" and "Bu," are used sparingly, mostly to convey the sense of respect that would be expressed in interpersonal interactions. Otherwise, individuals are referred to by their last name—or in the case of many Javanese, their singular name—as in most English-language scholarship.

Audio and Video Examples

Several chapters make reference to audio and video posted online, much of it on YouTube. For the convenience of readers, and to allow for updating or substituting links for content that becomes unavailable, links are also provided on this volume's companion website at https://blogs.cornell.edu/soundingoutindonesianmusic/. Links and media associated with Philip Yampolsky's chapter are available only via this site.

SOUNDING OUT THE STATE OF INDONESIAN MUSIC

INTRODUCTION

Andrew McGraw and Christopher J. Miller

In March 2018, Cornell University's Southeast Asia Program hosted "Sounding Out the State of Indonesian Music" (SOSIM), the fourth in a series of state-of-the-field conferences initiated in 2011 by the program's well-known Cornell Modern Indonesia Project.[1] The three-day gathering approached Indonesian music both as a subject of academic scholarship and as an artistic practice pursued within and beyond Indonesia. Overall, the event involved some four dozen participants, in four paper panels, three roundtables, three performances, and a video exhibition, the majority of which is represented by the contributions to this book.

In the interval since the conference, much has happened—not so much in Indonesian music itself to render the perspectives of individual chapters in this book obsolete but more than enough in the world at large to bring certain key issues to the fore. The killing of George Floyd in Minneapolis in May 2020 was a tipping point in the heightened attention to anti-Black racism. Anti-Asian violence has also seen a marked increase, which cannot be ignored. A broader reckoning with social injustice is under way in many spheres, including academia. The Society for Ethnomusicology, among other such organizations, has been grappling with systemic racism and arguments that ethnomusicology itself is inescapably colonialist (Brown 2020).[2]

While these particular points of reference are primarily American, the larger issues are global and long-standing.[3] And so, we feel compelled to add to the proceedings a more direct assessment of the state of our field with respect to the heightened imperative to decolonize. The point is not to dwell on what we might have done differently—certainly not at the expense of overshadow-ing the very real contributions the conference and this book make—but to look squarely at where our field does fall short, and to identify the questions we ought to ask moving forward. Our field lies at some remove from the center of the most heated dialogues, yet it also emerges from colonial history and is entangled with the post- and neocolonial present. A reckoning with this predicament, which to date has remained underexamined, is overdue.[4] Accordingly, we offer some pre-liminary reflections below, following an introduction to this book proper, and an overview of other contributions to the conference that have not translated to print. But first, there's a most fundamental question: What exactly is our field?

Defining Indonesian Music

Our invitation to conference participants, and the title of the conference itself, "Sounding Out the State of Indonesian Music," effectively announced our scope of interest as Indonesian music—not Indonesian music studies, but Indonesian music. The latter is, of course, the former's subject of inquiry, but it also exists as a field in itself. Do we mean to take "Indonesian music" as our field? Yes, but lightly, with qualifications. For only some of the contributors does Indonesian music act as their primary field, for few if any would it be the preferred identification, and for nobody is it the most precise. Broadly speaking, all of the Indonesian citizens whose musical activities are described in these pages practice Indonesian music, whether they are in West Timor (Yampolsky), Java (Hadiraharjo and Ishiguro), Bali (Moore; Collier), Jakarta (Byl), or the United States (Hiranmayena). More specifically, they sing Tetun poetry, play Javanese *karawitan*, create underground rock or perform traditional Balinese theater, merge Batak musical preferences with pop idioms, or "re-fuse" mathcore for Balinese gamelan. Others run private studios (Catra), compete in Islamic recitation competitions (Rasmussen), or cre-ate new music within niche networks, elite and underground (Miller; della Faille and Fermont). Those who research Indonesian music recognize all the activity within this field as worthy of study, even if their attention remains unevenly distributed. The differential in spread on the practice side is even greater: several forms of gamelan have a robust transnational presence (Clendinning), while a vast layer of traditional musics remain entirely limited to specific local commu-nities (Yampolsky), and many popular musics ubiquitous within Indonesia have negligible presence outside the country.[5]

As editors, we do not seek to narrow this broad field. Neither the confer-ence nor this book are intended to institutionalize particular genres or academic approaches. We certainly do not mean to claim the vast territory of Indonesian music as ours in an act of intellectual colonization. Our intent is instead aspirational: recognizing Indonesian music as the field within which we all operate, and thereby recognizing our links to something larger. The conference reflected a predominantly North American perspective on Indonesian music, with limited representation of the field's international scope. This limitation, however, allowed us to more fully highlight the remarkable fluidity across the apparent binaries of academic/nonacademic, center/periphery, nonnative/native, and research/practice.

A Gathering of Research and Practice

In convening the conference we spoke of bringing together those who work primarily as scholars, mostly within the field of ethnomusicology, with those from in, around, and outside academia who work primarily as practitioners: as performers, composers, ensemble directors, and organizers. These distinctions of field are too fundamental to not acknowledge, but our priority was to emphasize what we share across these distinctions. For although our priorities and attentions may differ, we are all committed to a common cause: furthering an understanding of and engagement in Indonesian music.

In organizing the conference, we sought to highlight the extensive overlap and connection between constituencies, and to resist compartmentalization. Rather than a sideshow to the main attraction of panel and plenary sessions, performances were an integral component. Several presenters and chapter authors, and both of us editors, performed, and those who are primarily practitioners participated in panels, including the opening roundtable, held in Indonesian, with the master Javanese gamelan musicians from the featured ensemble Ngudi Raras. We thus broadened the scope of the proceedings beyond verbal presentations of research and highlighted the shared intellectual concerns of both discursive and practice-based activity, giving rise to fruitful discussions and provocations not typically encountered in academic conferences.

We make no attempt to represent these nonverbal components of the conference in the body of this book but do wish to register the significance of their contribution here. They served to ground the ideas presented in papers and raised at roundtables. Most of all, they pointed to the complexity of Indonesian music, especially in its transnational aspect. The core members of Ngudi Raras, some of the most revered musicians in the greater Surakarta gamelan scene, were joined by I. M. Harjito and Sumarsam, who for decades have taught at Wesleyan University, to display their deep knowledge of Javanese *karawitan*. The next evening, Rumput, a group of Americans from Richmond, Virginia, newly devoted to *kroncong*, played an eclectic set with their guest artistic director Danis Sugiyanto, who in this book offers an assessment of their accomplishments and the novel phenomenon they represent.

Rumput's set, on a program of "Kroncong and Kontemporer," included both standard *kroncong*, itself a crystallization of a long history of hybridization, and innovative fusions of *kroncong* and American old-time music—or "re-fusions," as Jeremy Wallach suggested at the "Priorities in Practice" roundtable, a formulation Putu Tangkas Adi Hiranmayena takes up in his chapter. The remainder of the program featured other instances of fusion and exploration. Andrew Timar, a composer/performer and founding member of Evergreen Club Contemporary Gamelan, performed a composition for solo *suling gambuh*.[6] Timar joined other conference participants Sugiyanto, Darsono Hadiraharjo, Jessika Kenney, and Christopher Miller in an improvisation based on "Yen Ing Tawang," a *langgam* by the Javanese songwriter Andjar Any, which Rumput had just played. Miller and his colleague Kevin Ernste, of the Cornell Avant-Garde Ensemble, paired up with Dimitri della Faille, appearing as Szkieve, to offer a second improvisation, informed by the practices of sound exploration and noise Miller and della Faille examine in their chapters.

The "Kroncong and Kontemporer" program helped fill out the picture of Indonesian music beyond the central figure of traditional gamelan performance, revealing just how far gamelan's extra-Indonesian existence has expanded beyond the paradigm of the collegiate world music study group—although that facet was also represented by the participation of the Cornell Gamelan Ensemble in the first part of the *klenengan*. Nevertheless, most non-gamelan facets of Indonesian music in North America have sprung in one way or another from the teaching of gamelan at academic institutions. Most of the members of Rumput, for example, became aware of *kroncong* through their involvement in Gamelan Raga Kusuma, a community gamelan cofounded by I Gusti Putu Sudarta and Andrew McGraw, a professor at the University of Richmond. As Elizabeth Clendinning describes in her chapter, the relationship between collegiate and community gamelan ensembles in America is often symbiotic. It is, however, independent groups such as Tunas Mekar—a community ensemble based in Denver and led by Putu Tangkas Adi Hiranmayena and his father, I Made Lasmawan—that set the standard of artistic excellence, and groups such as Sari Raras Irama, the Buffalo-based community group whose founding Matt Dunning discussed in the "Priorities in Practice" panel, have emerged as formidable generators of enthusiasm for gamelan.[7] American gamelan has become more than enrichment for a liberal arts education or ethnomusicological training. Interpersonal relationships have also grown beyond prescribed roles such as teacher and student, researcher and informant—as called for several decades ago by Jody Diamond (1990). Of this, the "Tribute to Pak Saguh," an improvisational collaboration between the vocalist and composer Jessika Kenney and the musicians Maho Ishiguro, Darsono Hadiraharjo, and Sri Mulyana (Saguh Hadi Raharjo's two sons) was a particularly poignant example—no doubt all the more so for the participants after Pak Saguh's passing a year later.

As the references in the foregoing account make clear, the conference performances resonate through the current book. For those participants whose words do not appear in these pages, there thankfully exists ample documentation of their work elsewhere.[8] Special note should be made, however, of Jompet Kuswidananto, whose video work was exhibited at Cornell's Johnson Museum of Art and screened during the "Sound Beyond/As Music" roundtable, and whose installation work graces the cover of this book. The promise of venturing further beyond music, whether through attention to sound-engaging artistic practices like Kuswidananto's, or through a more thorough engagement with the burgeoning field of sound studies, awaits future conference organizers and editors.

Overview

We now turn to the chapters in this book. Most contributing authors take the invitation to sound out the state of Indonesian music through close examinations of particular case studies. Wallach and Yampolsky offer more meta and explicit assessments of the state of our field, through, in Wallach's contribution, a review of Indonesian popular music studies and a proposal for new directions it might take, and in Yampolsky's chapter, a discussion of the ways commercial media select among Indonesian regional musics and influence the manner in which those selected are depicted.

Some contributors take a different approach. Darsono Hadiraharjo and Maho Ishiguro analyze the appraisal of the present-day Solonese gamelan scene offered by the members of Ngudi Raras at the opening roundtable, offsetting their rather dire assessment with observations of a few more hopeful developments. Dimitri della Faille collaborated with fellow experimental musician Cedrik Fermont on a preliminary report on Indonesia's burgeoning noise scene. Putu Tangkas Adi Hiranmayena and Jessika Kenney contribute reflections from practice that suggest far-reaching implications for how others might reconceive their own engagements with Indonesian music.

Among the remaining chapters there is much diversity, although certain patterns may be noted. A trend common to Indonesians and non-Indonesians alike is a move away from what ethnomusicologists sometimes call "the music itself." This accords with Marc Perlman's analysis in his contribution to the Cornell

Modern Indonesia Project's initial state-of-the-field conference and volume. The comparatively small amount of technical analysis in this book is in part a consequence of Indonesian music scholarship moving beyond a consideration of the inner workings of gamelan musics, but also tracks with shifts in American ethnomusicology from "natural history to theory, 'sound' to 'context,' and 'authenticity' to 'hybridity'" (Perlman 2014, 293). Despite these trends there is, of course, still much to say about the nuts and bolts of Indonesian musics, as demonstrated especially by the contributions to this book from Byl, Fraser and Hadi, Wallach, and Miller.[9]

The organization of the book mostly follows that of the conference. The themes of the six parts are not intended to intellectually segregate the nineteen chapters; we instead encourage readers to jump between chapters to discover the connections between them, and to productively play them off one another.

Contributions by Julia Byl, I Nyoman Catra, Elizabeth Clendinning, Darsono Hadiraharjo, and Maho Ishiguro are collected within the first part, "Musical Communities." Byl describes what she calls "harmonic egalitarianism" in vocal performances at Toba palm wine stands and music studios, focusing on the compositions of Viky Sianipar, a young Toba Batak producer, composer, and arranger. By moving beyond harmonic analyses, Byl is able to demonstrate the aesthetic continuities between traditional *gondang* music and Sianipar's modern music. She analyzes the ways in which Sianipar "skillfully merges Batak musical preferences and modern sound possibilities" in ways that have garnered him a large audience of *pop Batak* listeners. Through analyzing blogs and comments on music videos, Byl outlines the ways in which Sianipar has struggled to reconcile *tradisi* (tradition) and *moderen* (modernity) in his own Batak world beat music and manage its critical reception.

In his chapter, I Nyoman Catra first outlines a general history of performing arts patronage in Bali in order to contextualize a detailed analysis of the role of contemporary arts clubs—*sanggar*—that have flourished on the island since Reformasi.[10] While prior forms of patronage were overwhelmingly hierarchical (via the courts) or communal (through village, temple, or neighborhood support), modern *sanggar* are often organized and controlled by charismatic individuals with independent means. *Sanggar* also afford forms of sociality independent of traditional social networks, aligned instead along aesthetic affinity. Their emergence represents a major new node in the Balinese art ecology, interfacing with the traditional scenes of educational institutions, festivals, and religious ceremonies.

In her contribution, Clendinning analyzes the role of Balinese gamelan in catalyzing global communities, focusing on *sanggar Manik Galih*, directed by I Madé Lasmawan and Ni Ketut Marni. Beginning with the ensemble's performance at the 2018 International Gamelan Festival (in which Clendinning took part), she examines the "local, regional, and transnational concepts of community formed by the interrelationship between academic and community gamelan in the United States and their affiliates in Indonesia." These "interlocking" and "overlapping" community affiliations enable both the development of "local" (both Indonesian and American) culture and new forms of transnational collaboration. Clendinning examines the various forms of community that coalesce around gamelan both in Indonesia and America, each in their own way manifesting the Balinese concept of *desa, kala, patra:* appropriate place, time, and context.

In a coauthored piece, Hadiraharjo and Ishiguro describe recent changes in the professional lives of contemporary Central Javanese gamelan musicians (*pangrawit*). Their contribution emerged from the roundtable with members of Ngudi Raras noted above. Their frank conclusion is that "the prospects for *pangrawit* and *karawitan* are grim." They outline a general decline in the "quality of music, opportunities to perform," and "institutional and governmental support" that have severely impacted the livelihood of traditional *pangrawit.* Hadiraharjo and Ishiguro outline profound shifts in forms of patronage, temporal ideologies, audience tastes and expectations, religious ceremony, and pedagogies. In sum, the combination of these changes has led to forms of compression—fewer and shorter pieces for shorter, predetermined ceremonial schedules—and shifts from long-term, complex forms of social patronage to short-term economic transactions mediated by cash. Accompanying these shifts is the overwhelming popular preference for "light" styles such as *campursari*, which many *pangrawit* hold in disdain. The irony here is that, according to Hadiraharjo and Ishiguro, "the number of people involved in the Javanese performing arts is higher than ever" even while the performance of the traditional, "deep" repertoire of Solonese *karawitan* is in a severe decline. (This relates to the general trend Yampolsky observes in his survey of regional music on VCD, in which there is a pronounced bias toward "light" repertoire.)

Part 2, "Music, Religion, and Civil Society," includes contributions by Jennifer Fraser, Sumarsam, and Anne Rasmussen. Each deals with the interaction of Islam and music in Indonesia, a topic in which there is growing interest but one that nevertheless remains less integrated and somewhat marginalized within Indonesian music studies. Fraser, in collaboration with Saiful Hadi, analyzes the expression of Islamic moralities in *saluang* performances in West Sumatra. They explore the "interactive intimacies" in *bagurau lapiak*, a form of *saluang* performance found in roadside stalls at the edges of town, and the fringes of Minang moral life, where "behaviors outside the normative standards of Islamic propriety occur." Some of these songs include explicit lyrics that may be described locally as *porno*, suggesting that widespread and romanticized narratives regarding Minang Muslim piety should be reconsidered and "expanded to take into account the plural realities of contemporary Minangkabau lives." Fraser's exploration of this scene is structured partly as an economic ethnomusicology of the financial interactions within *bagurau lapiak* performances.

Sumarsam's contribution continues his research program on the history of Islam in Indonesian performing arts. Here he is especially interested in problematizing the view of "Islam against the performing arts" that sometimes emerges in Indonesia (and globally). The vital connections between the arts and Islam go deep in Indonesia. In his chapter Sumarsam examines historical evidence of Islamic textual invocations in *wayang golek* performances from the North Coast of Java. He unravels a mysterious invocation used in both Javanese *wayang golek* and Balinese *wayang kulit* referring to the "hand, water, pen, and ink." Sumarsam argues that this invocation, often associated with the Bhima Svarga tale, is an ancient veneration of writing traditions that came to the *pasisir* (precolonial coastal cultures) through Islamic maritime trade networks.

Rasmussen picks up Sumarsam's historical thread, tracing the archipelago's Islamic musical traditions since 1945 and looking at how "the pendulum [swings] between the sound worlds of the Arab Gulf" and local Indonesian traditions. She analyzes a 2017 debate at the intersection of religion, politics, and the arts, in which Islamist hard-liners (*Islam keras*), aligned with contemporary Saudi forms of piety, vigorously protested a single performance of Qur'anic recitation in a style labeled *langgam jawa* rather than Arab *maqamat*. How does melody become politicized, Rasmussen asks, when, according to her interlocutors, those who decry the "aesthetic disobedience" of the recitation have only a vague understanding of the content and context of such melody? Rasmussen connects the incident to the rise in Indonesia of Islamic populism, and the effects of Saudi Arabian soft power.

Rebekah Moore, Danis Sugiyanto, Jeremy Wallach, and Philip Yampolsky offer analyses of popular musics and media, collected in the third part of the book. Moore analyzes the activist, "vernacular cosmopolitanism" of the Balinese rock band Navicula, demonstrating how they have "used their music and star power to encourage Indonesia and the rest of the world to take action on our most urgent environmental crises." Moore traces the "pathways" of Navicula's cosmopolitanisms, showing us how their global environmental awareness manifests in uniquely Balinese forms of activism, action, and protest. As in Wallach's contribution, Moore also describes how Navicula's style and success "contradicts old narratives about cultural flows from the West to the Rest." Resonating with an argument presented later in Wallach's contribution, Moore unambiguously positions herself as a hardcore fan of Navicula's music. This is, for her, good music, and this view has informed her analysis of its meaning and efficacy. More importantly, she focuses on the ways in which Indonesian popular musicians respond to the role the West has played in exacerbating local economic and environmental crises. Through close ethnographic storytelling Moore describes how, through their music, Navicula urges Western actors (scholars, tourists, and fans) to reconsider their ethical responsibilities to cultural others.

Sugiyanto describes trends in *kroncong* scenes, outlining the close aesthetic and social links between *karawitan* and *kroncong* communities in Solo, and the recent globalization of the genre, focusing on the Virginia-based ensemble Rumput, whose performance at the conference Sugiyanto led. He presents a reception analysis of local (Indonesian) responses to the globalization of *kroncong*, documenting a largely positive attitude.

In his chapter, Jeremy Wallach reconsiders the history of popular music studies in Indonesia and presents a novel paradigm for the analysis of post-Reformasi-era popular music studies. Prior analyses, Wallach suggests, were preoccupied with nationalism, democratization, totalitarianism, and identity, viewing popular music primarily (or only) as a form of political protest or resistance. Post-Reformasi analysis should, he argues, consider underground music studies and forms of localization in apparently globalized styles. As a response to the dissolution of "area studies" paradigms in anthropology and social sciences, Wallach argues for "solidarity in the face of general disciplinary fragmentation." Indonesian societies *do* exhibit strong forms of cultural coherence, alongside cultural difference, plurality, and global cosmopolitanisms. Such local cultural coherences, he argues, can be identified and analyzed in even apparently global forms such as metal and pop in Indonesia. Wallach argues that a narrowly political framework is not sufficient for such analyses, which would depend on "music's specific aesthetic properties." The challenge, according to Wallach, "is creating an analytical language that can access the distinctiveness."

Yampolsky's chapter, which was the keynote address at the SOSIM conference, ranges across the archipelago, assessing the influence of commercial media on cultural representation and change in regional music, both popular and traditional. Focusing on the VCD format, introduced in Indonesia in the mid-1990s, he analyzes what musics are and are not represented in this medium and the extent to which regional genres are "adapted to national conventions and standards." He ends his contribution with a critique of ethnomusicology's current focus on popular music and global media flows, which, he argues, tends to discourage scholarly attention to the documentation of regional traditions not represented in commercial media. Yampolsky maintains that such a preoccupation allows localized traditional forms to go unrecognized and undocumented.

Contributions by Dimitri della Faille and Cedrik Fermont and Christopher Miller make up "Sound beyond and as Music," part 4 of the book. Della Faille and Fermont's coauthored, descriptive contribution presents a scene analysis and biographies of some of the most important noise and sound artists working in Indonesia in the late 2010s. Their chapter explores in journalistic detail the emergence and evolution of underground noise scenes in Indonesia and their international connections to similar scenes distributed throughout Southeast Asia.

In his contribution, Miller focuses on a new approach to composition pioneered in the late 1970s by young musicians at the performing arts academy in Surakarta. In taking the "exploration of sound" as its "starting point," this approach relates to the broader "sonic turn" in music, which, as Miller argues, anticipated and fed the rise of sound studies. Miller triangulates between Indonesian sound exploration, sound studies, and the broader trend of sound as music, pointing out how prevailing understandings of the latter two fall short in explaining the rise of the former. Ultimately, he identifies a deeper cultural basis for sound exploration, identifying its roots in an acoustemology specific to Indonesia.

The fifth part of the book, "Music, Gender, and Sexuality," includes contributions by Bethany Collier, Henry Spiller, and Christina Sunardi. Collier analyzes the recent resurgence of children's *arja* theater troupes in Bali (*arja anak-anak*, *arja remaja*). She argues that the embodiment of gender in these ensembles has the "potential to disrupt the . . . endurance of conventional gender ideals as iterated and reinforced by Indonesian national and Balinese local ideologies." Such ideologies have traditionally sustained male authority while muting female voices in the public sphere. Collier argues that *arja*'s pedagogical process works against this dynamic by privileging female voices and exposing students to a wide range of "possible expressions of the feminine [while facilitating] the safe exploration of these roles." This affords young Balinese women the opportunity to experiment with alternate relationships between voice, body, and social space.

Spiller's contribution describes the emergence of female *rampak kendang* (choreographed group drumming) in West Java in the 2010s. While the form itself emerged in the 1970s, female performance is a new phenomenon, one that presents new implications for gender ideology in Sunda. Female *rampak kendang*, Spiller argues, "further illustrates the role of the performing arts in establishing, reinforcing, and challenging the norms of gendered behaviors in West Java." He concludes that while the form creates new spaces for "troubling" and "challenging" entrenched gender ideologies, *rampak kendang* primarily functions to reinforce existing ones.

In her contribution, Sunardi explores the intersection of gender, dance performance, and gamelan in Malang, East Java, focusing on the spiritual power of femaleness in cross-gender dancing. Ethnographic encounters with male, female, and transgender (*waria*) dancers reveal a fluid continuity of gender, including the performance of "female masculinity" and "male femininity" and the "layering" and "revealing" of performed gender roles. Nevertheless, Sunardi identifies an "underlying femaleness" in the *tayub* dances she analyzes, linking this "magnetic female power" to the ancient Hindu concept of *shakti*.

The sixth and final part, "Perspectives from Practice," opens with a poem by Jody Diamond, a veteran of the North American gamelan scene, followed by chapters by the practitioners and scholars Putu Tangkas Adi Hiranmayena and Jessika Kenney. Hiranmayena describes the aesthetic and social connections he experiences between American mathcore and Balinese *gamelan beleganjur*. By arranging a mathcore piece for *beleganjur*, he explores and problematizes his own multiple musical and cultural identities. According to Hiranmayena, his arrangement "critiques and frustrates genre categories" and "temporal ideologies" through "an auto-ethnographic inquiry." His central frame in this exploration is the Balinese concept of *benen mua*, or "fixing one's face," the performance of an outward attitude to social others. This lens allows him to explore issues of cultural appropriation that are often elided in the American gamelan scene.

We conclude the book with an experimental and reverential offering from the renowned singer Jessika Kenney in which she proposes a "transcultural Islamic feminist exegesis" through a sound philosophy linking Javanese and Persian sonic practices. Here she explores the "transdisciplinary" form of a verbal/visual score to invoke the sounding of text as a form of contemplative reading. Through this she connects spiritual musical practices to "Islamic feminism," "sound studies," "experimental practices," and "creative liturgy." Her inspiration and teacher for this practice is the Solonese *pesindhèn* (singer) Nyi Supadmi (Supadminingtyas), who for Kenney "offered the image of. . . [a] transcultural Islamic feminist *pesindhèn* engaged profoundly with the interpretation of sung text." Through shifting between Javanese and Persian mystical poetry and Qur'anic exegesis, Kenney is able to outline a powerful model for transcultural contemplative singing in which "multiple sources of knowledge and experiences do not cancel each other out in their multiple origins but rather are mutually and materially altered, resulting in surprising visions of the future." Hers, then, is a spiritual praxis that parallels what we hope to contribute to the scholarly study of Indonesian music and sound more generally.

Indonesian Music and the Challenge of Decolonialism

Returning now to the issues we raised at the outset of this introduction: What is the state of our field in terms of decolonialism and the persistent inequities that project seeks to address? There is no simple answer for the field as a whole.

Indonesian music as practiced by Indonesians is obviously not a colonialist enterprise. Neither is the study of Indonesian music by Indonesians, although that might be conditioned by an Indonesian analog to what Latin American theorists term "coloniality."[11] What about Indonesian music as practiced or studied by non-Indonesians?

The crux of the issue in the recent debate within the Society for Ethnomusicology (SEM) is the question of who studies whom. The charge from Danielle Brown that ethnomusicology *"is and can be nothing other than a colonialist and imperialistic enterprise"* (2020, emphasis in original) followed from her observation that the field consists of "predominantly white members" who "by and large research people of color." Related conversations on social media debated the ethics of writing about or performing the music of a social group to which one does not belong, tending toward a position sociologist Rogers Brubaker usefully characterizes as "epistemological insiderism," defined as "the belief that identity qualifies or disqualifies one from writing with legitimacy and authority about a particular topic" (Brubaker 2017). Some commentators realized that this stance, while potentially protecting Black musics from misrepresentation and misappropriation by white scholars and performers, also traps individuals with those identities within their racial domains. Brown herself did not argue that "those who spent decades studying a culture have no right to teach and write"; rather, she called for changing the system to put "people of color . . . at the forefront of telling their stories until some sort of equity is reached." The lack of equity, from Brown's perspective, stems not only from being in the minority—according to its 2014 survey, only 4.8 percent of SEM's membership identified as African American—but from white scholars insisting that they be recognized as the experts.

Indonesian music studies is by no means free of such imbalances. Out of the twenty-one conference participants who have contributed to this book, only five are Indonesian: I Nyoman Catra, Darsono Hadiraharjo, Sumarsam, Danis Sugiyanto, and Putu Tangkas Adi Hiranmayena. This is perhaps slightly better than the ratio in English-language publications and conferences overall, but far short of where we ought to be. All of those five were present in the United States at the time, supported by American institutions, but only one held a tenured position. Sumarsam remains the sole Indonesian ethnomusicologist at a professorial rank at an American university.

A number of factors make it far more likely that white Americans are the ones teaching in universities (and editing volumes such as this one), while many of our Indonesian teachers live in comparative poverty, unable to compete in the Western academic labor market or to access higher education's resources. Systemic racism is one of the reasons for this situation, but others more specific to Indonesian music studies are no less important. Compounding the linguistic and geographic divides, and that based in the substantial economic dispari-ties between Indonesia and the West, the expectations of North American and Indonesian academia differ significantly. Incentives and institutional support for presenting at international conferences and publishing in international journals are not robust in Indonesian performing arts institutions. Frustratingly, this has contributed to parallel and sometimes disconnected bodies of research and dis-course about the Indonesian arts between Indonesian and international academ-ics, institutions, and scholarly networks, perpetuating the colonial (and neoco-lonial) control of the production of knowledge. In the 1990s and early 2000s, American organizations such as the Ford Foundation and the Asian Cultural Council invested substantially in graduate training for Indonesian arts faculty and establishing graduate programs in Indonesia; these initiatives went a certain distance in bridging the gap, but there is farther to go.

Another factor is the hierarchical relationship between research and practice. Advancement in fields such as ethnomusicology in North American institutions is based overwhelmingly on one's publication record, reinforcing the sense of separation from one's subject of research. In this model, academics refine and abstract the "raw material" of local cultural workers. This bifurcation is less severe in Indonesia, as seen at the ISI and ISBI (Institut Seni Indonesia and Insti-tut Seni Budaya Indonesia) national conservatories in Bandung, Denpasar, Yog-yakarta, Padang Panjang, and Surakarta. Yet there remains a distinction between ISI faculty and *seniman alam*, the "natural artists" who are recognized as the true masters of performance traditions but are simultaneously marginalized due to their lack of academic credentials.

While scholars of Indonesian music are caught up in these paradigms, we also tend to be grounded by practice—whether that is playing and composing for gamelan, leading a *kroncong* group, running a *sanggar*, or acting as a tour man-ager for a rock band. This provides a means to maintain an ongoing direct con-nection with the communities we study, by moving beyond the walls of academia to engage non- and even anti-academic performers, composers, and thinkers, and to participate in new forms of community building and dialogue. Engage-ment in Indonesian music can thus function as decolonializing praxis, at the same time as our research derives strength from the ways in which we move flu-idly between performance, creation, collaboration, interpretation, and abstrac-tion, learning from the endless feedback loops emerging from different modes of intellectual inquiry and expression.

From this perspective, engagement in practice is positive. But for those of us who are not Indonesian, is it also problematic? North Americans involved in gamelan have remained somewhat insulated from the thornier issues surround-ing other musics, such as those connected to sizable diasporic communities.

Indeed, part of gamelan's appeal to liberal arts institutions is the apparently less complicated version of multiculturalism it offers, one apparently less compromised by the history of racism, exploitation, and violence that is impossible to ignore in African music ensembles, for example.[12] Nevertheless, one occasionally encounters the sentiment that the many gamelan in American institutions would be better off in storage.[13] This view is consistent with the logic of epistemological insiderism, and of moral contagion, in which *gamelan* in America are inextricably associated with colonialism, and assumes their performance by non-Indonesians necessarily constitutes an act of cultural appropriation.

Is it appropriation, in all the negative senses the term implies? To be sure, a great many non-Indonesian gamelan players—whether American, or Japanese, or British, or Australian—have made the music their own. But arguably they have managed to do so without taking it away from anyone else, in no small part because theirs remains an amateur endeavor. This is certainly not to say that our field is immune from such issues—Hiranmayena raises several in his chapter. But on balance, the attitude of Indonesians toward the American engagement with the Indonesian performing arts is one of approbation. Danis Sugiyanto presents several positive reviews of an American *kroncong* ensemble (cofounded by McGraw), in which his Javanese interviewees explicitly reject suggestions of appropriation. Promoting American gamelan ensembles is a strategic component of Indonesian cultural diplomacy. Such ensembles, as Dr. I Made Bandem once argued to McGraw (personal communication, July 2003), demonstrate the power of Indonesian culture to turn *bule* (white Euro-Americans) "partly into Indonesians." In 2007 the renowned composer I Wayan Sadra argued that, like Western art music, gamelan had achieved the status of a "global culture" owned by no one in particular and open to transformation by anyone. Do such positions reflect the attitudes of "colonized minds"? Are these actors cultural traitors? We do not think so. In Sadra's case, he articulated appeals to the potential universality of gamelan while simultaneously expressing decolonial stances and modeling forms of non-Western experimentalism.

Sadra's comments get at a reality on which the SOSIM conference and this book are predicated: that certain prominent aspects of Indonesian music, and Indonesian music studies—which in our working definition is a distinct but inextricable component part of Indonesian music—are now undeniably and irreversibly transnational. As with so much in the modern world, how this came to be is tied to a colonialist history. But rather than dooming us to repeat the past, we believe the current state of our field puts us in a better position to realize a more fully postcolonial future. The networks formed by the myriad individual connections between Indonesian and non-Indonesian researchers and practitioners provide a basis for increasing the level of interaction between English- and

Indonesian-language scholarship—a task easier to realize with the normalization of teleconferencing in the wake of the COVID-19 pandemic.[14] We believe this to be the best basis for correcting the imbalances in Indonesian music studies we have identified here: to increase not only the number of Indonesians working at US institutions and in American-dominated scholarly societies but also the international attention paid to Indonesians producing knowledge in the form of practice and publications in Indonesia. There remains, however, much work to be done, not only in the realm of scholarship but equally importantly in furthering social justice in Indonesia and for Indonesians living in the United States, and concretely advancing the lives of our Indonesian teachers, peers, students, collaborators and communities.

NOTES

1. The first conference resulted in the 2014 volume edited by Eric Tagliacozzo, current director of the Cornell Modern Indonesia Project. Several earlier generations of faculty involved with the project, which was initiated in 1956, played a major role in building Indonesian studies. The current initiative seeks to facilitate exchange between the field's numerous intellectual traditions.

2. See also Stephen Amico's call for "the end of ethnomusicology" (2020) along with responses from Aaron Fox, Anna Schultz, and Naomi Waltham-Smith.

3. Connecting explicitly with Black Lives Matter is the Papuan Lives Matter movement. See Gunia 2020 for a preliminary account. We thank Jessika Kenney and Jeremy Wallach for bringing this to our attention.

4. See, however, Sumarsam 2013; Spiller 2017; Wallach and Clinton 2019. At the SOSIM conference, several of its featured performances and collaborations modeled decolonial interventions, as did Jessika Kenney's presentation. Apart from these, and Putu Tangkas Adi Hiranmayena's critique, direct engagement with issues relating to the legacy of colonialism and the persistence of inequities, to the extent it occurred, did so primarily at the interstices of the paper sessions, sometimes in post-panel discussions.

5. There is, however, the intriguing case of burgeoning American interest in *dangdut*, alongside that in *kroncong* described by Sugiyanto in this book, notable for occurring largely outside academia. For a preliminary account see Wreksono 2018. Wreksono points to Andrew Weintraub, who in addition to authoring the first book-length study of the genre (2010) started the band Dangdut Cowboys, but he focuses on Rissa Asnan, an Indonesian music producer living in Delaware who is the driving force behind the singing competition Dangdut in America. See http://dangdutinamerica.com/ as well as the initiative's YouTube channel, https://www.youtube.com/channel/UCs1Y5GvoDETeq4I6-b1go2A.

6. The Evergreen Club is Canada's first gamelan ensemble, and one of the few anywhere outside Indonesia that operates as a professional new music group.

7. To these two we could add a very long list of well-established ensembles across North America, including Sekar Jaya, Kusuma Laras, and many others. See Clendinning 2020.

8. Diamond, whose presentation is only partially represented in this book by her poem, has archived much of her work, including the 1990 article referenced above, at http://www.gamelan.org/jodydiamond. Much of Timar's output as a music journalist, composer, and performer can be found at https://evergreenclubgamelan.com/music. Dunning's community-building efforts, now extending well beyond Buffalo, include the

online Gamelan Masters Guest Lecture Series he organized during the COVID-19 pandemic, archived at https://nusantaraarts.com/guest-lecture-series.

9. Also notable is the thread of scholarship concentrated on the technical analysis of Balinese gamelan, sustained in large part by the ongoing vitality of performative and compositional practice related to the *kebyar* and *kontemporer* aesthetics. We omitted this important corner of the field in anticipation of it being covered by a parallel symposium on contemporary gamelan, planned by Michael Tenzer in Vancouver, which unfortunately did not take place.

10. Reformasi refers to the period of political reform following Suharto's ouster in 1998.

11. In Anibal Quijano's initial formulation, "coloniality of power" points to the persistence of social, epistemological, and cultural hierarchies imposed by European colonialists, hierarchies whose specific force derives from the existence of European, mestizo, and Native populations in Latin America. Quijano and others such as Walter Mignolo have expanded the concept as intertwined with modernity; see Quijano 2007 and Mignolo 2011.

12. See the contrast between different cases in Solís's 2004 edited volume.

13. This sentiment was expressed by a departmental colleague to one of the contributors to this book.

14. The potential of teleconferencing, and of doing so bilingually, was admirably modeled by the inaugural conference on Indonesian studies co-organized by the American Institute for Indonesian Studies and Michigan State University. See https://asia.isp.msu.edu/aifis-msu-conference-indonesian-studies.

WORKS CITED

Amico, Stephen. 2020. "'We Are All Musicologists Now'; or, the End of Ethnomusicology." *Journal of Musicology* 37 (1): 1–32.

Brown, Danielle. 2020. "An Open Letter on Racism in Music Studies, Especially Ethnomusicology and Music Education." Email posted to the Society for Ethnomusicology's email discussion list, sem-l@indiana.edu, June 12. Posted also at https://www.mypeopletellstories.com/blog/open-letter.

Brubaker, Rogers. 2017. "The Uproar over 'Transracialism.'" *New York Times*, May 18. https://www.nytimes.com/2017/05/18/opinion/the-uproar-over-transracialism.html.

Clendinning, Elizabeth. 2020. *American Gamelan and the Ethnomusicological Imagination*. Chicago: University of Illinois Press.

Diamond, Jody. 1990. "There Is No They There: Global Values in Cross-Cultural Research." *Musicworks* 37: 12–23.

Fox, Aaron A. 2020. "Divesting from Ethnomusicology." *Journal of Musicology* 37 (1): 33–38.

Gunia, Amy. 2020. "A Racial Justice Campaign Brought New Attention to Indonesia's Poorest Region. Will It Translate to Support for Independence?" *Time*, December 15. https://time.com/5919228/west-papua-lives-matter-independence/.

Mignolo, Walter. 2011. *The Darker Side of Western Modernity: Global Futures, Decolonial Options*. Durham, NC: Duke University Press.

Perlman, Marc. 2014. "The Ethnomusicology of Indonesian Performing Arts: The Last Thirty Years." In Tagliacozzo 2014, 293–326.

Quijano, Aníbal. 2007. "Coloniality and Modernity/Rationality." *Cultural Studies* 21 (2–3): 168–78. https://doi.org/10.1080/09502380601164353.

Sadra, I Wayan. 2007. "International Gamelan Festival Amsterdam 2007. Menegakkan Identitas Global Gamelan." *Gong* 92 (7): 52–53.

Schultz, Anna. 2020. "Still an Ethnomusicologist (for Now)." *Journal of Musicology* 37 (1): 39–50.

Solís, Ted, ed. 2004. *Performing Ethnomusicology: Teaching and Representation in World Music Ensembles*. Berkeley: University of California Press.

Spiller, Henry. 2017. *Javaphilia: American Love Affairs with Javanese Music and Dance*. Honolulu: University of Hawai'i Press.

Sumarsam. 2013. *Javanese Gamelan and the West*. Rochester, NY: Rochester University Press.

Tagliacozzo, Eric. 2014. *Producing Indonesia: The State of the Field of Indonesian Studies*. Ithaca, NY: Cornell Southeast Asia Program Publications.

Wallach, Jeremy, and Esther Clinton. 2019. "Theories of the Post-colonial and Globalization: Ethnomusicologists Grapple with Power, Media, and Mobility." In *Theory for Ethnomusicology: Histories, Conversations, Insights*, 2nd ed., edited by Harris M. Berger and Ruth M. Stone, 114–40. New York: Routledge.

Waltham-Smith, Naomi. 2020. "For Transdisciplinarity." *Journal of Musicology* 37 (1): 51–62.

Weintraub, Andrew N. 2010. *Dangdut Stories: A Social and Musical History of Indonesia's Most Popular Music*. New York: Oxford University Press.

Wreksono, Amsara. 2018. "The United States of Dangdut: A Struggle to 'Shake' America." *Jakarta Post*, May 23. https://www.thejakartapost.com/longform/2018/05/23/the-united-states-of-dangdut-a-struggle-to-shake-america.html.

Part I
MUSICAL COMMUNITIES

1

HARMONIC EGALITARIANISM IN TOBA PALM WINE STANDS AND STUDIOS

Julia Byl

The 2018 production *Preman Parlente*—the "Stylish Street Tough"—boasts a screenplay by playwright Agus Nur, the comedy of Butet Kartaredjasa and Cak Lontong, and the backing of the Djarum Foundation, the cultural arm of Indonesia's largest clove cigarette manufacturer. This high-powered Javanese collaboration is all the more surprising considering that the action is set in the cultural domain of the Batak ethnic groups, who have long felt marginalized in what they often perceive as a Java-centric Indonesia. Essentialization is still partially at work here—the character of the *preman*, or gangster, is associated with the North Sumatran city of Medan and the Batak individuals who control it (Ryter 1998, 48). And yet the palm wine stand that provides the setting for the drama is a perfect corollary for the *warung*s (small eating establishments) that have nurtured Javanese and Indonesian televised comedy for years. *Preman Parlente*, then, is a significant addition to the mainstream national stage, adapting comfortable tropes to a different cultural conversation.

The musical talent behind the production is Viky Sianipar, a young Toba Batak producer, composer, and arranger whose career has been on the rise since his 2002 album, *TobaDream*, shook up the regional Batak music industry with its innovative world beat arrangements and production finesse. I recall seeing (with great interest) Sianipar's songs in rotation on Indonesian MTV in Sumatra in 2002 and 2004. Since then, Sianipar has released four more volumes of *TobaDream*, along with *Indonesian Beauty*, a collaboration with musicians from Aceh, Java, and West Sumatra. He also produced Tongam Sirait's 2004 album *Nommensen*, a tribute to the German missionary who brought Lutheranism to the Toba Batak in the 1860s, and choral harmony to its popular music. And if he but knew, Sianipar could also claim to be the most popular Toba Batak musician I have ever introduced to the North American students in the world music classes I have been teaching for more than a decade.

Assigning Sianipar's work was not my initial intent. Having studied Toba Batak music—ritual and popular alike—through ethnographic fieldwork since 1999, I was eager to introduce the informal music making of the palm wine stand (called a *lapo* in Toba Batak) to my students, and I turned to YouTube to familiarize them with the songs of the vocal trios most commonly sung there. They revolted. The unfamiliar falsetto harmonies, the stilted choreography, the clichéd production values, and above all the matching embroidered vests led students to openly deride this music. My solution was to switch in Sianipar's 2002 "Piso Surit," a video full of moody shots of the artist playing the piano in the rain forest, and a well-mixed, modern arrangement with hints of electronica. Yet although this piece was more popular with students, I felt that by privileging Sianipar and jettisoning the local songs on YouTube, students were missing out on understanding something key about Toba Batak musical communities.

Sianipar's movement—and with him, Batak cultural formations—into the national mediascape is predictable considering the diversification of media and the enhanced autonomy of the "outer islands" during Indonesia's post-Reformasi era. Media scholar Gareth Barkin has written on the "cultural bumpering" noticeable in television shows of this era, wherein regional cultural elements (a close-up of weaving, or a dancing hand) make it into a show's transitions or promotions, but not necessarily into the show itself (Barkin 2006, 365). Indeed, such a discussion is familiar from scholarship on Indonesia's *pop daerah*, as when Philip Yampolsky (1989, 14) or Jeremy Wallach (2008, 36) debates the true significance of a regional flute, constrained by the regular bars of a pop song. Viky Sianipar's music breaks free from these constraints—both musically and semantically—and this chapter will articulate how he skillfully merges Batak musical preferences and modern sound possibilities in a way that has resonated with many *pop Batak* listeners. And yet, reading Sianipar's oeuvre as an unmitigated triumph misses a more interesting story of cleavages between the rural, the regional, and the national, and the musical subjectivities of each of these constituencies. Although my larger understanding of Batak cultures is rooted in ethnographic research, in this chapter I write as a critic, analyzing Sianipar's aesthetic, his compositions, and their reception from afar. I train my analysis on a series of blog posts from the beginning of Sianipar's career, in which his listeners actively comment on the social and political aspects of musical creativity and ownership.

Taking a closer look at Sianipar's music and different responses to it—those of Jakartans, North Sumatrans, and of course, my own response contained tacitly in my analysis—allows us to parse the difference between representing Toba Batak culture in mainstream Indonesia and representing the musical experiences of Toba Batak individuals.

Batak Bildungsroman

Viky Sianipar, the youngest child of a mixed Toba Batak and Sundanese family, was born in Manggarai, a neighborhood to the south of Jakarta with very few Sumatran families. His father, Monang Sianipar, moved from Medan, North Sumatra, to Indonesia's capital as a part of a large migration of Batak families in the decades after the Indonesian War for Independence (1945–49) (Bruner 1972, 209). After first accumulating capital through growing a cargo business, his father opened a recording studio, MS Production, which took its place within a Toba Batak pop industry that had continuously released albums of soloists and vocal trios since the 1960s. And yet it was not this legacy that brought Sianipar to Toba Batak music, although Sianipar would release his 2002 debut through his father's studio. Rather, Sianipar was afforded enhanced opportunities from childhood, ranging from training at a local music academy to a trip to Berkeley, California, to learn English and jazz guitar. Pointedly, he admits to preferring the Beatles to *pop Batak*.

A revealing set of blog posts published in 2008 (and still available as of this writing) called *A Journal of Viky Sianipar* lays out in vulnerable detail the musician's movement from an adolescent ashamed of his *marga* (Toba Batak: clan name, in this case "Sianipar") to a mature musician who sees his ethnic heritage as a font of musical creativity. In a post titled "It Turns Out Batak Music Is Cool," he viscerally describes his feelings: "At that time all I knew of Batak was the endless boring *Bona Taon* parties [yearly gatherings of *marga*], the loud and often vulgar speech of my relatives from Medan, the three stones music of a shrieking vocal trio, and wedding parties with filthy food preparations that made me nauseous each time I attended one" (Sianipar 2008b).[1] Toba Bataks who have gone to enough wedding parties at *adat* halls (large rented buildings designed to hold the ritual activity, or *adat*, of Batak families) would not be bothered by the custom of divvying up raw meat among kinship groups (Byl 2014, 69). The simplicity of the three familiar chords (I–IV–V) that give the name to the description "three stones music" is precisely the reason that this music can be sung by audience members as well as performers. But Sianipar's reflections are an alternative view, refracted through the alienation of a modern, non-Toba-speaking second-generation teenager, forced to witness experiences he had no connection to. Naturally, the epiphany—that Batak music is actually *keren*, "cool"—comes to Sianipar not in Jakarta's steamy *adat* halls but at the high vantage point of Tongging Hill, when Sianipar visits Lake Toba in Sumatra as part of a music event planned by his father.

This natural landmark is the name of both the blog and the second track on *TobaDream* volume 2, "Tongging Hill," dramatized in a music video directed by Sianipar's older brother Bismark. The blog post, published online around five years after his debut album, is written at the pivot point between self-reflection and self-promotion—half reflection on Sianipar's own personal experiences, and half justification of them to a growing audience: "I admit that I can't speak Toba Batak, but I am learning," he states in Indonesian (Sianipar 2008b). Taken together, the blog and video are a sort of audiovisual bildungsroman—a coming-of-age story, through folly into true wisdom. Here I refer less to the local stories of Arjuna and Krishna than to European models of Young Werther and Goethe, for Sianipar finds his freedom through the Western mediums of staff notation and pen (or keyboard).

The video for "Tongging Hill" begins with a shot of Viky Sianipar in cutoff sweats, his feet propped on a table strewn with his drafts of musical manuscripts. The studio is well appointed, both modern and traditional: Toba Batak carvings and weavings are strategically placed in the background, while the panning shot foregrounds an old industrial fan, specifically curated for a retro vibe that is nonetheless very modern. The edit cuts to close-ups of the musician's pensive face and ink-stained fingers, fluently writing rests and notes with a ballpoint pen. In the musical track, a solo male voice sings a declamatory cadence in Karo Batak, the language of the group who live near Tongging. In short order the studio dissolves into a shot of Sianipar, wearing the same red-and-white hoodie, gazing at Lake Toba from this height, the focus of both the thoughts and the notes in the studio.

The portions of the video shot on site in North Sumatra differ markedly from the trope of choreographed women in costume characteristic of other *pop Batak* productions, although it participates in other clichés. Writing on Sianipar's guitar playing in the Indonesian magazine *Gatra* in 2003, music critic Carry Nadeak states that "what is lacking in this album is variation in guitar melodies" and characterizes his playing as "monotonous" (Nadeak 2003). When Sianipar is joined in village scenes by his electric guitar, that icon of musical cosmopolitanism—showing it to children seated around a traditional house, standing with it behind them as they jump naked off of a cliff into the water, soloing soulfully on the windswept peak—one can't help wonder where the amplifier is stashed and which audience it is directed at.

A novel element of "Tongging Hill" is the conscious decision to not subsume traditional elements into a modern sonic wash—a technique that Sianipar uses effectively in other tracks on the album. The village scenes are intercut with footage from the studio, and when Toba Batak musician Korem Sihombing and two other traditional musicians enter the studio, the electric guitar switches abruptly to the sound of the ritual *gondang sabangunan*. This is a considered decision as one of the instruments in *gondang*, a set of five tuned drums, is melodic as well as rhythmic, and it exhibits a vastly different tuning system from that played by Sianipar's electric guitar. Rather than trying to integrate the tunings, Sianipar arranges regular "trade-offs" between the guitar and drum kit, and the *gondang sabangunan*, linking them only by simple unison accents that coincide with the syncopation of the traditional patterns. In the video, Sianipar is seen emphasizing these accents as the musicians play, after having first conspicuously shown them his plans in the musical manuscript: the sense is of a master composer executing his vision. And yet, because the traditional musicians are given leave to play their ritual music as they see fit, the utility of such guidance is doubtful—they had certainly played such melodies countless times in the very Toba Batak ceremonies that Sianipar admitted to despising in the past, and Western notation was likely never a part of their performance.

Curiously, the video shows the traditional musicians arriving at the studio in their shirtsleeves, high-fiving the Sianipar enthusiastically. I should stress that the late Korem Sihombing, the singer and *sarune* player, was a long-term collaborator with Sianipar, suggesting respect and a shared vision. Still, a Toba Batak man in his shirtsleeves automatically connotes the milieu of the *lapo tuak*, or palm wine stand—the domain of the *preman parlente* and other ruffians. In contrast, ritual musicians are highly respected officiants, elevated by music meant to mediate with the divine, and they usually attend ceremonies in matching red, black, and white uniforms. This is not to say that the traditional musicians are not allowed to try on other elements associated with a Toba Batak social experience—the high five did not seem at all forced. But the scenes of the video, taken as a coherent narrative of Sianipar's musical transformation, show a conflation of musical traditions and audiences—in this case, ritual musics and popular audiences. Similarly, the electric guitar in the village does not convey a composer ready to absorb regional, rural music and the social experiences that frame it, as much as a Jakartan Batak bringing "coolness" to rural North Sumatra. For a national, urban audience that has never been to the Batak heartlands, it is natural to trust in Sianipar's ability to incorporate all of these cultural and musical perspectives. As we shall see, sometimes this trust is warranted, and sometimes it is not. For quite often, and with good reason, the village and the *lapo* prefer the music of the shrieking vocal trios of *pop Batak*.

Answering Back to Brother Viky

One of the hallmarks of Viky Sianipar's early years was his vulnerability and openness. He told the story of his transformation into a Toba Batak man proud of his musical heritage on multiple media platforms, which required a thorough rehearsal of his earlier ignorance—a brave narrative eschewed by many would-be media stars. This smart rhetorical technique was aimed at other culturally disenfranchised Batak youth, attempting to bring them to an appreciation of Batak music by way of his compelling story. (Of course, Sianipar also wanted to bring them to the store to buy the *TobaDream* album, revealing a key insight of the 2000s: that journaling can go hand in hand with marketing acumen.) At the end of every blog post on the website, most of them published in 2009, Sianipar opened up comments to his fans, and in the early years of the blog he read and answered them, sometimes engaging multiple times with the same person in a dance of mutual appreciation and persuasion. He was responsive and self-reflective: the blog post titled "Is Viky Ruining Batak Music??" received over one hundred responses, positive and negative, and still remains online ten years later as a transparent archive of the transformative moment when his music began to seep into the community of Batak listeners. For the most part, the responses were very positive, even effusive, such as the comment by Situmeang, recognizing the promise of Viky's new sound: "I hope Vikys upon Vikys are born, smart with no 'copy paste'" (Sianipar 2008a, comment from January 8, 2009). And yet the tensions between ritual Batak music, *pop Batak*, and Sianipar's newly coined "Batak world beat" also comes through—and are commented on by Sianipar himself, making the 2008 blog an archive of contrasting assumptions about Batak music.

The Musical Work: "Don't Forget Your Staff, Grandfather"

"HAS VIKY SIANIPAR'S MUSIC LOST ITS AUTHENTIC BATAKNESS?" Sianipar broaches this topic himself in the first line of his blog post, which rather good-humoredly replicates the all-caps challenges sometimes lodged at him. He counters, "Authentic Batak music is not TRIO songs, with shrill voices on high notes, "three stones" chords—i.e. only the chords I, IV, and V—and screaming saxophones. That is the result of MODERN ARRANGEMENT. And if they arrange Batak music in their way, yeah, I can do the same . . . make my own arrangement in my own way" (Sianipar 2008a). Sianipar's target here is what he feels to be the dated arrangement used in contemporary Toba pop songs. Indeed, even ten years later, contemporary Toba Batak songs still replicate many clichés: they are arranged for trios singing in three-part harmony, often at the top of their ranges; they feature fluty keyboards approximating the sounds of bamboo flutes in the transitions between verse and chorus, as well as an instrumental break with, more often than not, a robust, 1980s-era saxophone. In the words of Situmeang, they are "copy-paste." If Sianipar is anything like the undergraduate students in my classes, this arrangement style makes him as queasy as the wedding party food he describes above.

Sianipar, on the other hand, is a contemporary musician. Following North American music industry conventions developed to credit producers as music creators, Sianipar's name is listed on iTunes and YouTube as the author of tracks that only "feature" the songwriter and primary vocalist. The age of the remix is familiar to North American readers, but not everybody is used to its assumptions. The proposition of arranger/producer as composer is untenable to Roony, who writes on the blog: "Please brother viki sianipar don't ruin existing music, if you want to make a change in batak music, don't mix up the music or songs that are already out there, it is your own compositions that you need to mix up" (Sianipar 2008a, comment from August 6, 2008). Roony is not alone. He is joined in his critique by Lagubatak, who is "less than sympathetic with the style of adapting left and right, and adding our name as the owner" (Sianipar 2008a, comment from August 29, 2008). One of Viky Sianipar's primary contributions to "updating" Toba Batak music is his understanding of the process of arrangement as an essential component of the audio track—in the words of musicologist Albin Zak, "the recording process becomes one of deliberate composition, and its product, an original musical work" (Zak 2001, 13). But for Roony, there is something deeply unsettling in this extension of authorship. For him, arrangement and production does not count as a composition, a *ciptaan*—such a thing requires new melodies, harmonies, and lyrics.

Sianipar's response is cutting. He abandons his casual Indonesian for Toba Batak: "Olo, ompung, na uli, ompung" (Yes grandfather, very well grandfather). At first glance, this language appears respectful. "Ompung" is the word used for one's own grandfather as well as for elders occupying this kinship position. Sianipar's invocation of the words, then, could recall the cadence of formal kinship oratory, or perhaps an attempt of an urban grandson to engage respectfully with his Toba grandfather in the village. The subsequent lines, dripping with sarcasm, turn this feeling on its head, as "ompung" is translated as someone decidedly out of touch: "but do read the writing written above, grandfather … careful you don't stumble, grandfather, and don't forget your staff . . . . . grandfather" (Sianipar 2008a, response to comment, August 6, 2008). Although he purports to engage with Roony, Lagubatak, and those like him, he writes them off in a simulacrum of politeness. He assumes that their opposition is due to a lack of engagement with his music and methods, and that their protests are the feeble bleats of a dying generation.

Collaboration: "How Can I Get the Cassette?"

For the commentators who felt so engaged by Viky Sianipar's music to seek out
and answer back on his blog, the prevailing feeling is a pride in a new domain
of representation for Batak culture, one with enhanced musical innovation
and production values. And yet the ability to represent the category "Batak" is
not automatically conferred by a clan name: the Batak group is not one discrete ethnolinguistic category but is made up of at least five distinct groups,
all with their own land, language, and musical traditions. Because the Toba
Batak group is one of the largest and most recognizable nationally, many of
the other Batak groups—the Karo, the Simalungun, the Mandailing—tend to
feel as if they are an afterthought, and they resent the Toba for a tendency to
cancel out difference. Such a criticism can certainly be lobbed at Sianipar—
TobaDream features songs that are known as Simalungun and Karo, sung in
these languages by Toba Batak musicians. In the *lapo* in Medan, I have heard
criticism of Sianipar's co-optation of non–Toba Batak music—for instance,
that the musicians on his album get the ornamentation wrong, drown out a
subtle melody with an overpowering church vibrato, or simply sing the wrong
lyrics. Certainly, some level of wistfulness or even envy may be at work here,
such as a wish that Karo or Simalungun singers might gain a level of compa-
rable acclaim, and that their ethnic groups might gain representation in the
Indonesian mediascape.

This perspective is not evident in the blog. On the contrary, many non–Toba
Bataks praised Sianipar's efforts, such as Thomy Mariyono Tarigan's assessment
of the interpretation of the Karo song "Piso Surit": "As long as I've lived, perhaps
this is the first time I've heard a Karo song played on MTV. Don't ever stop being
inspired!" (Sianipar 2008a, comment from April 25, 2008). Others reached out to
ask that Sianipar turn to their traditions for inspiration, such as M. A. Nasution
(a Mandailing Batak name), who urges Viky to use Mandailing songs and the *gordang sambilan*, a drum tradition related to (but distinct from) the Toba *gondang*
we have already seen. Sianipar's response deserves an airing: "Actually, I've long
wanted to develop [*manggarap*] *Gordang Sambilan* but until now I haven't found
a player. . . . I need a person who will collaborate, who can be directed, who is open
to Western music. If not, we will argue the whole time. If I can find a player, I will
wipe up [*melibas habis*] Mandailing music" (Sianipar 2008a, response to comment, May 5, 2008). Sianipar's difficulties in finding collaborators are detailed
more thoroughly later on in the year, when a cool-headed commentator (who
decries both "the tendency of Bataks to criticize" as well as the "emotional pro-
[Sianipar]-contingent") exhorts him to work together with traditional musicians
instead of simply being inspired by traditional music. Sianipar responded with

a numbered list of complaints about traditional musicians. Some concern a lack of facility with Western musicianship:

1. Not all understand the tempo, beat and language of international music.
2. Not all are able (or want to study) to memorize music parts.

Other complaints concern professionalism:

5. Not all of them can come ONTIME. . . .
7. Not all of them want to be directed by a "snot-nosed junior musician" like me.

The frustration of fieldworkers in adapting to the habits of traditional musicians is legendary, so we can certainly understand the friction between the studio and the *adat* hall. And yet, Sianipar's invocation of "quality standards" raises the question of whether true collaboration with ritual musicians is even possible: "Not all are idealistic"; "not all understand the mission that I am pursuing"; "not all understand the essence of traditional Batak music" (Sianipar 2008a, response to comment, October 2, 2008). There is a whiff of the zealotry of the recent convert here. I am reminded of a comment Sianipar, who admits to just beginning to learn his ancestral language, left elsewhere, in Toba Batak, to a German-dropping Toba Batak expatriate: "If you have already achieved success across the sea, don't let yourself not want to speak Batak, okay? JBU" (Sianipar 2008a, comment from April 5, 2008). This is a surprisingly conservative position for such a globalized musician to make online—indeed, one that an *ompung* or grandfather in the village might voice—but like the industrial fans in the music video, retro conventions are often used for modern ends. Of course, Sianipar is speaking from his own complex cultural experience, but he risks jettisoning and writing over the lived musical experiences of the individuals he uses for source material. Technological mediation is evident in the collaboration as well as the composition and execution. Sianipar's response to a Simalungun Batak man offering up the tradition of *gonrang Simalungun* is not to find a traditional musician to study from but to ask, "How do I go about getting the cassette?" (Sianipar 2008a, comment from March 18, 2008).

Social Life: "Singing in the Bathroom"

Occasionally, Viky Sianipar would garner praise from readers who, on further reading, wished to put Sianipar's songs into rotation with the older *pop Batak* that Sianipar himself derided. One reader commenting on the blog apparently did not get the brief about avoiding cliché instrumental breaks: "But if I can give you a suggestion Brother Viky, it might be even more amazing [Toba Batak: *makyos*] with a saxophone" (Sianipar 2008a, comment from August 29, 2008). Parrude-Rude likes Sianipar's "modern Batak music" but nevertheless asks that his next album feature a trio: "If there is a trio, it is fun . . . even more so for the down-and-out who can forget about their stress when singing together . . . and drinking *tuak* in a wine stand. The positive side of singing in a trio is the philosophy of togetherness" (2008a, comment from August 18, 2008). Sianipar consistently exhorts his fans to not only read his words, as above, but to listen to his music intently—a practice that can be done alone, with earphones on, after the purchase of a CD. This suggestion is reminiscent of Thomas Turino's characterization of the "capitalist-cosmopolitan formation" (Turino 2000, 119) that often stands at odds with the participatory social ethos of traditional musical communities. Parrude-Rude rejects the suggestion that listening is the ultimate musical activity by suggesting that the trio style that formed the past three decades of *pop Batak* is better suited to the Batak social ethos than the single-voiced, experimental sound compositions of Sianipar: "If Batak music is only solo singing, then Batak people will only sing alone in the bathrooms, becoming egotistical and individualistic" (Sianipar 2008a, comment from August 18, 2008).

More than semantic sparring, the comment field of Sianipar's blog is an ontological battlefield. At stake are three major issues: whether the recorded track is a legitimate composition; whether musical collaboration that eschews engagement with different Toba constituencies can result in meaningful representation of them; and whether the act of individual listening can replace the social act of performance. Each issue challenges the embedded social experience of Batak music. Casting arranging as a modern, prestigious form of composition can deemphasize the acoustic domain of sung words and strummed chords. To rearrange the words of media scholar Douglas Kahn (who writes of the recording as a "machined fusion of orality and literacy"), literacy has outflanked orality (Kahn 1992, 5), as is the case in the video, when Sianipar waves his inked manuscript at hereditary musicians who have learned through oral tradition. Drawing inspiration from sound recordings rather than from traditional musicians turns "collaboration" into the extraction of sonic data from sterile recordings, rather than a process of working with complex, irritating people who open up their musical worldviews to each other—and the resulting "representation" is arguably the musical divorced from the social and the cultural. Recasting the "three stones" chords of trio harmony as a cliché stylistic remnant from the 1980s, rather than a linked social and musical structure, writes over the experience of the *lapo tuak*, in which these conventions are still very much in mode. And yet, the overwhelmingly positive response to Sianipar's music from his very engaged audience—who, like the high-fiving ritual musician, can presumably exist in multiple musical styles and ontologies at once—demands a more subtle analysis. This requires both taking Sianipar's music seriously as compositions and understanding how *pop Batak* music is realized socially, in informal musical settings in Jakarta and Medan.

Harmonic Egalitarianism

The track "Ansideng Ansidoding" was released on the first *TobaDream* album in 2002. The song was originally composed by Nahum Situmorang, a prolific 1950s songwriter whose work makes up the corpus of much Toba Batak popular song. Part of Sianipar's brilliance is his ability to make songs sound "traditional" within innovative arrangements. "Ansideng Ansidoding" is sung by Korem Sihombing, a singer whose voice sounds surprisingly like a traditional bamboo flute with its breaks and quivers—and the text of the song also revels in the precolonial (or at least prechoral), as it is about Sisingamangaraja XII, a hereditary Batak ritual and resistance leader who was killed in 1909 by the Dutch. Although early songbooks confirm that "Ansideng Ansidoding" was written by Situmorang, I had not heard of the song before hearing Sianipar's arrangement of it. And yet elements of the song sound much more like precolonial musical traditions than popular music from the 1950s or the 2000s—for instance, the words of the chorus, "o among amonge" (oh, oh father) harken back to an almost extinct mourning tradition called *andung*. Picking this particular song shows a subtle taste that is not governed by the demands of the pop market but is rather the act of an artist curating a particular sonic palette.

The arrangement is where Sianipar's skills are best exhibited. Like major producers in other realms of world music, such as Bollywood's A. R. Rahman, Sianipar creates an additive texture, where a sparse first verse is updated the next time around by a wash of strings, then intensified with a choppy rhythmic motif on the guitar. A high chime sound is subtly mixed into the interstices of the phrases, able to consistently break through the arrangement's increasingly layered frequencies. And yet the acoustic realm is prioritized as well, whether in the tentative, flutelike sounds of Korem Sihombing's voice, or the way the guitar is recorded—so that the sound of fingers stopping or starting strings provides not only the piece's rhythm but also a sense of its intimacy. Sianipar's complaint about "three stones" music— that is, compositions that rely overly much on the tonic, dominant, and subdominant chords—is also taken seriously: in the third verse of "Ansideng Ansidoding," the synthesized strings and strummed guitars progress downward chromatically from the tonic by four half steps, realizing all of the complex harmonies that such a movement requires. But how does such a piece play in the social spaces of Medan or Jakarta—the *lapo*, or on the front porches of houses where young people gather to sing and make music? The obvious answer is that it is not played, or rather, not performed. Sianipar is right—we really do need to listen to the track. His major contribution is the arrangement of the song, and if the mix of the recording is the true musical realization of a digital arrangement, then the piece is fundamentally altered each time it moves outside of the recording. If such a song—written in the 1970s by Nahum Situmorang and recently popularized by Sianipar's arrangement—is then sung by the multiple voices in the *lapo*, the logic of the remix fails, the song ceases to be Sianipar's, and it reverts to Situmorang. The difference between these different types of authorship is that Sianipar's exclusive claims are bound up with copyright and sales, whereas Situmorang's creative output—born of, debuted in, and reportedly even composed in the *lapo*—is decidedly more egalitarian and communal in character (Byl 2014, 138–39).

Unlike their regional neighbors—the Malays in North Sumatra, or the Javanese in Jakarta—Toba Bataks are well known for their egalitarian social structure. Different clans are endowed with spiritual power through their ancestors, but any member of the clan is able to assert the title of *raja*, and his daughters, *boru ni raja*—daughters of kings. A social display of hierarchical deference, such as that described in Central Java by Benjamin Brinner (1995, 18), would be absolutely out of place in Toba musical life, even in the ritual realm. This tendency often comes across in social singing traditions in both formal and informal settings, reflecting precolonial traditions and colonial transformations.[2] The polyphonic SATB arrangements sung by the Toba Batak church choir on Sundays (and practiced in rehearsals held in the houses of community members throughout the week) are a relatively egalitarian musical setting when compared with, say, liturgy guided by a cantor: it is a lay practice in harmony with Protestant traditions that emphasize the right of all believers to come to God and interpret scripture. In fact, many Toba Batak churches will have so many choirs that even the role of conductor, a talented man or woman from the congregation, is not as elevated as it might be otherwise. Similarly, *lapo tuak* singing is notable for its extension of the right to participate to anyone who knows the song, or who will sit long enough to learn it. And although the *lapo* too is a site where many works of songwriter Nahum Situmorang are sung—as well as those of Gypsy Tampubolon and Iwan Simatumpang, prolific songwriters of the 1980s and 1990s—these songwriters are not autocratic. Their songs neither assert the right of artistic expression due to a composer nor demand the aural attention of their audiences: their ascendancy is determined by popular voice.

Even the charge that conventional *pop Batak* songwriting is nothing but three easy chords—reserving the complex harmony and voicing for those who have studied Western music and can write it on staff paper—is far from the truth. Moreover, this assumption misses how the tradition of Toba Batak songwriting has been conditioned by the local aesthetics. For the moment, let's grant the I–IV–V critique: that conventional Toba Batak music is limited in its harmonic language. A cursory analysis of traditional *gondang* patterns shows why (*gondang* is the name of the ensemble, while the instrument of the five tuned drums, *taganing*, is one of two melody bearers within the *gondang* ensemble). Because the tuned drums allow for a range of only five notes, a common pattern entails playing a phrase on three drums (or an accompanying flute/double reed instrument), then repeating the entire melody as a sequence, moving up or down a drum; another approach involves repeating a pattern but ending the phrase on an adjacent drum. If the *taganing* tune seen in figure 1.1 was arranged for a pop vocal trio—as it was in the mid-twentieth century—you can easily see how the translation of a melodic sequence and the up-down pairings might rely on a I–V progression. In the initial iteration, the first and third *taganing* drums suggest a tonic, while the concentration on the second and fourth notes in the next four measures graphs onto a V^7 chord. The basic functional harmony suggested by these patterns might appear simplistic when compared to the functional harmony of Protestant hymns—but this comparison decidedly misses the point. The *gondang* repertoire was banned for decades by the colonial government and Lutheran missionaries (Purba 2005, 214), and so a brief progression with its suggestion of *gong*s and *gondang* might not have been a poor imitation of European music but rather a respite from it.[3]

Yet I'll not concede that most Bataks inhabit a world of diminished chords, either. Quite the opposite. The sum total of harmonic knowledge is not a hoard for the trained but is dispersed generously among every person in the palm wine stand or church choir, even the ones who never can quite hit the high note. I have argued elsewhere that the three-part harmonic voicings of the Toba Batak *lapo* repertoire are worked out collaboratively between whoever is available to sing, on the fly (Byl 2014, 180). In the informal contexts of Toba Batak music making, vocal harmonization is not a rarefied skill but a social activity that even the most amateur musicians engage in, even if with imperfect intonation. These skills are honed primarily by listening to and singing *pop Batak*. Its songwriters' harmonic language originated in Lutheran chorales and American revival hymns, both of

FIGURE 1.1 Sequential melodic motives played by the *taganing* (tuned drums)

which were sung by Bataks from church benches beginning in the first decades of the past century. As you can see in the transcription in figure 1.2, many such songs have more than three chords (or "stones"). The common *lapo* song "Songon Bulan" uses a ii–V–I progression, followed by a secondary dominant seventh of IV. Crucially, the ii chord progression is suggested by moving the first phrase's musical motive up one pitch—an absolutely commonplace gesture in songwriting, but also in the melodies of the *gondang* ensemble. The secondary dominant seventh chord, on the other hand, is certainly derived from hymnody—indeed, the missionaries who proselytized in the Batak lands were Pietist Lutherans who loved (and taught) nineteenth-century American hymns, a tradition replete with such harmonic features. In less technical language, trios call the latter chord an "escort" or *pengantar* chord—a homey metaphor suited for an aspect of social music making rather than for a compositional technique. Far from a pale comparison, then, "pre–Viky Sianipar" Toba song is a resilient tradition with deep roots in the lived social experience of Toba music—of churchgoers and gong lovers.

I have not yet heard Viky Sianipar's songs sung in the *lapo tuak*, perhaps because their cunning features are not well suited for that particular social context. The subtle mixing of gonglike sounds is unavailable in the palm wine stand, and so his compositions—his tracks—have a comparatively small sound print there. The tuned drum, *sarune*, electric guitar, and keyboard are mixed to share sonic space in Sianipar's tracks, but the only mixing one encounters in the palm wine stand involves the drinks.

FIGURE 1.2 "Songon Bulan" (Dakka Hutagalung), first verse in a *lapo* arrangement

And yet, perhaps there is a way to recognize Viky Sianipar's considerable skill and ambition and the prestige his work bestows to Toba Batak music, while validating the music making that goes on alongside and outside of his musical and aesthetic milieu. A suggestion by blog respondent Togi Sianipar may allow us to have it both ways. Togi Sianipar very much enjoys the music of the musician from his own *marga* and concedes that the style of the older trio music belongs to a "past time" (though neglects to specify if he listens to it nevertheless). But at the end of his comment, he also suggests that "it is possible that even Viki Sianipar's music will be STALE in 8 to 10 years." As I write now, thirteen years after the posting of this comment, I can testify that Sianipar's singular musical vision is still the primary national exponent of Toba Batak music. In addition to headlining regular events held in the nation's capital, he has recently garnered national recognition with two Anugerah Musik Indonesia awards in the category of Production of a Regional Language Song—in 2015 for *TobaDream* volume 4, and in 2016 for a song on the soundtrack of *Toba Dreams*, a film that boasted national actors realizing a distinctly regional story.

Viky Sianipar's career, fostered by a rich and well-connected father, also tells a *national* story about economic and cultural power in post-Reformasi Indonesia. The sponsor of *Preman Parlante*, the 2018 play described at the beginning of this chapter, was the Djarum Foundation, an organization that supports a diverse array of cultural programming, well produced and well advertised. In truth, this organization's very existence is really a prong of a corporate social responsibility campaign that is meant to detoxify a toxically fragrant clove cigarette company, PT Djarum (Welker 2014), a corporate strategy that has become more and more important in the diversified industries of post-Suharto Indonesia. Sianipar too seems sincere when he describes the larger engagement with Toba Batak music that he hopes his music to foster, for which he has opened the Viky Sianipar Music Centre, a large compound housing a studio and music club. This endeavor, though, is also founded on capitalist aspirations whose benefits are accumulated rather than dispersed: the authentic Toba-style house carving that adorns the music center also frames a 7-Eleven and incorporates a small billboard that has been rented out by clove cigarette companies. Of course, the late New Order period originated the co-optation and coercion of the cultural signifiers of Indonesia's "outer islands," most notably in the Taman Mini theme park described by John Pemberton, in which a Javanese child marvels at Sumatran singing (Pemberton 1994, 156). The post-Reformasi era has witnessed the increased commodification of these cultural signifiers, in which the ostensibly noble goals of cultural promotion and national integration are sometimes inseparable from marketing and distinctly noncultural promotion. The website for the music center states that the 7-Eleven is only there to support the Batak music that goes on in the studio. And yet when we recall (for one final time) the blog post in which Sianipar explains why he does not collaborate with traditional musicians, this altruistic impulse is alloyed: "8. Not all musicians are willing play music without demanding MONEY, even though in the end they will be paid as well" (Sianipar 2008a, comment from September 20, 2008).

Of course, getting one's money in the end may be acceptable for investors, but most ritual musicians demand to be paid on the day of the party. Perhaps a better metaphor for what Sianipar is trying to do is the ritual compensation system used in Toba Batak *adat* halls, where a portion of raw meat and a meal for the musicians is given not in compensation but as a gesture of respect. For surely, Sianipar holds Toba Batak musical heritage in high regard. There may be an arrogance in requiring someone to listen, really listen to you, as if the mere act of listening would dissolve all critique, even critique lodged outside of the domain of the musical. But there is also an earnest desire to *be heard*, and though Sianipar's songs are rare in the *lapo*, they are heard on the phones of eager young musicians and then rendered acoustically in performance spaces (by none other than the sons of my own principle *gondang* informant, G. Sitohang, among others). This collaborative reimagining of Sianipar's compositions occurs through live performances in Medan's Taman Budaya (Culture Park), in the ethnomusicology program at Universitas Sumatera Utara, and on tour with Viky Sianipar's group throughout eastern Europe.

The interpretation of Sianipar's work vis-à-vis the wells of Batak musical thought that animate it, then, is not a black-and-white proposition due to the multiplicity of Toba musical experiences—*gondang* music, but also notated chords, creativity expressed collectively in the palm wine stand *and* individually in the studio. I find it easy to be shaded one way or the other, as I watch the politics of representation shift in other contexts. On the one hand, consider the controversy surrounding the 2019 Indigenous Music Awards in Canada, in which Inuk musicians Tanya Tagaq, Kelly Fraser, and Piqsiq boycotted the awards due to the inclusion of a song by the Cree musician Cikwes, who used *katajjak* (Inuit throat singing) techniques herself without sufficiently engaging proper means of transmission. By suggesting that *katajjak* must be connected to "the land (nuna) of the far north" (Cecco 2019), Tagaq explicitly refutes ownership based in general categories of indigeneity rather than engagement with a specific land and its singers and speakers— and I suspect that some of Sianipar's online detractors might recognize this insistence on mutual experience. On the other hand, consider Joshua Tucker's study of highland elements in Peruvian *huayno* music, in which he argues that "indigenous people's engagement with urban modernity is often used as evidence to deny their rights" (Tucker 2011, 388), or the genre of South African *maskanda*, a music represented as "precolonial" by colonial and apartheid regimes alike, which in actuality "articulates the distinction between deep Zulu and contemporary urban experiences, by hovering in between them" (Titus, forthcoming 2022, 13).

Sianipar's license to be at once an urbane Jakartan and a musician of Toba descent is in fact eagerly invoked by others. The hip hop group Siantar Rap Foundation, for instance, is a group of Batak city dwellers who hail not from the Indonesian capital but from Siantar, the rough-and-tumble city an hour from Lake Toba, where the streets are full of Batak languages. Significantly, I knew of this group because of their participation in the Jakartan production *Preman Parlante* (with Viky Sianipar as music director), their rap segueing directly into the sound of the *gondang*; on listening to the group's recent YouTube offerings, I can discern in the mix the sounds of a village bamboo flute, the songs of Nahum Situmorang, and a trap-inflected drum track. Sianipar's Toba Dream has become, in the words of the Siantar Rap Foundation's logo, "Batak Swag Ethnic."

More than a decade has passed after the flurry of controversy on the blog, contesting Sianipar's right to arrange music created in a ritual realm not his own and to hold judgment on aesthetic preferences rooted in a social experience he is not part of. Sianipar is now a successful popular musician by every metric. Yet strangely, he has chosen not to take down the blog posts that document these earlier dissensions. This may be a function of fame. Perhaps the singer/producer/composer has transcended his origin story and has not given them a second thought. I prefer to consider the retention of this ephemera as a democratic impulse, though, and as a testament to music made communal through the diverse audience members that engage with it.

NOTES

1. The word "Batak" can have two meanings. It can refer to the larger ethnic category of inland Sumatran tribes, which is then split into subgroups, of which Toba Batak is one. It is also used to refer to the most prominent of these subgroups, the Toba Batak. In this chapter, I use "Batak" with elements that apply to the larger grouping, and I specify Toba Batak when I speak of the subgroup that is the primary focus of the discussion. It is unclear which meaning Sianipar intends here, although I suspect it is the latter. All Toba Batak and Indonesian passages are translated by the author.

2. It may seem as if the esoteric nature of *gondang sabangunan* contravenes this claim; after all, Toba traditional music may not be played by just anyone, and the ritual knowledge of musicians is strictly guarded. However, the key here is that these musicians may be hired by any member of any *marga*, and their esoteric knowledge is placed at the service of many different people. Finally, although musicians gain prestige from their knowledge in ritual contexts, in normal life they are treated like any other member of society, and they often have nonritual professions as well (teacher, farmer, banker).

3. There is evidence that the gong-based *gondang sabangunan* ensemble was banned while a related tradition, *gondang hasapi*, was not. Both ensembles shared repertoire. The flutes and lutes of *gondang hasapi* music could accommodate harmony and became integrated into popular traditions, whereas the nondiatonic tuned drums of the *gondang sabangunan* could not. Yet the regular gong alternation glossed onto a basic harmonic bass pattern, aesthetically preserving the feeling of the *gondang sabangunan* instrument in *gondang hasapi* music. Now that neither ensemble is banned by Toba Batak churches, both ensembles are part of popular and ritual music making.

WORKS CITED

Barkin, Gareth. 2006. "The Foreignizing Gaze: Producers, Audiences, and Symbols of the 'Traditional.'" *Asian Journal of Communication* 4: 352–70.

Brinner, Benjamin. 1995. *Knowing Music, Making Music: Javanese Gamelan and the Theory of Musical Competence and Interaction*. Chicago: University of Chicago Press.

Bruner, Edward. 1972. "Batak Ethnic Associations in Three Indonesian Cities." *Southwestern Journal of Anthropology* 28 (3): 207–29.

Byl, Julia. 2014. *Antiphonal Histories: Resonant Pasts in the Toba Batak Musical Present*. Hartford, CT: Wesleyan University Press.

Cecco, Leyland. 2019. "Canada: One Indigenous Group Accuses Other of Cultural Appropriation in Award Row." *Guardian*, April 9. https://www.theguardian.com/world/2019/apr/09/canada-indigenous-music-awards-inuit-cree-cultural-appropriation.

Feld, Steven. 2000. "A Sweet Lullaby for World Music." *Public Culture* 12 (1): 145–71.

Fraser, Jennifer. 2014. *Gongs and Pop Songs: Sounding Minangkabau in Indonesia*. Athens: Ohio University Press.

Kahn, Douglas. 1992. "Introduction: Histories of Sound Once Removed." In *Wireless Imagination: Sound, Radio, and the Avant-Garde*, edited by Douglas Kahn and Gregory Whitehead, 1–30. Cambridge, MA: MIT Press.

Nadeak, Carry. 2003. "Mimpi Toba Kedua." *Gatra*, December 27. http://arsip.gatra.com/2003-12-20/majalah/artikel.php?pil=23&id=34461.

Pemberton, John. 1994. *On the Subject of Java*. Ithaca, NY: Cornell University Press.

Purba, Mauly. 2005. "From Conflict to Reconciliation: The Case of the 'Gondang Sabangunan' in the Order of Discipline of the Toba Batak Protestant Church." *Journal of Southeast Asian Studies* 36: 207–33.

Rodgers, Susan. 1988. "Me and Toba: A Childhood World in a Batak Memoir." *Indonesia* 45: 63–84.

Ryter, Lauren. 1998. "Pemuda Pancasila: The Last Loyalist Free Men of Suharto's Era?" *Indonesia* 66: 44–73.

Sianipar, Viky. 2003. *TobaDream*. MP Production, B000TD7J8OP. CD.

Sianipar, Viky. 2008a. "Si Vikki Merusak Musik Batak??" *A Journal of Viky Sianipar*, February 25. https://tongginghill.wordpress.com/2008/02/25/esensi-musik-tradisional-dan-lagu-batak/.

Sianipar, Viky. 2008b. "Ternyata Musik Batak Itu Keren." *A Journal of Viky Sianipar*, May 5. https://tongginghill.wordpress.com/2008/05/05/ternyata-batak-itu-keren/.

Titus, Barbara. Forthcoming, 2022. *Hearing Maskanda: Musical Epistemologies in South Africa*. London: Bloomsbury.

Tucker, Joshua. 2011. "Permitted Indians and Popular Music in Contemporary Peru: The Poetics and Politics of Indigenous Performativity." *Ethnomusicology* 55 (3): 387–413.

Turino, Thomas. 2000. *Nationalists, Cosmopolitans, and Popular Music in Zimbabwe*. Chicago: University of Chicago Press.

Wallach, Jeremy. 2008. *Modern Noise, Fluid Genres: Popular Music in Indonesia, 1997–2001*. Madison: University of Wisconsin Press.

Welker, Marina. 2014. *Enacting the Corporation: An American Mining Firm in Post-Authoritarian Indonesia*. Berkeley: University of California Press.

Yampolsky, Philip. 1989. "'Hati Yang Luka': An Indonesian Hit." *Indonesia* 47: 1–17.

Zak, Albin. 2001. *The Poetics of Rock: Cutting Tracks, Making Records*. Berkeley: University of California Press.

2

THE EVOLUTION OF PERFORMING ARTS PATRONAGE IN BALI, INDONESIA

I Nyoman Catra

The performing arts in Bali are a rich integration of dance, music, drama, literature, fine arts, and other elements. Traditionally, they have been supported by organizations hosted by *banjar* (neighborhood hamlet meetinghouse), *desa adat* (traditional village organization), *pemaksan* (temple congregation), and *sekaa* (traditional arts club within a *banjar*). Today, an increasing number of artists in Bali are earning certificates and degrees from formal institutions and are making artistic endeavors a profession. The majority of these individuals are engaged in creative work in *sanggar*, private studios for art activities, for financial gain.[1]

The newly created *sanggar* are an addition to more traditional and communal organizations, and they are growing in popularity and drawing more participants. The *sanggar*, many of which are fully equipped studios, are free from formal legal regulations and are popping up all over the island, especially in urban areas. Yet they remain social organizations that assemble and employ artists who have the talent, ability, commitment, and dedication to the *sanggar*'s programs. A healthy competition among *sanggar* is providing new vibrancy to the arts scene in Bali, with multiple activities and frequent opportunities for involvement in formal government festivals and performing for private organizations or ritual occasions, where expressing the performers' devotion to the gods is the priority of the gathering. *Sanggar* also train artists to perform for secular tourist shows in hotels or in small tourist entertainment locales in the villages.

To get a broader picture about the current state of *sanggar* in Bali today, we need to consider how arts activities were managed and recognized in previous generations. Accordingly, in this chapter I first outline a general history of performing arts patronage in Bali, setting the stage for a more detailed analysis of the recent emergence of *sanggar*.

Traditional Forms of Patronage

The earliest Balinese inscription describing professions in the performing arts dates from the reign of King Kesari Warmadewa in the tenth century. The inscription identifies several types of performing artists, such as mask performer (*atapukan*), drummer (*parpadaha*), flute player (*anuling*), and shadow master/puppeteer (*pabwayang*). In recognition of the performers and their profession the king made their honorariums tax free. In the fifteenth century, known as an artistic golden era under the leadership of King Dalem Waturenggong, the performing arts enjoyed great support from the palace. Every royal family (*raja-raja*) in Bali was affiliated with a group of village performing artists with defined relationships to the *Puri* (palace), *Para* (people), *Pura* (temple), *Purana* (religious holy book), and *Purohita* (priests). All of these aspects of life were intertwined and mutually reinforced the welfare of both inner and outer aspects of artists' lives. Many new performance genres emerged during this era, when artists were dedicated and devoted to the religious functions of their practice, to society at large, and to their king.

During the reign of these kings, at least four major movements occurred in Bali that had a significant impact on the development of ceremonial art and culture. First, the sage Rsi Markandya came to Bali around the eleventh century and introduced the Bhumisuddha ritual for the purification of the earth. This ritual, which asks for the blessing of Mother Nature, requires the burning of five elements of precious metal that correspond to the spatial mandala: silver representing the east, copper the south, gold the west, iron the north, and soil in the middle. It was during this time the mother temple of Bali, Besakih, was constructed. The irrigation system (*subak*) was also introduced during this time and remains intact today, with performance a necessary component of its associated religious offerings.

The second movement was led by Empu Kuturan, also around the eleventh century, who successfully unified sects who quarreled because of their different beliefs and ceremonial practices. Empu Kuturan developed the concept of oneness of the almighty God with the personification of deities known as Tri Murti that dwell in the Kahyangan Tiga temples in each village. Tri Murti deities include Lord Brahma as a creator, Lord Wisnu as a preserver, and Lord Shiva as a destroyer. They dwell in the Temple Desa, the Temple Puseh, and the Temple Dalem. During this era, it became common practice for each compound in the community to include corresponding house shrines known as Sanggah Kemulan (Rong Tiga). At the island level, the Temples of Kahyangan Jagat and Dang Kahyangan protect the Balinese at each of the cardinal directions.

The third movement was led by Priest Danghyang Nirartha (Peranda Sakti Wawurawuh) who, in the fifteenth century, introduced several ritual concepts and practices, such as recognizing the oneness of God by worshipping communally—regardless of sect or caste—at the Padmasana shrine, bringing together all castes: Bramana, Ksatria, Wesya, and Sudra.

The temples have annual ceremonies based on the calendar cycle of 210 days, or one for every year in the lunar calendar, based on the new/full moon cycle. The ceremony can last for one day, three days, eleven days, or forty-two days. Performances are part of the rituals and may include music, dance, dance-drama, shadow puppetry, and other art forms. All the performances are offerings embodying the concept of balance. A man or woman living in this world achieves peace and prosperity through what is today known as Tri Hita Karana, or a balanced relationship to the almighty God(s), to others, and to the natural environment. The organization responsible for managing these ceremonies is mainly the *banjar*, functioning as an organ of the traditional village association (*desa adat*). The performers might be permanently committed to the *banjar* or can be contracted individually on special occasions.

The local community organization (*banjar adat*) and *desa adat* are strongly related to the communal kinship systems that carry on traditional, cultural, religious, and social life. A *banjar* is a neighborhood organization, an aggregate of member families that plan, organize, and execute the great majority of activities that make up Balinese life (Eiseman 1995, 72–73). *Desa* literally means "village." *Adat* means "customary" or "traditional" and is usually associated with the practice of Balinese Hinduism and a village's religious life. For a long time, the growth and development of Balinese artistic activity and organization has been centered in these village organizations. *Banjar* are directed by a leader called *kelihan banjar*. Most of a *banjar*'s *adat* and *dinas* (state or governmental) services can be managed by a single *kelihan banjar*. He has a secretary, treasurer, and assistant (*kasinoman*) who are in charge of sharing information and summoning the members for meetings and information. Sometimes selected people will function as advisers known as *kerta banjar*. The *banjar* organization includes subbranches (*sekaa*) such as a traditional music organization (*sekaa gong*), a religious singing organization (*sekaa kidung*), a youth organization (*sekaa truna-truni*), and a womens' organization (PKK, Pembinaan Kesejahteraan Keluarga). The structure of those traditional subbranches is very simple. Most important is the mutual work (*gotong royong*) and the ethos of togetherness.

Each temple has a number of people who become temple congregants (*pemaksan*). Each temple is associated with a specific resident deity and associated performance styles such as *sanghyang, barong, baris, rejang*, and other sacred performances that must take place during the annual temple ceremony (*odalan*). Members of the various *banjar* organizations provide these ceremonial performances.

New Forms of Patronage Post-Independence

Formal education in the performing arts at the high school level was established in Bali in the 1960s through the Konservatori Karawitan (KOKAR), originally located on Jalan Ratna in the capital city of Denpasar. Here the students studied dance (*tari*), traditional music (*karawitan*), and puppetry (*pedalangan*). Today the school is located in Gianyar and is known as SMKN 3 Sukawati, and it includes both performing and fine arts curricula. The former KOKAR remains a high school for the performing arts in Denpasar; another arts high school, known as SMK, was later established in Bangli.

Formal education at the college level was established in 1967 in Denpasar. The arts college, previously known as Akademi Seni Tari Indonesia (Indonesian Dance Academy, ASTI), and later Sekolah Tinggi Seni Indonesia (Indonesian of College of the Arts, STSI), is now known as Institut Seni Indonesia (Indonesian Institute of the Arts, ISI). In this school the major fields of study are performing arts and fine arts. A third major program in *seni media rekam* (recording arts) is in development. There are seven similar campuses spread throughout Indonesia. Recently, several Institut Seni dan Budaya Indonesia (Indonesian Institute of Arts and Culture, ISBI) have been established in several locations in Indonesia. All of these campuses are supervised by the Ministry of Research, Technology, and Higher Education in Jakarta. In these various institutions, students can earn a variety of degrees, including a two-year diploma, bachelor's, master's, and doctorate in various fields of expertise. The ministry of education categorizes these majors into five fields: composition (*pencipta seni*), reviewer/researcher (*pengkaji seni*), presenter (*penyaji seni*), management (*pengelola seni*), and instructor (*guru seni*). This categorization has gradually replaced the dichotomy between "natural artist" (*seniman alam*) and "academic artist" (*seniman akademis*) that was frequently used from the 1970s through the early 2000s to categorize artists.

The performing arts have become part of the extracurricular offerings in most preschools, elementary, middle, and high schools in Bali, both public and private. Today there are annual school contests known as Pekan Olah Raga dan Seni Pelajar (I: Student Athletics and Arts Week, PORSENIJAR) for middle and high school students. Most students selected for these programs have received training privately through *sanggar* that employ specialists in the area the student wishes to study.

The increasing use of seven-tone ensembles such as *semarpagulingan, semaradana*, and *slonding*, and the emergence of new musical instruments (*barungan gamelan baru*), as seen in *sanggar* including Gamelan Manika Santi, Gamelan Nawanada, Gamelan Salukat, Gamelan Pesel, and others, require players who have extraordinary technique and understanding of the repertoire. Such *sanggar* have helped augment students' extracurricular arts activities.

Since Indonesia gained independence on August 17, 1945, government offices have had the responsibility of fostering, preserving, and developing both classical and traditional arts as well as new art forms. Cultural heritage is also managed through government offices. The hierarchy begins at the grassroots level of arts activities, which is sponsored by the *banjar* system in the *desa adat*, linked to the local government (*desa dinas*) providing activities and creative opportunities for its constituents, up to the central government. Linkages between the *sekaa* at the *banjar* level, affiliated at village level (*dinas*), subdistrict level (*kecamatan*), district region level (*kabupaten/kota*), provincial level, and up to the central government ideally advance the art and culture of the nation.

The Division of Culture in the province of Bali (Kantor Dinas Kebudayaan Provinsi Bali) was established in 1996 and is tasked with fostering, developing, and preserving the province's cultural values. This office is affiliated with the lower offices in the nine regions, charged with the same task. Some regions merge the culture division with the youth sport division and the tourism division under one regional minister. The provincial government established an organization called Majelis Pertimbangan dan Pembinaan Kebudayaan LISTIBIYA (Cultural Consideration and Development Assembly), whose members are selected from artists, cultural specialists, and scholars, as a team to review Balinese art and cultural activities and report to the governor. In 1971 this institution held a seminar on sacred and secular Balinese performing arts with the goal of shielding Bali from foreign cultural influences. This institution has branches in each region throughout Bali.

Cultural heritage is a crucial component to both Bali's tourism industry and its agricultural economy, through the ceremonies associated with the *subak* irrigation system. Tourists are attracted to Bali because of its vibrant culture and natural environment. Cultural activities coupled with natural beauty—open land, mountains, rice terraces, and beaches—have been and remain alluring to tourists. Although the history of tourism in Bali started in the early twentieth century, mass cultural tourism was officially started in the 1970s when Bali was promoted as a tourism destination by the central government. The provincial government, under the leadership of Governor Prof. Dr. Ida Bagus Mantra, promoted "cultural tourism" in an effort to reverse the negative impacts of "tourist culture."

The provincial government of Bali has hosted the Bali Arts Festival since 1969. This program consists of parades, performances, contests, exhibitions, seminars, and, most recently, documentaries and films. The annual Bali Arts Festival, which always starts during the second weekend of June and runs for a month until the second weekend of July, when schools are on vacation, celebrated its fiftieth anniversary in 2019. This festival is supported by the regional governments (*kabupaten/kota*), which provide groups to perform as representatives of their district's talent and artistry. The festival was originally intended to upgrade village ensembles through the intensive preparation and observation of other village groups.

In 2013 the government added another performing arts festival, known as Bali Mandara Mahalango (BMM), which starts after the Bali Arts Festival. BMM hosts around seventy performances that are presented nightly until the end of August. In 2016 another festival, known as Bali Mandara Nawanatya (BMNN), was also established. The government mission statement for this event is to promote the creation of innovative artwork that improves the material and spiritual welfare of society in a sustainable manner. The BMNN's activities are expected to encourage innovative artworks, provide education, promote healthy entertainment, and promote tourism all in an effort to support Balinese cultural development. At these events, performances are geared toward the younger generation and are performed every weekend from Friday to Sunday all year long at the Bali Art Center, except during the periods of the Bali Arts Festival and BMM.

To avoid redundancy, the curators from the government's organization committee categorized performances at these festivals as performances from classical/traditional arts, popular arts, and contemporary arts according to the percentages described in table 2.1.

The governor of Bali, through the Dinas Kebudayaan (provincial department of culture), is the leading organizing force behind these festivals. As mentioned, the Bali Arts Festival is affiliated with the regional governments (*kabupaten/kota*) who select groups to participate in the program. While approximately 250 referrals are submitted annually, only fifty performances are approved by the Dinas

TABLE 2.1 Relative proportions of genres at major annual festivals

PESTA KESENIAN BALI	BALI MANDARA MAHALANGO	BALI MANDARA NAWANATYA
60% classic/traditional	60% popular	60% contemporary
20% popular	20% contemporary	20% classic/traditional
20% contemporary	20% classic/traditional	20% popular

Kebudayaan. Every day at least five performances are staged from 11:00 a.m. until late at night. More than twenty genres of performing arts are prepared by representatives of the nine regions. In this situation, *sanggar* play important roles as representatives of the regencies for the Bali Arts Festival. Here the opportunity for *sanggar* participation is openly accepted.

For the BMM and BMNN festivals, the repertoires are programmed, selected, and appointed by the curator's peer team. Here too *sanggar* can propose work and be accepted to perform. In order to receive financial support for production costs through the Dinas Kebudayaan, *sanggar* must be officially registered by their regional department of culture.

The Role of *Sanggar* in Contemporary Balinese Culture

Sanggar have grown intensively in Bali since the 1970s. While the first *sanggar* were predominantly dance studios, today there are many *sanggar* focusing on gamelan and other kinds of music, as well as shadow puppetry (*pedalangan*) and fine art. According to I Wayan Dibia and Rucina Ballinger, *sanggar* "first started to sprout up in the city of Denpasar due to the demand at the time for dance lessons," a demand that increased with the "onset of tourism." The studios mostly run short courses for groups, "mainly during the weekend," in dance and traditional gamelan repertoire, training young people to participate in secular and sacred cultural production. *Sanggar* also give private lessons (Dibia and Ballinger 2004, 15).

As mentioned, all new *sanggar* must register with the regional cultural office after being recognized by the village head (*perbekel/lurah*) and subdistrict head (*camat*). The regional cultural office then issues a certificate as legal recognition of the *sanggar*'s operations. Similar organizations such as *yayasan* (arts communities) must satisfy similar legal requirements. Most of these are considered nonprofit organizations.

Sanggar have given rise to a new sight in Bali today: a child carrying his or her favorite instruments, perhaps a *kendang, rebab, suling*, or *jembe*, in a sling to and from *sanggar*, much as other musicians carry guitars, saxophones, and flutes. Many children learn solo drumming (*mekendang tunggal*) from their teachers in these organizations. This child or person is sharpening his or her skills to be able to play certain instruments so that he or she can demonstrate their skill in public at contests and/or to win trophies and certificates of recognition.

Sanggar have various purposes and priorities. Some *sanggar* work on creative productions while others might hold regular classes (I: *kursus*) to practice repertoires. Some *sanggar* might have a regular paying engagement in hotels or restaurants for tourist entertainment, or at other venues and events. In addition to the government-run festivals described above, there are those run by private organizations, such as Nusa Dua Festival, Kuta Carnival, Lovina Beach Festival, and Sanur Village Festival.

Most every region in Bali hosts an annual festival. Some regions might be more sporadic in their programming depending on available funding and overall budgetary concerns. Festival Seni Budaya Badung takes place in Badung regency and generally runs for two or three weeks. This festival is a celebration of the anniversary of the Mangupura Government Office. Denpasar Festival (DenFes) is usually held at the end of the year. The city of Denpasar also schedules late-afternoon performances on the stage at the Lapangan Puputan Badung square where people can mingle, watch, and relax after work. This programming also targets *sanggar* involvement, providing them chances to perform. Similar ideas have been presented in Gianyar, Klungkung, Bangli, Karangasem, Jembrana, and Tabanan.

Utsawa Bali Sani organized by Hindu Indonesia University in Denpasar regularly hosts a performance festival that draws participation from *sanggar*, *sekaa*, arts communities, and individuals. In addition, many arts and culture contests are held around the island, such as the Lomba-lomba Beleganjur, Lomba makendang Tunggal, Lomba Bapang Barong, Lomba Tari Jauk Manis/Durga/Keras, Lomba Tari Kekebyaran and so on. These contests provide additional participation opportunities for any *sanggar*.

A *sanggar* may be patronized by several institutions simultaneously: governmental offices, nongovernmental organizations and businesses, festival organizers, individual donors, and other social organizations. Many *sanggar* and *yayasan* receive support from a wide range of organizations. Those that have been most successful in combining support from multiple sources include Sanggar Bajra Sandhi, Sanggar Cahaya Art, Komunitas Seni Pancer Langit, Sanggar Seni Gumiart, Sanggar Makara Dwaja, Yayasan Geoks, Sanggar Çudamani, Sanggar Semara Ratih, Sanggar Dwi Mekar, and many others. Several of these have received support from international organizations and donors.

The *sanggar* I organize, Seni Citta Usadhi in Badung, serves as an example. We have received support from many sources on several occasions. Our dance drama "Dramatari Arja" has been supported by the Badung regional government as part of the Bali Arts Festival program annually since 2007. Other productions, such as traditional *Baris Melampahan* and *Janger* dance dramas, as well as innovative musical and dance projects, have been regularly supported by the regional government. Our productions of *Saraswati Puja* (2015) and *Bondres Busul Mincid* (2016) were supported by the Bali Mandara Mahalango Festival. In

2008 the Nusa Dua Festival (2008) supported our production of several innovative dances including *Gandrungwangi*, *Chess Dance*, and the *Kebo Iwa* ballet, each performed as the main opening program of the festival. Our dance production *Krisna Pamrascitaning Jagat, Amerthaning Bhuwana* (2012) was sponsored by the Krisna Oleh-Oleh tourist gift shop. In addition to these productions, our *sanggar* regularly presents ritual performances at temples across Bali.

In the span of five decades *sanggar* have grown from community/societal associations to private studios. Among the factors influencing this shift is the increasing number of artists in Bali earning certificates and degrees from formal institutions and making artistic endeavors a profession. The rise of the Balinese middle class, related primarily to the tourism industry, enabled private individuals to purchase studio spaces and supply them with the equipment needed for their activities and creativity. Free from the binding rules, obligations, restrictions, sanctions, and regulations of traditional communal organizations, *sanggar* can provide a gathering space for professional artists and teachers who have the training and degrees to improve the artistic standards of the community. These professionals can guarantee higher standards of technique and clearer understanding of new aesthetics in music, dance, and other arts. It is interesting to note that the traditional call to meeting is marked by the sound of wooden slit drums (*kulkul*, or I: *kentongan*). The village *kulkul*, hamlet *kulkul*, and *sekaa kulkul* are used to summon its members. Today, members of communities are more likely to use social media on mobile phones as a medium to communicate and organize. Members are informed about their obligations by creating groups on WhatsApp, BBM, and other available services. This is becoming the primary tool of communication. While the recent growth of *sanggar* may be compared to such apps, the traditional *banjar* organizations will continue to exist because of Hindu religious rituals, ceremonies, and activities. *Sanggar* may increase in the years to come, but they will not undermine or threaten traditional societal structures and forms of patronage. Both systems are useful in supporting Balinese art and culture.

NOTES

All non-English text is Balinese, except for Indonesian text indicated by the abbreviation "I."

1. The majority of the information in this chapter is derived from my own experience as a member and director of several *sanggar* over several decades. However, readers should also consult descriptions of *sanggar*, and their activities, in the following sources: Clendinning 2020; Collier, in this book; Downing 2019; Harnish 2007; McGraw 2013; Mora 2011; Yamin 2019.

WORKS CITED

Clendinning, Elizabeth. 2020. *American Gamelan and the Ethnomusicological Imagination*. Champaign: University of Illinois Press.

Dibia, I Wayan, and Rucina Ballinger. 2004. *Balinese Dance, Drama and Music: A Guide to the Performing Arts of Bali*. Tokyo: Tuttle.

Downing, Sonja. 2019. *Gamelan Girls: Gender, Childhood, and Politics in Balinese Music Ensembles*. Champaign: University of Illinois Press.

Eiseman, Fred B., Jr. 1995. *Bali: Sekala & Niskala*, vol. 2: *Essays on Society, Tradition, and Craft*. Singapore: Periplus Editions.

Harnish, David. 2007. "'Digging' and 'Upgrading': Government Efforts to 'Develop' Music and Dance in Lombok, Indonesia." *Asian Music* 38 (1): 61–87.

McGraw, Andrew Clay. 2013. *Radical Traditions: Reimagining Culture in Balinese Contemporary Music*. New York: Oxford University Press.

Mora, Manolete, 2011. "Negotiation and Hybridity in New Balinese Music: Sanggar Bona Alit, a Case Study." *Perfect Beat* 12 (1): 45–68.

Yamin, Tyler, 2019. "One or Several Gamelan? Perpetual (Re)construction in the Life of a Balinese Gamelan Semara Pagulingan." *Ethnomusicology* 63 (3): 357–92.

3

BEYOND THE *BANJAR*

Community, Education, and Gamelan in North America

Elizabeth A. Clendinning

More than a thousand spectators were gathered inside the white, crumbling walls of colonial Fort Vastenburg in Solo, Java. We had been among the audience the night before, but tonight, we were backstage in our jackets and *kebaya*, the *udeng* perched on the men's heads and long hairpieces complete with flowers affixed to the women's—all part of the traditional uniforms worn to play Balinese gamelan music. Hundreds of paper lanterns hanging above the stage fluttered in the cool summer breeze, casting a more intimate light over us than the moody, jewel-toned lights that bathed the stage.

We were the musicians and dancers of Sanggar Manik Galih, a loose, mul-tisited collaborative of Balinese and American gamelan musicians and dancers directed by I Made Lasmawan and Ni Ketut Marni.[1] Our group had only fully coalesced a week before as musicians from the United States and a few "ringers" from other parts of Bali had descended on Lasmawan's home village hamlet of Bangah, Bali, to meet and prepare for the performance. Despite one rehearsal being interrupted by a 7.0 magnitude earthquake and our travel to Java beset with complications and delays, we had all made it. We chatted in English, Bali-nese, and Indonesian as we waited for the group before us, a women's gamelan from Solo, to complete their set. Having prayed together and been blessed with holy water just minutes before, we were ready to step onstage. But unsurprisingly, the program was running a bit late, so the musicians variously passed the time smoking, being interviewed by local schoolchildren, or taking some last-minute selfies together. Finally, their set finished and we made our way to the front of the stage.

This performance was part of the second night of concerts for the International Gamelan Festival held in Solo, Indonesia, in August 2018. The weeklong event was sponsored by the Indonesian government and designed to highlight the global vibrancy of gamelan culture. Nightly performances featured a roster of nineteen foreign ensembles as well as dozens of Indonesian ensembles, largely drawn from Java. The opening ceremony on the evening of August 10 established the tone of the event and its symbolic importance. The opening piece, *ketawang* "Puspawarna" (Kinds of Flowers), had famously been included on the Voyager Golden Record that had been launched into space forty-one years before as a time capsule of human life and culture. In an opening speech, Indonesian Minister of Education and Culture Muhadjir Effendy announced that the Indonesian government would be seeking UNESCO Intangible Cultural Heritage status for gamelan the following year. For the application to be successful, he requested support from members of the entire gamelan community—not only Indonesians, many of whom have primarily passive knowledge of these rich artistic traditions, but musicians involved in the hundreds of gamelan ensembles active outside Indonesia.[2]

As a musician, dancer, and scholar of Indonesian performing arts who has been involved in the Indonesian performing arts in the United States and in Bali for a decade, I was pleased to note the emphasis on gamelan as a transnational phenomenon. Gamelan communities have existed outside of Indonesia since the mid-twentieth century, and while their artistic and cultural relationship to gamelans in Indonesia has been debated in scholarly and public forums for decades (for example, Becker 1983; Diamond 1990), only recently has there been sustained investigation into their history and social structure (Brinner 2013; Lueck 2012; Mendonça 2002; Steele 2013; Strohschein 2018; Sumarsam 2013). Gamelan as an art form has taken root in a variety of different settings globally, including at colleges, in prisons, in outdoor festivals, and played by live musicians and in robotic form (McGraw 2016; Mendonça 2010; Solís 2004). As a result, non-Indonesian gamelan ensembles take on different pedagogical and creative approaches and cultural meanings than they do in Indonesia (Clendinning 2020; Harnish 2004; Harnish, Solís, and Witzleben 2004; House 2014; Khalil 2016; Mendonça 2002; Miller 2005; Spiller 2015; Steele 2013; Strohschein 2018; Sumarsam 2004; Vetter 2004; Witzleben 2004). Yet, like their Indonesian peers, gamelan players across the world unite in local groups in common cause of learning, performing, and sharing Indonesian performing arts. Although such musicians emerge from vastly different sociocultural and national backgrounds than Indonesian gamelan musicians, the ensembles also have great importance to foreign musicians. What else but deep devotion to the music and the musical community would lead a half dozen

American musicians to fly across the world join their Balinese colleagues for a weekend performance in Java?

The news coverage of the festival presented one interpretation of the international gamelan phenomenon and what it might mean to Indonesian and non-Indonesian communities. In English, the festival was termed a "homecoming," and in Indonesian, foreign groups were said to *mudik*—the word most often applied to describe the return of Indonesian workers to their family homes for the Idul Fitri celebrations at the end of the Islamic holiday Ramadan. In a certain sense, this description is fitting; gamelan music inarguably originates from specific regions within Indonesia, and foreign individual ensembles that travel to study or perform in Indonesia often treat their visit as a pilgrimage. But, in that foreign musicians are not returning but rather visiting, the metaphor only carries so far. Foreign gamelan ensembles form communities that are made cohesive by a sense of shared geography, roots, and artistic lineages even as they encompass an ever-shifting, cosmopolitan array of new influences. While each group carries recognizable ties to gamelan practices and communities in Indonesia, each grows in its own ways in its own home, developing as is appropriate to its own time, place, and situation. When the groups travel to Indonesia, they represent an overlapping intercommunity dialogue rather than a repatriation of a singular tradition, as suggested by calling it a "homecoming."

Using the model of a community that extends "beyond the *banjar*"—a neighborhood ward in Bali around which traditional arts and community events revolve—this article examines local, regional, and transnational concepts of community formed by the interrelationship between academic and community gamelans in the United States and their affiliates in Indonesia. Although the path to the establishment of gamelan communities in North America is detailed in a variety of publications (Brinner 2013; Clendinning 2020; Lueck 2012; Solís 2004; Sumarsam 2013), I provide a brief history and overview of gamelan culture in North America for context. Second, drawing on examples primarily from my own work among musicians performing on Balinese gamelan in the United States, I examine how rootedness in one or more cultural and artistic lineages, creation of local culture, and the concept of transnational collaboration creates interlocking and overlapping sets of community affiliation to illustrate this point. I focus on a set of gamelans that are primarily instructed or sponsored by a single long-term teacher, I Made Lasmawan, as a case study. These interlocking gamelan communities provide unique opportunities for Indonesian and American musicians alike, fostering small-scale but energetic transnational connections that animate and energize broader Indonesian-American cultural exchanges.

Establishing Gamelan Communities in North America

The 1893 Columbian Exposition in Chicago marked the initial introduction of live gamelan music to North America; however, it was not until over half a century later that the first gamelan ensembles would be founded on the continent. While the 1930s and 1940s brought an increasing American awareness of Indonesian music through the circulation of recordings, live tours of Indonesian musicians and dancers, and more local imitations of Indonesian arts (Cohen 2010; Spiller 2015), the first opportunities for Americans to study gamelan on their own soil appeared at the end of the 1950s, with the arrival of two sets of gamelan instruments at the University of California–Los Angeles. The Central Javanese and Balinese gamelans, imported alongside other non-Western instruments by Mantle Hood with funding from the Ford Foundation, came to be used in world music "study groups" led by Hood and expert native musicians. In addition to enriching the musical variety available at the university, the gamelans served as a primary model in the development of Hood's concept of bimusicality (1960)—the idea that students needed to play a musical genre to some degree in order to understand it, and more specifically to the time, Western musicians who were presumed to primarily be musical "natives" in the Western classical tradition could and should become familiar with other musical systems. As the concept of experiential learning gained traction within ethnomusicology and academia more broadly, gamelan came to occupy a canonical place in non-Western collegiate ensemble education.

The early gamelans in North America were not the first to be played primarily by non-Indonesian musicians; Hood had encountered one of Europe's early community gamelan ensembles, Gamelan Babar Layar, through his dissertation director and Indonesianist music scholar Jaap Kunst (Mendonça 2011). However, they were the first to be used in a specifically pedagogical setting, a situation that affected the way in which gamelan communities were founded and grew in North America in subsequent decades. The next gamelan groups that appeared in the United States in the late 1960s and early 1970s were largely founded by Hood's former students and Indonesian colleagues within university settings. In 1979, non-collegiate community gamelans Gamelan Sekar Jaya (Balinese) in California and the Boston Village Gamelan (Central Javanese) in Massachusetts were formed by musicians who had learned about the music from academic courses or university-sponsored summer workshops in the United States, listening to recordings, and traveling to Indonesia. According to a survey by the author in 2019, just over sixty years after the first gamelans were founded at UCLA, over 150 gamelan groups provide opportunities for North Americans to play and hear live gamelan music.

The ways that contemporary gamelan ensembles in North America are founded, sustained, and related to other ensembles are largely dependent on their geographic location; their institutional structure; and their ties to other groups through shared instructors and members. The first element, geography, is perhaps most significant in influencing the structure of communities. Gamelan ensembles are still most numerous along the Atlantic and Pacific Coasts in urban areas with diverse and thriving arts scenes, dense concentrations of colleges and universities, and sometimes historic or contemporary connections to Asian immigrant communities. In contrast, in some areas such as the southeastern United States, the nearest two gamelans may be separated by hundreds of miles. Densely populated urban areas may support an array of both academic and community gamelans, often including ones founded or maintained by musicians originally affiliated with another group. In less populous or culturally vibrant settings, a single gamelan, often hosted at a university, serves as the sole representative of Indonesian performance culture. Because of the relatively case-by-case basis on which gamelan ensembles are founded, the ensembles' founders and directors play a substantial role in establishing the culture of the group, including creating local community and fostering feelings of transnational community.

The reasons why non-Indonesian musicians play gamelan are varied, and writings about gamelan by non-Indonesian authors generally include detailed information about how they first encountered and began to play gamelan music, ranging from hearing recordings to learning about gamelan in college to hearing live ensembles perform (for example, Bakan 1999; Gold 2005; McGraw 2013a; Tenzer 2000, among many others). Although American gamelan ensembles may still be populated primarily by white, middle-class men (McGraw 2013b), the past few decades have seen a substantive expansion of those demographics (Clendinning 2020). While Indonesian gamelan groups are generally still gender-segregated, American gamelan groups have long been mixed gender; in the 2010s, their memberships are nearly evenly divided between men and women. American community-based gamelans are still generally dominated by white, middle-class individuals with time and resources to devote to studying the music. However, in academic gamelan courses, the demographics of students who choose to learn gamelan often mirror those of their institutions, yielding collegiate gamelan groups with high percentages of Asian and Latin American members. Some Indonesian students who have arrived in North America to study other academic subjects even find themselves learning to play gamelan for the first time. These communities with their varied demographics and localized conditions foster a variety of different interpretations of Indonesian performing arts.

Balinese Gamelan, Community, and *Desa, Kala, Patra*

It is difficult to describe the omnipresence and cultural importance of gamelan in Bali to those who have not traveled there. At night, the air near villages' *bale banjar* (neighborhood ward meetinghouses) become electrified with the sounds of gamelan, the low hums of the great gongs felt far beyond the compounds where musicians practice. Along with the related performing arts genres of dance, vocal music, and shadow puppetry, music played on one of the island's over thirty varieties of gamelan serves as a primary devotional offering and entertainment within the religious practice of Balinese Hindus, who constitute more than 80 percent of the island's population. The predominant industry in Bali, the tourist industry, has substantially capitalized on the Balinese performing arts as well, with nightly staged performances of carefully chosen repertoire available for tourist consumption. Though performing artists worry about the potential decline in quality or prevalence of specific genres of performance, Balinese traditional arts are supported by the island's conservatories, showcased in local and regional competitions and the annual Bali Arts Festival (Pesta Kesenian Budaya), and maintained and developed by a variety of private arts clubs (*sanggar* and *yayasan*). In short, though not all Balinese perform or care passionately about the islands' native performing arts, the level of artistic production permeates daily life in a way that is almost unimaginable in North America (Dunbar-Hall 2016).

Outside Indonesia, gamelans take on several different artistic forms and social roles, depending on their membership demographics, location and setting, and artistic vision. Gamelans outside of educational settings embody a particularly wide variety of models. While some ensembles are devoted to studying and performing traditional repertoires or new pieces in relatively traditional styles, others perform new and highly experimental compositions—a contrast that can be seen, for example, in comparing the performances of Balinese ensembles Gamelan Sekar Jaya and Gamelan X, both based in the San Francisco Bay Area. Community-based gamelans also lie on a spectrum between true amateurism—ensembles with open membership that generally perform for free—to semiprofessional groups that require members to audition and generally accept paid gigs only. Some groups, like those supported through the Indonesian embassies, are explicitly geared toward education and cultivating gamelan as representation of the Indonesian nation.

Within academic gamelans in North America, which are explicitly educational in their goals, helping others understand the artistic and cultural dimensions of gamelan practices is a central task. Basic musical, cultural, and ethical challenges of such an endeavor have already been discussed substantively elsewhere

(Clendinning 2020; Macy 2017; Solís 2004; Sumarsam 2016; Sudirana 2018), and each individual teacher takes a different approach to these issues. However, both North American and Balinese instructors with whom I have worked have, in their own ways, articulated three important principles for representing Balinese music and culture in a way that is fitting with the Balinese concept of *desa, kala, patra*—appropriateness to time, place, and situation. First, music should be taught at a level appropriate to players' abilities while still being rendered as accurately as possible. This principle can require choosing repertoire carefully; simplifying more difficult parts in a musically idiomatic way; or performing select portions of longer pieces well rather than struggling with the whole work. Second, the culture of the group should be authentic to Balinese practices in spirit, if not precisely in execution. Finally, groups in America should "remember their roots"—that is, be knowledgeable about how the group is coming to learn the music and how it relates to the broader landscape of Balinese gamelan performance.

The creation of community within an individual ensemble is most strongly related to the second principle, evoking an authentic spirit within ensemble culture. Although united by their shared choices to participate in the gamelan ensemble at any given time, college students do not share the deep-seated cultural heritage, long-term community sensibility, or broader sense of belonging within an artistic system that is integral to Balinese performing groups, or the alternative types of affinity and community culture (Strohschein 2018) developed in long-lived community gamelan outside of Indonesia. Rehearsal schedules are often fixed in length, and performance dates are chosen according to availability on the semester calendar rather than any sense of musical preparedness. The ensemble's internal sense of identity and its relationship to other ensembles, whether local or distant, shifts with each new term with the introduction of new members.

Yet the incorporation of even simple ensemble traditions on a regular basis helps foster group identity for both collegiate and community gamelans in North America. Some social practices, such as taking off one's shoes to play and not stepping over instruments, are directly teachable aspects of Balinese culture. However, more intangible characteristics, such as the *rame* spirit of liveliness and energy that animates group practices in Bali, must be captured in new ways, often by creating American twists on Balinese traditions. Some such traditions relate to the groups' performance activities themselves—for example, Colorado College's tradition of playing *beleganjur* (marching gamelan) during homecoming. Creating and wearing group T-shirts may also foster community spirit through creating a unified feel to practice and performance and through creating shared group cultural practices. For example, at Florida State University, members of the gamelan reveled in wearing the group's bright red shirts that featured a line drawing of the Florida state capitol on the back because of the descriptive, risqué ensemble motto written in Balinese that accompanied the image.[3] Within the context of the university, only group members understood the motto and its humor. On a more daily basis, the consumption of snacks and tea, a core element of musical rehearsals in Bali, has manifested itself at gamelan practices across North America in its own distinctive fashion. Desserts made of sticky rice that are commonly found in Indonesia might be replaced by brownies; hot sweet tea, by its iced counterpart.

The third principle, honoring one's roots, animates the work of individual ensembles but also more broadly shapes a community superstructure that loosely relates academic and community gamelans in North America to each other and to arts practitioners in Bali. Within North America, geography plays some role in the dissemination of music. Balinese teachers frequently travel to work with several different groups, and American gamelan enthusiasts often join or form new groups when they move to a new location. Yet it is the connection through the teacher that brings musicians from different ensembles together—and with some exceptions, Balinese teachers are most often supported financially and logistically through work with an academic institution. The broader types of community connections are illustrated in the opening anecdote about Sanggar Manik Galih, a group I have been involved with since its founding in 2011. The type of community created by this group can be more fully understood through an overview of the life and work of its central teacher, I Made Lasmawan, whose family has served as the pedagogic and artistic lifeblood for Balinese gamelans in the Front Range region of the Rocky Mountains for nearly three decades.

Case Study: Communities of I Made Lasmawan

Community can be understood as the ways that individuals within a single, specific group with shared practices relate to each other and also as the way that different groups that recognize some points of kinship—shared histories, belief systems, practices, or members—interact with each other. Understanding this superstructure is crucial to modeling flows of people and ideas that animate these shared histories and practices. Brinner (2013) has suggested understanding academic gamelans as part of a musical ecosystem—a model that, like its counterparts in ecology, focuses on gamelan ensembles and teachers as embodying certain niches and who must adapt and change symbiotically with their environments. Considering academic gamelan as an influential part of this model is important because it changes the rhetoric that the "one-semester" gamelan student is entirely disconnected from broader gamelan communities. Individual teachers serve as both grounding factors and points of change within these ecosystems; their pedagogical lineages, the way that musical and cultural material is transmitted and different parts of the ecosystem are connected. The ecosystem and pedagogical lineage of Lasmawan, who is both normative and exceptional in the approach and scope of his teaching, provides a compelling model for understanding how large-scale community can flow through and in between academic and community gamelan groups in North America.

Lasmawan, who was born in the province of Tabanan, Bali, in 1958, was formally educated at the Indonesian arts conservatories both in Bali and in Solo and occupied the post of lecturer in Balinese music in Solo during and after completing his master's degree in the 1980s. He additionally studied with *seniman alam*, artists with no formal conservatory training who were considered experts in their fields. In 1990, a chance encounter brought Lasmawan into contact with Robert (Bob) Brown, who hired him to teach at San Diego State University. A few years later, he was offered a more permanent, half-time faculty position by Victoria Levine at Colorado College, a position that provided sufficient financial support to teach other ensembles in that area. In the following years, his teaching engagements would expand, encompassing gamelans in both community and academic settings, including the semiprofessional community group Gamelan Tunas Mekar. In partnership with his wife Ni Ketut Marni—who teaches dance and takes care of logistical matters for the groups, such as food and costuming—and with assistance from his three adult sons and long-term students, Lasmawan instructs more than a half dozen gamelans on a regular basis, not including more occasional guest residencies (Clendinning 2013).

In Bali, the family additionally hosts study abroad programs and conducts performances as a part of their transnational *sanggar*, Sanggar Manik Galih, as well as regular rehearsals of *banjar*-based club groups. The *sanggar* was founded and maintained in partnership with one of Lasmawan's first Colorado College students and subsequent collaborators, ethnomusicologist Elizabeth Macy. While performing arts study abroad programs in Bali are popular and it is recognized that foreign interest provides an important effect in sustaining Balinese traditional performing arts cultures, the conception of the activity taking place within an explicitly transnational *sanggar* is still unusual (Clendinning 2017; Dunbar-Hall 2016).

Not all Balinese gamelans in North America are connected to a single family of teachers; however, the phenomenon is not uncommon. Lasmawan's network, due to its size, is an interesting and fruitful context in which to consider how seemingly separate ensembles may share certain elements and find themselves as part of a larger community. The repertoire that Lasmawan uses as core material for his academic groups and as easier literature for some of the community groups contains a combination of standardized *kreasi baru* pieces from the mid- to late twentieth century, some more regional or ensemble-specific favorites, and his own new compositions. Teachers who use those pieces—whether they are in regular contact with each other or not—are related via this source material.

The sharing of repertoire as well as the movement and sharing of musicians between these Front Range groups creates a sense of distant kinship between them. More experienced musicians, especially those from Gamelan Tunas Mekar, have frequently assisted with the academic groups, including serving as "ringers" for end-of-semester performances. In return, the local academic programs serve as a crucial source of new members for Gamelan Tunas Mekar. Michael Fitts, longtime president and coordinator of the ensemble, described their relationship with the nearby academic groups to me: "They're like AAA baseball, and we're the major leagues . . . when he [Lasmawan] finds somebody who's really switched on, he asks them, 'So—do you want to come rehearse with Tunas Mekar?' [It is often] people who are really musicians and composers, really wondering what it's about" (quoted in Clendinning 2020). Other new arrivals to the ensemble are recruited locally, often through a friend or through encountering the ensemble at a local performance. Finally, other gamelan musicians who have studied Balinese music with a college or community group elsewhere may move to the Denver area and join, bringing in a variety of experience on which the ensemble can expand.

The community connections made through the distinct ensembles and the *sanggar*, though at times situational and fleeting, can also turn into long-term relationships as American gamelan musicians build friendships with each other through gamelan; when they travel to Bali, they also form relationships with individuals of all generations from Bangah who are involved in the arts at Sanggar Manik Galih.

For some American students, studying in Bali is a once-in-a-lifetime event. Other musicians, however, return to Bali long after they have graduated. This pilgrimage allows them to build long-term friendships with some of the Balinese performers as well as with other American gamelan musicians whom they might only see in Bali. After the practices and performances end, members keep in touch via Facebook, WhatsApp, Instagram, YouTube, and other forms of social media until they see each other again, often after a year or more has passed. Ultimately, the most enthusiastic young gamelan musicians often grow into long-term musicians, many in turn supporting themselves and their interest in gamelan music and communities through teaching within educational settings. Though some individual gamelan groups, academic and community alike, have prospered for decades on their own, gamelan ecosystems in North America are fragile due to their niche nature. The symbiosis between academic and community groups in

North America and their partners in teaching and learning in Indonesia helps create the infrastructure that enables entire artistic and educational communities to thrive.

Making Meaning in Community and Academic Gamelan

The nature of Americans' attraction to the gamelan and the relationship or nonrelationship of American practitioners of Indonesian arts to arts practice in Indonesia has been a common theme in both journalistic and scholarly writing for over three decades. Writings about academic gamelan have largely focused on issues of authenticity in instruction and representation in performance (Harnish 2004; Harnish, Solís, and Witzleben 2004; Sumarsam 2004; Vetter 2004; Witzleben 2004), both from native and non-native practitioner perspectives. Some musicians have consistently highlighted the collaborative nature of many groups and argued that, after decades of playing, American gamelan musicians should be able to call gamelan "my music" too. Some highlight that the potential for mischaracterization, exoticization, or generally insensitive or inaccurate representations of Indonesian culture within American gamelan communities (McGraw 2013b; Spiller 2015). Other writers, drawing on Slobin's concept of "affinity intercultures" (Slobin 1993), construct Americans' continued participation in gamelan ensemble subcultural groups outside of Indonesia as being based on a specific attraction to the music in a culture that is initially not rooted in prior ethnic, national, or religious identity (Mendonça 2002; Lueck 2012), but one that develops through shared experience into love for some element of the broad spectrum of activities that constitute gamelan outside of Indonesia (Strohschein 2018). As more academic and community gamelans have been founded outside of Indonesia and have been increasingly easy to find due to their online activity, a greater number of interested musicians from around the world have been able to make gamelan a part of their life for years or even decades.

The impact of playing in gamelan on a community musician's life is profound, especially for gamelan "superenthusiasts" who frame their lives and identity around gamelan (Lueck 2012). The individual reasons that musicians cite for their interest in gamelan, invariably addressed in nearly all works on gamelan by non-Indonesian authors, are ultimately as distinctive as the writers themselves. The overall social result, however, is more easily observed. It is not uncommon for serious musicians to move to specific areas of the country to live close enough to perform with a high-level group, or to travel for hours every week to attend rehearsals and perform. Romances bloom, both among American gamelan musicians and between them and their Indonesian counterparts, leading to a small but significant number of sustained relationships within the community. Freed from the dictates of academic schedule and educational norms, many community groups embrace their own interpretations of Indonesian culture—including, for members of Gamelan Sekar Jaya, the regular practice of speaking in Balinese. The more that members of the group live shared experiences, the more tight-knit the group tends to become.

Despite the shorter amount of time that students spend in academic versus community gamelan ensembles, the impact of gamelan culture in North America can be felt keenly in higher education. Gamelans are perhaps the most prevalent representation of Indonesian culture within American society. As such, they serve not only to expose students to Indonesian culture but more generally to increase students' appreciation of musical and cultural diversity in a hands-on form. The results of this engagement, though often intangible in the short-term, are viewed as a positive way of creating more thoughtful engagements between Americans and Indonesians. In an online petition designed to garner continued institutional support for the University of Michigan gamelan, Sumarsam wrote, "Having taught gamelan for more than 40 years in the US, I can testify that teaching gamelan is one of the best educational enterprises for American students to be exposed to non-Western music" (McLain 2014). Studying gamelan can help musicians of all ages broadly strengthen and gain clarity on the aural, intellectual, and physical fundamentals of their musicianship. This sense of "opening minds," as Lasmawan likes to call his primary mission in teaching, is not limited to music; students also gain intercultural competence as they connect directly through shared performing arts endeavors with artists from and located on the opposite side of the world (Clendinning 2020).

Correspondingly, teaching foreigners provides distinctive personal and professional opportunities for Indonesian musicians. Though individual artists and entire gamelan ensembles have toured the world for over a century, the ability for Indonesian performing artists to partner with academic institutions in the United States and Canada (and in England, Australia, and elsewhere) provides new opportunities for artistic collaboration, travel, and the chance to experience ways of life outside of Indonesia, as well as distinctive opportunities for sharing Indonesian culture. Lasmawan and Marni, for example, not only bring Balinese artistic culture to the classroom and the stage; they also bring students and community gamelan musicians into their lives and their homes. These relationships create a sense of belonging found in few other types of educational experience.

Finally, it is important to note that even as gamelan music remains officially emblematic of Indonesia and retains greater or lesser prominence and popularity in its historic regions of origin, musicians who avidly play gamelan as adults are still in the minority in most Indonesian communities. The choice to perform or teach gamelan at a high level—or even to passionately study it as an adult novice—is a purposeful choice. Uniting to play gamelan can create certain types of musicians' bonds that transcend ethnic heritage, nationality, language, religion, and other potential points of social separation, even if only within an artistic context. This possibility for transcendence is a central but elusive goal of intercultural education, one whose promise is hinted at within the brief points of contact that student gamelan players have in educational settings and that is more fully realized and fulfilled among the long-term members of international gamelan communities.

Energy, Spirit, and Community

The audience was in high spirits as the musicians of Sanggar Manik Galih finally took the stage. Coming in the middle of an evening set featuring traditional and fusion presentations of Javanese gamelan, the promise of the shimmering sounds of Balinese gamelan and the elegant silhouettes of Balinese dancers seemed to be a welcome interlude. As we waited for the *pak* of the drum that would call us to attention, I looked to the faces of the musicians around me. We were American and Balinese, young and old, but all devoted to the ideal of teaching, performing, representing, and purely having fun with this music. Beyond us, in the rows of chairs below, dozens of cell phones were raised aloft, ready to capture this fleeting half hour when we would all play together. Moments later, the *pak* sounded, we raised our mallets, and our hands began to fly.

The individual teachers, scholars, and musicians of the past half century who brought gamelans to North America had built the infrastructure for gamelan communities to exist both in North America and within a transnational context. It will be the task of the younger generations to continue to define and refine these communities. To what extent will academic institutions and community groups in close geographic proximity collaborate? How can musicians and teachers transcend the remaining barriers that make equality in transnational collaborations difficult? What importance will future musicians and dancers attribute to these experiences? One model for both media and message was provided by Putu Hiranmayena, Lasmawan's eldest son, who as usual provided a comprehensive concert rundown after the festival. In an inspirational note on Facebook in which he tagged every musician and dancer who had performed together, he wrote, "The energy was high and the spirit was full; we made mistakes but who gives a shit, shred on, baby!!!" With a consistent commitment to energy, spirit, and community among musicians on both sides of the Pacific, gamelan communities will continue to thrive as not only a facet of Indonesian culture or an isolated American practice but a shared human heritage.

NOTES

1. The *sanggar*, brainchild of Lasmawan and former student Elizabeth McLean Macy (a professor at Metropolitan State University of Denver), was founded in 2011. Unlike most Indonesian *sanggar*, private arts clubs whose members are drawn from a local geographic range, Sanggar Manik Galih was meant from its founding to be multisited.

2. The proposal for Indonesian gamelan to be inscribed on the Intangible Cultural Heritage Representative List (RL), a designation emphasizing continued visibility and awareness of a cultural practice, was submitted in March 2019 for consideration in 2020. The application was successful, and gamelan was added to the list in December 2021.

3. The state capitol of Florida, located in Tallahassee about one mile from the Florida State University College of Music, consists of a twenty-three-story tower flanked on either side by two lower domed buildings. The ensemble motto, "Kota Kalingga Jaya" (City of the Victorious Phallus), was bestowed on the ensemble by I Ketut Gede Asnawa in the mid-1990s.

WORKS CITED

Bakan, Michael B. 1999. *Music of Death and New Creation: Experiences in the World of Balinese Gamelan Beleganjur*. Chicago: University of Chicago Press.

Becker, Judith. 1983. "One Perspective on Gamelan in America." *Asian Music* 15 (1): 81–89.

Brinner, Benjamin. 2013. "The Ecology of Musical Transmission between Indonesia and the United States." Paper presented at Performing Indonesia: A Conference and Festival of Music, Dance, and Drama, at the National Museum of Asia Art of the Smithsonian Institution, November 3, 2013. https://asia.si.edu/essays/article-brinner/.

Clendinning, Elizabeth A. 2013. "Air Mengalir: I Madé Lasmawan, Pedagogy, and Musical Kinship in the Transnational Balinese Gamelan Community." Paper presented at Performing Indonesia: A Conference and Festival of Music, Dance, and Drama, at the National Museum of Asia Art of the Smithsonian Institution, November 3, 2013. https://asia.si.edu/essays/article-clendinning/.

Clendinning, Elizabeth A. 2017. "Learning in the "Global Village': Performing Arts Tourism in Bali, Indonesia." In "Music and Tourism," ed. Monique Desroches and Jessica Roda, special issue, *MUSICultures* 43 (2): 89–114.

Clendinning, Elizabeth A. 2020. *American Gamelan and the Ethnomusicological Imagination*. Urbana: University of Illinois Press.

Cohen, Matthew Isaac. 2010. *Performing Otherness: Java and Bali on International Stages, 1905–1952*. New York: Palgrave Macmillan.

Diamond, Jody. 1990. "There Is No They There: Global Values in Cross-Cultural Research." *Musicworks* 37: 12–23.

Dunbar-Hall, Peter. 2016. "Balinese Gamelan: Continual Innovation, Community Engagement, and Links to Spirituality as Drivers for Sustainability." In *Sustainable Futures for Music Cultures: An Ecological Perspective*, edited by Huib Schippers and Catherine Grant, 145–78. Oxford: Oxford University Press.

Gold, Lisa. 2005. *Music in Bali: Experiencing Music, Expressing Culture*. New York: Oxford University Press.

Hood, Mantle. 1960. "The Challenge of 'Bi-Musicality.'" *Ethnomusicology* 4 (2): 55–59.

Harnish, David. 2004. "'No, Not "Bali Hai"!': Challenges of Adaptation and Orientalism in Performing and Teaching Balinese Gamelan." In Solís 2004, 126–37.

Harnish, David, Ted Solís, and J. Lawrence Witzleben. 2004. "'A Bridge to Java': Four Decades Teaching Gamelan in America." In Solís 2004, 53–68.

House, Ginevra. 2014. "Strange Flowers: Cultivating New Music for Gamelan on British Soil." PhD diss., University of York.

Khalil, Alexander. 2016. "The Gamelan Project: Teaching, Playing with, and Learning from American Schoolchildren Playing Balinese Gamelan." *Ars Orientalis*. https://asia.si.edu/essays/article-kahlil/. Accessed November 28, 2021.

Lueck, Ellen. 2012. "'Sekaha Gong Amerika': Affinity and the Balinese Gamelan Community in the United States and Canada." Master's thesis, Wesleyan University.

Macy, Elizabeth McLean. 2017. "'Can I Write It Down?': Repetition, Imitation, and Transmission in Situ." In *Proceedings of the 4th Symposium of the ICTM Study Group on Performing Arts of Southeast Asia*, 219–22. Penang: Universiti Sains Malaysia.

McGraw, Andrew C. 2013a. *Radical Traditions: Reimagining Culture in Balinese Contemporary Music*. Oxford: Oxford University Press.

McGraw, Andrew C. 2013b. "The Gamelan and Indonesian Music in America." Oxford University Press blog, November 27. http://blog.oup.com/2013/11/gamelan-indonesian-music-america/.

McGraw, Andrew C. 2016. "Atmosphere as a Concept for Ethnomusicology: Comparing the Gamelatron and Gamelan." *Ethnomusicology* 60 (1): 125–47.

McLain, Elizabeth. 2014. "Save the UM Gamelan," petition on change.org. https://www.change.org/p/university-of-michigan-school-of-music-theatre-dance-save-the-um-gamelan.

Mendonça, Maria. 2002. "Javanese Gamelan in Britain: Communitas, Affinity and Other Stories." PhD diss., Wesleyan University.

Mendonça, Maria. 2010. "Gamelan in Prisons in England and Scotland: Narratives of Transformation and the 'Good Vibrations' of Educational Rhetoric." *Ethnomusicology* 54 (3): 369–94.

Mendonça, Maria. 2011. "Gamelan Performance Outside Indonesia 'Setting Sail': Babar Layar and Notions of 'Bi-musicality.'" *Asian Music* 42 (2): 56–87.

Miller, Christopher J. 2005. "Orchids (and Other Difficult Flowers) Revisited: A Reflection on Composing for Gamelan in North America." *World of Music* 47 (3): 81–111.

Slobin, Mark. 1993. *Subcultural Sounds: Micromusics of the West*. Hanover, NH: University Press of New England.

Solís, Theodore, ed. 2004. *Performing Ethnomusicology: Teaching and Representation in World Music Ensembles*. Berkeley: University of California Press.

Spiller, Henry. 2015. *Javaphilia: American Love Affairs with Javanese Music and Dance*. Honolulu: University of Hawai'i Press.

Steele, Peter. 2013. "Balinese Hybridities: Balinese Music as Global Phenomena." PhD diss., Wesleyan University.

Strohschein, Heather A. 2018. "Locating Affinity and Making Meaning: Gamelan(ing) in Scotland and Hawai'i." PhD diss., University of Hawai'i at Mānoa.

Sudirana, I Wayan. 2018. "Meguru Panggul and Meguru Kuping; The Method of Learning and Teaching Balinese Gamelan." In *Lekesan: Interdisciplinary Journal of Asia Pacific Arts* 1 (1), https://jurnal.isi-dps.ac.id/index.php/lekesan/article/view/341.

Sumarsam. 2004. "Opportunities and Interaction: The Gamelan from Java to Wesleyan." In Solís 2004, 69–92.

Sumarsam. 2013. *Javanese Gamelan and the West.* Rochester, NY: University of Rochester Press.

Sumarsam. 2016. "Gamelan, Etnomusikologi, dan Kurikulum Perguruan Tinggi di Amerika Serikat." In *Bunga Rampai Pemikiran Akademisi Indonesia di Amerika Serikat,* edited by Deden Rukmana and Ismunadar, 185–98. Yogyakarta: ANDI.

Tenzer, Michael. 2000. *Gamelan Gong Kebyar: The Art of Twentieth-Century Balinese Music.* Chicago: University of Chicago Press.

Vetter, Roger. 2004. "A Square Peg in a Round Hole: Teaching Javanese Gamelan in the Ensemble Paradigm of the Academy." In Solís 2004, 115–25.

Witzleben, J. Lawrence. 2004. "Cultural Interactions in an Asian Context: Chinese and Javanese Ensembles in Hong Kong." In Solís 2004, 138–52.

4

DECLINE AND PROMISE

Observations from a Present-Day *Pangrawit*

Darsono Hadiraharjo and Maho A. Ishiguro

This project (and the resulting chapter) was conducted collaboratively between Maho Ishiguro, an ethnomusicologist, and Darsono Hadiraharjo, a prominent pangrawit *active in Solonese* karawitan *scenes. Written in first-person singular, "I" signifies the voice of Hadiraharjo. All interviews, as well as events such as weddings and rehearsal sessions discussed in this article, were conducted and witnessed by both authors. While setting the theoretical framework, organizing discussions, and reflecting on relevant literatures and scholarship in the field of ethnomusicology is within Ishiguro's expertise, the rich content and opinions in this article come directly from Hadiraharjo. The writing, however, is the result of extensive discussion concerning how we wanted to tell the stories of our project.*

During a roundtable discussion at the SOSIM conference about how *pangrawit* (gamelan musicians, literally practitioners of *karawitan*) view their present-day situation, participants of the event appeared to reach one particular conclusion: the prospects for *pangrawit* and *karawitan* are grim. This roundtable included ethnomusicologists present at the event, the members of the ensemble Ngudi Raras,[1] at Cornell as part of a month-long tour of the United States, and the Javanese scholar-musicians Sumarsam, I. M. Harjito, and Danis Sugiyanto. Most of the comments from the Ngudi Raras members focused on how *karawitan* practices are *turun*—on a decline. This decline has affected the quality of the music, opportunities to perform, economic livelihood, institutional and governmental support, as well as changes in the art industry that have impacted the lives of *pangrawit* and the tradition of playing *karawitan*.

Among the nine Javanese musicians present at the roundtable, I (Darsono Hadiraharjo) was the youngest. I have been among the younger generation of *pangrawit* active in Solo for about a decade, though more recently I have been in the United States serving as an artist-in-residence at Bates College (2017) and a visiting artist at Cornell University (2018–20). In my view, representing the younger generation, the condition and direction of *karawitan*'s future is notably different from the gloomy condition painted by the older musicians at the roundtable. In this article, I first revisit the questions and topics explored at the roundtable, discussing the social, economic, political, and cultural landscape of the network with which *pangrawit* engage in Solo today. I then illustrate the kinds of transformation *karawitan* has undergone in recent times and the direction it may take in the near future.

In order to more fully represent the larger but still relatively small, tight-knit, yet diverse network of *pangrawit* in Solo, I visited a handful of *pangrawit*. Having grown up in a family of *dhalang* (puppeteers) and *pangrawit* serving the communities in Klaten and Semarang as well as governmental and private institutions in Solo and Yogyakarta, I hold knowledge and memories of my family's history and how they have navigated the world of *karawitan*. As an active performer in Solo, I have been engaged with the network of *pangrawit* there for a decade since graduating from Sekolah Menengah Kesenian Indonesia (SMKI) and Institute Seni Indonesia (ISI) Surakarta, national conservatory institutions. Here, I present my own personal views that stem from my experience as a young *pangrawit*. Readers must keep in mind that as each *pangrawit* experiences the socioeconomic and cultural landscape differently, mine is only one understanding of the world of *karawitan*.

I begin by illustrating and contextualizing the grim conditions of the *karawitan* world described by some members of Ngudi Raras. In conversations with me in Solo, older generations of *pangrawit* have highlighted a change in the way people in Javanese society sense and manage time as the primary factor behind the decline of *karawitan*. Simply put, people's lives today are increasingly busy and are managed differently from previous eras. This has affected patronage, people's tastes in entertainment, and musicians' choice of repertoire, as well as matters of *garap* (the interpretation of musical passages), how *karawitan* is learned, and the nature of events at which *karawitan* is performed. I then identify the underlying causes of change, as well as some reasons for optimism about the future prospects for *karawitan*.

The Nature of Events: Two Weddings in July

In early July 2018 I attended a wedding in Gombang, Boyolali, which hired Ngripto Laras, a group of musicians from Klaten consisting mostly of my family and relatives. It was held at the groom's house instead of a rented hall, which would be a typical place to hold a wedding in cities like Solo today. In the case of this Gombang wedding, while the musicians coordinated with the emcees who conducted the wedding, the musicians had great flexibility in what pieces to play and how to play them. Here, Ngripto Laras played some sophisticated classic pieces such as *gendhing* "Lokananta," *slendro manyura* and *gendhing* "Babar Layar," *pelog barang*, to name a few. A few *pesindhèn* took turns singing various *langgam* and *jineman* playfully. The musicians had more time, allowing them to play longer pieces and explore their *garap*, as they were not subject to a strict schedule, which would be the case in a wedding at a rented hall. The whole atmosphere was relaxed, and musicians were given much more liberty in what pieces to perform and how to perform them.

A week before the Gombang wedding, as a member of Langen Praja, the musical troupe at the Mangkunegaran palace, I performed at the marriage of one of the court dancers. Langen Praja was invited to provide musical and dance performances at the wedding.[2] The *pangrawit*, numbering around twenty including myself, gathered at 6:00 p.m. at the venue for the wedding, which began around 7:00 p.m. Ibu Umiyati, the dance teacher of the bride and the wife of the former head of Langen Praja, Bapak Hartono, coordinated this performance. The wedding, which lasted for two hours, was held at Graha Saba Buana, a large rental hall owned by the current president of Indonesia, Joko Widodo. Langen Praja performed the following pieces:

1. *Ketawang* "Mijil Wigaryntas," *pelog nem*
2. *Ladrang* "Semar Mantu," *pelog nem*
3. *Ketawang* "Kodhok Ngorek," *pelog nem*
4. *Ladrang* "Sri Widodo," *slendro manyura*
5. *Ketawang* "Tirta Kencana," *pelog nem*
6. *Ladrang* "Mugi Rahayu," *slendro manyura*
7. *Gambyong Retnokusumo* dance, with *Ladrang* "Sumyar," *pelog barang*, shorter version
8. *Lancaran* "Kebo Giro," *pelog barang* (2–3 cycles)
9. *Gatutkaca Gandrung* dance, comedic version (about thirty minutes with cassette tape accompaniment)
10. *Lancaran* "Sarung Jagung," *pelog barang* (with *ciblon*)
11. A short *langgam*
12. *Ayak-ayakan, pelog barang*
13. *Ladrang* "Tedhak Saking," *pelog barang* (only *irama* 1 and 2 for closing)

In contrast to the pieces played at the Gombang wedding, all the pieces played at this wedding were in the forms of *lancaran, ketawang,* and *ladrang,* which have relatively short cycles. Furthermore, the pieces were played in short rendi-tions, moving briskly from one section to another. *Gambyong Retnokusumo* was similarly shortened by omitting some of the middle sections. Bu Umiyati gave me signs as I played the drums, indicating when to stop and start, coordinating tightly with the emcees' announcements. How Langen Praja played at this wed-ding was typical of today's Javanese weddings, which take place in a rented hall. Everything was delivered on a tight schedule, the music adjusting to a fast-paced event that unfolded like clockwork over just two hours. I played in two other weddings in Solo that July, which followed a similar design.

Most weddings in Solo are held in rented halls today. In order to maxi-mize business, the venues book two events a day. Most guests are aware of the typical set schedule of wedding events. After receiving a sign the event is coming to an end (usually when cold dessert is served at the end of the series of dishes provided to the guests), the guests begin to leave, whether or not the wedding reception is over. "When there is no longer any audience, why would we keep playing? That would be a waste of time and energy" (Suripto, per-sonal communication, August 2018). Even at the wedding for a well-known dancer from the Mangkunegaran court, the management of the limited time ironically took priority over the arts, restricting the repertoire of *karawitan* and its performance. At many weddings and similar events today, I empha-size that the ways the time is managed impact not only the repertoire but also the *garap* (interpretation of performance styles), *rasa* (feeling and the general atmosphere), and one's sense of values for their labor in performing *karawitan*.

People's Tastes in Entertainment Today

"The audience's taste has been changing. They no longer ask for classic pieces that take time to enjoy and understand." Thus observed Sri Mulyanto, the current head of Ngripto Laras (personal communication, July 2018). When the group is asked to perform at an event, the patron may inform the head of the group which pieces she or he would like to hear. For example, when my wife (Maho Ishiguro) and I hired Ngripto Laras for our wedding anniversary in July 2018, we specifi-cally requested classic pieces. In order to fulfill such requests, Mulyanto chose the repertoire to perform and hired a female singer known for her classical technique and style. If no specific request is made, Mulyanto decides what repertoire to play in relation to the event and audience.

Mulyanto commented that it was rare for Ngripto Laras or the other *karawi-tan* groups he was involved with to play a series of classic pieces at events today.

Long, refined, and philosophically deep classic pieces and their performances are simply not in demand, both in and outside of the cities. Mulyanto's group performs for both *klenengan* (performance of instrumental and vocal music) and *wayang kulit* (puppetry performance). In these performance contexts, responding to what pleases the audience, Ngripto Laras increasingly plays lively and short pieces rather than classic pieces.

This preference is also reflected in how performances of wayang are designed. In traditional wayang performances in Solo, *lakon* (stories) are divided into three sections indicated by musical modes. Between these sections, particularly in a contemporary practice, there are *limbukan* and *goro-goro*, two breaks of substantial length that highlight guest singers and feature comedians.[3] Sometimes, a *dhalang* invites important personnel and sponsors from the audience to the stage to sing, chat, or dance. *Dhalang* these days frequently invite female singers specializing in *campur sari*, a style of music with an upbeat nature and catchy, memorable vocal lines that are easy for the audience to enjoy, dance to, and sing along with (see below for further discussion). This accessible entertainment is similar to other forms commonly enjoyed in Java today on TV programs, YouTube, and social media on cell phones. This contrasts with the poetic language and refined art of *karawitan*, which asks the audience to take time and work to understand the performance. Saguh Hadi Raharjo (Pak Saguh), my father, a *dhalang* active from the 1970s to the 1990s and known for his classical style, commented on how audiences in the past used to be satisfied with hearing narration from *dhalang* and seeing the screen with moving puppets and listening to *karawitan*. Today, on the other hand, audiences demand a type of entertainment that is instantly exciting and easy to understand. Pak Saguh lamented that the *dhalang*'s craft of beautiful poetry and ways of narrating and unfolding *lakon*, orchestrating the music and performers, and singing were being overshadowed by the practice of highlighting well-known singers as star guests to attract the audience.

Today, the *limbukan* and *goro-goro* are getting increasingly long, commonly lasting over two hours. This takes away the *dhalang*'s time to narrate the *lakon* and leaves the *pangrawit* less time to perform the music. The types of pieces performed in these sections also tend to be more lively, employing *sragenan*, which features exciting interlocking figuration between two *saron demung* (lower-register metallophones) rather than the longer classic pieces. Audiences' changing tastes have thus significantly reshaped performance styles in wayang as well as *klenengan* events. Here is where we continue to find how people's sense of time results in the ways the *karawitan* performances are shaped today.

The Learning Process of *Karawitan*

"Learning *karawitan* takes time" (Suripto, personal communication, August 2018). In my experience, most *pangrawit* agree with this statement. However, the current curriculum for *karawitan* seems to be heading in the opposite direction. The program at SMKI was shortened from four to three years in 1994 to conform to the national curriculum. I was the second graduating class after the program was changed to three years, though it covered as much material as the previous four-year program. Furthermore, both ISI and SMKI use notation extensively as a pedagogical tool in what they believe is a quicker and simpler learning process for students. By being written down, musical patterns are standardized and, subsequently, often simplified. Such standardization reduces variation, helping students learn patterns in a shorter time.

After I graduated from ISI, my main method of studying *karawitan* was attending rehearsals and *klenengan* by *empu* (master musicians). The Mangkunegaran had routine rehearsals where a number of *empu* gathered on the west side of the palace and practiced large classic pieces that were rarely played. I frequently sat on a bench by the rehearsal room with my notation books, following how these *empu* played pieces that included many special passages. I also began to sit and listen to the musicians at the Mangkunegaran court's *Rebon*, a routine weekly dance rehearsal for Langen Praja. After a few months, they noticed how regularly I attended their rehearsals, observing and quietly studying, and they invited me to play when there were open spots. At these rehearsals outside of school, I learned to make variations, polished the sense of time in *karawitan*, broadened my repertoire, and acquired the skill to work with other musicians. In other words, I matured as a *pangrawit* at these rehearsals outside of school.

Suripto, one of the members of Mangkunegaran's Langen Praja, a former musician at Radio Republic Indonesia (RRI, national radio station), and teacher to many young musicians, emphasized the importance of *pergaulan* (I: to mingle and socialize with others) in the process of learning *karawitan*. Students at the conservatories may have a good handle on technique. However, playing among themselves and their teachers in classes with fixed conditions—in terms of sequence of sections, changes in tempi, and choices of repertoires practiced, for example—the students' exposure is limited in terms of variety of styles, repertoire, and the skills to be adaptable and follow others. This is something I also often observe among my foreign students who have studied *karawitan* for years before coming to Java. Some of these students are highly skilled, having a good handle on various complex melodic and rhythmic patterns. However, when there is a small alteration to the way a familiar piece is rendered, many have a difficult time following the music. The skills needed to do so take a long time to acquire, because it requires the performer to know more than one way of playing a piece and be observant of others.

Furthermore, Suripto expressed the difficulties of bringing young students to practice *pergaulan* at his open rehearsals. He constantly encourages his young students to get out of the classroom. I have also witnessed several ISI teachers bringing their students to Mangkunegaran's rehearsals to introduce them to opportunities to study performance practice. However, only a few of the students from ISI stick around for such rehearsals, because they are likely outside of their comfort zone. The students must also follow the social etiquette practiced by older generations of musicians. Today, as most youth have mobile phones and motorbikes, it should be much easier to coordinate occasions to gather and show up to practice. However, it appears that the more comfortable life becomes, the more difficult it is to manage the time to venture out to an unfamiliar territory, even to broaden one's knowledge. Perhaps the younger generations who are so immersed in the world of internet, which provides quick access to everything, are finding it difficult to travel to the events that require them to engage with others in real time and be physically and mentally present.

Not only the attitudes of the students but also their chances of attending rehearsals and the nature of these rehearsals have changed significantly in recent decades. Marc Benamou observed during his fieldwork in Solo in the early 2000s that there were several types of rehearsals and *klenengan*, such as SMKI's Selasa Kliwon (also known as Malam Anggara Kasih) and routine rehearsals at the house of Rahayu Supanggah, one of ISI's professors (Benamou 2010, 25). I also recall a number of other rehearsals and performances at the Mangkunegaran court and other places such as Balai Soedjatmoko, which helped me learn repertories I did not encounter at ISI. Today, these practices are no longer held regularly. Some of the reasons for their termination include the deaths of charismatic *pangrawit*, such as Martopangrawit, Mloyo Widodo, and Mitro Pradonggo, to name a few, who attracted others to play, ask questions, and learn from them. Today, it is rare to find *pangrawit* who are willing to volunteer their time to organize events and help others learn without compensation. This is because contemporary Javanese society (and the communities of *pangrawit*) increasingly expects cash payment for their labor. With the decreasing number of opportunities to listen and study outside of the conservatory, students and young *pangrawit* do not have the kind of learning environment to which I had access. This has certainly had a direct impact on the quality and repertoire of performances. From the current curriculum designs at the major teaching institution in *karawitan*, to students' learning style today, styles of interactions between musicians, and limited number of rehearsals, I suggest that the changing sense of time in Solonese society has been once again echoed definitively in various conditions in today's *karawitan* world.

Campur Sari

"*Campur sari* destroys *pangrawit*'s sense of *irama* (tempo, rhythm, and timing) and refinement" (Sri Mulyanto, personal communication, July 2018). A number of *pangrawit* have described *campur sari* as aesthetically antithetical to *karawitan*. Practicing *campur sari* thus ruins the musicality required for playing *karawitan*. "I know a *pangrawit* who used to be pretty good. But after playing *campur sari*, he is no longer that great" (Saguh Hadi Raharjo, personal communication, August 2018). As I describe below, according to many *pangrawit*, *campur sari* has turned into *karawitan*'s archenemy, for economic as well as aesthetic reasons.

A handful of scholars have studied *campur sari*, whose Indonesian name means "mixture of essences." Sutton (2013) described the formation of *campur sari* in the 1960s and its revival and popularization in the 1990s, initiated by Campur Sari Gunung Kidul and its group leader, Manthous. *Campur sari* is a hybrid form that integrates the singing style of *karawitan* and its instrumentation primarily with *kroncong*'s light repertoire of *langgam Jawa* and various electronic instruments such as synthesizers and electric guitars. Described as an open-ended genre, *campur sari* continued to absorb a variety of musical genres such as *dangdut* and Indonesian pop music. Sutton describes *campur sari*, which is mostly sung in Javanese, as "re-Javanizing the musical" scene (Sutton 2013, 89). Notably, in his early study of *campur sari*, Supanggah (2003) discussed how the form has come to be associated with modernity, which Indonesia strived to achieve in a short time after the end of World War II. The use of diatonic scales and the addition of electronic instruments in some *campur sari* ensembles evoke modernity for many Javanese.

Cooper's (2015) ethnographic article on *campur sari* covered a wide range of issues around the genre, including its relationship to the music industry and the livelihood of *campur sari* musicians. Just like the musicians she interviewed outside of Yogyakarta, some of the young *pangrawit* in Solo have been drawn to *campur sari*. Ari, a young musician I met at the Mangkunegaran's Pakarti rehearsals, commented how he had refused to play *campur sari* as long as he could, because he very much enjoyed playing *karawitan*.[4] However, about two years ago, one of the senior players in his *karawitan* group began recruiting young musicians to play *campur sari*. One day, his friend came to his house, begging him to join the *campur sari* group. They did not have enough people for a gig that evening as it was during the busy Idul Fitri season. Ari explained that most of his friends in *campur sari* groups around Solo come from a *karawitan* background (Ari, personal communication, August 2018).

While still prioritizing gigs in *karawitan* groups, Ari stated that playing *campur sari* is less of a time commitment, and also less stressful. For example, he explained, when he is in *karawitan* groups, he usually plays *kenong*. When playing in a wayang troupe that often employs *sirep*—where most of the ensemble stops playing to provide a quieter accompaniment to narration by the *dhalang*—he feels highly exposed. In *campur sari*, on the other hand, the keyboard is constantly being played. Therefore, if he does not know a specific piece, he can still derive his parts by listening to the keyboard, unlike in *sirep*, where *bonang*, the easiest part to follow, does not play.[5] Furthermore, when hired as a *campur sari* player, the playing time is shorter but with the same pay, as both *campur sari* and *karawitan* musicians are typically hired per evening of performance rather than by the hour. Supanggah (2003) also discusses the economic advantages of *campur sari*. While gamelan instruments take up a lot of room in venues, the usual setting for an ensemble of *campur sari* only requires a keyboard and a handful of gamelan instruments, which is much more practical to set up, saving time, energy, space, and ultimately money. In other words, *campur sari*, in comparison to traditional *karawitan*, is much more manageable, in terms of space, performance skills, and time.

I asked Ari who listens to *campur sari* and why audiences seem to like it. My young nephews and nieces in their teens and twenties listen to American pop as well as Indo-pop. I cannot imagine them listening to *campur sari* through their MP3 players or cell phones. Ari explains that people across generations love *campur sari* at events like wayang and weddings because they can dance to it. Also, with its dominant vocal line, the pieces are easy to remember and audiences can sing along. *Campur sari* is thus more inclusive, not only in its integration of various genres of music but also for audiences seeking to participate in the music through song and dance. I recall here the *halal-bihalal* event of my family in June 2018.[6] Even though about 60 percent of those who gathered at this event were practicing *pangrawit*, we hired a *campur sari* singer and a keyboard player. Before the close of the event, a number of women in the family, most of them *pesindhèn* or wives of *pangrawit*, went up to the front, took the microphone, and sang along and danced to *campur sari*. Even my eighty-seven-year-old aunt joined the dance floor!

Campur sari maintains some local styles of music such as the repertoire of light *gendhing*, songs by Ki Nartosabdho (1925–85), and *langgam Jawa*, while integrating new elements of the audience's choosing.[7] Its participatory nature and memorable melodies appeal to today's tastes in entertainment. While the ongoing existence of *karawitan* has been bolstered by government-funded institutions such as RRI, ISI, and SMKI, *campur sari*'s popularity rose out of its direct appeal to the audience. It is the flexibility and adaptability in the very nature of *campur sari* that allowed the genre to transform and develop in accordance with its audience's tastes at particular times.[8]

Underlying Causes of Change

To summarize the analysis of the contemporary *karawitan* world I have discussed so far, it appears that the older generations of *pangrawit* who experienced a "better" world of *karawitan* in earlier times lament today's performance contexts. The limited time given to playing *karawitan* at events such as weddings, anniversaries, and wayang force *pangrawit* to choose short pieces that are played in quick succession. With a packed schedule at these events, the music serves as an interlude between the emcees' announcements and the *dhalang*'s narration. Changes in audiences' tastes inform the choices *pangrawit* make in the selection of repertoire. Looking for immediately understandable, fun, and exciting entertainment such as *campur sari* or light and popular *gendhing*, today's public does not want pieces deep in philosophical meaning. This has impacts also in the recording industry, which no longer records *karawitan* and finds higher sales in *campur sari*, both in cassette and VCD or, more recently, DVD formats.

Moreover, the way *pangrawit* manage their economic livelihood today reflects the social and cultural changes impacting the *karawitan* world. One of the reasons for the paucity of *klenengan* relates to how *pangrawit* prioritize their time. In the past, *pangrawit* took pride in the tradition they maintained—as seen in the rehearsals at the Mangkunegaran that focused on rarely played classic pieces. There was no significant compensation for showing up and rehearsing these pieces. Rather, the musicians found value and honor in being the carriers of the traditions their ancestors had practiced for generations. I articulate that the common factor for the various transformations in the *karawitan* world I discussed here—the "declines" in the eyes of many traditionalist gamelan musicians in and outside of Java—is the change in the ways the Solonese society perceives and values the passing of time today.

I believe *karawitan* today has become too associated with monetary gains and too distanced from its values in connection to the courts and its functions in everyday lives of people. The offering of *syukuran* (I: an act of giving thanks) for anniversaries and *bersih desa* (I: a traditional practice that is performed to cleanse villages from bad spirits) events in the past frequently involved *klenengan* or wayang. Central Javanese traditionally believed in the values and power these performing arts had, and such *syukuran* events kept *pangrawit* busy. Today, it is much less common for people to hold *sykuruan* events, let alone to hire *karawitan* groups for them. The decrease in the number and quality of *klenengan*, changes in the nature of events and pedagogical styles, and competition with *campur sari* have led the older generation of *pangrawit* to view *karawitan* as having a bleak future, both economically and culturally.

Socialization of *Karawitan* Today

The kinds of *klenengan* where I deepened my experience of *karawitan* when I was in my teens and twenties do not exist anymore. Today, I rarely get to play the deeply philosophical and abstract classic pieces. However, looking at the young generation of *karawitan* practitioners today, I feel that they are springing back, figuring out how to be engaged in the world of *karawitan* in new ways.

First, it is evident that the number of students involved in the performing arts has been increasing. Enrollment at ISI—both in Solo and Yogyakarta—is steadily growing each year in the *karawitan* and wayang as well as other departments. Mulyanto, who has taught at ISI Yogyakarta for a decade, commented that the enrollment in the *karawitan* department has more than doubled since he began teaching. Interestingly, he stated that *campur sari* has brought new types of students who are not from traditional musical families to ISI. At neighborhood events, through the radio, and wayang, people are widely exposed to *campur sari*. As it is a genre of music capable of integrating various styles, some of the pieces sung in *campur sari* are songs by Ki Nartosabdho and reference other popular *karawitan* pieces. Therefore, young people are getting more exposure to gamelan instruments and the repertoire of *karawitan* through *campur sari*, leading some to enroll at ISI to study *karawitan*.

The exposure of the general population to *karawitan* also comes from the government's effort in education. During the presidency of Susilo Bambang Yudhoyono (2004–10), the central government created a program called *muatan lokal* (I: regional curriculum), through which schools in various areas in Indonesia choose teaching material focusing on local practices. In Java, *karawitan* became part of *muatan lokal* as well as extracurricular afterschool programs supported by BOS (Bantuan Operasi Sekolah), a national program that has funded student activities in school since 2005 with a significant boost in funding since 2009. When I was in middle school in Delanggu, my school was well known for having a *karawitan* program. It was rare for K–12 schools to have a *karawitan* program prior to the implementation of *muatan lokal* and BOS. Through school programs such as these, *karawitan* has become more widely practiced today.

The wider circulation of *karawitan* among the general population is also discussed in a dissertation by Jonathan Roberts (2015) that focused on community gamelan groups attended by middle-aged women and men. In Solo since 2005, when Joko Widodo (Jokowi) became the mayor, there have been many programs for restoring local traditional and cultural practices. "Solo, the spirit of Java," a well-known slogan seen on many billboards and stickers on cars in Solo today, emerged from Jokowi's effort to preserve the unique traditional and cultural practices the Solonese are proud of. Besides renovating traditional markets and cleaning up the streets, Jokowi's programs have been continued by his successor, FX Hadi Rudyatmo, who has expressed the goal of providing a full gamelan set to every *kelurahan* (the lowest level of governmental administration) in Solo. As of September 2018, twenty-six of the fifty-four *kelurahan* in Solo have been given a set of gamelan.[9]

In some cases associations of businesses gather money to buy gamelan instruments. In small villages outside of Solo, community groups often use instruments that are rented out by individual owners. The practice of gathering in local villages to play *karawitan* has taken place for several decades, possibly emerging from the legacy of Pembinaan Kesejateraan Keluarga (PKK), a New Order program that aimed to gather neighborhood women to socialize. Roberts (2015) noted that these groups typically do not reach high technical levels of performance, and some groups may view socialization as their primary purpose for gathering. Nevertheless, many are enthusiastic about performing at competitions and weddings as well as recording and broadcasting through RRI programs. Some of these amateur groups have also applied for grants from Pemkot (I: *pemerintah kota*, city office) to support their performances and practices.

A Solonese royal court has also begun to not only widen the opportunities for learning courtly practices of traditional Javanese performing arts but also make them more inclusive.[10] In 2014 the Mangkunegaran court founded Akademi Seni Gaya Mangkunegaran (ASGA, Academy of Arts in Mangkunegaran Style) to provide instruction in dance, music, and theater repertoire to a new generation of artists.[11] ASGA offers Diploma 3 (similar to an associate's degree) to its students, most of whom work during the day and attend classes in the evening. The degree is recognized by ISI Yogyakarta, which accepts ASGA graduates as transfer students if they wish to continue their study and receive an undergraduate degree. ASGA is financially supported by local government offices as well as through private donations, which make student tuition much lower than ISI and other universities. Graduates of ASGA are often given the opportunity to perform at events at the Mangkunegaran such as Sabtu Ponan, restoring and maintaining the performing arts styles specific to the court. Finally, in Solo there are countless informal arts communities such as Pakarti and Sanggar Soeryo Soemirat that make the traditional arts more accessible than in the past, when the traditional arts were passed down within artist families.

Today, the number of people involved in the Javanese performing arts is higher than ever, both among youth and adults, as the general population of Solo are engaged in *karawitan* in comparison to the past when the practice of *karawitan* was more exclusive to families that have been involved in the arts for generations and to court personnel. Governmental as well as grassroots interest has resulted in the wide accessibility of practicing *karawitan*. Though there has been some decline in institutions such as RRI, the downward trend identified by the *pangrawit* in the panel may change in the near future as ISI graduates enter governmental sectors. Today, ISI has broadened its curriculum, offering majors in arts management, media studies, and ethnomusicology. A number of graduates with degrees in these disciplines enter *dinas*, local offices that deal with tourism, culture, and education, which previously had been filled with administrators without arts experience.

With the greater accessibility of the performing arts, changes have occurred in the nature of *karawitan*. But many *pangrawit* are concerned with the quality of performances. As discussed earlier, training in *karawitan* requires a long period of study and constant exposure to the arts. Gathering to practice at *sanggar* (I: private studios; see Catra's chapter in this book) or schools once or twice per week is simply not enough for one to master a broad repertoire of *karawitan*. Older generations of *pangrawit* have commented that while the younger generation active in *karawitan* today may have better technique due to their formal studies, they struggle to embody *rasa*—the essence of each piece, leaving their performances without blend, without *rasa*.

The issues regarding *rasa*—the loss of them and also changes in them—are evident also at the professional level. When I participated as part of Langen Praja from the Mangkunegaran at the International Gamelan Festival (IGF) in August 2018, the *pangrawit* decided to play a medley of *gendhing*, which consisted of seven pieces for a total duration of forty minutes. Rather than playing a single long *gendhing*, which would better represent classical court practice, the *pangrawit* put together a continuous medley for the audience to enjoy the flavor of several different pieces. The pieces in this medley were undoubtedly classic, yet Langen Praja's performance catered to the tastes of today's audience.[12] As the *kendhang* player, following the choice of a senior musician who, for one part of the medley, selected a certain vocal part known to be appropriate for wayang performances, I added the wayang style of *ciblon* drumming as well as patterns often heard in lively *gambyong* dances.[13] A similar trend was seen in the performance by the group from the Paku Alaman (the minor court from Yogyakarta) at IGF, where its *pangrawit* played a couple of popular pieces including a *langgam*. Even in the courts, where the classic *gendhing* and the deep philosophy and refinement of *karawitan* originate, popular styles have been adopted in performance. Finally, at the same event, the Kraton Kasunanan brought out its *rebab* (a type of bowed string instrument), which is considered a *pusaka* (heirloom), as a number of *pangrawit* processed behind the instrument. This was one of the very rare occasions where the Kraton has shared their treasure with the general public, a sign of the wider socialization of their sacred possessions.

The current popularization of *karawitan* through the socialization of traditional practices and adaptation of popular styles is not new. Some earlier examples of adaptation of popular folk style arts (I: *kesenian rakyat*) are recorded in various historical periods. For instance, *tayuban*, a village dance tradition and the parent form of a more well-known *gambyong* dance, and its lively music styles that use *ciblon* drumming have been witnessed in the courts as a result of fluid movement of people between rural villages and cities (Widyastutieningrum 2004). More recent practice of incorporation of popular styles into traditional forms are seen in the works of Ki Nartosabdho, a composer who created many memorable, singable vocal parts for existing complex pieces, making them more accessible to the general audience. Such changes were met with opposition in the 1960s, especially among the die-hard classicists. Teaching staff at ISI and court-serving *pangrawit* in the past have been known to have ripped and burned books of notations that contained Nartosabdho's compositions. However, his pieces today are increasingly popular and widely played, because they are deeply loved by the general audience as well as many *pangrawit*. Resistance to change has been common among older *pangrawit* for generations.[14]

As I enjoy playing classic and philosophical *gendhing* and also see great importance in popularizing *karawitan* among the general public, I hope, as a member of the younger generation of *pangrawit*, the community of *pangrawit* can be part of both maintaining classic *gendhing* and making *karawitan* accessible to the general public. As Suripto stated, we *pangrawit* are only servants to this wonderful tradition, which our ancestors have practiced for generations (Suripto, personal communication, August 2018). Rather than lament the decreasing demand for classic *gendhing*, I hope *pangrawit* can remind the public of the great cultural values our ancestors have carried through the practice of *karawitan*.

NOTES

All non-English text is Javanese, except for Indonesian text indicated by the abbreviation "I." We would like to thank Chris Miller and Andy McGraw for all the encouragement and opportunity to work on this project. Finally, we dedicate our first collaborative project to the late Bapak Saguh Hadi Raharjo, the father of Darsono and Maho, and artistic mentor to many, both in and outside of Java.

1. The members of Ngudi Raras on tour in 2018 were Wakidi Dwidjomartono, Mulyani Soepono, Paimin, Sularno Martowiyono, Sri Mulyana, and myself, Darsono Hadiraharjo.

2. The Mangkunegaran is one of the two courts in Solo, the other being Kasunanan. Both have contributed significantly to the continuation of *karawitan* in Solo; however, the Mangkunegaran court has been known to have higher-quality musicians and performances (Benamou 2010). Today, Langen Praja represents one of the highest levels of performance and the strongest commitment to classical repertoire in Solo.

3. See Mrázek 2005 and Emerson 2016 on the changes in roles and content of *limbukan* and *goro-goro* from classical to Nartosabdho-style wayang performances. Originally a small section where a chaotic condition in a wayang story is played out, *limbukan* and *goro-goro* today typically last over two hours and feature guest musicians and comedians hired specifically for these sections. This style of *goro-goro* was popularized by Nartosabdho and practiced widely by *dhalang* today. Such contemporary characteristics of *goro-goro* reflect the increasing focus on the entertainment value for the audience in performing arts, corroborating Mulyanto's comments.

4. Pakarti is a gathering of musicians at the east side of the Mangkunegaran palace that began in the 1950s. Today it is open to anyone interested in practicing, with a focus on the repertoire of dance and music frequently performed at the Mangkunegaran court.

5. Only the soft instruments, plus *kenong, kempul*, and *gong*, play in *sirep*.

6. *Halal-bihalal* is an Indonesian-Muslim practice of gathering people after the end of Ramadan. Typically families and relatives and neighborhood come together to celebrate Idul Fitri and to greet each other to deepen their ties and friendship.

7. See Perlman 1999 for a detailed and comprehensive discussion on *campur sari* as an ensemble that fuses various musical characteristics of existing music genres and repertoires, including *langgam Jawa, kroncong*, and pieces by Nartosabdho, all popular among the general public in Solo at the time of this writing. Perlman further illustrates the works by Manthous, which resulted in a significant development and popularization of *campur sari*.

8. On the topic of governmental supports for the arts under Sukarno and Suharto's administration, see Lindsay 1995, Yampolsky 1995, and Harnish 2006.

9. "Upaya Melestarikan Budaya dan Seni, Pemkot Surakarta Hibahkan Gamelan ke Kelurahan dan Sekolah" [In effort to preserve culture and arts, Surakarta city government grants *gamelan* to villages and schools], *Tribun Kaltim*, August 12, 2018, http://kaltim. tribunnews.com/2018/08/12/upaya-melestarikan-budaya-dan-seni-pemkot-surakarta-hibahkan-gamelan-ke-kelurahan-dan-sekolah.

10. Felicia Hughes-Freeland illuminates the changing roles of court dance traditions in Yogyakarta's Keraton Kesultanan in her 2011 book. At the end of World War II, especially with the establishment of Kridha Beksa Wirawa, the practice of court dance experienced a significant transformation, including the use of dance as education of Javanese minds and bodies. At this point, along with the activities at Taman Siswa, court dance traditions that had been exclusive inside the court walls became part of the identity-building process of the Central Javanese and the nation of Indonesia, which was politically dominated by the Javanese. Among royal Javanese courts, the Mangkunegnaran in Solo is known to have been more open to changes, adopting new styles of music and dance as well as art practitioners and students. It is the first court to formally establish a performing arts academy to teach its particular repertories and styles.

11. ASGA is an institution attached to the Mangkunegaran court, which gives particular focus on the performing arts in Mangkunegaran court style. Located in the east side of the court, ASGA attracts students in their late teens and early twenties from Solo and its

vicinity. As ASGA is a Diploma 3 program, it follows the national curriculum guideline, which requires general education courses such as religion, Indonesian language, *pancasila* (the state philosophy), and *pendidikan kewarganegaraan* (I: civics). There are three majors, study of *wayang kulit* performance, dance, and art management, which the students can pursue at ASGA over six semesters.

12. The medley began with *gendhing* "Bondhan," *pelog nem minggah* "Saratruna," then continued to *ladrang* "Semang" in *bedhayan* style and a section of *patethan pelog nem ageng*, followed by *ketawang* "Puspanjala," *ayak-ayakan* "Kemuda," finishing with *ayak-ayak* "Mijil" in *irama wilet* with *ciblon* and returning to *ayak-ayak* "Kemuda" with wayang-style drumming and singing.

13. Sukamso, a faculty member at ISI Solo, had a significant part in choosing the repertoires for Langen Praja's performance at IGF this year, including a *gerong* (male chorus) melody for *ayak-ayak* "Kemuda" composed by Nartosabdho. As this melody was written for and frequently used in wayang, I chose to employ wayang-style drumming.

14. Perlman notes the interesting relationship between the popular pieces of Nartosabdho from the 1970s and 1980s and older generations of *pangrawit* who found Nartosabdho's arrangements of already-existing *gendhing* "shallow and incompetent" (1999, 5). I have also heard accounts where well-known *pangrawit* from the courts did not agree to play Nartosabdho's pieces and burned notations of his compositions. I agree with Perlman's argument that the popularity of Nartosabdho's pieces endured long after the deaths of these *pangrawit*, as many gamelan musicians continued to create pieces in his style.

WORKS CITED

Benamou, Marc. 2010. *Rasa: Affect and Intuition in Javanese Musical Aesthetics*. New York: Oxford University Press.

Cooper, Nancy. 2015. "Retuning Javanese Identities: The Ironies of a Popular Genre." *Asian Music* 46 (2): 55–88.

Emerson, Kathryn Anne. 2016. "Transforming Wayang for Contemporary Audiences: Dramatic Expression in Purbo Asmoro's Style, 1989–2015." PhD diss., Leiden University.

Harnish, David D. 2006. *Bridges to the Ancestors: Music, Myth, and Cultural Politics at an Indonesian Festival*. Honolulu: University of Hawai'i Press.

Hughes-Freeland, Felicia. 2011. *Embodied Communities: Dance Traditions and Change in Java*. New York: Berghahn Books.

Lindsay, Jennifer. 1995. "Cultural Policy and the Performing Arts in Southeast Asia." *Bijdragen tot de Taal-, Land- en Volkenkunde* 151 (4): 656–71.

Mrázek, Jan. 2005. *Phenomenology of a Puppet Theatre: Contemplations on the Art of Javanese Wayang Kulit*. Leiden: KITLV Press.

Perlman, Marc. 1999. "The Traditional Javanese Performing Arts in the Twilight of the New Order: Two Letters from Solo." *Indonesia* 68: 1–38.

Roberts, Jonathan. 2015. "The Politics of Participation: An Ethnography of Gamelan Associations in Surakarta, Central Java." PhD diss., Oxford University.

Supanggah, Rahayu. 2003. "Campur Sari: A Reflection." *Asian Music* 34 (2): 1–20.

Sutton, R. Andy. 2013. "Musical Genre and Hybridity in Indonesia: Simponi Kecapi and Campur Sari." *Asian Music* 44 (2): 81–94.

Widyastutieningrum, Sri Rochana. 2004. *Sejarah Tari Gambyong: Seni Rakyat Menuju Istana*. Surakarta: Citra Etnika Surakarta.

Yampolsky, Philip. 1995. "Forces for Change in the Regional Performing Arts of Indonesia." *Bijdragen tot de Taal-, Land- en Volkenkunde* 151 (4): 700–725.

Part II
MUSIC, RELIGION, AND CIVIL SOCIETY

5

SINGING "NAKED" VERSES

Interactive Intimacies and Islamic Moralities in *Saluang* Performances in West Sumatra

Jennifer Fraser with Saiful Hadi

Saiful Hadi was my key collaborator in this research on saluang. *He shaped the design of the project, helped facilitate attendance at events, introduced me to performers, and assisted in textual transcriptions and interpretation.*

When Saiful Hadi, known on the circuit as Pak Ketua, and I arrived at the café on the outskirts of Payakumbuh, a town in the heartland region of West Sumatra, around midnight on a July evening in 2015, three women were sitting on a stage. They were *padendang* (vocalists) in a Minangkabau genre known as *saluang* for the flute that accompanies the vocals. Santi (a stage name), then thirty-five, and her younger sister, Si Tel, were wearing skimpy, short-sleeved T-shirts, glittery headbands, and heavy makeup. One man, the *janang* (emcee), sat cross-legged on the edge of the stage, while another initially sat behind the keyboard and later moved to play the *saluang*.[1] There was a scattering of *pagurau* (attendees) seated at the tables in the café. This was a kind of *saluang* known as *bagurau lapiak*. Technically, its name derives from the context; *bagurau* means "to joke around" while *lapiak* refers to the mats on which the performers sit. But performances known as *bagurau lapiak* come with a host of other associations, including those about places where they are held (markets, coffee shops, and roadside stalls); musical style (a mix of songs from the repertoire now marked as *saluang klasik*[2] and various pop styles, including *pop Minang* and *dangdut Minang*); instrumentation (*saluang* mixed with keyboard); and guiding moral codes. Several performers and devotees told me that *bagurau lapiak* are venues where activities and behaviors outside the normative standards of Islamic propriety occur. In other words, things happen in these contexts that you would not witness in other Minangkabau contexts, including other kinds of *saluang* performances. Most importantly, however, the term *bagurau lapiak* makes reference to the economic frame of these performances; when performers are not contracted for private or community celebrations on a given evening, they might gather to work at one of these events. Rather than receiving a fixed fee as they do at other engagements, they work for tips, dividing the earnings between themselves and the manager of the space. *Pagurau*—who almost exclusively identify as cisgendered men— pay for the privilege of making requests, often for a particular song or singer.[3] A financially successful *bagurau lapiak* is dependent on the performers' ability to engage and keep an audience, a duty that falls largely to the vocalists and emcee.

In this chapter I draw on fieldwork with *saluang* that spans eighteen years, involves more than forty hours of field recordings with some three hundred songs and formal interviews with singers, flute players, and other people engaged in the genre, to offer a close reading of the song "Upah Kasua." The chapter focuses on the lively interactions, what I call here "interactive intimacies," between the vocalists and audience members, which extended this song's duration from a more typical six or seven minutes to twenty-three. What was so special about this song? Why was the audience so engaged in it? The song, like most in any evening, was specifically requested by an audience member. Its title, translated as "Fees for the Mattress," metaphorically references financially supporting one's children in order to secure sex with one's wife. When such references, in both song titles and lyrics, are made through allusion to sexual organs, sexual acts, or particular people, they are identified locally as *porno*. In mainstream Minangkabau sensibilities, discussion of human anatomy pertaining to reproduction and sexual acts is taboo, especially so between men and women. Discursive formations—both scholarly and vernacular—of the people who identify as Minangkabau celebrate their Islamic piety and position them among Indonesia's most devout Muslims. But the stories, practices, and behaviors I witnessed while doing research on *saluang*, including vocalists' choices to deliver lyrics identified as *porno* and their audiences' delight in them, suggest that these romanticized narratives of Minangkabau piety should be revised and expanded to take into account the plural realities of contemporary Minangkabau lives.[4] Moreover, by alluding to the possibility of erotic play in these performances, I am fulfilling Deborah Wong's call to counter an "ethnomusicology devoid of erotics" (2015, 179).

In *saluang*, a song is defined by melodic content, not text; vocalists have some freedom in choosing texts within a specific performance. It is possible, then, for the singers to deliver the melodic content of songs with *porno* titles but refuse to sing lyrics that would be classified as *porno*, or the more salacious varieties of texts where there is no attempt to veil the references to body parts or people that are labeled either *pantun telanjang* (I: naked verses) or *pantun vulgar* (I: vulgar

FIGURE 5.1 Te E and Si Nor, senior *padendang,* dressed modestly, at a *saluang* performance for a wedding in Suayan, August 1, 2015. Photograph by the author.

verses), depending on the interlocutor. Te E (Aunty E), the most celebrated singer when I was in the field in 2015 and 2016 (figure 5.1), told me on several occasions that she refused to sing *porno* lyrics (interview, Payakumbuh, July 15, 2016). The vocalists that night at the *bagurau lapiak,* however, made different choices.

In *saluang,* texts can be created in the moment of performance by responding to the general mood or sentiment of the song and the performance context. Pak Ketua estimated that about 80 percent of the texts are *baku* (fixed), meaning they are relatively standard in form, known by different singers, repeated, and sometimes connected with a specific melody, while some 20 percent are created anew, what Pak Ketua and others call *spontanitas* (I). All texts in *saluang* should be structured according to rules of *pantun,* a poetic form found throughout the Malay world. *Pantun,* which feature lines that are eight to nine syllables long, are structured in two halves; the first, what *saluang* performers call the *batang,* draws on references to the natural environment, local places, or the context of performance, while the second, the *isi,* contains the content, the moral or message. The two halves, moreover, must rhyme. Many of the verses are four lines in total, although I have recorded some examples that are as long as twenty-four. Almost all songs, moreover, are strophic in form with *saluang* interludes between verses. However, there are no predetermined number of times performers will sing a strophe nor which singer will sing when. There is considerable flexibility in the moment of execution.

"Upah Kasua" that evening was almost entirely spontaneous, driven by interactions with the audience, including their commentary and requests as delivered through the emcee. The nature of the discourse—both the commentary and the lyrics—was highly sexualized by Minang standards, suggesting a kind of social intimacy between performers and audience. In delivering this song, Santi, the lead *padendang,* included a *porno* reference in the very first verse, alluding to sleeping with one's wife without having intercourse.[5] After the second verse, the emcee delivered a request to prolong the song, along with a jab at Santi about eating *kueh rayo* (sweets served during Lebaran) alone, thereby making her plumper. She responded to their provocation in sung verse, inviting the listeners over to Tanjuang Aro, her neighborhood, to eat cake. She wants the audience to think about her, to not get "drunk over someone else," that is, obsessed with another singer.

Ka Tanjuang Aro sajo makan kue	Come to Tanjuang Aro [my house] to eat cake
Iyo dek alah kueh den asiangkan	The cakes are ready to serve
Elok lah kanduang bajaleh-jaleh	Don't think about someone else
Oi jaan dak diek dimabuak angan-angan	Don't get drunk with those thoughts.

After Santi delivered this particular verse, Pak Ketua whispered to me that the offer to "come eat cake" was *kata sindiran* (I: an allusion) for audience members to "come play at her house," a direct sexual invitation. This verse therefore can be considered "naked." Its inclusion blatantly challenges normative Minang moralities. As Pak Ketua told me, in the *klasik* style of *saluang*, you are not allowed to issue such an invitation. But it is part and parcel of the *lapiak* scene, a context that was viewed as morally corrupt by a number of performers I encountered. As a young singer in her twenties (her identity has been veiled for her protection) commented to me, there were "no limits" to what vocalists would sing about; no refinement or allusion; they started late at night; and they were often held in locales where attendees would consume beer. There was, in her mind, nothing respectable about these performances (personal conversation, 2015). Mila, a singer in her early thirties, was equally disparaging of the vulgar lyrics, but she also made reference to the practice of vocalists dancing directly with men for *saweran* (tips) (informal interview, August 1, 2015). I've never personally witnessed such dancing at a *saluang* performance. Several vocalists, including Te E and Mila, directly told me they do not participate in *bagurau lapiak* out of personal choice and a sense of morality, while the young singer quoted above told me her husband expressly prohibited it. This context for *saluang*, then, has a bad reputation in some circles.

Interactive Intimacies

The inclusion of "naked" verses, like the one above, is predicated on what I call "interactive intimacies" between the vocalists and their almost exclusively male audience members. In some ways, these intimacies parallel what Nancy Cooper calls "seduction scenarios" (2000) and Bader and Richter call "*nyawer* encounters" (2014). This phrase also is inspired by the work of other scholars interested in performer-audience relationships, including Ali Jihad Racy's "ecstatic feedback model" in regard to Arab *tarab* (1991, 1998) and Jang's study of vocal exclamations (or increasing lack thereof) by the audience in Korean *p'ansori* (2001). Racy found interactions with the audience key to a musician's creative impulses, the unfolding of the musical event and, ultimately, "the nature of the created musical product" (1991, 8–9). Contexts for *saluang* were extremely intimate in the days before amplification;[6] audiences had to sit close to and be attentive to the musicians, but the nature of the interactions was comparatively limited, restricted to requests for particular songs, which were conveyed, moreover, in a discreet way, whispered to a performer or conveyed on a slip of paper. Historically, Minangkabau moral codes required a sense of modesty and self-effacing reserved behavior, which held for both performers and their audiences. Performers were not to engage in direct eye contact with the audience but should look down. It was even appropriate for performers to close their eyes during performance (Phillips

1992). When we attended performances together in 2016, Pak Ketua often commented on the posture and stance of the singers, commenting when singers erred or correctly embraced the old standards. In the past, there was little eye contact or discussion, then, between performer and audience.

The nature of the interactions has changed and expanded radically over the years, tied with the increasing participation of women as vocalists since the 1960s. In the past, women's participation in *saluang* was limited. As Adriyetti Amir relates: "According to some interpretations of Islam, women cannot be the focus of view or of hearing. Their voice itself is considered 'aurat' [part of the body that should not be exposed, according to religious law]." This perspective, she argues, has historically limited women's participation in Minangkabau oral traditions as it was "not suitable for women to sing in front of men," moreover in the middle of the night (1995, 28, 32). Writing in 1995, Adriyetti Amir suggested that men were still the dominant vocalists in *saluang*, whereas Peggy Sanday, writing in 2002, only referenced vocalists who were women. During my fieldwork in 2015 and 2016, I encountered no active male vocalists at the performances I attended.

The "interactive intimacies" I discuss, therefore, are particular to contemporary performance contexts, though Philip Yampolsky and Hanefi (1994), Adriyetti Amir (1995), and Sanday (2002) all mention the inclusion of erotic texts in *saluang*, suggesting lyrics called *porno* today have existed for some time. While there can be a sense of physical intimacy between performers and their audiences based on proximity of seating, the intimacies I reference are more of a social, and sometimes sexual, nature. They are reliant on personal familiarity. On the *saluang* circuit *padendang* and *pagurau* often know each other by visage, name, current and previous relationships, and other information. *Pacandu*, a term reserved for the most devoted fans, have the cell phone numbers of their favorite *padendang* so they can find out where they are singing on any given night. Vocalists, for their part, are seen actively responding to texts and calls on their cell phones in the course of performances.

In contemporary *saluang* performances audience engagement is key to the creative process. As Racy suggests for *tarab*, the creative "process derives its significance and effectiveness from its immediate physical and temporal contexts." In other words, what happens during any *saluang* performance is "essentially place and time specific" (1991, 9). Each performance and the way it unfolds is unique, constituted by a series of intersecting axes, including performance context, location, and style of *saluang*. Each of these parameters influences who the performers will be, along with their individual talents and abilities. The flow of an evening—which songs will be performed, how those songs are structured, the types of *pantun* used, and the nature of interactions—is constituted in part by the audience who attends (see figure 5.2, which shows the various

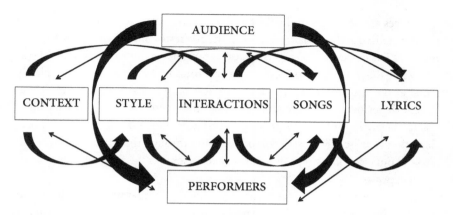

FIGURE 5.2 The interplay of elements structuring *saluang* performances.

interplay of factors). *Padendang*, therefore, need to be nimble and responsive to a variety of requests made by the individuals who constitute the audience over the course of an evening. While one might be tempted to think of the performance practice as "improvisational," that perspective, according to Racy, is "a categorical distinction that may stem mostly from Western analytical perspectives." There is no local term that is equivalent: rather, just as in *tarab*, there is a "fundamental acceptance of flexibility and spontaneity as norms of musical creativity" (1991, 18).

A successful *bagurau lapiak* is financially contingent on the interactions—verbal and gestural exchanges in the course of performance—because this is where men depart with their money and the performers make money. When the men want to make a request at a *lapiak* performance, they come up to the stage, folding a bill over the edge of the cardboard box, whispering their request to the emcee or delivering a written note, using slips of paper set out on the tables. *Pagurau* can request particular songs, selecting from hundreds in the *klasik* repertoire, or even a pop song; though they never know what might be requested on any given night, singers need to be prepared to cover the repertoire. I've also heard *pagurau* ask to prolong a song, repeat a text, respond to a verse or phrase, or prolong a specific ornament. At some performances, men use requests to flirt with the vocalists or make sexual overtures, such as asking a singer to remove her jacket or asking her personal questions. Enamored of a particular singer, *pagurau* might ask her to sing. For example, at the *bagurau lapiak* that evening, someone made a request for "Santan junior" to sing. This was a reference to Santi, who is considered beguilingly plump and nicknamed for her resemblance to a well-known singer, Santan, who was then in her fifties.

Emcees are necessary to the flow of the evening at *lapiak* performances; their job is to enhance the joviality and keep the requests coming, thus boosting the revenue. The emcee mediates the requests, announcing them over the sound system while the *saluang* continues in the background. Their interjections typically come at the end of a song, but they can also occur, as was the case in "Upah Kasua," at periodic intervals during the song after a verse or two. These exchanges create a lively interplay between singers and attendees. Although audience participation is principally restricted to mediation through the emcee, listeners will also call out cries of appreciation or other comments as the song unfolds. Silence is not expected.

For the singers in the *lapiak* scene, it is a financial imperative to establish and maintain intimacy with one's audience. A vocalist needs to be able to gauge her audience and keep them engaged. The request of "Upah Kasua" set the stage for intimacy, for it opened up greater likelihood for *porno* content. As Mila said, the singers in the *lapiak* contexts are "brave to bring these [naked] *pantun* because they want to get the money" (informal interview, Payakumbuh, August 1, 2015). A year later, Pak Ketua reinforced this idea, stating that "the [singers] do as they wish in order to captivate people [listeners]" (personal conversation, July 22, 2016). Moreover, as one *tukang saluang* (flute player) asserted, vocalists ultimately "have to consider the feelings of those making the requests" and "satisfy their viewers" (personal conversation, August 1, 2015). Singing racy verses helps attract the men—and keep their attention. Another strategy for success is to tease attendees through their texts, using stage names or allusion. Santi, the lead singer that night, performed most of the song; her familiarity with the men in attendance that evening allowed for a particularly vibrant interaction, just as the attendees' knowledge of each other enhanced the sense of camaraderie and allowed them to get her jokes.

Another tool singers employ to attract audiences is to dress provocatively. Sartorial choices are significant and culturally charged. By mainstream Minang standards, singers should dress modestly, like Te E (see figure 5.1), with long sleeves, long skirts, and, for the most modest, a headscarf. In comparison, the women at this *lapiak* performance with short sleeves and close-fitting T-shirts would be considered by many Minang to be scandalously dressed. Their choice in attire didn't go unnoticed at the performance, either. Putra Panampuang relayed a comment, announced by the emcee to all in attendance, "I am looking at your shirt, Santi, there is a brand. What is the brand? It's not evident to us." The implication behind his comment was that Santi might lean over more so the men could see the logo, thereby revealing more of her cleavage. Clearly, some men are responsive to these sartorial presentations.

Men are attracted to *bagurau lapiak* for different reasons. Hanging out in the market one night, Pak Ketua ranked men's motivations for me, saying the first consideration is about a particular singer's attractiveness and sartorial choices; the second is the racy verses; and lastly a singer's voice (personal conversation, July 31, 2015). Mak Lenggang, a faculty member at Institut Seni Indonesia (Indonesian Institute of the Arts) in Padang Panjang who is a semiprofessional *saluang* player, agreed that for most attendees, a pretty face and body trumped singing ability, but he also added that men also attend for the camaraderie with other audience members (personal conversation, Padang Panjang, July 23, 2015). During a performance, men compete for the singer's attention, trying to one-up the others in their requests, but the community of devotees is, as Pak Ketua pointed out, also a close one. The men—at least the regulars on the circuit—know each other well. The performance space allows for conversation, and the most devoted *pagurau* stay up all night, many nights in a row, seeking this entertainment. The devotees check in with each other about when and where performances are happening, sharing knowledge gained by word of mouth, through SMS text messaging and social media. Sometimes they even meet up in order to travel together in a pack of motorbikes. Like the performers, the *pagurau*, or at least the regulars, have what Pak Ketua referred to as *nama pentas* (I: stage names) or nicknames on the *saluang* circuit known to others. For example, Pak Ketua is one of his current nicknames because he used to be the head of a *saluang* organization. At this performance, he was called Mak Datuak, referring to an appointed leadership role within his clan. Formerly his nickname was Roda-Roda Gila (Mad Wheels) because he was fanatical about driving around the countryside in search of *saluang* performances and often drove his motorbike a little wildly. In performance, the name of the *pagurau* making the request is announced by the emcee, which is one way that familiarity is built over the course of a performance.

I have heard stories—or rather, gossip—about behaviors *padendang* engaged in that I have not personally witnessed. Anthropologists and folklorists have theorized the concept of "gossip," shedding light on its cultural meanings, value, and import for anthropological inquiry. Van Vleet, for example, suggests it is important to "examine gossip as culturally and linguistically situated sets of practices that shape moral discourses and social relationships (including that between the ethnographer and her interlocutors) in particular cultural contexts" (2003, 492). It is a way, in other words, through which individuals "make sense of relationships and events, creating order and coherence from the complicated and contingent occurrences of everyday experience" (2003, 492). In the context of *saluang*, it helps people parse competing discourses and behaviors associated with normative Islamic piety. For example, a number of individuals felt it important to tell me that some singers engage in morally questionable behaviors, such as dancing with men during a performance or arranging encounters beyond the stage. Some people used the term *teman gelap* (I: literally, "a friend in the dark") to refer to the behavior where an unrelated man would escort a singer to and from a performance for a tip. As Abrahams asserts, "Gossip, like joking, takes place between individuals who stand in a special relationship to each other. We can therefore discern a good deal of the formal and informal social structure of a community by noting those categories of people who joke or gossip with each other." It is important to note that the stories of the most "outrageous" behaviors came from men, perhaps an attempt to "increase the gossiper's base of esteem" (Abrahams 1970, 290), whereas virtually no singer was willing to acknowledge such practices when talking with me, unless she was trying to deliberately distance herself from these behaviors. Gossip, as Van Vleet suggests, is "one type of evidence upon which ethnography might be based," but it is also important "for how we understand the process of knowledge production in anthropology: the politics and power relationships involved in how an ethnographer comes to know, what an ethnographer is permitted to know, and how these might be incorporated or left out of ethnography" (Van Vleet 2003, 492). Most of the singers with whom I spoke positioned themselves on record as modest, pious Minang women. Many of them expressed some concern, at least in theory, about the degradations to lyrics, even if in practice they incorporated *porno* lyrics.

Finally, if we consider gossip as a "technique for maintaining community control through the elucidation of a public morality" or policing a "community-held public image in the face of internal conflicts and external pressures" (Abrahams 1970, 290–91), then the stories people tell about drug and alcohol consumption, extramarital affairs, and high divorce rates tell us something. In this close performance scene, it is common knowledge who is dating whom, how many times a singer has been married, and who her current husband is. Many of these singers end up marrying men from the world of *saluang*, whether male performers or the attendees, and that knowledge becomes part of the performance practice, when men are teased in song lyrics. In this *saluang* scene, the line between gossip and the public sphere can be ambiguous, difficult to tell where one ends and the other begins, though I would argue when the stories about individuals enter the sphere of performance through lyrics and requests, it is more firmly in the realm of the latter.

Close Reading of "Upah Kasua"

The rendition of "Upah Kasua" that night, the only one I have recorded to date, lasted for almost twenty-three minutes, two to four times longer than any other song I documented in 2015 or 2016.[7] It engendered some of the most animated exchanges between vocalist and audience members I've ever witnessed, suggesting the conditions that night were prime for optimal interactive intimacies. Santi read her audience well and was responsive to their demands, interjections, and commentary; the men were primed to listen carefully; and the members of the audience gelled during this particular song. Even though there were three *padendang* on stage that night, it was almost exclusively Santi singing. The emcee played an active role in fostering the jovial environment, enhancing and encouraging increasing intimacies between the vocalists and the audience members through commentary and interpretative explanations. How men in the audience react to the delivery of the texts (for example, through shouts, jeers, amusement, or contemplation) also influences the way a particular song and event unfolds. In this rendition of the song, there were eleven verses, two of which were partial: just half a *pantun*. Ten of these eleven *pantun* were sung by Santi and one by her younger sister, Si Tel. As Mak Lenggang said, most of the younger singers don't know the tunes in the more *klasik* repertoire, like "Upah Kasua," just the pop tunes, so they often just sit there letting the more capable singers do all the work (informal interview, Padang Panjang, July 25, 2015). Curious about the relative amounts of time spent on text, *saluang* interludes, and emcee narration, I mapped out the relative division of time. The delivery of text constituted about 39 percent of the performance, the *saluang* interludes just 20 percent. The remaining 41 percent— a significantly greater percentage than other songs I witnessed in 2015–16—was constituted by the emcee's conveyance of audience requests and commentary.

Why were the men so engaged in this particular song? One factor was the quick wit of Santi in responding to their requests, in rhyming couplets no less; her lyrics were not only playful but demonstrated a high level of artistry. Another factor is the actual content of the text. In the third verse, as seen above, Santi invited the attendees over to her house to eat cake. The following verses and interactions involved discussion of the kind of cake she'll make and how she'll make it, with different men in the audience contributing to the dialogue. Many of the attendees are identified individually by their nicknames, but sometimes, as at this performance, collectively by a group name, for example, Lumuik Simpang is the name of a group. In the back and forth, starting at 04:22, the group promises to stop by Santi's house. Santi in turn promises a big cake, and Lumuik responds saying a slice would be enough for them. Putra Pasena specifies that Santi doesn't need to make a big cake, but rather "a round cake with lots of chocolate sprinkles," and if it is a round cake, he wants a big slice, not a small one. In response, Santi states one slice is not enough; she'd give him the whole cake. In return, Putra Pasena comments that if it's not a small cake, then she should give it all away, while the group Lumuik Simpang asks, "If the cake is that big, how many eggs are used? Please clarify, Santi." The third request delivered in this particular interlude after the fifth verse also includes the request to see the logo on her T-shirt more clearly. This segment of requests lasts well over a minute, suggesting this interaction is as important as the delivery of text by vocalists. The *saluang* plays a brief interlude and Santi doesn't take up the cue to enter where a vocalist might, so the emcee jumps in again, with a request from Pak Ketua, here called Mak Datuak, that he made partially, much to my chagrin, on my behalf: "If Santi makes a cake, how delicious is it? Because her triceps are strong to mix it. The cake will be finished in a minute with the shaking of her upper arms," a comment on her physique and generous triceps, which engenders considerable laughter. In retort, she sings another half verse: "[Even] if the eggs are not that many, mixing is still needed." It's unclear the reason for the delivery of just a half *pantun*: Was she consumed with laughter, couldn't think of a matching, rhyming couplet, or something else? Technical errors, like the failure to deliver a whole *pantun* or use the correct rhyming scheme, do happen in these performances. Bujang (a term that is used interchangeably with Putra here) Pasena counters her verse: "Santi, if there aren't that many eggs to put into the mix, but the [egg] whites are necessary, add margarine and sugar." Santi's response to this verse is worth looking at closely, because it illustrates the depth of these interactive intimacies and generated the most robust laughter.

Biaso buek kueh di Lubuak Bangku	Usually to make a cake in Lubuak Bangku
Iyo putiah jo nan balabiahkan	The [egg] whites are used more
Oi kalau itu kami lah tahu	If that's the case, we already know
Indak paralu kanduang kato kan	You don't need to talk about it.

This verse generated such a response because she was referencing a specific person in the audience, Putra Pasena, and his ex-girlfriend from Lubuak Bangku. As Pak Ketua told me, everyone in the audience and the performers were aware Pasena used to date this woman. Therefore, this would be another verse that veered into the territory of "naked" verses by "gossiping" directly about people. Emboldened by her direct reference, Pasena responded yet again (remember he was paying at least 10,000 rupiah each time he made a comment): "If in Lubuak Bangku, there are two eggs. If in Tanjuang Aro, there are lots of eggs. Just one egg container is not enough, you need a *sacabek* (a container that holds hundreds of eggs), because Santi your upper arms are big. In Lubuak Bangku, the upper arms are small." This was another direct reference: people who knew his ex-girlfriend knew she had small upper arms and that now he liked Santi's plump upper arms and their power. Two verses later, Santi comments on Pasena's changing tastes:

before he used to like this skinny woman in Lubuak Bangku, whom she named directly in the verse, but now he liked a woman who is "meatier," that is, herself. These explicit references are yet more examples of how "naked" these verses became in this rendition.

There is one final interaction worth focusing on. The emcee announces, "If the strength of the big upper arms is known, how is the strength of the small upper arms?" In other words, the attendees know the strength of Santi, but they don't know about the strength of Si Tel, her younger sister. This was an indirect request for Si Tel to sing. In the same break between verses, the emcee conveyed a comment from the oldest man in the audience: "Who is the one singing with that voice? I am really affected by it." It's hard to catch the full exchange on the recording, but I am also certain there was a comment that stated, "Although I am already old, I still have *saleronyo*." The reference to *salero* implies sexual appetite and can more specifically reference an erection. Si Tel does sing in response to the request—the only verse she takes in the whole song. The first half is a stock verse, but the second was, "If those stirring are not good, please point out to us how to do it." It's not clear if she's referring to stirring the eggs, the appetite, or both. How an audience member interprets a verse in the moment affects how it might get categorized. And that's part of the point of these verses: how much innuendo you want to read into the metaphor of making a cake, breaking the eggs, beating the eggs, use of egg whites, and so on, is contingent on one's previous exposure to these kinds of exchanges and one's personal capacity to infer sexual innuendo. As Pak Ketua explained to me, not everyone gets these metaphors or references. Any *pantun* has the capacity to be interpreted on multiple levels: some people think about it literally, while other people have the requisite internal context to get the joke, especially when it is about specific people. Part of the attraction to and enchantment in *saluang* for engaged listeners are their enjoyment of the vocalists' skillful wordsmithing, their ability to get the double entendres.

In the rendition of "Upah Kasua" discussed above, the men clearly became more animated as the song progressed, with more individual members of the audience becoming involved in the dialogue and encouraging the verbal sparring to continue, deliberately issuing provocative comments that would engender response from the vocalists, largely Santi. While critics complain that such lyrics are far from the subtle allusions that have been a hallmark of the genre for generations, this performance clearly illustrates the quick wit of vocalists. Interactive intimacies are key to the creative process of *saluang* performances: the particular nature of them shapes the way the rendition of a particular song unfolds. The delivery of this song took so long precisely because the audience became highly engaged and invested in it, in part, I argue, because of the "naked" verses and racy content, but also because of Santi's ability to capture and hold their interest.

These interactive intimacies—through the nature of the performance context, the performative stances of these vocalists, the lyrical content, and commentary by audience members—rub against the normative middle-class, Minangkabau narratives of Islamic moralities. I deliberately waited until I was older to return to ethnography of the *saluang* world, knowing that my presence as an unmarried woman at these performances late at night would present some logistical challenges. It was part of the reason I hired Pak Ketua, an older, respected man within the scene, to travel with me to performances. His experience, standing, and position within the *saluang* scene and investment in the genre and my research about it engendered our close collaboration. Until this research began in the summer of 2015, I had spent the majority of my time in West Sumatra among very devout Muslims. It was precisely my limited experience that attracted me to navigate the murky waters of *saluang* and its nonnormative behaviors, to complicate the romanticized notions of Minangkabau people as pious Muslims. As an ethnographer, I feel compelled to represent these other realities. Even though these events are part of the public sphere, I face the challenges of how to represent them and the engagement of individuals ethically, protecting the rights of human participants. In the *saluang* world, I did encounter behaviors and stories I have not witnessed in other contexts, such as stories about performers using *sabu* (methyl amphetamine) and getting jailed, or stories about a singer being married seventeen times. On our way home from a performance around 2:00 a.m., Pak Ketua pointed out a café where, in his words, "bad things" happen: alcohol and *sabu* are consumed and sex workers hang out. Caught between contemplating the ethics of exposing a more unsavory depiction of Minangkabau life and challenging those romanticized images, I solicited advice from colleagues in West Sumatra. One Minang ethnomusicologist agreed it was important to write about this world, to include the pornographic, and not just the flattering images of Minang people as pious. Pak Ketua himself agreed it was important to share the stories but suggested that I anonymize identities when discussing specifics of lives that occur off stage or outside the performance realm, such as people's marital status, extramarital affairs, or drug habits. The performance I discuss in this chapter was part of the public sphere, open for anyone to attend, and shared with the neighborhood through loudspeakers. The song texts and interactions that were verbalized, shared with all to hear, are part of the public record. I am reminded of anthropological discussions of gossip suggesting that everyone has a personal stake in the narrative, that we must consider *why* people are telling the stories. While it might be tempting to read this *saluang* world as a liminal space in Minangkabau society, a place that is betwixt and between the norms of behavior for everyday life, it is the everyday reality for these singers and their audiences. Communitas is created through performance.

The singers have some agency over what to wear and the lyrics to sing, even if economic realities structure the range of possibilities. When I was working in Sumatra in the summers of 2015 and 2016, there was no discussion among participants of government or religious bodies officially policing and contesting these performances. When I questioned Pak Ketua about it, he responded that those who are devout—he used the phrase "Islam *murni*" (I: pure Islam) to explain what he meant—choose not to participate in the *saluang* scene, concerned with maintaining their reputations and avoiding the gossip that might ensue if they were seen attending events. For example, my host father, recognized as a devout man within the community, admitted he was no longer so comfortable attending *saluang* performances. In other words, these performances, especially those within the *lapiak* scene, have a reputation that challenges dominant Islamic moralities in West Sumatra. I think it is important to document the plurality of practices, the multiple ways of being Minang in the world today.

NOTES

All non-English text is Minangkabau, except where otherwise specified. The abbreviation "I" indicates Indonesian.

The research for this chapter was made possible through a Harold H. Powers Travel Grant from Oberlin College for fieldwork in the summers of 2015 and 2016. I especially thank Saiful Hadi for his assistance and invaluable contributions, along with all the other individuals named or not within the chapter. This research received clearance from Oberlin's Institutional Review Board.

1. Because of the sensitive nature of this material at this performance, I have elected not to include photographic evidence until I can have a more explicit conversation with the key performers. I have decided to retain the vocalist's stage names, following Saiful Hadi's guidance on which material it was important to anonymize.

2. The term has been created retroactively and used in both live practice and the recording industry to distinguish the so-called original repertoire and performance style from contemporary descendants, like *saluang dangdut*, a style borrowing repertoire, rhythm, and instrumentation from *dangdut* (Fraser 2013).

3. While I am alert to moving beyond the gender binary, in my more than twenty years of experience in West Sumatra, I have found most people identify as cisgender men or women, including the participants—performers and attendees—at *saluang* performances. However, I use this term cautiously, recognizing it is one imported from discussions of gender identity in the United States and not a term I have encountered in Sumatra.

4. Readings of Islamic piety should also be intersectional; specifically they should also be crosscut with gender, location, and socioeconomic class. Such a reading, however, is beyond the scope of the current paper.

5. The *isi* of the verse translates literally as "Take your body to the well [the bathroom] / If you don't shower, just wash your face." See "Rendition: 'Upah Kasua' 07/31/2015" in Fraser et al. 2021, https://songinthesumatranhighlands.com/song-in-the-sumatran-highlands/

rendition-upah-kasua-073115, for an audio recording of the performance along with a complete transcription, translation, and analysis. The page is part of a digital project on *saluang, Song in the Sumatran Highlands*, funded, in part, by the National Endowment for the Humanities.

6. Some musicians and audiences still prefer this setting, engaging in a type of performance labeled *saluang lamak* ("*saluang* that is pleasing"), which are small gatherings involving true connoisseurs dedicated to the poetic and musical artistry involved.

7. Again, see the webpage noted above for the recording, transcription, translation, and analysis of this song.

WORKS CITED

Abrahams, Roger D. 1970. "A Performance-Centred Approach to Gossip." *Man* 5 (2): 290–301.

Amir, Adriyetti. 1995. "Women Performers in Minangkabau Oral Tradition." *Tenggara* 34: 23–35.

Bader, Sandra, and Max M. Richter. 2014. "Dangdut Beyond the Sex: Creating Intercorporeal Space through *Nyawer* Encounters in West Java, Indonesia." *Ethnomusicology Forum* 23 (2): 163–83.

Cooper, Nancy I. 2000. "Singing and Silences: Transformations of Power through Javanese Seduction Scenarios." *American Ethnologist* 27 (3): 609–44.

Fraser, Jennifer. 2013. "The Art of Grieving: West Sumatra's Worst Earthquake in Music Videos." *Ethnomusicology Forum* 22 (2): 129–59.

Fraser, Jennifer, with Saiful Hadi, Arzul Jama'an, Martis, Syahril, Gabriela Linares, Megan Mitchell, and Benjamin Simonson. 2021. *Song in the Sumatran Highlands*, last updated July 12. https://songinthesumatranhighlands.com/song-in-the-sumatran-highlands/index.

Jang, Yeonok. 2001. "P'ansori Performance Style: Audience Responses and Singers' Perspectives." *British Journal of Ethnomusicology* 10 (2): 99–121.

Phillips, Nigel. 1992. "A Note on the Relationship between Singer and Audience in West Sumatran Story-Telling." *Indonesia Circle* 58: 67–70.

Racy, Ali Jihad. 1991. "Creativity and Ambience: An Ecstatic Feedback Model from Arab Music." *World of Music* 33 (3): 7–28.

Racy, Ali Jihad. 1998. "Improvisation, Ecstasy, and Performance Dynamics in Arabic Music." In *In the Course of Performance: Studies in the World of Musical Improvisation*, edited by Bruno Nettl and Melinda Russell, 95–112. Chicago: University of Chicago Press.

Sanday, Peggy R. 2002. "Songs and the Performance of Desire." In *Women at the Center: Life in a Modern Matriarchy*, 149–70. Ithaca, NY: Cornell University Press.

Van Vleet, Krista. 2003. "Partial Theories: On Gossip, Envy and Ethnography in the Andes." *Ethnography* 4 (4): 491–519.

Wong, Deborah. 2015. "Ethnomusicology without Erotics." *Women and Music* 19: 178–85.

Yampolsky, Philip, and Hanefi. 1994. Liner Notes for *Night Music of West Sumatra: Saluang, Rabab Pariaman, Dendang Pauah*. Washington, DC: Smithsonian Folkways CD SF 40422.

6

FROM TEXTS TO INVOCATION

Wayang Puppet Play from the North Coast of Java

Sumarsam

Toward the end of my research in 2017, when my new research topic was still up in the air, I met Gunawan Suwati, a musician, *dhalang* (puppeteer), and leading artist in Tegal. I met him for the first time in my second visit to the area. In my first visit, I interviewed a number of *wayang golek dhalang* and attended their performances, including a performance of one of the most popular *dhalang*, the late Ki Enthus Susmono, who was also the governor of Tegal. He was known for his kitschy, humorous style, but also for the Islamic nuances in his performances.[1] Knowing that I was interested in studying *wayang golek*, Gunawan suggested that I document an older form of this genre unique to Tegal. He felt that the older style had been diluted by modern *wayang kulit* and the new style of Ki Enthus Susmono's *wayang santri*.[2] I enthusiastically accepted Gunawan's suggestion. I agreed to work with him to organize a performance, assemble musicians, and find *dhalang* who were interested in participating in this documentation project. This documented performance of *wayang golek* proved to be a treasure trove of information. I would like to thank Gunawan Suwati for his suggestion.

Before discussing this performance and documentation, I would like to mention briefly in what way the subject matter in this article, *wayang golek*, intersects with my broad interest in the history of Javanese performing arts, the interest that has resulted in the publication of two books (Sumarsam 1995, 2013) and numerous articles. While looking back and thinking about the contents of my past publications in relation to the sociopolitical realities we are living in the post-9/11 world, especially its impact on Muslim communities and their cultures, I feel that it is timely for me to return and expand my research on Islam and performing arts.[3] The post-9/11 era has brought issues of religion and culture to the fore of public consciousness. In this regard, debates about a perception of the view of "Islam against performing arts" often surface. Dialogues between the recently emerged radical Islamic voice and the localization of the Western-influenced, global cultural trend have brought about a discussion of pros and cons on the place of traditional performing arts in today's Indonesian society. It is with this rather overarching background in mind that two years ago I carried out field research on, among other genres, *wayang golek* in the North Coast areas of Java (especially the area from Batang to Tegal) and the inland of South Central Java—the former is the focus of this study. Unlike two-dimensional wayang leather puppet play, this three-dimensional wooden puppet performs without a screen. In Tegal's area and Indramayu it is called *wayang golek cepak*. Unlike *wayang kulit*, this wayang genre reenacts Islamic stories and the stories of *babad* (local chronicles), instead of Hindu epics as in *wayang kulit* performance.

Essentially, this present study is an investigation of recent discourse around Islam and the performing arts among the Javanese. Because *wayang golek* reenacts Islamic stories, this study will broaden the scope of my inquiry regarding Java's long tradition of performing arts and its interface with the Islamization of the area. It is also worth mentioning that amid the discussion on Islam's perspective toward the performing arts, certain Muslim communities on the North Coast of Java maintain and even revitalize the existence of *wayang golek* as a marker of their local identity, as well as for celebrating social events and individual rites of passage.

Documentation and Performance

Returning back to my encounter with Gunawan, continuing conversation with him led to the performance and documentation of *dhalang* Ki Warnoto's *wayang golek* performance. On the morning of November 28, 2017, the wayang stage and gamelan was set up under the tent in front of Suwati's house. Like many *wayang golek* performances nowadays, a sound amplification system was used. On their arrival, *dhalang* Warnoto and the musicians rehearsed, guided by Gunawan. They focused their rehearsal on a few pieces that the musicians seemed to be having a hard time remembering. It was mentioned to me that the drummer who used to accompany Ki Warnoto's performance had passed away. Therefore, Warnoto invited a drummer from out of town who had never accompanied his performance before; hence the rehearsal often focused on matching the drum rhythms and the rhythmic movements of the puppets. The rehearsal finished at around noon. Lunch was served for them. Afterward, the musicians dispersed, some went to another rehearsal in a different location, and Ki Warnoto went home to rest and prepare for the upcoming evening performance for documentation.

At around 7:00 p.m., the musicians and *dhalang*, in a full traditional costume, gathered, ate dinner, and prepared for the performance, which began with a musical overture. Unlike the musical overture for *wayang kulit*, which consists of pieces in *pathet manyura*, the musical overture for *wayang golek* consists of pieces in *pathet sanga*.[4] After the overture ends, the *dhalang* signals the play to begin. The musicians play a piece named "Kawitan Tegal" to accompany the first scene. After moving *kayon* (a puppet representing the tree of life) from the middle of the screen, signifying the opening of the play, Ki Warnoto introduced two puppets of ladies-in-waiting, dancing in turn to lively rhythms. Then a puppet representing a king entered, sitting on a throne, followed by a signal from Warnoto for the music to accelerate. At a certain point, most of the instruments dropped out, except for a few quiet instruments. This is known as *sirep*, used to accompany the *dhalang*'s narration. In the Tegal style of *wayang golek* this is called *ngabor*.[5] Below is the beginning of his narration:

Sareng sakenyarira Sanghyang Predangga Pati, gumantya mring Sanghyang Ratri, kapanjutan ima-ima, gambura lawan ancala. Ima-ima mega, gambura segara, ancala puncaking gunung.

When the sun is going down, changing the day to nighttime, it illuminates *ima-ima, gambura*, and *ancala*. *Ima-ima* means cloud, *gambura* ocean, *ancala* the tip of the mountain.

Sanghyang Anon methik pupusing gebang siwalan tunggal, nedak kinen dha-padha, tinetesan asta gangga ganggané wirantanu. Asta namaning tangan, gangga banyu, wira tulis, tanu mangsi.

God picks the tip of the single leaf of *gebang siwalan*, cutting it in the same length, sprinkled by *asta gangga wirantanu*. *Asta* means hands, *gangga* water, *wira* pen, *tanu* ink.

Samyå rebutan papan mboten wènten ingkang saged nututi antawisipun. Saweneh wonten ingkang nuwakaken papan, saweneh wonten ingkang nuwakaken tulis.

People debate about tablet [and writing], no one can confirm the difference. There are those who consider tablet as older than writing, and vice versa.

Awit praptané balé dumadi inggih minati anyar pinanggih al warak al wahi, dumugunipun akhiré jaman.	Because of the arrival of new life, we find a new creation in the form of books of revelation until the end of the world.
Kamangka saderengipun papan gumelar, tulis sampun gumantung. Saderengipun tulis gumantung, papan kang sampun gumelar.	The issue is that, before the tablet exists, writing has existed. Before the writing exists, the tablet has been available.
Saicaling papan tulis, para pujangga sami manunggal ngregengaken, sami nggunggung aksara.	After the disappearance of the tablet and writing, poets get together for reckoning the letters.
Tibaning mangsi aneng papan nimbulaken leksara sawidak kalih cacahe. Leksara suwidak-kalih kapundhut tigang-dasa kabucal mengaler dhawahipun wonten tanah Bandi Israel inggih wonten tanah Arab inggih tanah Mesir	As the ink falls on the tablet, it has led to the creation of sixty-two letters. Of the sixty-two letters, thirty of them are thrown to the direction of the north, falling on the land of Bandi [India?], Israel, and Arab or Mesir.
Leksara punika terik tesih gundhul dereng dipun paringi sandhangan mbenjang lamun sinandhangan saged ngawontenaken kitab Jabur, Injil kelawan Torek lan al-Quran.	The letters are still plain, haven't yet been given vowel symbols. In the future, when the vowel symbols are added, the form of books of revelation until the end of the world. They will lead to the creation of holy books of Jabur, Bible, Torah, and Qur'an.

Hearing Ki Warnoto's narration of the opening of the play, my immediate response was that it is very different from the opening narration of *wayang golek* I have seen before, and strikingly different from that of *wayang kulit* performance.[6] I expected that it would be different, but not *this* different!

Regardless of the difference, what we should know is that the narration of the first scene in any wayang performances is actually an invocation, a literary yoga of some sort, "a hymn to the power and potency" (Foley 2002, 88), or an apology (Zurbuchen 1987), to the gods. This invocation, presented in stylized language and accompanied by a soft music, is meant to have what Turner (1982) calls a liminal effect for the listeners, while the story is only mentioned in passing. Although I am aware of this phenomenon, I am completely at a loss regarding the line: "The Almighty picks the top of *gebang siwalan* leaf, to be cut in the same length, sprinkled by *asta gangga wirantanu*. *Asta* means hands, *gangga* water, *wira* pen, *tanu* ink." I asked myself, what is *dhalang* Warnoto talking about? I understand that *gebang siwalan* is a leaf and tree of the palm family. When he mentions hand, water, pen, and ink, taken together, he is describing the elements and process of archaic writing, using dried palm leaf, or *lontar*. The subsequent sections of the invocation I found even more confusing. He mentions the origin of the alphabet, which was transformed to Arabic letters, which bring about the birth of the holy books of the Jews, Christians, and Muslims. Later on he also mentions the origin and meaning of the Javanese alphabet, the *hanacaraka*.

As I mentioned, Ki Warnoto's invocation is very unique when compared to *wayang kulit*. In traditional *wayang kulit*, after a few opening sentences of narration, the *dhalang* will mention the name of the location of the scene, usually a kingdom or gods' abode. In Warnoto's *wayang golek*, a large part of the beginning narration does not in any way touch on the story presented in the scene. While the story line presented in the first scene in our documented performance concerns a king who is looking for ways to reject suitors for his daughter, the content of Warnoto's narration is about the practice of ancient writing and the birth of the alphabet and scriptures. In this study, I will focus only on the beginning section of the invocation, the section that mentions *asta gangga wirantanu*.

Realizing that I hadn't seen enough *wayang golek*, I viewed more performances on YouTube. I found that a few *dhalang* in Pemalang, Indramayu, and Cirebon, all near Tegal on the North Coast, also used variants of the same text Warnoto used. Subsequent research led me to discover the use of variants of the same texts by *dhalang* in the Pasundan area of West Java and in Banyumas and Cilacap, in South Central Java. The same line of texts is used by both *wayang golek* and *wayang kulit* performers. Interestingly, I also found out, after rereading Zurbuchen's (1987) and Hooykaas's (1973) books, that the same line is also recited by Balinese *dhalang*.

All things considered, three questions come to my mind. First, what is the significance of an invocation using ancient texts that describe ancient writing technologies? Second, how do we explain the distribution of *asta gangga wirantanu* texts, especially its concentration in the north coastal (*pesisir*) area, extending to Bali? Lastly, what is the origin of the texts?

From *Pustaka* to *Pusaka*

With regard to the first question, I would like to suggest the following explanation. In the early centuries of Javanese history, during the process of the Hinduization of Java, the Javanese were not only introduced to the Hindu religion but also underwent a technological revolution, namely, writing tradition. In India, the earliest Hindu sacred writing of *veda* (collections of poems and hymns composed in archaic Sanskrit) took place a thousand years before the Common Era. Indian writing was introduced to Indonesia in the first millennium CE, in the form of inscriptions written on stone or copper plates (Hunter 1996). This development brought about the rise of Hindu-Javanese kingdoms. Subsequently, these centers promoted not only sociopolitical and religious life but especially literary and artistic endeavors, such as the introduction of the Hindu epics, the *Ramayana* and *Mahabharata*. Because this tradition of writing, however rudimentary it was at the time, was a highly valuable tool to document and disseminate knowledge and literary works (the manuscript, *pustaka*), the Javanese treated *pustaka* and the physical object (in the ancient times *lontar*, dried palm leaves) on which the manuscript was written as venerated objects.

The reason for considering them as such can trace its origin from one of the main aims of the poets in writing their literary works: as an act of worship. In his study of *kakawin*, Zoetmulder identifies the Old Javanese words *lango, lengeng, lengleng* as a way for the poets to express their emotion in worshipping the god of beauty. "What they convey is a feeling that is perhaps best rendered by 'rapture.' It is a kind of swooning sensation, in which the subject is completely absorbed by and becomes lost in its object, the appeal of which is so overwhelming that everything else sinks into nothingness and oblivion" (Zoetmulder 1974, 172). This magico-religious observance of the poets resonated in the minds of and was observed by the Javanese, so much so that they treated *pustaka* (manuscript) as *pusaka*, an heirloom or magically charged object from which power can be absorbed. Perhaps the idea of manuscript containing power was similarly deeply felt by the author of *Bhima Svarga*, discussed below, so much that he felt it necessary to describe in detail the technical means of writing as a way to show his readers the technical intricacy of writing to reinforce the notion of venerating writing tradition.

The adaptation of certain texts used for invocation also relates to this veneration of expressing knowledge through written documents and the physical objects on which they are written. One might also think of this phenomenon as analogous to a symbolic expression of *curiga manjing warangka* (the union of the dagger and its sheath) when Javanese people talk about the mystical union between the content (*isi*), that is, the blade of the dagger, and the receptacle (*wadhah*), the sheath of the dagger.

Maritime Trade and Networks, and the Origin of the Texts

With regard to the second question—the distribution of texts along the North Coast—my research led me to trace the maritime world of trading in Southeast Asia, which began in the fifteenth century. As Vickers (1993) points out, the Southeast Asian maritime world made it possible for a cosmopolitan interweaving of cultures to develop. In the case of Java's North Coast area, maritime trading led to the formation of a *pesisir*-community complex, which made possible the movements of ideas, people, and their literary and performing arts in the area. Vickers has eloquently explained intraregional interactions as reflected in Balinese *kidung* poetry, *malat*, and other literary forms. Pigeaud (1967, 6–7) has mapped the expansion of literature in this period, starting from East Java and going both eastward and westward, through the literary centers of Gresik, Demak, Cirebon, and Banten.

One of the most widely disseminated stories in that period, not only within the *pesisir* trading network linking Java to other insular islands but also reaching as far as the mainland of Southeast Asia (Cambodia, Thailand, Malaysia, and Myanmar), was the Javanese story of Panji. According to Vickers (1993, 68), Panji stories provided a model of Java's exemplary qualities for the kingdoms in the archipelago.

With the wide distribution of the Panji story in Southeast Asia in mind, I assumed that the text recited by *dhalang* Warnoto was also disseminated through the Panji story. However, I cannot find evidence to support this assumption. Instead, my research led me to the village of Kabuyutan Ciburuy in West Java, following up on research conducted by a philologist at the National Museum of Indonesia, Aditya Gunawan, who has recently published an article titled "Manuscript Production and Aksara Mysticism in *Bhima Svarga*" (2016). In this study, he describes a collection of *lontar* manuscripts from the village of Kabuyutan (now housed in the National Museum of Indonesia). He describes a number of manuscripts containing the story of *Bhima Svarga*, written in Old Javanese. It was in the *Bhima Svarga* that the texts of *dhalang* Warnoto's invocation originated.[7]

In the story of *Bhima Svarga* the second of the five Pandhawa brothers, Bhima, wants to rescue his father Pandu from hell, where he was being punished for killing a deer. After going through many trials and battling the guardians of hell, Bhima was able to rescue his father. Subsequently, he has a dialogue with God Siva (Guru). One of the topics of the dialogue concerns the origin of *pustaka*:[8]

[Bhīma:] guru mǝne dak atakon iri kita, paran rika kamūlaniṅ pustaka hirǝṅ iku, mantañen sinaṅguh lǝvih, paran kaṅ ginave.

[Guru:] Bhīma dak varah ta kita, mūlaniṅ pustaka hirǝṅ, roniṅ gǝbaṅ, pinukah pinaḍapaḍa lvane lavan davane, tinitisan gaṅgā vīra tanu, gaṅgā riṅ bañu, vīra riṅ panuli, tanu riṅ mañsi (66.2–4).

Kukusiṅ lǝṅa dilah, ghināṣa riṅ lavak tambaga, jineran laṇḍaniṅ kǝpuh, vinoran lāka, iṅulig iṅǝnah riṅ pamaṅsen, ya ta mañsi arane, ikaṅ ta prasiddha ṅgvaniṅ agave pustaka (66.6–8).

[Bhīma:] There is more, Guru. I would like to ask you. How did the earliest manuscript turn black, until it was said to be the best, how was this done?

[Guru:] I would like to talk to you, Bhīma. The earliest manuscript turned black. The gebang leaf, cut in the same manner lengthwise and widthwise, [is then] transformed into life by the gaṅgā, vīra, and tanu. Gaṅgā is water, vīra the pen, tanu the ink.

The smoke of the oil lamp, rubbed in copper shells, dissolved in the laṇḍa of the kepuh tree, mixed with lac, [and then all] mixed in the right doses into the inkwell. This is what is called ink. Its role in the making of books is well known.

The *Bhima Swarga* texts include a description of the process of producing ink, by mixing the residue of the smoke of the oil lamp with the liquid from *kepuh* fruit. This description is also mentioned in the invocation used by Balinese *dhalang*. This fact suggests that the two manuscripts came from the same period when intercultural exchanges happened during the heyday of *pesisir* maritime trade in the sixteenth century.[9]

There is no colophon to indicate when this version of the *Bhima Svarga* was composed, but in the context of other manuscripts that mention this story, the manuscript must have been written in the early part of the sixteenth century, before Java was fully Islamized. This conjecture is corroborated by other evidence, including the presence of a Bhima cult during the Majapahit period (Duijker 2010) and the popularity of Bhima in iconographic forms, such as figures carved on the walls of the Candi Sukuh temple (fourteenth to fifteenth century) in Central Java depicting a scene of Bhima in conversation with God Siva.

The paucity of evidence prevents us from knowing the exact form of wayang performance before the subsequent arrival of Hinduism and during the Hindu-Javanese period. We know, however, that the Hindu epics the *Mahabharata* and

Ramayana encouraged the development of many forms of wayang plays, hence the importance of written documents for introducing and spreading the story. It makes sense, therefore, that Javanese society treated written documents (*pustaka*) as venerated objects—the old manuscripts are often considered to be magically charged heirlooms (*pusaka*). A handful of wayang stories reflect this point of view, including the story of *Pusaka Sastra Jendra* and *Jimat Kalimasada*; both of them are believed to refer to written documents. Interestingly, these two examples became venerated objects (from *pustaka* to *pusaka*) due to a "misinterpretation" of their original meanings. For the former, the original text was "sang stryahajeng," which means "beautiful lady," but it seems to have been read as "sastra hajeng" and eventually transformed to "sastra arjendra," or "sastra jendra," which means "a book of sacred knowledge" (Supomo 1997, 228). For the latter, the original text is "Kalimahoshadha," the name of Yudhistira's spear (a transformation of a sacred book), which he used to kill Salya in the final Bharatayudha war. Subsequently, Kalimahoshadha was read as Kalimasada, which according to tradition derives from Kalimah Syahadat, a letter containing the Confession of Islamic Faith (Supomo 1997, 231–33). This transformation reflects a tendency in Javanese to venerate written texts and to transform the original meaning of a magical object to suit socioreligious and cultural changes. In the case of the transformation of the *Bhima Svarga* texts in *dhalang* Warnoto's invocation, I suggest that this is another example of the Javanese practice of venerating ancient written documents and transforming them in ways that still resonate in twentieth-century cultural practices.

NOTES

All non-English text is modern Javanese, except where otherwise specified. The abbreviation "I" indicates Indonesian.

1. I should mention that Ki Enthus Susmono earned his fame as a *dhalang* through his performance not of *wayang golek* Tegal style but his own creative work of *wayang golek*, which he calls *wayang santri*. I consider Ki Enthus's *wayang santri* an Islamic popular cultural performance (a kitsch, as he himself characterized his wayang performance), which he uses, for the most part, as a tool for his political and ideological agenda. To enhance its popularity, vulgar jokes, swear words, and sexual innuendo are not uncommon in Ki Enthus's wayang performance, as well as a flashy gamelan accompaniment. I sense that Enthus's fame has made other *dhalang* envy and lament for an older Tegal wayang performance. It was partly in this context that Gunawan encouraged me to document an older, "authentic" *wayang golek cepak* Tegal style and its gamelan accompaniment. Ki Enthus Susmono passed away on May 14, 2018, when on his way to lead a Qur'anic study (I: *pengajian*) a stroke took his life.

2. For discussion of today's *wayang kulit* performance, see Mrázek 2001, Kayam 2001, and Sumarsam 2013. Marking the difference between *wayang* performance in the past and today (starting at around the 1980s) are the extended scenes of Limbukan and Gara-Gara, two scenes that contain lighthearted musical interludes and humorous dialogues (with no relation to the story of the play) between clown servant puppets with

the *pesindhèn* singers, guest artists, and VIP audience. On *wayang santri*, see Boonstra 2014, 2015.

3. I have written about this particular topic in my 2011 article "Past and Present Issues of Islam within the Central Javanese Gamelan and *Wayang Kulit*."

4. The names of the pieces are "Lompong Keli," *ayak-ayakan sanga*, and "Kratagan." *Pathet* is a modal classification of gamelan composition.

5. In *wayang kulit*, the narration of *dhalang* is called *janturan*. It is interesting that in *wayang golek* Tegal it is called *ngabor*. In Javanese *wayang kulit* a piece called "Kabor" is often performed for the first scene of the kingdom of Hastina.

6. I must admit that before I saw this documented performance, I had seen only a limited number of *wayang golek* performances.

7. Gunawan also mentions that the same texts appear in another *lontar* manuscript, *Sang Hyang Sasana Mahaguru*.

8. The original is a transliteration by Aditya Gunawan from his 2016 article, using a modified version of the system from Zoetmulder's 1982 *Old Javanese-English Dictionary*. The numbers in parentheses refer to the canto and the verses. The translation is my own.

9. Here is the text used by Balinese *dhalang*: "Hirika ta hana pupusing gebang / sewala tunggal / hika ta pinék pwa tatas pinada pada panjangnya tekeng lwarnya / hik ta tin-estesan hasta gangga / uwira / tanu ndya ta ingaranan mangkana / hasta / nga / tangan / gangga / nga / toya / uwira / nga / panuli / tang / nga / mangsi / ndya ta hingaranan mangsi / ta pwa kang haranya / nora ta lyan / kukus hikang lengan silah ginera / landan hikang kepuh / dinasar ing lawan tambaga / hika ta piniketiket pinaratista ring patra hinusan" (Zurbuchen 1987, 268).

WORKS CITED

Boonstra, Sadiah. 2011. "Performing Islam." *Inside Indonesia* 106. https://www.insideindonesia.org/performing-islam.

Boonstra, Sadiah. 2014. *Changing Wayang Scenes: Heritage Formation and Wayang Performance Practice in Colonial and Postcolonial Indonesia*. PhD diss., Vrije Universiteit Amsterdam.

Boonstra, Sadiah. 2015. "Defining *Wayang* as Heritage: Standardization, Codification, and Institutionalization." In *Sites, Bodies, and Stories: Imagining Indonesian History*, edited by Susan Legêne, Bambang Purwanto, and Henk Schulte Nordholt. Singapore: NUS Press, 159–79.

Duijker, Marijek. 2010. *The Worship of Bhima: The Representation of Bhima on Java during the Majapahit Period*. Amstelveen: EON Pers.

Foley, Kathy. 2002. "First Thing: Opening Passages in Southeast Asian Puppet Theater." In *Puppet Theater in Contemporary Indonesia: New Approaches to Performance Events*, edited by Jan Mrázek, 84–91. Ann Arbor: Center for South and Southeast Asian Studies, University of Michigan.

Gunawan, Aditya. 2016. "Produksi Naskah dan Mistisisme Aksara dalam *Bhima Svarga*." *Manuskripta* 6 (1): 11–39.

Hooykaas, C. 1973. *Kama and Kala: Material for the Study of Shadow Theatre in Bali*. Amsterdam: North-Holland.

Hunter, Thomas. 1996. "Ancient Beginnings: The Spread of Indic Scripts." In *Illuminations: The Writing Traditions of Indonesia*. New York: Weatherhill.

Kayam, Umar. 2001. *Kelir Tanpa Batas*. Yogyakarta: Gama Media for Pusat Studi Kebudayaan UGM.

Lysloff, René. 2014. *Srikandhi Dances Lènggèr: A Performance of Music and Shadow Theater in Central Java*. Leiden: KITLV Press.

Mrázek, Jan. 2005. *Phenomenology of a Puppet Theatre: Contemplation on the Art of Javanese Wayang Kulit.* Leiden: KITLV Press.

Pigeaud, Theodore G. 1967. *The Literature of Java*, vol. 1. The Hague: Nijhoff.

Sumarsam. 1995. *Gamelan: Cultural Interaction and Musical Development in Central Java.* Chicago: University of Chicago Press.

Sumarsam. 2011. "Past and Present Issues of Islam within the Central Javanese Gamelan and *Wayang Kulit.*" In *Divine Inspiration: Music and Islam in Indonesia*, edited by David D. Harnish and Anne K. Rasmussen, 45–79. Oxford: Oxford University Press.

Sumarsam. 2013. *Javanese Gamelan and the West.* Rochester, NY: University of Rochester Press.

Supomo, S. 1997. "From *Sakti* to *Sahada*: The Quest for New Meanings in a Changing World Order." In *Islam: Essays on Scripture, Thought and Society*, edited by Peter G. Riddell and Tony Street, 219–36. Leiden: Brill.

Turner, Victor. 1982. *From Ritual to Theatre: The Human Seriousness of Play.* New York: Performing Arts Journal Publication.

Vickers, Adrian. 1993. "From Bali to Lampung on the Pasisir." *Archipel* 45: 55–76.

Zoetmulder, P. J. 1974. *Kalangwan: A Survey of Old Javanese Literature.* The Hague: Nijhoff.

Zoetmulder, P. J. 1982. *Old Javanese-English Dictionary.* With the collaboration of S. O. Robson. 2 vols. The Hague: Nijhoff.

Zurbuchen, Mary. 1987. *The Language of Balinese Shadow Theater.* Princeton, NJ: Princeton University Press.

7

THE POLITICIZATION OF RELIGIOUS MELODY IN THE INDONESIAN CULTURE WARS OF 2017

Anne K. Rasmussen

From January to July 2017 I conducted ethnographic research in Java and Sumatra on the intersection of music, religion, and politics. I visited individuals and communities from Banda Aceh on the western tip of Sumatra, to Malang, East Java, building on relationships I established twenty years earlier in the course of research on the culture of Qur'anic recitation and Islamic music (see Rasmussen 2005, 2010a, 2010b, 2016a, 2016b, 2019). In addition to engaging interlocutors in conversation and presenting my own research and teaching through lectures, classes, and workshops, I also frequently found myself "in the course of performance" (Rasmussen 2010a). Musical performance, that is, playing the Arab lute, the *'ud*, and singing Arabic and Indonesian/Arabic language songs, has become an important aspect of my research methodology, and one that permits an entrée into discussions and demonstrations of musical matters as they pertain to Islamic musical arts, or *seni musik Islam*, and to cultural politics as well. In 2017 the subject of my earlier research, namely, the cultural realm of Qur'anic recitation and knowledge among Indonesian Muslims, had become a lightning rod for intense public debates around issues of morality, appropriate behavior, and Islamic etiquette (*adab*) in this Muslim-majority country. In the political arena, the controversy centered on Jakarta's mayor, Basuki Tjahaja Purnama (a.k.a. Ahok), a Christian of Chinese descent, whose general demeanor and supposed irreverence toward a particular verse from the Qur'an fueled the fires of Muslim extremism. In the cultural arena, a lesser drama shadowed the accusations and eventual persecution of Ahok. This debate centered around, of all things, melody.

In this chapter I ask the following questions: What are the sources for Muslim musical expression in Indonesia? How does the pendulum of musical inspiration swing between the sound worlds of the Arabian Gulf and Peninsula and the Eastern Mediterranean Arab world (Egypt, Jordan, Lebanon, Palestine, Syria)? How do the musical aesthetics and techniques of the global and the local inform spiritually based music making? What is it about the power of music, or just melody as is the case with the examples presented here, to support or subvert communities, ideologies, and authorities? As Laudan Nooshin writes in the introduction of *Power and the Play of Music*: "What is it about music that facilitates and sometimes disrupts the exercise and flows of power? And who controls such flows, how and for what purposes?" (2009, 3).

My analysis highlights one incident where the exercise of power played out in the objection to and support of melody—in this case the melody deployed by a Qur'anic reciter in performance at the presidential palace. To unpack the vehement objections to this performance, I consider Simon Frith's explanation of "bad music" and employ Jonathan Neufeld's concept of "aesthetic disobedience." In analyzing melodies that are thought to be either "obedient" or "disobedient" in the contemporary moment, I listen also to the creeping soft power of Saudi Arabia, which is made audible in the reciters' world through economies of mass media. Although arguments against change or variation are central to the musical delivery of sacred and spiritually infused language performance, I suggest here that any perception of melodic stability may be more of a mirage in the shifting sounds of this aestheticized political terrain. My intent in this chapter is to expose the ways in which political muscle and religious subjectivities are expressed through a variety of media, even through melody.

Some Background

In my earlier work, I document the ways that cultural and musical practices of the Arab Gulf and the Eastern Mediterranean Arab world made their way to the Indonesian archipelago through travel and trade by way of a maritime "silk road." Early Indian Ocean trade and travel led to the eventual Islamization of Indonesia, resulting in an even more purposeful exchange of peoples, ideas, and commodities around the Indian Ocean. The obligatory pilgrimage to Mecca, with its concomitant activities of commerce, education, and social relations, further stimulated the circulation of people, ideas, and materials in an Indian Ocean world. Indonesia's early pilgrims to Mecca were of interest to the archipelago's colonial occupiers, particularly the Dutch Orientalist Christiaan Snouck Hurgronje (1857–1936), who, in the late nineteenth century, recorded their images on photographs and their voices on wax cylinder recordings, more than three hundred of which were made in both Mecca and Batavia (now Jakarta) between 1905 and 1909.[1] Together, these photographs and phonograms, along with written accounts, provide a partial record of the early sights and sounds of an Indian Ocean ecumene. In 2017 about 221,000 Indonesians made the annual pilgrimage to Saudi Arabia, the highest number from any country, and thousands more embark on the lesser pilgrimage, the Umrah, every year. In spite of the vigorous global flow of ideology and praxis between Indonesia and a Muslim, Indian Ocean world, the archipelago's Islamic musical traditions have only begun to be taken seriously by scholars in the past couple of decades.[2]

We can see the diffusion of material culture and musical practice from the Indian Ocean cultural ecumene to the Indonesian archipelago in such things as musical instruments and musical genres.[3] Alongside the dissemination of Arabic as a language of intellectual, social exchange and ritual performance, musical practices, repertoires, instruments, and related terminology from the Hadramaut region of what is now the country of Yemen and elsewhere in the Arabian Peninsula migrated to Southeast Asia, where they prevail to this day. Here are three examples. *Gambus,* the term derived from the Arabic *qanbus,* refers to (1) the original lute type that migrated from Yemen to Indonesia; (2) the modern Arab lute, the *'ud;* and (3) the Indonesian instrumental and vocal genre of Arabic and local language songs with Arab stylings and Islamic flavor (Berg 2011; Capwell 1995). The second of my examples, *hajir marawis* is a more recent Islamic musical genre, also named for the instruments in the ensemble. It is an exciting, contemporary style involving the Arab drums, the *hajir* (s.) and several *marawis* (pl.) that are played in rapid-fire, interlocking patterns to accompany Arabic-language, and thus de facto Islamic songs (Rasmussen 2019). Finally, "Dana Dana" songs from the Arabian Peninsula with their predictable choruses and interludes that use the syllables "dana dana" have been adapted by Indonesian Islamic singing stars and amateur *qasidah modern* or *qasidah rebana* groups alike. The religious intent of all of this music—*gambus, hajir marawis,* and *qasidah*—can be enhanced by dances, such as *sharh* and *zapin,* and other creative choreographies and elaborate, theatrical music and dance packages are commonly commissioned and presented for religious ritual, recreation, and ceremony (Berg 2011; Nor 1993; Rasmussen 2019).

What about that foundational element of music: melody? In a country renowned for its nontempered, nondiatonic pentatonic or heptatonic scales of regional traditions or the scales (*laras*) and modes (*pathet*) of the courtly gamelan styles, can we also identify a Muslim melodic profile that takes its cue from the Indian Ocean cultural ecumene? The earliest Indonesian religious performers and reciters of the Qur'an likely chanted according to their abilities and what they learned from Arabs or other South Asians who traveled to the region. Numerous professional reciters explained to me that once regular travel to Mecca was established, reciters learned a set of authoritative "Meccan melodies" known as *lagu Mekkawi*, which were transmitted orally and used for recitation and religious singing (Rasmussen 2010b, chap. 3). *Lagu Mekkawi* were eclipsed beginning around the time of Indonesian independence in 1945 and progressively throughout the rest of the twentieth century. Melodies from Mecca were replaced by the performance practice of the great Egyptian reciters of the mid- to late twentieth century whose vocal virtuosity was transmitted *not* by the waves of Indian Ocean trade and travel but rather by radio, recordings, and air travel between the Arab *Mashriq* (Eastern Mediterranean Arab world) and Indonesia. The complete adaptation and normalization of the Eastern Mediterranean Arab system of *maqamat* in both terminology and performance practice was facilitated by educational and government institutions and a competition system to teach, measure, and reward *murattl* (simple, plain) and *mujawwad* (florid, virtuosic) styles of recitation.[4]

As I have written elsewhere, the systematic study of and with Egyptian reciters, and the institutionalization of their style and technique in schools and through a system of competitions, led to flawless command, among Indonesian reciters, of *maqam* melodies and *tajwid*, the system of pronunciation, timing, and dividing the text that governs the reading of Qur'anic Arabic. People in the business of religion were also bolstered by government patronage nurturing the efflorescence of a "recitation culture" throughout the country among males and females, from children through adulthood, eventually propelling Indonesian reciters (both male and female) to victory at international competitions. Along with the superstar reciters of Egypt, the singers of Arab radio, recordings, and films were also influential among the country's Muslims, washing the archipelago in successive waves of the musical styles—in melodic singing practices—of such Arab-world luminaries as Umm Kulthum, Muhammad Abd al Wahab, and Fayrouz, and later Amer Diyab and Nancy Ajram, all of them "secular singers" whose songs were borrowed and adapted for the extraordinarily rich field of Indonesian Islamic musical arts (Rasmussen 2005, 2010b, 2011, 2019).[5]

The following example is a case in point. Champion reciter and teacher of the Qur'an, composer, player of the Arab tuned *suling* or side-blown flute, and ensemble leader Nur Asiah Djamil (1947–2014), whom I interviewed in Medan, Sumatra, in 1999, borrowed liberally from popular songs of the Arab world that she heard on radio, in films, and on the record and cassette recordings that circulated between the Arab world and the Indonesian archipelago (see also Weintraub 2011a). Along with her ensemble, Nada Sahara, literally translated as "Melody of the Desert," composed of women singers and instrumentalists, Djamil released a series of cassettes of *qasidah modern* and *gambus* music, the two major genres of Islamic musical arts popular from the 1960s through the 1990s. It is not uncommon to hear direct melodic quotations or contrafacts of popular "secular" songs from the Arab world singers, some of whom are Christian, in Djamil's "original" compositions. During the era when this music was popular (the 1970s through the 1990s) there was apparently no dissonance perceived in the adaptation of secular folkloric songs, even songs by Arab Christian artists, to convey Muslim piety in Indonesia, as long as the melodies sounded Arabic.[6] In this case and many others like it, the artist repurposed music originally created for one particular cultural context for use in another, confirming my affirmation that meaning is created not in the music itself but at the site of its reception. The point is that the reassignment of meaning to musical melody and style is something that has transpired with ease in the context of Muslim Indonesia. Before moving on to the "predicament at the palace," when melody itself was perceived as objectionable, let's review the historical precedent for adaptation, appropriation, and bricolage in expressions of piety through the Indonesian performing arts.

The *Wali Songo*

The performing arts have always been associated with the spread of Islam throughout the Indonesian archipelago in contrast to their precarious status in Muslim communities elsewhere. Common knowledge of the alliance of art and religion is based on the stories of the *Wali Songo*, the "nine saints" who spread the teachings and practice of Islam, through a variety of media. Principal among them was wayang, the comprehensive performance art that encompasses storytelling, communication of current events, comedy, history, and moral teaching through dramas involving puppetry, singing, musical accompaniment by gamelan, visual arts, and, when human actors are involved, dance.[7] The story of the *Wali Songo*, and particularly one *wali*, Saint Sunan Kalijaga, operates as a kind of "origin myth" for Indonesian Islam and the arts, and it is repeated and engaged imaginatively and efficaciously to the advantage of a vision and version of Islam that is tolerant, varied, expressed through and inspiring to the arts, and uniquely Indonesian.

We can probably attribute the richness of the Islamic soundscape in Indonesia to a number of factors, among them the *Wali Songo*, who, at least in the public imaginary, set the stage for creative fusion at the intersection of piety and the performing arts. The result is a soundscape of religious performance that reverberates, live and mediated, in the public sphere. This soundscape can include exquisite renditions of call to prayer (*azan*; also transliterated from the Arabic as *adhan*) and Qur'anic recitation performed in the Arab modal system, or *maqamat*, along with, of course, rather unremarkable renditions of the call to prayer and plain and tuneless recitations rendered by everyday amateurs. This soundscape also features devotional rituals such as *zikr*, the communal, musical-rhythmic chanting in remembrance of God, and songs, called *sholawat*, for which performers use Arab *maqamat*, along with regional melodies and vocal timbres that draw from the *slendro* and *pelog laras* and *pathet* of gamelan and folk styles. Adding to the uniquely indigenous genres, like *qasidah modern, gambus,* and *hajir marawis*, mentioned above, Islamic music is also saturated with Western, globalized pop music aesthetics and techniques including crooning vocals, tri-adic harmonies, functional bass lines, and electronic effects like pitch correction. However, in counterpoint to a long-established mix of various genres and styles of Islamic music, a more contemporary chorus of intolerance toward diverse and locally Indonesian or indigenous forms of religious expression can be heard in the intersection where aesthetics meets religious ideology and social politics, and this was the unfolding drama that framed my research in spring 2017.

The Predicament at the Palace

An emergence of hard-line Islam (*Islam keras*) or Islam *extrem* (extreme) or *kanan* (right-wing) with their ideologies of modernist or Wahhabi Islam, puri-tanical Salafism, and a literalist, text-centered approach to religion has discour-aged Indonesia's long history and culture of a musical Islam. Several factors are at play here. First, the religious authority, financial investment, and soft power of Saudi Arabia conveyed through mass media, educational institutions, and capitalism are manifested in the propagation of Saudi-style recitation, clothing, lifeways, and ideas. Second, inspiration from authoritative forms of Arab culture can be refracted in Indonesia through an Orientalist lens that renders anything Arab as "everything Islam." Third, a love-hate relationship with globalization and influences from the West further enrich and complicate the picture and the soundscape of Indonesian Islam.

In spring 2015 intense political culture wars were sparked by the use of local Javanese melodies, referred to during this entire debacle as *langgam Jawa,* for a presentation of Qur'anic recitation, which took place at the presidential pal-ace on May 15, 2015, by reciter Muhammad Yaser Arafat.[8] In the proceedings of the Ar-Rainery International Conference on Islamic Studies, the reciter (who is originally from Sumatra, not Java) states:

> I was invited by the minister of religious affairs of the Republic of Indo-
> nesia, Lukman Hakim Saifuddin, to present the TLJ (*Tilawa Langgam*

Jawa, or recitation with Javanese melodies) at the event of Isra' Mi'raj [the flight from Medina to Mecca of] Prophet Muhammad (May 15, 2015). . . . The flash point of the TLJ controversy lies in its peculiarity. The TLJ is considered to violate the common practice; recitation with Arabic *adab* [custom, etiquette, aesthetic]. The supporters of the TLJ understood it as a form of fusion between religion and culture. [But] the opponents of the TLJ accused the TLJ of being ridiculous, an attempt at de-Arabization, the liberalization of Islam, and "playing" with the Qur'an. For them, the Qur'an is a holy book that must be chanted with Arabic rhythms (*irama*) as has been the habit all these years. (Yaser 2016, 395–96, translation from Bahasa Indonesia by the author)

This then, was the predicament: the reciter used a Javanese melodic style, what everyone referred to as *langgam Jawa*, a term more exactly associated with popular musics like *kroncong* or *campur sari*. The label *langgam Jawa* notwithstanding, the gesture was immediately recognizable to some of the people in attendance, who then objected to his recitation on the basis that the Arabic-language Qur'an should only be melodized using "Arabic *adab*," a complex concept that conjures Arab and thus Muslim etiquette, custom, aesthetics, and also in this case melody (Rasmussen 2019; Rozehnal 2019). Further, as the reciter, Muhammad Yaser Arafat, states above, "The holy book must be chanted with Arabic *irama*," a term from the Indonesian language that, among reciters, refers to rhythm and melody, and in this case to the Arab *maqamat*, or system of melodic modes. While it is well known that improper *tajwid* (the rules governing the pronunciation of Qur'anic Arabic) can alter the meaning of a text, here we have a case where attendants objected to the inappropriate use of melody.

In spring 2017, as I conducted interviews and attended social and spiritual assemblies, often participating as a musician, everyone seemed to be asking my opinion of this event. Was it appropriate to recite using local Javanese tunes? Was it even possible? The event came to be interpreted as polemical, and it seemed that melody had become political. My longtime consultant and colleague Maria Ulfah and I discussed the matter at length.

> Even before he finished reciting people were upset. Habib Rizieq Shihab from Islamic Defenders Front [Fron Pembela Islam or FPI] came and said—"you can't do that!" The followers of Hisbut Tahrir and the leader of FPI are religious hard-liners [*extrem*]! "That's *haram*" [forbidden], they said. . . . Yes, so all of these people arrived on the steps of the Ministry of Religious Affairs, and the minister was confused [*bingung*]. "If this is the way it is going to be," the minister said, "then all of the Islamic institutes should have seminars [to resolve the controversy]."

So, they did. The Maejlis Ulema Indonesia [the Association of Muslim Clerics] did and the Institut Ilmu al Qur'an [the Institute (for Women) for the Study of the Qur'an] did. (Maria Ulfah, personal communication, January 25, 2017)

And she went on to list the important men in the recitation world (who are known to both of us) and their opinions. "Some said: 'Why! We already have established the correct melodies for reciting. We do not need to introduce new melodies.' But others recognized the practice as a long-standing 'natural' expression of Javanese Islam. *Yaaaa*, this generation, they don't know. And they don't know about the relationship of gamelan with *Wali Songo*. At the time of the *Wali Songo*, they also performed the religious texts this way." Maria Ulfah described the opponents as associating this music or melodic style with things that are *heboh*, a term that can be translated as exciting, titillating, or even smutty. She mimed the following scenario:

Say there is a wedding and they have a Javanese woman [*orang jawa*] who comes with this certain hairstyle *dandang*. And she is dressed like this [she gestures] and wears a *kabaya* [Javanese traditional dress] and is attractive. She wears the skirt [*kein*] and the top but without a jacket [like a strapless dress]. And the songs she sings are Javanese. Then the men come, and they have money and they put it here [she indicates that men put bills into the woman's cleavage]. Into her bra [*B.H.* or *bay-haa*, the abbreviation for the Dutch term, *bustehouder*] but it doesn't have any straps. Then there is *gamelan* [music]. And she has a big bun in her hair [*sanggul*, the typical hairstyle and hairpiece of Javanese women, especially of singers and dancers]. And she has a long *slendang* [scarf] that she manipulates like this [she demonstrates].

Maria Ulfah opined that the *tilawa langgam Jawa* recitation in Javanese modes triggered an association of *langgam Jawa* with Javanese entertainments. As she put it, those who objected, "they think those with such an intention" (*yang punya hajat itu*), namely, the intention of enjoying the entertainment that might transpire at a Javanese wedding, "are not real Muslims" (*bukan orang Islam*).

Bad Music

In his contribution to the book *Bad Music: The Music We Love to Hate,* popular music scholar Simon Frith offers "The label 'bad music,' . . . is only interesting as a part of an argument" (2004, 17). According to Frith, it is not the music itself that is necessarily "bad"; rather, "the apparent judgement of the music is something else altogether, something more akin to the judgement of a social institution or social behavior or group for which the music simply acts as a sign" (17). Frith's distinction is useful here. It was natural, as Maria Ulfah points out above, for the carpers at the palace and beyond to object to the melodic aspect of the recitation, not because of the intervallic relationships that distinguish *langgam Jawa* from Arab *maqamat* but because they associated such melodies with communities and contexts outside of the realm of performative piety.

René Lysloff investigates and interprets the kinds of Javanese public entertainments that may well have titillated the imaginations of the auditors at the palace and beyond when they heard, or even pondered, the reciter's *langgam Jawa*. Lysloff writes on *tayuban*, *ronggeng*, and *lengger*, all of them traditions "in which women dance for money" (2001, 3). He describes this cultural realm in opposition not to religious propriety but rather to New Order nationalism.

> *Lengger* represents everything that palace dance in the cultural centers of Solo and Yogya is not. While the refined female dance of the palace symbolizes an idealized realm of feminine grace and beauty, even godliness, *lengger* is earthy, representing the fleshy sexuality of the potentially available, and even dangerous woman. [Such performances may also be viewed as] crude and primitive: crude because the (female) dancer's movements draw (male) audience attention to her body in an overtly sexual way; and primitive because it arose out of behaviors and attitudes no longer appropriate to modern, New Order Indonesian values. (Lysloff 2002, 3–4)

As Muhammad Yaser Arafat and Maria Ulfah recall above, the controversy erupted almost before the recitation was finished. While Minister of Religious Affairs Lukman Hakim Saifuddin defended the recitation and even espoused it as an example of long-standing Indonesian Islamic tradition, others, for example, the deputy secretary-general of the Maejlis Ulema Indonesia (the Association of Muslim Clerics), Tengku Zulkarnaen, warned that the Qur'an could only be recited in an Arabic way. He and his cohort described the incident as "embarrassing."[9] The number and variety of people from the religious Right who chimed in on what might seem a rather superfluous incident was a harbinger of what was actually happening in spring 2017, a political scenario that transcends melody.

Widening the Lens

A wave of nativism, racism, xenophobia, populism, and hard-line Islam effected a sociopolitical tsunami in Jakarta in 2017, the repercussions of which were felt throughout the rest of Indonesia and through the presidential election of April 2019. This Islamic populism, a trend that parallels populist inclinations in the United States and Europe, was sparked and then fueled by the Javanese gubernatorial campaign, election, and runoff vote, combined with the accusation, trial and conviction, resignation, and imprisonment of the incumbent governor, Basuki Tjahaja Purnama (aka Ahok), a Christian of Chinese descent, whose general demeanor and supposed irreverence toward a particular Qur'anic verse fueled the fires of Muslim extremism.[10] Although prosecutors recommended dropping the blasphemy charges based on their conclusion that it was impossible to prove that Ahok violated Article 156A of the Criminal Code (KUHP 156), judges pushed forward, disregarding prosecutors' recommendation and convicted Ahok to two years in prison based on a speech he gave on September 27, 2016, when he urged voters not to be deceived by Islamists who misused verse 51 from Sura al-Ma'idah to persuade citizens that Muslims weren't allowed to vote for non-Muslims.[11]

News of vigorous anti-Ahok demonstrations flooded the press, and although I was curious about such protests, my family and I hoped that I would never be caught up in one of these hostile and potentially dangerous mass rallies. My curiosity was satisfied when I stumbled right into the middle of a demonstration staged (with a permit from the city police department) by several religious hard-line groups in Surakarta (a.k.a. Solo), Central Java. A carnivalesque demonstration of rage and militant jihadist posturing was enhanced through creative costumery, ski masks, Arab headdress, and military fatigues, invoking presumptive martyrs and suicide bombers of the Arab world.[12] Organization leaders referred specifically to Ahok's misuse of the Qur'anic verse and at one point led the crowd into a refrain of "gantung, gantung, gantung si Ahok" (hang Ahok).[13]

To return to Frith's explanation of "What Is Bad Music?" it seems possible that what the opponents heard, saw, and imagined in Muhammad Yaser Arafat's performance, and the YouTube video of it that went viral, was not only a representation of rural, Javanese, smutty (heboh) performing arts, such as the tayuban and lengger described by René Lysloff and Maria Ulfah. They may also have been reacting to a moment of "aesthetic disobedience," to borrow a term from Jonathan Neufeld (2015).[14] As voices from the country's Islamist extremist activists arose in hostile objection to the recitation at the palace, even the "middle of the road" (wasatiyyah) pious public began to hear the reciter's use of langgam Jawa as "bad" and "disobedient": the perfect example of the flaws, immorality, and objectionable permissiveness of Indonesian Islam vis-à-vis the models of puritanical Salafism and literalist modernism that today guide globalized Islamic movements in Southeast Asia.

Aesthetic Disobedience, Obedient Recitation, and the Sonic Soft Power of Saudi Arabia

I am applying the concept of "aesthetic disobedience" as it was introduced to me by philosopher of the arts Jonathan Neufeld. Neufeld explores aesthetic disobedience using the examples of a number of pivotal moments in the Western (European) art world reminding us that "to describe the beginnings of great art movements by pointing to transformative moments where the rules were fruitfully broken is commonplace" (2015, 115). I think his definition of aesthetic disobedience suits our predicament at the palace rather well: "an act of aesthetic disobedience is characterized as a public communicative act that beaks an artwork norm in order to draw attention to and to reform perceived conflicts between an entrenched norm of the artword and other, broadly speaking aesthetic commitments" (2015, 116). Like civil disobedience, aesthetic disobedience has several pillars, according to Neufeld. Among these, it is "public and communicative," "risky," and "violates a deeply entrenched norm or norms of the art world" (118). Although the recitation was probably not meant to promote a definitive change in recitation styles, it was meant to challenge increasingly rigid and entrenched sensibilities about what constitutes good Islamic behavior in Indonesia. This leads us to ask, if Muhammad Yaser Arafat's recitation was "disobedient," what does obedient recitation sound like? How stable is the performance practice of melody among reciters in Indonesia and throughout the Islamic world?

Indonesia's remarkable institutionalization of the Egyptian style of recitation is renowned in the Muslim world, which has been established and recognized since at least the middle of the twentieth century (Rasmussen 2010b, chap. 4). It should be remembered, however, that, "although it may be perceived as 'from the time of the prophet,' the melodic system most men and women strive to master was actually formally institutionalized fairly recently, only in the second half of the twentieth century" (Rasmussen 2010b, 77). Prior to the institutionalization of the melodic style and techniques of the great Egyptian reciters was, we presume, the circulation of a mix of melodic materials learned through Indian Ocean trade and travel, as well as local practice. While the Egyptian melodic style with its virtuosity of ornamentation, vocal timbre, and range and its performance practice of the Arab system of musical modes, the *maqamat*, has been institutionalized in Indonesia and circulates globally through mass media, it is not entirely resistant to alteration. I contend that, swept up in the tsunami of nativism and the vociferous presence of religious hard-liners (*Islam keras*), both Indonesian musical expression and the beloved and world-famous Egyptian performance aesthetics have been on the chopping block. In some circles, even the long-established "correct Arab way" has yielded to new trends in Qur'anic recitation, trends that, I submit, are also examples of aesthetic disobedience; because these modern styles emanate from reciters in Saudi Arabia and the Arabian Gulf, they have come to assert a great deal of influence in recitation cultures in Indonesia and beyond.

The soft power of Saudi Arabia is ever present in Indonesia. For example, men and women of means may be tempted by elite hajj travel packages they can barely afford so that they can complete pilgrimage to Mecca in style. Or college-age students may be seduced by a free education through the network of Saudi-funded schools, called LIPIA (Lembaga Ilmu Pengetahuan Islam dan Bahasa Arab or College for the Study of Islam and Arabic), where music is considered *bid'ah* (an unnecessary innovation) and is prohibited, along with television, loud laughter, and men and women learning alongside one another. Saudi television, broadcast media, and the information stream of the internet and social media is omnipresent and permeates region, gender, and socioeconomic class. Much of what is broadcast involves the many kinds of language performance inherent to Islam. It should not be surprising, then, that Saudi reciters and people who perform the call to prayer are heard throughout the global *umma*. Saudi Arabia's reciters have challenged long-standing aesthetic systems of recitation in Muslim communities as close to the kingdom as Egypt (Frishkopf 2009) and as far away as China (Harris 2014). As studies by Frishkopf and Harris concur, accompanying this change in praxis is the suggestion of a change in ideology. Detailed analysis of recitation styles is beyond the scope of this chapter; suffice it to say that Saudi reciters prefer the faster, less decorated *murattl* style of recitation with fewer pauses, a limited melodic range, and fewer modal modulations among the melodic modes (*maqamat*) than is characteristic of the Egyptian *mujawwad* and even *murattl* styles of recitation long normalized in Indonesia.

One Indonesian reciter whose voice was new on the scene in 2017 and whose influence was audible in the Islamic soundscape, particularly among younger reciters, is Muzammil Hasballah, then a student at the Institute of Technology in Bandung.[15] In his popular YouTube videos, Muzammil is clad either in a flannel shirt and wool cap with an Arab *kufiya* (checkered scarf) around his neck—his hipster look—or in a collared shirt, sweater vest, and suit coat, both looks an obvious departure from Indonesian Muslim fashion (*busana Muslim*) or the Western suit with an Indonesian cap (*peci*) typically worn by male reciters. Muzammil's style of recitation is remarkable for the soft, gentle timbre produced by the use of the head voice in his midrange as opposed to the piercing chest voice employed by Indonesian male and female reciters, especially in their higher range. His recitation is further notable for the repeated motives and patterns established by a sequence of descending phrases, and the recurrence of familiar melodic patterns renders his recitation as much like a song as an improvisation.[16]

Like the Saudi style described above, Muzammil Hasballah does not modulate between the *maqamat*. The combination of his gentle vocal timbre, his use of the diatonic *maqamat* (*Nahawand*, *Kurd*, or *Ajam*), the quickly recognizable repeated phrases, and the dramatic pauses on the subtonic that resolve to the tonic suggest as much a relationship to Western practices of melody making as they do to the Arab improvisatory praxis that has been so successfully normalized in Indonesia and other countries beyond the boundaries of the Arab world.

If the popular style of Muzammil is acceptable among the vociferous critics of Muhammad Yaser Arafat's performance at the palace, and thus "obedient," I suggest strongly that any perception of an aesthetic commitment to the notion of melodic stability—or a single right way, what Muhammad Yaser Arafat, the reciter at the palace, referred to as Arabic *irama*—is merely discursive rhetoric colored by the politicized aesthetics of the moment. In other words, while the cultural tenets of hard-line Islam attempt to censor one melodic style, they are accepting of another that is also "disobedient" or noncompliant in comparison to the traditional parameters of Qur'anic recitation that have been solidified by an institutionalized pedagogy, at least a half century of practice, and a system of recognition and reward, all of which are in place to ensure and safeguard the accuracy of the holy Qur'an.

While alarming, the religious radical extremism, ethnonationalism, and sociopolitical populism in Indonesia (like these tendencies in the United States) have also served as a catalyst for lively discussions, including among Indonesia's prominent religious leaders, of tolerance, nonviolence, and the importance of sustaining and preserving local culture, as a part of the unique qualities of Indonesian Islam or *Islam Nusantara*. Two indicators of this climate of precocity are the choice of Dr. Ma'ruf Amin, then current chair of the Maejlis Ulema Indonesia (MUI, the Council of Islamic Clerics) as incumbent president Joko Widodo's vice presidential running mate in 2019 and the initiative of the MUI to exert some sort of quality control on religious spokespeople who seem to be learning to craft their positions and public speech through misinformation on the internet, what some refer to as "Islam Google." My goal over the past two decades has been to engage performance, and especially musical and religious performance, as a part of this discussion. Questions about Indonesian Islam are even more relevant today than when I lived in the country in the late 1990s, just after the fall of President Suharto in 1998, and the turbulent context of Reformasi politics and *krismon* (monetary crisis) economics. Some of the discursive exchange around these issues happens through language but, as this chapter illustrates, also through and with music and its performance. I am fortunate to be able to engage both words and music as discursive streams of exchange, and my return to numerous consultants and communities in 2017 was enriched by the invitation to participate, with voice and instrument, toward an ever-enriched soundscape of cultural particularities that speak volumes to the cognitive ear, the open heart, and the inquisitive mind.

NOTES

The Fulbright Foundation and the AMINEF, the American Indonesian Exchange Foundation, supported my research in Indonesia from January to July 2017. Many thanks also to Andrew McGraw and Christopher Miller for the invitation to participate in the SOSIM conference. I am further indebted to Elizabeth Clendinning and Jacqui Carrasco of Wake Forest University and to Anne van Oostrum and Julia Kursell of the University of Amsterdam Department of Musicology. Thank you also to Dr. Arnoud Vrolijk, director of the Leiden University Library, to the graduate students in the Kampung Melayu in Leiden, and to my colleagues from William and Mary, Kathy Levitan and Jonathan Glasser, who facilitated my visit to Leiden where they were in residence for the semester. Just prior to completing this chapter, Tom Pepinsky pointed me to a few more recent articles on the Ahok scandal. In addition to numerous interlocutors and teachers in Indonesia, among them Maria Ulfah and Mukhtar Ikhsan, Leo Zaini, Peny Ayagari, Das Rizal, Dadi Darmadi, Masykuri Abdillah, and Mokhamad Yahya, I am grateful for the support of these individuals and institutions.

1. Anne van Oostrum (2021) is working on an online catalog of the more than three hundred wax cylinder recordings made or commissioned by Snouck Hurgronje at the University of Leiden in the Netherlands.

2. Indonesianist ethnomusicology has tended to privilege studies of the courtly arts along with regional traditions. Following the fall of Suharto and during the era of Reformasi, several anthropologists turned their attention to Islam as a cultural and political force. For post–New Order sources on music and performance culture, see Rasmussen 2010b and the fourteen case studies in Harnish and Rasmussen 2011; see also Van Doorn-Harder 2006 and Gade 2004. To underscore the paucity of studies on Muslim Indonesia among ethnomusicologists in general, we could look at the contributions to *Islam and Popular Culture*, edited by Karin Van Nieuwkerk, Martin Stokes, and Mark Levine (2016). Twelve of the eighteen chapters treat Islam and popular culture in the Arab world. Of the remaining six chapters, two focus on Iran, one on Turkey, one on Pakistan (and England), one on Ghana (and Egypt), and one—my own—combines work in the Arabian Gulf and Indonesia. For suggestions on why scholars have been slow to interpret Islam as a cultural force in Indonesia, the country with the world's largest Muslim population, see the introduction to Harnish and Rasmussen 2011. See also Weintraub 2014.

3. Indian Ocean trade networks beginning as early as the ninth century were a harbinger of the subsequent introduction and institutionalization of Islam later in the twelfth to the fourteenth centuries. One example of early exchange is the shipwreck of an Omani dhow found in 1998 off the coast of Bilitung, an island east of Lampung, Sumatra, and just north of West Java. The shipwreck was used as a model for a reconstructed vessel called the *Jewel of Muscat*, which sailed from Muscat, Oman, to Singapore in 2010.

4. *Murattl* is a simpler style akin to chant with a smaller range and less modulation and decoration when compared to the *mujawwad* style, in which a reciter exploits his or her entire range, employs virtuosic improvisation, and engages melodic construction and modulation within the system of Arab *maqamat*. See Rasmussen 2010b, chap. 3.

5. With her background performing at Muslim festivals and her musical education among religious singers, Umm Kulthum always conveyed a sense of religiosity and pious

propriety. The poetry of her songs also contained religious references. She was, however, primarily a concert artist whose performances were also transmitted through radio, television, and film. See Danielson 1997.

6. Djamil's composition "Fajar Menyingsing" (The Dawn Dawns) is a direct contrafact of the Lebanese song "Shatti ya Dunya," a folkloric song for the festive *dabkah* line dance, composed by Mansur and 'Assi Rahbani and made famous by the Lebanese (Christian Maronite) diva Fairouz. Djamil adds an original if derivative introduction and interlude but copies the tune in the Arabic *maqam Hijaz* (D E-flat F-sharp G A B-flat C D), with its characteristic move to a *maqam Rast* tetrachord in the upper part of the octave (G A B-half-flat C) and the canceling of the B-half-flat and return to B-flat in a descending gesture. Djamil's text describes the dawn of morning, dew on flowers, birds, bees, and butterflies in a fertile garden until the last verse, when she sings: *Tuhan maha pengatur lagi maha kaya*; *Semua yan diciptakannya indah semua. Hewan dan tumbuh-tumbuhan bertasbih kepadanya* [x2]; *Marilah kitapun semua taat padanya* [x2]. Almighty God, the governor, is most rich; All of his creations are beautiful; Animals and plants glorify him [x2]; Let us all obey him [x2]. See https://www.youtube.com/watch?v=4KdVXTteBKc.

7. The most common forms are *wayang kulit*, using shadow puppets; *wayang golek*, using three-dimensional puppets; and *wayang orang*, involving human actors/dancers.

8. See https://www.youtube.com/watch?v=pH_0ltT71tE. Note that while *langgam Jawa* was the term used in the ensuing debate, here the announcer uses the term *langgam nusantara* to flag the reciter's use of traditional melodies for his recitation. The footage also captures the reaction and recognition of the special quality of this performance among some audience members.

9. Numerous articles from Indonesian periodicals such as *Tempo* and *Republika* may be found on this topic beginning in May 2015. See, for example, Sadewo 2015 from *Republika* and "Quran Langgam Jawa, Menteri Agama: untuk Pelihara Tradisi" [Qur'an in Javanese Melody, the Ministry of Religious Affairs: to Safeguard Tradition] from *Tempo*, May 18, 2015, https://nasional.tempo.co/read/666985/quran-langgam-jawa-menteri-agama-untuk-pelihara-tradisi.

10. For more on this trend, see Pepinsky et al. 2018; Hatherell and Welsh 2017; Osman and Waiker 2018; Setijadi 2017.

11. That controversial verse "al-Ma'ida" is widely believed to prohibit Muslims from electing a non-Muslim leader. But many people also told me that religion wasn't the problem: "there have been many good Christian leaders." It was just his demeanor. Although he was honest and got things done, he was rough (*kasar*), not *halus* (refined) like the Javanese. It seemed that the deck was stacked for the downfall of Ahok, and as one man exclaimed with glee when I returned to Jakarta after a few weeks absence: "It was like everyone in Java was sacrificing a goat in celebration of his conviction!" ("Sampai momotong kambing di seluru Jawa!")

12. See McDonald 2009 on the performativity of violence in the Palestinian context.

13. See a short video clip of this demonstration, as well as an image of the poster, on the Society for Ethnomusicology's Sound Studies Section blog. Many thanks to Juan Carlos Meléndez-Torres and Davindar Singh for their curation. https://sites.google.com/view/semsoundstudies/soundingboard03/demonstration-in-solo.

14. Complicating the matter even more is the fact that the reciter himself is from Sumatra. See Puspitasari 2016.

15. University campuses like the Bandung Institute of Technology have been incubators of religious extremism. See Dunne 2018.

16. To easily find his performances and his official channel, search for Muzammil Hasballah on YouTube. That a recitation is improvised is key to its authenticity. According to the sources for my study (2010b), the Qur'an is not made by a human, and the melody of

the recitation should be improvised, based on a spontaneous compilation of already internalized and appropriate materials. Like instrumental improvisation, recitation should not be rehearsed and re-sounded over and over in the same way. That would render it a human and individual creation. What reciters are trying to do is model an archetype in the moment of performance (Rasmussen 2010b, chap. 3).

WORKS CITED

Berg, Birgit A. 2011. "'Authentic' Islamic Sound': *Orkes Gambus*, Music, the Arab Idiom, and Sonic Symbols in Indonesian Islamic Musical Arts." In Harnish and Rasmussen 2011, 207–40.

Capwell, Charles. 1995. "Contemporary Manifestations of Yemeni-Derived Song and Dance in Indonesia." *Yearbook for Traditional Music* 27: 76–89.

Danielson, Virginia. 1997. *The Voice of Egypt: Umm Kulthum, Arabic Song, and Egyptian Society in the Twentieth Century*. Chicago: University of Chicago Press.

Dunne, Patrick. 2018. "A Youthful Intolerance Takes Hold in Indonesia." *Asia Times*, June 19.

Frishkopf, Michael. 2009. "Mediated Qur'anic Recitation and the Contestation of Islam in Contemporary Egypt." In *Music and the Play of Power in the Middle East, North Africa and Central Asia*, edited by Laudan Nooshin, 75–114. Farnham, UK: Ashgate.

Frith, Simon. 2004. "What Is Bad Music?" In *Bad Music: The Music We Love to Hate*, edited by Christopher Washburne and Maiken Derno, 15–36. Abingdon, UK: Routledge.

Gade, Anna M. 2004. *Perfection Makes Practice: Learning, Emotion, and the Recited Quran in Indonesia*. Honolulu: University of Hawai'i Press.

Harnish, David D., and Anne K. Rasmussen, eds. 2011. *Divine Inspirations: Music and Islam in Indonesia*. Oxford: Oxford University Press.

Harris, Rachel. 2014. "The New Battleground: Song and Dance in China's Muslim Borderlands." *World of Music* 6 (2): 35–56.

Hatherell, Michael, and Alistair Welsh. 2017. "Rebel with a Cause: Ahok and Charismatic Leadership in Indonesia." *Asian Studies Review* 41 (2): 174–90.

Lysloff, René T. A. 2001. "Rural Javanese 'Tradition' and Erotic Subversion: Female Dance Performance in Banyumas (Central Java)." *Asian Music* 33 (1): 1–24.

McDonald, David. 2009. "Politics and the Performance of Violence in Israel/Palestine." *Ethnomusicology* 53 (1): 58–85.

Neufeld, Jonathan A. 2015. "Aesthetic Disobedience." *Journal of Aesthetics and Art Criticism* 73 (2): 115–25.

Nooshin, Laudan. 2009. "Prelude: Power and the Play of Music." In *Music and the Play of Power in the Middle East, North Africa and Central Asia*, edited by Laudan Nooshin, 1–32. Farnham, UK: Ashgate.

Nor, Mohd Anis bin Md. 1993. *Zapin, Folk Dance of the Malay World*. Singapore: Oxford University Press.

Osman, Mohamed Nawab Mohamed, and Prashant Waikar. 2018. "Fear and Loathing: Uncivil Islamism and Indonesia's Anti-Ahok Movement." *Indonesia* 106: 89–109.

Pepinsky, Thomas B., R. William Liddle, and Siaful Mujani. 2018. *Piety and Political Opinion: Understanding Indonesian Islam*. New York: Oxford University Press.

Puspitasari, Tika. 2016. *Gaya Tilawah Jawi Muhammad Yaser Arafat*. Thesis, Program Pascarsarjana, Institut Seni Indonesia, Surakarta, Jawa, Indonesia.

Rasmussen, Anne K. 2005. "The Arab Musical Aesthetic in Indonesian Islam." *World of Music* 47 (1): 65–89.

Rasmussen, Anne K. 2010a. "Plurality or Conflict? Performing Religious Politics through Islamic Musical Arts in Contemporary Indonesia." In *Music and Conflict*, edited by John Morgan O'Connell and Salwa el-Shawan Castelo-Branco, 155–76. Urbana: University of Illinois Press.

Rasmussen, Anne K. 2010b. *Women's Voices, the Recited Qur'an, and Islamic Music in Indonesia*. Berkeley: University of California Press. Book website (with additional content including 25 audio examples): http://www.ucpress.edu/book.php?isbn=9780520255494.

Rasmussen, Anne K. 2011. "'The Muslim Sisterhood': Religious Performance, Transnational Feminism(s), and the Particularity of Indonesia." In Harnish and Rasmussen 2011, 111–31.

Rasmussen, Anne K. 2016a. "Women Out Loud: Hearing Knowledge and the Creation of Soundscape in Islamic Indonesia." In *Theorizing Sound Writing*, edited by Deborah Kapchan, 191–215. Middletown, CT: Wesleyan University Press.

Rasmussen, Anne K. 2016b. "Performing Islam around the Indian Ocean Basin: Musical Ritual and Recreation in Indonesia and the Arabian Gulf." In Van Nieuwkerk et al. 2016, 300–322.

Rasmussen, Anne K. 2019. "*Adab* and Embodiment in the Process of Performance: Islamic Musical Arts in Indonesia." In Rozehnal 2019, 149–68.

Rozehnal, Robert, ed. 2019. *Piety, Politics, and Everyday Ethics in Southeast Asian Islam: Beautiful Behavior*. London: Bloomsbury Academic.

Sadewo, Joko. 2015. "Wasekjen MUI: Baca Alquran di Istana Pakai Langgam Jawa Adalah Memalukan" [Secretary-General, Maejlis Ulema Indonesia: Qur'an Recitation at the Palace Using Javanese Melodies Is Embarrassing]. *Republika*, May 17. https://www.republika.co.id/berita/dunia-islam/islam-nusantara/15/05/17/nohjmt-wasekjen-mui-baca-alquran-di-istana-pakai-langgam-jawa-adalah-memalukan.

Setijadi, Charlotte. 2017. "Ahok's Downfall and the Rise of Islamist Populism in Indonesia." *ISEAS Perspective* 38: 1–9. https://www.iseas.edu.sg/images/pdf/ISEAS_Perspective_2017_38.pdf.

Van Doorn-Harder, Pieternella. 2006. *Women Shaping Islam: Indonesian Women Reading the Qur'an*. Urbana: University of Illinois Press.

Van Nieuwkerk, Karin, Mark Levine, and Martin Stokes, eds. 2016. *Islam and Popular Culture*. Austin: University of Texas Press.

Van Oostrum, Anne. 2021. "Gender and Genres of Arab Music in the Collection of Christiaan Snouck Hurgronje (1857–1936)." In *Music in Arabia: Perspectives on Heritage, Mobility, and Nation*, edited by Issa Boulos, Virginia Danielson, and Anne K. Rasmussen. Bloomington: Indiana University Press.

Van Zanten, Wim. 2017. "Recordings of Indonesian Music and Speech in the Snouck Hurgronje Collection (1905–1909) in Leiden—Preliminary Remarks." Unpublished manuscript, Leiden University.

Weintraub, Andrew N., ed. 2011a. *Islam and Popular Culture in Indonesia and Malaysia*. Abingdon, UK: Routledge.

Weintraub, Andrew N. 2011b. "Morality and Its (Dis)contents: Dangdut and Islam in Indonesia." In Harnish and Rasmussen 2011, 318–36.

Weintraub, Andrew N. 2014. "Decentering Ethnomusicology: Indonesian Popular Music Studies." In *Producing Indonesia: The State of Indonesian Studies*, edited by Eric Tagliocozzo, 347–66. Ithaca, NY: Cornell Southeast Asia Program Publications.

Yaser, Muhammad [Muhammad Yaser Arafat]. 2016. "Memperkenalkan Tilawah Langgam Jawa" [Introducing Recitation with Javanese Melody]. In *Mengkaji Kembali Peradaban Islam: Menata Ulang Tradisi Umat Islam dalam Aspek Etika-Etika Sosial, Intelektual dan Spiritual* [Reawakening Muslim Social Ethics, Intellectual and Spiritual Tradition]. Conference Proceedings of the First Ar-Raniry International Conference on Islamic Studies, edited by Anton Widyanto and Rahmat Yusny, 394–407. Banda Aceh: Bandar Publishing. http://jurnal.ar-raniry.ac.id/index.php/aricis.

Part III

POPULAR MUSICS AND MEDIA

8

THE VERNACULAR COSMOPOLITANISM OF AN INDONESIAN ROCK BAND

Navicula's Creative and Activist Pathways

Rebekah E. Moore

In July 2005 I stepped into a small, sweltering cassette shop on the main artery of the village of Kerambitan in West Bali. The shop's owner was Made Pasek, a vocalist for a local heavy metal band and the brother of Nyoman Suadin, a noted gamelan instructor for several colleges and community groups on the East Coast of the United States—and my host for my first brief stay in Bali. Pasek flicked a wall switch to light the bare bulb hung overhead and expose the rows of dusty shelves stocked with hundreds of cassette tapes documenting a broad history of music in Bali. A mélange of *gamelan gong kebyar, angklung, dangdut, pop Bali* (Balinese-language pop music), and recorded *wayang kulit* materialized from the shadows. "Just give me anything rock and original," I said to Pasek. After weeks of intensive study with Gamelan Banjar Wani, I was saturated by everything bronze and bamboo and in the mood for the sonic familiarity of home that the electric guitar and drum kit would provide.

Pasek offered me an assortment of recent releases by Bali-based rock bands: pop punk trio Superman Is Dead (2003), rockabilly act The Hydrant (2005), and Balinese-language hard rockers Lolot, who gained national media attention when they sold more than a hundred thousand copies of their album *Bali Rock Alternative* (2004) and garnered a significant following in Java. My eye was drawn to a cassette with a psychedelic cover, melding sweeping paisley and art nouveau in garish hues of purple, green, and yellow, framing an abstractly depicted yet undeniable vulva. The album title was *Alkemis* (Alchemist), and the cassette's provocative cover foreshadowed the surprising sounds trapped within its magnetic ribbon: allusions to Jimi Hendrix in guitar solos, vocal stylings that danced between Chris Cornell and Eddie Vedder, and a heavy-handed rhythmic pulse that suggested a propensity for death metal drumming. This was Navicula.

I listened to the cassette of *Alkemis* more than a hundred times, until the tape degraded and sounds emitted became maddeningly warped. I puzzled: How did musicians born more than ten thousand miles from my front door come to share so many of my musical memories? I could intuit, through the flux of the tape, that like me, Navicula had soothed teenage angst with 1990s Seattle sound and the likes of The Melvins, Nirvana, Alice in Chains, and Soundgarden. Like them, I had diligently studied these bands through copied cassettes passed among friends, in fanzines, and on MTV.[1] Years later during our first interview, front man Robi confirmed my suspicions of our shared musical affinities, when he likened his first encounter with Nirvana to "falling in love" (*jatuh cinta*). In what I would come to know intimately as his personal, poetic turn of phrase, he claimed that his love affair with grunge transformed into spiritual devotion: "Music became like religion to me. I worshipped these bands like my gods" (Gede Robi Supriyanto, interview with author, February 25, 2009).

Thousands of miles separated Nirvana and Navicula—and Nirvana and me: we weathered our teenage years in Bali and North Carolina, respectively, far from grunge rock's epicenter in Seattle. But the affinity we felt for this music from a far-flung "elsewhere" (Baulch 2007) would, over our time getting to know each other, forge an intimacy of shared musical memories that would deepen our research collaborations and nourish our long friendships.[2]

This chapter compiles, through ethnographic observations, long conversations, and years of personal memories and deep friendship, the biography of an Indonesian band with a twenty-five-year history of recording original music, touring nationally and internationally, and mobilizing for social and environmental justice. Navicula has achieved a level of success that challenges the primacy of rock ingenuity by artists and labels in the United States and United Kingdom. They have also used their music and star power to encourage Indonesia and the rest of the world to take action on our most urgent environmental crises. As a result, they have pioneered direct action for social and environmental justice as a benchmark of ethical responsibility among their creative peers.

After more than a decade of knowing the musicians, managers, producers, and publicists behind Navicula, as our relationships have charted complex pathways through research collaboration, professional collaboration, friendship, and activism, I stake no claim on removed objectivity.[3] Rather, as a fan and friend, interlocutor and cotheorist I offer this chapter as homage to humanistic research that foregoes impartiality and prioritizes deep participation and intersubjectivity, whereby humanistic knowledge arises from the intimacies of research coparticipation (see Agar 1986; Sanjek 1990; Stewart 1998). Such intimacies engender ethical *responsibility* to "nurture," to "take care" of these relationships (Titon 1992, 321, cited in Hellier-Tinoco 2003, 25), long after the so-called fieldwork or book chapter concludes. Moreover, and owing to indigenous researcher calls for decolonized research methods (see, e.g., Tuhiwai Smith 2012), ethnographic intimacy requires intentional *engagement* and *reciprocity*: talking or writing *about* the human subjects of research should intentionally support those subjects' creative, professional, or activist undertakings in an ongoing feedback loop of "mutual and cooperative exchange" (Brereton et al. 2014, 3).

Navicula is a four-person outfit that, for the majority of its lifespan, has featured lyricist, guitarist, and lead vocalist Gede Robi Supriyanto (Robi); lead guitarist and backing vocalist Dadang SH Pranoto (Dadang); renowned kit player Rai Widya Adyana (affectionately called Gembull); and electric bassist and backing vocalist Made Indra (Made). The band's name was borrowed from an encyclopedia entry on the Latin name for a strange genus of golden algae, shaped like a ship. Since the 1998 release of their first album of original songs, *Self Portrait*, Navicula has established a national and international reputation among fans, music critics, and environmental activists as Indonesia's "green grunge

FIGURE 8.1 Navicula performing at an earthquake relief fundraising concert at Black Dog, Bali. September 25, 2009. Photograph by the author.

gentlemen," an English-language appellation bestowed by an entertainment news reporter, in reference to both their aesthetic and activist preoccupations.

My first encounter with Navicula's music predated my entrée into their lives as an ethnomusicologist researching rock music in Bali and wider Indonesia by more than three years. It followed the band's signing with Sony Music Indonesia by more than two. *Alkemis* was the only album Navicula released under their major label contract. Shortly after its launch, the label and the band reached a mutual decision to part ways, as Sony turned its attention to more lucrative mainstream pop, and the band chose the creative freedom of their independent roots. Ten years after our first face-to-face encounter, as I began preparing this chapter, the band celebrated the launch of their ninth full-length studio album, *Earthship*, and completed a two-week tour of Europe—their fifth international tour to date.

The notion of the "pathway" presents an opportunity to explore the metaphorical and physical travel composing the story of this Indonesian band. Much as Ruth Finnegan's 1989 study illuminated music-related activities as pathways that are deeply meaningful, actively forged, and connect individuals to communities, Navicula's creative pathways have been forged through their commitment to the craft of rock music. They draw on the familiar instrumentation and song structure of rock music and signify their predecessors in grunge, metal, and psychedelic rock through vocal and playing style, dress, and onstage gesture. While they acknowledge the roots of such rock genres on US and UK soil, they, like their Indonesian rock predecessors, also stake claim to rock as both a globally circulating and definitively local music.

The history of rock music in Indonesia charts its own complex pathway through the colonialism, nation building, and global neoliberalism that have determined the long-standing precedent to exploit "foreign" (*asing*) resources for "local" (*lokal*), creative undertakings (see Wallach 2008). In the late 1950s, Indonesians were listening to artists like Elvis Presley and Bill Haley and the Comets via radio station broadcasts from the Philippines (Wendi Putranto, interview with author, February 19, 2010). Later, aspiring rockers would absorb the sounds and styles of US and UK rockers, from the Rolling Stones, Led Zeppelin, and Jimi Hendrix to Deep Purple and Black Sabbath through mail-order catalogs, cassettes delivered by cruise ship workers, and, in the case of Deep Purple, Metallica, Iron Maiden, Green Day, and others, concerts on Indonesian soil (Rudolf Dethu, interview with author, April 10, 2010). Later still, the nation's formative rock bands, Koes Plus (formed in 1963), God Bless (1973), and Iwan Fals (who began recording in 1980), would influence a generation of rockers born under Suharto's authoritarian New Order. Collectively, rock and metal bands like Puppen, Burgerkill, Seringai, Naif, KOIL, SID, and Navicula would establish an underground rock movement steeped in political dissidence and connecting metal, punk, and grunge scenes, as well as student activists opposing the Suharto regime, across Jakarta, Bandung, Yogyakarta, Surabaya, Medan, and Denpasar over the course of the 1990s and early 2000s (Wallach 2008).

Going International

In 2010, Navicula released a single titled "Metropolutan" (Metro-pollutant) for free digital download, prior to embarking on a multiday tour of Jakarta. The song, which documents the heavy traffic and stifling pollution of Indonesia's capital and megacity, was an instant hit among fans and critics. Each night of their tour, hundreds of Navicula fans crammed into city venues, large and small, and many sang this song along with the band, having memorized the lyrics after just a few days of repeated listening. "Metropolutan" reinforced the band's activist orientation and desire to direct the collective attention of their fan base toward an urban socio-environmental plight. It also marked their first steps toward national and international acclaim. Shortly after the song's release, Canadian filmmaker and Bali resident Daniel Ziv approached the band to request the use of "Metropolutan" in his new documentary about Jakarta street buskers (*pengamen*). *Jalanan* (The Streets) (Ziv 2014) would go on to become a major cinematic release and winner in the Best Documentary category at the Busan International Film Festival.[4]

Two years after the song's initial release, Navicula recorded a music video for "Metropolutan," as part of their yearlong effort to secure a tour to the United States. The song was submitted to the global band competition "The Next Røde Røckers," sponsored by Australian recording equipment company Røde Microphones. A panel of expert judges, including Matt Sorum from Guns N' Roses and Velvet Revolver, David Catching of Queens of the Stone Age, and Howlin' Pelle Almqvist of The Hives, handpicked the ten finalists from more than five hundred acts from forty-three countries, each selected for their video's quality, artistic flair, and prominent product placement—every video was required to feature Røde equipment. Rock fans worldwide voted online to declare a final victor. They chose Navicula. The band received a contract to record at Hollywood's Record Plant, under the tutelage of producer Alain Johannes, who has shaped albums by Queens of the Stone Age, Arctic Monkeys, and Chris Cornell. Thus, like many of their musical heroes, from the Velvet Underground and Jimi Hendrix to Frank Zappa and the New York Dolls, Navicula's 2013 album *Love Bomb* included tracks recorded, mixed, and mastered in this legendary studio.

Los Angeles was one of several international destinations for the band that year. Just prior to joining the Røde competition, Navicula was selected for Quebec

City's premier alternative rock festival, Envol et Macadam. They also landed a slot at the Sydney Festival in Australia and headlined a show at Sydney's famed Manning Bar. While in the United States, Navicula added tour dates in Berkeley, San Francisco, and New York City. In 2012, after a serpentine path through Canada, Indonesia, Australia, and the United States, Navicula returned to Bali nearly broke, exhausted, and having gained only a small international following and a slight profit from merchandise sales. But making money and luring fans were not the primary goals of their international touring that year. Rather, they sought and successfully gained both national media attention and financial support for future projects. Shortly after their return, *Rolling Stone Indonesia* named Navicula the country's "Rock Ambassadors" in a five-page editorial spread (Hidayat 2013). They inked an endorsement deal with Volcom Entertainment, a California-based skate, swimwear, and clothing company popular in Jakarta and Bali, earning them a recording advance and two-year distribution and promotions contract. The signing enabled the band to complete the remaining eleven songs for *Love Bomb* and release a limited-edition album, featuring a cover handmade by Javanese artists and eco-activists from recycled Tetra Pak packaging.

As the bandmates entered their late thirties and family and community responsibilities expanded, their commitment to music rarely waned. They followed the success of *Love Bomb* with an ambitious live-recorded acoustic video album, *Tatap Muka* (Face to Face), shot at Setia Darma House of Mask and Puppets in Ubud. In 2017 they returned to Australia for tour dates in Sydney, Melbourne, Brisbane, and Byron Bay. In early 2018 they started production on their ninth album, *Earthship*. The music video for the album's first single, "Ibu" (Mother), hinted at the album's environmentalist subject matter and iconography of Mother Earth that would adorn the album's cover (figure 8.2). While still mixing the album, the band traveled to Sumba with rural community empowerment organization Kopernik to shoot a music video highlighting the organization's new project to supply locals with solar and bio-sourced power for lighting and small motors. The video features Navicula's fifteen-year-old song "Terus Berjuang" (Keep Up the Fight), rearranged and recontextualized through a new music video celebrating Indonesian farmers as the front line for social and environmental justice. In October 2018, on the heels of the *Earthship* release, Navicula completed their first European tour, including stopovers in Germany, Austria, Slovakia, Hungary, Poland, and the Czech Republic, while their management back home in Bali laid the groundwork for their eventual return to the US East Coast.[5]

In his 2012 book on jazz players in Accra, Steven Feld argues that musicians' way of knowing and being in a world of musics and cultures beyond Ghana's national borders challenges assumptions that (1) jazz belongs only to America and (2) African jazz is only a creative hybrid, or a localization of a globally circulating genre. Ghanaian jazz musicians assert a cosmopolitan knowledge of

FIGURE 8.2   The cover of Navicula's 2018 album, *Earthship*. Artwork and design by Sweeneypen, used with permission.

jazz history and its leading players and a cosmopolitan desire to engage through music, in conversation with artists like John Coltrane and Elvin Jones. Where Feld describes "jazz cosmopolitanism" as "the agency of desire for enlarged spatial participation" (2012), Navicula's metaphorical travel through musics and subject matters of local and global relevance combines with their physical travel through national and international touring to *achieve* enlarged spatial participation. As musicians located at the periphery of the music industry's global conglomerates—and like so many independent artists around the world—Navicula has achieved both creative freedom and the freedom of mobility afforded the most successful Western pop stars. But their achievements merit more than accolades for an indie act gone global: they have achieved a global mobility that, for many Indonesians, has been severely limited by the oppressions of colonialism and global capitalism, yet flaunted by the many traders, travelers, and tourists arriving from the West. And while, like the jazz players of Accra, Navicula's story dispenses with old narratives about cultural flows from the West to the Rest, it also challenges scholars of Indonesian music to think critically about which musical stories we continue to privilege and what binaries we might reinforce—traditional and modern or local and foreign—that set such stories off course.[6]

The Green Grunge Gentlemen

Through domestic tours across Bali, Java, Sumatra, and Kalimantan and international tours through Europe, Canada, Australia, and—the axis of artistry for many of the rock legends they admire—the United States, Navicula has reached diverse audiences abroad and reaped industry accolades at home. They have also gained national and international attention for environmental action campaigns, staged in partnership with a number of NGOs and environmental watchdogs. Navicula's international travel has significantly widened their carbon footprint, but it has also empowered them to educate on the environmental issues most concerning in Indonesia and to compel audiences to take up what they hold to be a universal responsibility to "save ourselves, from ourselves,"[7] to borrow a phrase from their 2009 song "Overkonsumsi" (Overconsumption). We are all obligated to fight for environmental justice, before we eliminate the very resources needed for our own survival.

On September 23, 2012, I waited alone in a dimly lit, nearly vacant parking lot outside a newly erected four-star hotel on the outskirts of Pangkalanbun, Kalimantan. It was well past midnight. They would have arrived hours earlier, but they were delayed by missteps and unforeseen obstacles: a motorbike accident, a broken-down van, and a standoff between angry Dayak villagers protecting the forests and hired militia protecting the employees of a palm oil company. Minutes later, they finally materialized from the dark highway. An entourage of more than forty included two vans and pickup trucks adorned with flapping flags and banners proclaiming their mission, flanked by seven motorbikes donning tiger stripes, mounted by riders in matching jumpsuits. In circuslike flair, the Kepak Sayap Enggang (Flapping Wings of the Hornbill) Tour arrived, composed of members of the Greenpeace Indonesia deforestation action team, Mata Harimau (Eye of the Tiger); Wahana Lingkungan Hidup Indonesia (Indonesian Forum for the Environment, WALHI); Aliansi Masyarakat Adat Nusantara (Indigenous Peoples Alliance of the Archipelago, AMAN); documentary filmmaker Rahung Nasution; and the road-worn members and crew of Navicula.

I immediately handed over the items the band had requested I bring from Bali: extra guitar strings; their limited-edition CD, *From Bali, for Borneo*, produced exclusively for distribution during this most unusual of band tours; and a liter of Jack Daniels. My own route to Kalimantan had been straightforward; I landed in Pangkalanbun just five hours after departing from Denpasar, Bali, with only a short transit in Surabaya. Navicula, on the other hand, arrived in Kalimantan after a two-day journey from Canada, where they performed at the Envol et Macadam alternative music festival and toured Quebec City and Toronto. In order to finance their Kalimantan tour, Navicula's manager, Lakota, and I set up a Kickstarter campaign using my family's US mailing address to raise the required budget. After successfully meeting their goal, Navicula became the first Indonesian band to support their music through online crowdfunding.

From Pangkalanbun, we traveled for twelve days and 2,000 kilometers across Indonesian Borneo, ending in Pontianak. Navicula would rarely plug in their amps or take to a stage, as one would expect on a typical band tour. Rather, they took turns donning the tiger-striped jumpsuits and mounting matching motorbikes to serve as eyewitnesses to the new wastelands, where rain forests and peatlands had been illegally razed to make way for row upon row of oil palms.

We rode up to 200 kilometers each day, making multiple stops at roadside repair shops to address flat tires, broken axles, and threadbare brakes—the consequences of the rough terrain we traversed. Each night we found respite in a Dayak village and met with residents to learn about their struggles with encroaching mining, logging, and agribusinesses intent on leveling the remaining trees. Following a formal welcome ritual featuring traditional music, dance, and libations in the form of a local palm or rice liquor, we would gather in community halls and listen to heated testimonials from the villages' bitter elders and impassioned youth: "Indonesia is a free country! But where is our freedom? We are imprisoned in our village, surrounded by companies who take away our freedom, when they raze the forests." "We are Dayak. Our identity is synonymous with the forests. When the forests are gone, so are we." "The government only shuts its eyes and opens its pockets."[8] Such were the comments of the rightful stewards of the Kalimantan interior, engrained forever in our memories.

Throughout their career, Navicula has been at the forefront of eco-activism within Indonesian music. Following in the tradition of protest balladeers like Iwan Fals and joining contemporary social dissenters like the metal band Seringai and the Jakarta punk band Marjinal, Navicula employs both song lyrics and offstage activism to take on issues as diverse as mass consumerism, palm oil's impact on indigenous peoples and wildlife, and government corruption. All nine of their studio albums and numerous compilation albums feature songs with social or environmental messaging. "Suram Wajah Negeri" (Land of Grim Faces) (Navicula 2005), for example, was recorded in response to rising interreligious conflict in Indonesia and became an anthem of survival for many Balinese following the 2002 bombings. In 2005, when the government drafted a controversial anti-pornography law,[9] Navicula responded with the song "Supremasi Rasa" (Supremacy of the Senses). The 2009 release of *Salto* (Somersaults) included songs like "Overkonsumsi" (Overconsumption), indicting Indonesia and other powerful Asian and Western nations for global environmental crises. Their 2013 album, *Love Bomb,* released shortly after their Kalimantan tour, focused largely on Indonesian deforestation and palm oil, as reflected in songs like "Orangutan," "Bubur Kayu" (Wood Pulp), and "Di Rimba" (In the Forest).

These titles represent the breadth of issues explored in Navicula's music, as well as their trademark dedication to social and environmental justice. Beyond lyrics, their long-term cooperation with environmental watchdog groups and NGOs has deepened their specialized knowledge on the issues most important to them, inspired direct action among their fans, and served as a source of spiritual affirmation for environmental activists nationwide. It has also led to other creative awareness-building projects, such as *Pulau Plastik* (Plastic Island), a television series and upcoming feature-length documentary film on Bali's plastic waste crisis, produced by Navicula front man Robi and his wife, Lakota. Following the Borneo tour, guitarist Dadang has continued to support the Indigenous Peoples Alliance (AMAN). In September 2018 he attended the Global Climate Action Summit in San Francisco as a representative of AMAN, and to promote a series of documentary films on the impact of climate change on indigenous peoples, produced by the US NGO If Not Us Then Who? and featuring Dadang's scoring. Navicula's eco-activism has also gained them international media attention from outlets including *The Guardian* (Smith 2014), the Australian conservation site *Mongabay* (Hance 2012), and the now defunct site for global band news, *MTV Iggy* (Bakkalapulo 2013). These milestones mark Navicula's success in drawing global attention to Indonesia's environmental crises, many of which have been exacerbated by the country's commerce and trade partnerships with Western nations. They have also helped disseminate indigenous Indonesian knowledge on the environment to an international audience and asserted their own agency as informed environmental leaders who are owed a seat at the table for global climate change conversations.

Pnina Werbner has described vernacular cosmopolitanism as a presumed "oxymoron that joins contradictory notions of local specificity and universal enlightenment" (2006, 496). Finding confluence rather than contradiction, Kwame Anthony Appiah described a "rooted" cosmopolitan as one who is "attached to a home of one's own, with its own cultural particularities, but [also] taking pleasure from the presence of other, different places that are home to other, different people" (1997, 618). Throughout their career, Navicula has been both rooted in their lived experiences growing up in Denpasar, Bali, and reaching for broader spatial participation in both the global music industry and global environmental activism. Navicula's environmental concerns span the Indonesian archipelago—and, indeed, the globe—yet their activist roots run deep in Balinese soil. As an organic farmer and permaculture designer, Robi is particularly concerned about land rights and clean water access for Balinese farmers. As the "locals" of a major tourist destination marketed for a century as an Edenic last paradise, they acknowledge the mutual dependency of tourism and capitalism binding Bali, Jakarta, and rich nations together, yet they have often joined Balinese activists and artists to protect the cultural and environmental integrity and vitality of home from "foreign" exploitation. For example, along with other Bali-based bands, Navicula has been engaged in the Bali Tolak Reklamasi (Bali Rejects Reclamation, BTR) protest movement for several years. BTR was spearheaded by WALHI Bali in 2013, in response to a presidential degree sanctioning a land reclamation project on the island's southeastern coast. In 2018, large-scale investors tendered development contracts, ranging from a Formula 1 racetrack to private luxury residences, a mega mall, a golf course, and a Disneyland. While the project has been temporarily stayed, it is still strongly endorsed by Bali's governor. Further, current president Joko Widodo has yet to make a presidential proclamation to prohibit further tourism development in this region. If it moves forward, it will squeeze out small-scale businesses, deny local fishers and residents access to the area, and cause significant repercussions for Benoa Bay's marine ecosystem, as a result of the disruption of seawater flow (Bell 2014). Since 2013 Navicula has frequently participated in street protests (*demo*) organized by WALHI and donned the distinctive campaign T-shirts when they perform in Indonesia. Robi also participated in a collaborative recording of the song "Bali Tolak Reklamasi," written by Balinese folk trio Nosstress to promote the Change.org petition to halt the development project.

Navicula's latest album, *Earthship* (2018), highlights environmental crises that are locally and globally urgent, including the pollution, land damage, and loss of biodiversity caused by mining and oil drilling and the microplastics polluting oceans and poisoning food sources. The album concludes with the acoustic song "Saat Semua Semakin Cepat, Bali Berani Berhenti" (When Everything Else Is Getting Faster, Bali Is Brave Enough to Stop), a reference to the Balinese New Year and Nyepi (Day of Silence). On Nyepi, air traffic to and from—and even over—Bali is halted. Everyone on the island is required to remain indoors. Travel, cooking, and the use of electricity are forbidden, and Hindu Balinese are encouraged to use the time for fasting, prayer, and meditation.

The lyrics of "Saat Semua Semakin Cepat, Bali Berani Berhenti" cite Nyepi as a source of spiritual rejuvenation for activists. It provides time to self-reflect on achievements and goals and prioritize the self-care needed to keep up the fight. The reference to Hindu ritual also purposefully evokes the romantic depiction of Bali as the "Island of the Gods," one repeatedly imposed by European explorers, Dutch colonizers, wandering artists, anthropologists, and Indonesia's own tourism development boards. Navicula knows that Bali is revered for its spiritual exoticism and, like many artists and activists before them, appropriates this characterization as a means to draw attention to local knowledge and assert their right to global conversations on global environmental crises. Thus, the song reflects a vernacular cosmopolitanism in which, as Homi Bhabha has written, belonging to a "cosmopolitan community [is] envisaged in *marginality*" (1996, 195–96). As citizens of a small island in a postcolonial Asian nation, far from the Western power centers for geopolitics and summits on climate crisis, Navicula draws attention to Balinese ways of knowing that could inform the rest of the world on how to save ourselves from the environmental crises the most wealthy and powerful have created.[10] Nyepi, for example, results in tangible, positive environmental impacts, due to the near elimination of nonrenewable energy consumption for a period of twenty-four hours. Thus, as acknowledged in 2009 by Balinese activists and cultural leaders who spearheaded the World Silent Day campaign to encourage a worldwide commitment to reducing energy consumption, Nyepi could be viewed as both an important Balinese ritual for purification and self-reflection and an effective action on climate change.

Early in our research relationship, I questioned Robi about the effectiveness of music to advance environmental justice. Why not spend more time engaged in direct action, I asked? He countered that music's capacity to explain and amplify an issue and motivate activists proves that Navicula's music *is* direct action. He also argued—from a position of deep experience working with nonprofit partners—that NGOs are not necessarily any more effective than musicians at inspiring behavioral change. So, he argued, "Let music convey something that is also fun. Let us take pleasure in it. Through more 'serious' means like NGO reports or nonprofit workshops, there is no guarantee that there will be a radical change within society, let alone one that has been going in the same direction for years. But I believe that water can make a hole in a stone" (Gede Robi Supriyanto, interview with author, May 2, 2010).[11] In 2016 Robi was honored with an invitation to join the Asia Society's Asia 21 Young Leadership Initiative, in recognition of his role as a musician mobilizing for social change. The accolade is a powerful endorsement of the impact of Navicula's music as important activism.

Alongside other requisites of the recording artist, including paid performances and touring, album and merchandise production, promotion, and distribution, and social media engagement, Navicula has added an important benchmark for success among their rock peers: social and environmental activism. Bands who commit to this important work can draw on their creative prestige to defend disenfranchised local communities and conserve environmental resources. Thus, Navicula's activism is both an important aspect of their creative and celebrity identity—what music marketers would call their branding—*and* important work to motivate environmental action among Bali-based musicians and fans.

The momentum propelling Navicula down their creative and activist pathways does not always lead away from the local. They have always circled back home to Bali, in both their music and their activism. Their lyrics reference the specific social, environmental, and political landscapes of Bali and greater Indonesia. Occasionally, the band even makes space for Balinese instrumentation, or the ambient sounds of the island's natural and human cacophony.[12] Home is depicted on album covers and vibrant concert and tour flyers that celebrate Balinese ecology and the iconic figures of Balinese cosmology. Robi and Lakota have also spearheaded a number of campaigns to address tourism overdevelopment, agrarian pesticides, ocean microplastics, and poor waste management impacting their island home. By merging knowledge gained from national and international activists and NGOs with their localized knowledge of Bali's natural and cultural resources and their collective dependence on the land and sea, Navicula has cultivated an ethical responsibility among their fans, at home and abroad, to and beyond the local. They believe their music not only *can* but *must* encourage a change in how we all respond to global environmental crisis—in how we honor a dual commitment to a specific local context and to "the global tribe we have become" (Appiah 2006, 100). Navicula has forged creative and activist pathways that reflect their personal geopoetics—their own sense of the world out there, and its impact on home. They have never been content as mere devotees of the bands they admired as teenagers and young adults. Rather, they have composed hundreds of original works in their twenty-two-year history. They have never been willing to be passive pawns of a domestic music industry that insists on adherence to depoliticized pop music norms. Rather, they have identified new sources of financial support for their music and activism. Navicula's story resists a reduction of their work to symbolic resistance or xenocentrism (Wallach 2005) and illustrates how collaborative work and a visionary ethos rocket-launched an off-the-radar band from Bali to Borneo, the United States, Australia, Canada, Europe, and back home again.

Coming Home

The music video for Navicula's song "Days of War, Nights of Love," one of the tracks they recorded with Alain Johannes at Record Plant, portrays moments in the studio and on the stage during their Australian and US tours, travel by air and road, and banter over beers and *kretek* (clove cigarettes). The story line finds each band member reveling in the magic of an international tour but also dreaming of *home*. Home means something different to each: for Robi, home is his wife, Lakota, and their vibrant organic garden in Ubud. For drummer Gembull, it is cooking in his Denpasar kitchen with his young son. For guitarist Dadang it is casual moments of hanging out, drinking coffee, and trading jokes with his Balinese neighbors. For bassist Made, home is dancing through the waves of a Bali beach, in the good company of his dog. The symbols of home are at once intimately nostalgic and personal to each musician, and reminiscent of the security, comfort, and familiarity of home an audience almost anywhere would recognize.

On Friday, March 23, 2018, shortly after Navicula wrapped a show celebrating their collaboration with Kopernik in Sumba, bassist Made and his fiancée, Afi, were returning to Denpasar by car when Made veered off the narrow road and collided head-on with a tree. Afi was killed instantly. Within hours of the accident, I spoke with Robi by phone from Boston to ask about Made's condition. Robi's voice, calm and resigned, intensified my fear that Made would pass. His words then bring great comfort now in the loss of someone I count among my dearest friends: "I think we must let Made choose the path that is best for him now." Two days later, after lingering briefly in a coma, Made also left this world.

While Made and Afi's loved ones have been overwhelmed by the loss, they have also been deeply moved by the thousands of messages of gratitude shared via social media, that Made and Afi could be united in eternity. Friends, venues, and community organizations around Bali rallied together to raise money for Made's medical expenses and care for Afi's young daughter. Navicula was resilient in the wake of their loss. Within weeks of the accident, they recruited a new bassist and staged a tour across Bali, to every community and venue that contributed to fundraising for Made and Afi. They called it the Home Sweet Home Tour.

As an agnostic and activist, I generally associate agency with human choice and action rather than divine intervention. But over ten years spent living in Indonesia I have also cultivated a personal spirituality that allows for the possibility that some things are beyond rational explanation. One night before his accident, Made and Deny Surya, a senior sound engineer at Antida Studios in Denpasar, worked late into the night, laying down all of Made's bass and vocal tracks for *Earthship*. Made's diligence and expediency surprised Deny and his bandmates, who expected him to be the last to finish recording, as he had been on every album before this. After his death, bandmates and friends have told me that Made must have known he would not return to the studio. But he now continues on as the deep pulse linking melody and harmony for Navicula's tribute to Mother Earth, and to the home we all share.

In Indonesia I have witnessed, time and time again, the potency of music to educate, inspire, heal, and connect people. In ceremony, Hindu Balinese perform special repertoires of music, dance, and theater as the pathway connecting those dwelling in *sekala*, the seen world of living human beings, with *niskala*, the unseen world—where both ancestors and contemporaries taken before their time now dwell. Through *Earthship*, and all of the albums that preceded it, friends, family, and fellow musicians and activists continue to find a pathway back to Made—to invite his spirit to accompany them in this seen world, this home of his thirty-six years.

In the weeks following Made's death, I often found myself rummaging through the digital clutter of my memories of Navicula, captured in ten years of photographs and videos. I have grieved deeply for Made, partially because he, Gembull, Dadang, and Robi have all provided a brotherly love that my own brother has withdrawn, due to our political disagreements and impasse over the 2016 US presidential election. Navicula has been the center of my social, professional, and activist universe for a very long time; grief has become dynamite for that foundation of cultural, critical, and emotional distance that I imagined was necessary for my storytelling to become scholarship. Music connects me to them, in this world and beyond. The ethos of the vernacular cosmopolitan, which has charted our often overlapping pathways in music, profession, and activism, requires an openness to learn and *care* for each other, and to continuously expand our ethics of care to include the people and places we have yet to know or understand. Cosmopolitanism is never rootless; metaphorical and physical travel enable an ongoing interplay between notions of home and away, and of friends and strangers. My home discipline of ethnomusicology, and all others employing humanistic means to connect, in Appiah's words, to a "world of strangers," affords an intimacy that fervently resists binaries of home and field, as well as research interlocutors and friends. After all, what is the ultimate goal of this work if not a deepening sense of our shared humanity?

Navicula's creative and activist pathways have created a forward momentum for their steadfast dedication to making new music, expanding their fan base, and safeguarding the natural environment of their island and the planet. I have been lucky to travel these pathways with them for many years. And I have been inspired to forge my own—to take a deep interest in and value, as Appiah has charged us, *particular* human lives (2006), and to travel, make music, write stories, and advocate for the well-being of friends and strangers, in Indonesia and my own backyard.

Appiah wrote, "Each human being has responsibilities to every other" (2006, 129). I hope Navicula's story will encourage the reader to consider the deep and persistent significance of both the *local* and the *global*, and of music's capacity for cultivating our ethical responsibility to one another. As Kay Kaufman Shelemay (2013) has urged, let us consider our moral responsibilities to both the people with whom we work and the wider communities we might impact, as scholars whose work brings us into frequent contact with strangers, turned research interlocutors, turned friends.

In memory of Made Indra Navicula. Cinta kami selalu bersamamu.

NOTES

1. Media deregulation in the 1990s brought international recording companies and MTV to Indonesia (Baulch 2007), making more readily available to young musicians and fans the albums and music videos of their favorite European and American performing artists.

2. Baulch examines reggae, metal, and "alternapunk" (Baulch's term) as political strategies to resist "dominant Balinese identity discourses" (2007, 18). She argues that young urban musicians and fans gestured toward Western "elsewhere(s)" in their co-optation of these genres, as a strategy to define their own sense of Balinese identity.

3. See Moore 2013 for a description of the professional relationships I developed with Navicula and other music industry professionals in Bali. Since 2017, I have also worked as Navicula's North American tour manager.

4. Navicula's lead guitarist Dadang also composed the film's score, in collaboration with Ernest Hariyanto.

5. Navicula's second US tour was repeatedly delayed due to difficulties securing US visas under the Trump administration and, in 2020, the spread of COVID-19. Their future international touring remains uncertain.

6. While the predominance of Javanese and Balinese gamelan studies within Indonesian music scholarship has been well documented, many authors represented in this book have endeavored to critique and move beyond this research scope.

7. Bahasa Indonesia: "Selamatkan diri kita dari kita sendiri."

8. Quotations were logged in the author's field journal during village meetings. Names of individual speakers are unknown.

9. The law passed in 2008.

10. Even at the 2007 UN Climate Change Conference, which was held in Bali, no Balinese delegates were among the more than sixty participants from Indonesia (UNFCCC, 2008).

11. "Iya, maksudnya, jangankan yang lewat musik yang lebih banyak menyampaikan sesuatu lewat *fun*, secara *fun* gitu ya. Lewat cara-cara serius aja seperti LSM atau *NGO* aja, belum tentu bisa mengubah, mengubah sesuatu masyarakat secara radikal. Apalagi untuk mengubah suatu kultur yang sudah berjalan selama bertahun-tahun. Tapi saya percaya, air bisa membuat lubang batu gitu, apabila kamu melakukannya secara konsisten."

12. Navicula included recorded samples of the bustling streets of Ubud; the *ketuk*, the gamelan's timekeeper gong; and the *suling*, a bamboo flute, on their 2005 album, *Alkemis* (Alchemist).

WORKS CITED

Agar, Michael H. 1986. *Speaking of Ethnography*. Beverly Hills: Sage.
Appiah, Kwame Anthony. 1997. "Cosmopolitan Patriots." *Critical Inquiry* 23 (3): 617–39.

Appiah, Kwame Anthony. 2006. *Cosmopolitanism: Ethics in a World of Strangers*. New York: W. W. Norton & Company.

Bakkalapulo, Maria. 2013. "Navicula Live: Rock Against Environmental Destruction." *MTV Iggy*, August 23.

Baulch, Emma. 2007. *Making Scenes: Reggae, Punk, and Death Metal in 1990s Bali*. Durham, NC: Duke University Press.

Bell, Loren. 2014. "Bali Uprising: Plan to Convert Protected Area into Golf Courses, Mall Spurs Outrage." *Mongabay*, August 16. https://news.mongabay. com/2014/08/bali-uprising-plan-to-convert-protected-area-into-golf-courses-mall-spurs-outrage/.

Berger, Harris M. 2009. *Stance: Ideas about Emotion, Style, and Meaning for the Study of Expressive Culture*. Middletown, CT: Wesleyan University Press.

Bhabha, Homi. 1996. "Unsatisfied: Notes on Vernacular Cosmopolitanism." In *Text and Nation*, edited by Laura Garcia-Morena and Peter C. Pfeifer, 191–207. London: Camden House.

Brereton, Margaret, Paul Roe, Ronald Schroeter, and Anita Lee Hong. 2014. "Beyond Ethnography: Engagement and Reciprocity as Foundations for Design Research Out Here." *Proceedings of the SIGCHI Conference on Human Factors in Computing Systems*, 1183–86. New York: Association for Computing Machinery.

Feld, Steven. 2012. *Jazz Cosmopolitanism in Accra*. Durham, NC: Duke University Press.

Finnegan, Ruth. 1989. *The Hidden Musicians: Making Music in an English Town*. Middletown, CT: Wesleyan University Press.

Hance, Jeremy. 2012. "Featured Video: Plight of Orangutans Highlighted with New Rock Song." *Mongabay*, January 17. https://news.mongabay.com/2012/01/featured-video-plight-of-orangutans-highlighted-with-new-rock-song/.

Hellier-Tinoco, Ruth. 2003. "Experiencing People: Relationships, Responsibility and Reciprocity." *British Journal of Ethnomusicology* 12 (1): 19–34.

Hidayat, Adib. 2013. "Rolling Stone Indonesia Editors' Choice 2013: Rock Ambassadors: Navicula." *Rolling Stone Indonesia* 97, May 2013.

Moore, Rebekah E. 2013. "Work in the Field: Public Ethnomusicology and Collaborative Professionalism." *Collaborative Anthropologies* 6: 103–29.

Sanjek, Roger. 1990. "On Ethnographic Validity." In *Fieldnotes: The Makings of Anthropology*, edited by Roger Sanjek, 385–418. Ithaca, NY: Cornell University Press.

Shelemay, Kay Kaufman. 2013. "The Ethics of Ethnomusicology in a Cosmopolitan Age." In *The Cambridge History of World Music*, edited by Philip V. Bohlman, 786–806. Cambridge: Cambridge University Press.

Smith, Jed. 2014. "How Bali Punks Navicula Took On the Palm Oil Industry." *Guardian*, April 25. https://www.theguardian.com/music/australia-culture-blog/2014/apr/25/how-bali-punks-navicula-took-on-the-palm-oil-industry.

Stewart, Alex. 1998. *The Ethnographer's Method*. Thousand Oaks, CA: Sage.

Titon, Jeff Todd. 1992. "Music, the Public Interest, and the Practice of Ethnomusicology." *Ethnomusicology* 36 (3): 315–22.

Tuhiwai Smith, Linda. 2012. *Decolonizing Methodologies: Research and Indigenous Peoples*. 2nd ed. London: Zed Books.

UNFCCC. 2008. "Report of the Conference of the Parties on its Thirteenth Session, Held in Bali from 3 to 15 December 2007." UNFCCC Framework Convention on Climate Change, March 14, 2008. https://unfccc.int/resource/docs/2007/cop13/eng/06a01.pdf.

Wallach, Jeremy. 2005. "Underground Rock Music and Democratization in Indonesia." *World Literature Today* 3: 16–20.

Wallach, Jeremy. 2008. *Modern Noise, Fluid Genres: Popular Music in Indonesia, 1997–2001*. Madison: University of Wisconsin Press.

Werbner, Pnina. 2006. "Vernacular Cosmopolitanism." *Theory, Culture, and Society* 23 (2–3): 496–98.

AUDIO/VIDEO RECORDINGS

The Hydrant. 2005. *Saturday Night Riot*. Electrohell. Cassette.

Lolot. *Bali Rock Alternative*. 2004. Bali Music Group. Cassette.

Navicula. 1998. *Self Portrait*. Self-release. Cassette.

Navicula. 2005. *Alkemis*. Sony Music Entertainment Indonesia. Cassette.

Navicula. 2007. *Beautiful Rebel*. Electrohell. Compact disc.

Navicula. 2009. *Salto* (Somersaults). Zygote Records. Compact disc.

Navicula. 2013. *Love Bomb*. Røde Microphones and Volcom Entertainment. Compact disc.

Navicula. 2013. "Days of War, Nights of Love." Video directed by Erick EST. EST Film. https://www.youtube.com/watch?v=vftepzIZ9s0.

Navicula. 2015. *Tatap Muka*. Volcom Entertainment, Antida Records, and EST Movie. Compact disc and DVD.

Navicula. 2018. *Earthship*. Self-release. Compact disc.

Navicula. 2018. "Ibu." Video directed by Erick EST. EST Movie. https://www.youtube.com/watch?v=Ae_CL6AhdLE.

Navicula. 2018. "Terus Berjuang." Video directed by Erick EST. EST Movie and Kopernik. https://www.youtube.com/watch?v=7SrmwXzAgJE&t=1s.

Superman Is Dead. 2003. *Kuta Rock City*. Sony Music Entertainment Indonesia. Cassette.

Various artists. 2013. "Bali Tolak Reklamasi," by Nosstress. ForBali. https://www.youtube.com/watch?v=m62Ha35mQ-Y.

Ziv, Daniel. 2014. *Jalanan*. DesaKota Productions, DVD.

9

KERONCONG IN THE UNITED STATES

Danis Sugiyanto

Keroncong has been described by several researchers as an Indonesian music that has been deeply influenced by Western (primarily European) music.[1] Since its emergence in the seventeenth century, *keroncong* has developed into a dynamic and unique form, distinct from its original influences. The term *keroncong* itself has received many different definitions. The term can be understood to refer to any of the following:

1. An onomatopoetic term referring to the sound of a specific instrument called the *cuk* or ukulele, if it is played in a way to create a "*crong . . . crong . . .*" sound.
2. A traditional string-band ensemble.
3. A "beat" associated with that ensemble, often referred to as *irama keroncong*.
4. A musical form within the context of the *keroncong* ensemble, alongside the forms named: *langgam keroncong, langgam Jawa, Stambul I, Stambul II, Jenaka, Bentuk Bebas* (free form), among others.[2]

Recently, *keroncong* has developed quickly due to both internal and external influences. Both the interests of players and the highly dynamic, interconnected historical era they are living in has furthered the development of *keroncong*. The form has already spread to several other countries, including the United States.

American students have been increasingly attracted to *keroncong*. At least two US groups have emerged in recent years, supported by university music faculty: first an ensemble in Riverside, California, followed shortly by one in Richmond,

Virginia. As is well known, Balinese, Javanese, and Sundanese gamelan ensembles have been established in the United States for many decades. In comparison, *keroncong* has been far less performed and studied. It has not received the kind of institutional support and popularization, in either Indonesia or America, that gamelan has. So what attracts these American students to *keroncong*? When were they first exposed to it? Why do they study and play this music?

My hunches about the interest in *keroncong* in the States were confirmed by the American *keroncong* researcher Russ Skelchy, who currently resides in England. According to Skelchy, there is ample research on gamelan available in the States, but very little to be found in English regarding *keroncong* (personal communication, February 10, 2018).[3] Many of the English-language publications by Western researchers regarding *keroncong* are rather dated.[4] The Indonesian language literature has, however, grown steadily over the past two decades.[5]

The Growth and Development of *Keroncong* in the United States

I first learned of an American interest in performing *keroncong* in 2000, when a researcher from Hawaii reached out to me with questions about *langgam Jawa*. This was a master's student studying at Gajah Mada University in Yogyakarta. Unfortunately, I do not know the results of the researcher's work, and I have forgotten his name. Then, in 2008, I heard of a *keroncong* ensemble established that year by Deborah Wong, René Lysloff, and their students at the University of California at Riverside. This ensemble was called Orkes Pantai Barat (OPB) and was one venue in which Skelchy developed his interest and expertise in *keroncong*. The ensemble performed at the Solo Keroncong Festival (SKF) in 2012.

In 2013 Andy McGraw and his wife, Jessica Zike, played recordings of *keroncong* for some of the musicians in Gamelan Raga Kusuma, the Balinese gamelan he and *dhalang* Gusti Sudarta had established at the University of Richmond in Virginia in 2006, and asked if they might want to start an ensemble.[6] They enthusiastically agreed. In 2014 Raga Kusuma member Hannah Standiford had just been awarded a Darmasiswa award, so she decided to focus on *keroncong* repertoire during that year, working with me and sending parts recordings and videos back to the newly formed group in Virginia. In 2016 the University of Richmond invited me, Gusti Sudarta, and the Javanese singer Peni Candrarini to collaborate with the new *keroncong* ensemble (which McGraw and Standiford had named Rumput) and the Appalachian musicians Elizabeth LaPrelle and Anna Roberts-Gevalt. We staged six performances, which we called the Shadow

Ballads project, in Richmond and at Wake Forest University, Bucknell University, Cornell University, the Indonesian consulate in New York, and the Indonesian embassy in Washington, DC.

Through the collaboration in 2016 I was better able to grasp the American interest in and understanding of *keroncong*, and its relationship to gamelan in the United States. Javanese and Balinese gamelan, as well as *keroncong*, are well established in Richmond. I was frankly surprised at the level of interest and ability in *keroncong* in the former capital of the Confederacy.

According to McGraw, in 2014 he was exploring new ways to expand the group's musical activities when Zike, also a member of the ensemble, recommended *keroncong*. McGraw noticed that many members of the gamelan ensemble were experienced string players who also played Americana or Appalachian music. Virginia is not only (in)famous for tobacco but also for its outstanding bluegrass, country, and old-time musicians (Andy McGraw, personal communication, February 12, 2018). The new group Rumput was formed out of their enthusiasm for the idea. But how did the group come to be named after the Indonesian word for grass? I had thought this was because the R also referred to "Richmond," but it instead refers to a spirit and philosophy of "grassroots" community making, which is deeply shared in old-time and bluegrass music and Indonesian *keroncong* and gamelan (Andy McGraw, personal communication, February 16, 2018).

How did they study this music? Who ran rehearsals? Where did they find instruments? At first they found videos on YouTube and picked instruments without yet having a teacher. They used local instruments, such as a Western cello and ukulele, retuning them in the *keroncong* manner. In the summer of 2014 McGraw traveled for research to Indonesia and purchased local instruments—*cak*, *cuk*, and *selo*—and recorded several lesson videos with performers based in Denpasar. McGraw himself focused on *selo*, having studied Javanese *kendang* for many years. They began rehearsing once weekly, after potluck dinners at McGraw's home.

In August of that year Hannah Standiford traveled to Solo as a Darmasiswa student (Hannah Standiford, personal communication, February 9, 2018). During that academic year she studied both gamelan and *keroncong*, studying the latter intensively with me. Every Wednesday evening she joined our rehearsals with Orkes Keroncong Swastika. She videotaped each recording, sending them back to the musicians in Richmond. On my recommendation, she studied with several ensembles around Solo, absorbing the wide range of styles and repertoire. She is rather famous in Indonesia now as a *keroncong* singer and musician, having played in Jakarta, Bandung, Semarang, Yogyakarta, and other cities. Rumput itself has now toured Java twice, in July 2017 and July 2018.

In 2018 I had the opportunity to teach at the University of Richmond and the College of William and Mary (in Williamsburg) as a visiting Fulbright artist-scholar. During that time I was the visiting artistic director of both Orkes Keroncong Rumput and Gamelan Raga Kusuma. That semester we had the opportunity to perform throughout Virginia, as well as in Washington DC, New York, and Baltimore. I found that Andy and Hannah, as codirectors of the ensemble, had provided a solid base for Rumput's continued development. Most interesting for me was their unique approach to the music, based on their American musical aesthetics, and their innovative combinations of *keroncong* with American and British Isles music.

Rumput's Style

Rumput is most attracted to, and most proficient at, the *langgam Jawa* style. In Central Java, *keroncong* is often described as being divided into two overarching styles: *keroncong asli* and *langgam Jawa*. *Keroncong asli* uses essentially Western musical structures such as scales, tonal harmonies, chords, equal-tempered tuning, and playing techniques associated with Western light orchestral music. *Langgam Jawa* imitates and is influenced by Central Javanese gamelan but performed by the same instruments as are used when playing *keroncong asli*. In this case the *piul* (violin) imitates the *rebab*, the Western flute the *suling*, the guitar the *gambang*, the *cak* (high ukulele) the *siter*, the *cuk* (low ukulele) the *kenong*, the *selo* (cello) the *kendang* (using a pizzicato technique), and the bass the *slenthem*, *kempul*, or *gong*.

Although the *keroncong asli* style is deeply influenced by Western musical elements, *keroncong* as a form has evolved into a uniquely local expression over the centuries. This process of local adaptation and reinvention is seen throughout Indonesian culture. While the physical materials of the *keroncong* ensemble can be directly linked to Western forms, their treatment and its styles of orchestration and elaboration are distinctly local, in accordance with local *rasa* (feeling or aesthetic). As an analogy, while Indonesian *baju* or *kemeja* are clearly derived from the Western dress shirt, the use of local tailoring and batik patterns have transformed the form into an expression of distinctly local culture. While *keroncong* instruments can be traced to a Western historical origin, *keroncong* music is uniquely Indonesian.

According to Sunarno, the basis of all Western (or "universal") music is that of European classical music, in which instruments such as violins and flutes are responsible for carrying the melody (personal communication, September 2018). In this system, the more complex the musical texture, the more value the music is perceived to hold. However, *keroncong* incorporated many techniques, both instrumental and vocal, that are unique to traditional Indonesian forms of musical organization. And yet, *keroncong* is also capable of incorporating many of the sophisticated styles and techniques of Western classical and jazz music. Some forms of contemporary *keroncong* are quite sophisticated, and far from the derogatory descriptions of *keroncong* musicians as street buskers and their *ngroncongi* sounds.

The styles and techniques of *langgam Jawa* are more specialized, representing the local genius of the Central Javanese for adopting elements of foreign cultures and adapting their styles to new influences. *Langgam Jawa* does not employ Western harmony but instead the modal forms of Central Javanese gamelan. Each of the instruments, and the vocalist, emulates the techniques and instruments of the gamelan ensemble. Rumput has studied both the *langgam Jawa* and *asli* style, and while they are proficient, they have much yet to learn. Most interesting to me are their mixtures of Javanese, Balinese, Sundanese, Appalachian, and Irish musics, combinations that it would be difficult for Indonesian musicians to realize.

The Motivation to Study *Keroncong* in Richmond, Virginia

So what attracted the members of Rumput to *keroncong*? Were they not satisfied studying Javanese and Balinese gamelan? Or was it that studying gamelan sparked and conditioned their interest in *keroncong*? What similarities between these two musics might explain their interest?

I was born in the city of Solo, and my father was a renowned *kendang* player, regularly performing for the Ramayana shows at Prambanan. I was expected to follow in his musical footsteps but instead I became devoted to *keroncong* music. At first, I thought these two musical worlds were quite distinct, but as I have gotten older I have met many *gamelan* musicians (*pangrawit*) who are attracted to and perform *keroncong*, both *asli* and *langgam Jawa* styles. In this section I mention just a few.

According to the late Wakidjo, his father played *keroncong selo* and guitar. His nephew, Murtanto (the son of Wakidi Dwijomartono), is an outstanding *selo* player who often plays with my group, Orkes Keroncong Swastika. Hartono, a musician at the Mangkunegaran, is also a well-regarded *keroncong* musician. Sutarman, a vocalist and vocal teacher, used to often sing *keroncong*, along with his younger brother, Sunardi. Waluyo, a *keroncong* singer at RRI Surakarta, is the younger brother of Walidi, a *pangrawit* and gamelan teacher at SMKI Surakarta.

Others involved in gamelan, *campur sari*, and *keroncong* include Teguh Palur, Pahang Sunarno, and Sutarso, a renowned *gendèr* player and a *selo* player with Radio Orkes Surakarta. Eventually, I came to learn that many Javanese who enjoy *karawitan* also enjoy *keroncong*, and vice versa. This tendency is shared by the members of Gamelan Raga Kusuma and Rumput.[7]

There are many musical and cultural similarities between Central Javanese gamelan and *keroncong*. Both are comparatively soft musics, and they share many of the same social stigmas, both negative and positive. Among many contemporary Solonese youth, both are considered "old people's music," music for sleeping to, conservative, slow, without dynamic contour. But of course, it is difficult for these young people to appreciate musics they do not fully understand. Those who have studied these musics understand that these stereotypes are incorrect.

The Relationship of Gamelan and *Keroncong* Scenes

There are many *keroncong* ensembles in Solo. According to the data collected by Wartono, the current director of HAMKRI (Himpunan Artis Musik Keroncong Indonesia, the Indonesian Keroncong Artists Association), based in Solo, there are more than fifty groups in Solo today (Joglo Sriwedari, personal communication, March 13, 2016). However, it is clear that many musicians play in several ensembles. It is common for musicians to hop from one rehearsal to another each evening. These are occasions for focused rehearsals, open-ended jam sessions, and laid-back hanging out while eating Javanese snacks. Amateur groups tend to allow anyone to sit in at any time, whereas professional groups tend to be more exclusive, with a relatively stable lineup of musicians. This is the case for the professional group I perform in, Swastika, of which I have been a regular member since 1994.

Foreign fans of *keroncong*—primarily from Japan, England, Hungary, Australia, and America—often come to Solo to study and attend jam sessions and concerts. Solo currently hosts many public performing contexts for *keroncong*: there is the Keroncong Lesehan at Taman Budaya each third Tuesday of the month, the Cakrawala Musik Keroncong broadcast at RRI every third Sunday, the Keroncong Bale at the Balai Soedjatmoko every Tuesday, the regular performance at the Keroncong Joglo HAMKRI at Sriwidari every Friday night, and a new series at the Gesang Stage at Omah Sinten every fifth Tuesday (*selasa wage*).[8] When foreign students attend these events, they are learning about not only the musical forms of *keroncong* but also its surrounding culture, a specifically Solonese way of being together through music.

Keroncong music has evolved and developed through intensive processes of rehearsal, study, and composition among its musicians. Many workshops, seminars, contests, discussions, and publications concerning *keroncong* also have furthered this development. The Indonesian culture of musical study and rehearsal is quite different from that in America, and this is related to various factors such as available materials, spaces, education systems, cultural attitudes toward time, artistic economies, and even the weather!

Orkes Keroncong Rumput organizes its study of and approach to *keroncong* in ways rather similar to those employed in Solo. Every rehearsal is preceded by a potluck meal at McGraw's home, where they usually rehearse. This is common in Indonesia as well, where food almost always accompanies the rehearsal and performance of traditional music. The practice of providing and making food collectively is an embodiment of the *gotong royong* that is also necessary for making music together. Even those Rumput members who are not able to make or bring food almost always bring beer or wine. The approach toward musical rehearsal itself is rather different, however. In Solonese *keroncong* ensembles it is common practice for musicians to frequently switch instruments, such that more experienced players eventually are able to play all instruments in any style. As a beginning group, Rumput members have specialized in particular instruments. This reflects the specialization that is typical in Western ensembles but rather uncommon in—for instance—Central Javanese gamelan. However, Rumput members are just now starting to switch instruments between songs.

Reception by Central Javanese *Keroncong* Musicians

Rumput has received an enthusiastic response from Indonesian observers, especially those in Central Java, who for the most part have expressed happiness and pride. I haven't encountered anyone who has expressed offense or sentiments of appropriation or cultural theft. Instead, Indonesian observers tend to read Rumput's efforts as a form of respect. According to Andi Prihtyastoko, a leading *keroncong* musician in Yogyakarta:

> As the saying goes: "you can't love what you don't know." Their music is a sign of respect to those of us who are the caretakers of *keroncong*. It makes us feel proud to know there are foreigners who want to study our culture. And we are happy because they have taken this very seriously; they are studying the traditional forms and songs and are striving to embody the real character and feeling of *keroncong*, through their

repertoire, playing techniques, and vocal embellishments. This isn't easy, but we already see the results! And we are proud! (Andi Prihtyastoko, personal communication, December 12, 2017)

Andi is happy to have "made new friends through *keroncong*," and he is impressed with Rumput's attempts to understand the subtle *rasa* of this style. The same sentiment was expressed by Solonese musicians, such as Sunarto:

> As I get older, my love and pride for *keroncong* has only increased. Now there are many Westerners who are studying our refined [Javanese: *adiluhung*] *keroncong* music. Through this they must study Indonesian language, Javanese (high Javanese!), new instruments, and new forms of melody that are nowhere notated. They must study how *slendro* and *pelog* are transformed through *langgam Jawa*; they must study the difficult nuances of *cengkok*, *gregel*, *luk*, and *vibrasi* embellishment. So I really must salute their efforts! (Sunarto, personal communication, November 6, 2017)

Sunarto feels that Rumput's efforts have deepened his own appreciation and love of *keroncong*, an old form that persists throughout many cultural transformations. He points out that culture is expressed through music and that by learning *keroncong* forms, techniques, and melodies, the members of Rumput are learning about Indonesian and specifically Central Javanese culture. Learning the subtleties of language pronunciation is certainly a challenge here, one that members of Rumput still need to work hard on.

The Solonese *keroncong* musician Wawan Listanto has commented specifically on their instrumental playing: "I really think they are tight and clean in their playing. But they also have their own style. Their hybrid and collaborative pieces are the most interesting to me. They have an approach toward arranging that is really different and I think Solonese audiences find very riveting. It's *keroncong*, with which we're familiar, but we're not sure what might happen next!" (Wawan Listanto, personal communication, August 7, 2018). According to Wawan (who is often called Mbolo in the Solonese *keroncong* scene), Rumput has succeeded in both performing traditional pieces and adding their own style to the form. The musician Yessy Rianto agreed and is especially impressed with Hannah Standiford's ability to simultaneously sing and play the *cak* (personal communication, August 1, 2018).

In general, Solonese audiences have been very impressed with the ensemble's ability to learn a wide range of traditional repertoire in a relatively short time. Yet some older Solonese *keroncong* musicians, including Budiyono, Wilbordus Sumarno, and Martanto (Canthing), hope that they will study more seriously the *asli* style so that it is balanced with their performance of *langgam Jawa*. Ironically, it is this style, with its tonal harmony, straightforward tempos, and chords, that is technically more similar to the Western musics the members of Rumput are already familiar with!

Grass Roots

Grass is hardy. It can grow in many kinds of climates and conditions. Crushed underfoot, it keeps coming back up. Without special attention or care, it will spread where it can. *Keroncong* in Indonesia is a lot like grass. Without mass media or governmental support, it continues to survive and grow. I believe Orkes Keroncong Rumput, like so many *keroncong* ensembles in Indonesia, has developed similarly strong roots. The ensemble is committed to both tradition and exploration. According to McGraw, *keroncong* encourages a laid-back sociality that strengthens the connections between players. According to Standiford, studying *keroncong* is a means to respect and possibly contribute to Indonesian culture. For them, new exploration must take place on a solid foundation of traditional understanding. For Indonesian musicians and audiences, *keroncong*'s value is enhanced by the foreign appreciation and contributions by ensembles such as Rumput.

NOTES

1. There is no standard spelling for the term. According to Yampolsky, prior to World War II it was always spelled *krontjong* (personal communication, October 2020). *Kroncong* and *keroncong* appear equally common in Indonesia today.
2. The term can also refer to a form of East Javanese (Madurese) jewelry.
3. Skelchy completed a dissertation on the *keroncong* singer Waljinah at UC Riverside in 2015.
4. See Becker 1975; Heins 1975; Kornhauser 1978; Taylor 1983; Hatch 1985; Yampolsky 1991; Tan 1993; Kartomi 1998. For more recent accounts, in addition to Skelchy 2015, see Tan 2004; Cohen 2006; Ganap 2011; Yampolsky 2010, 2013; Mutsaers 2014; McGraw 2022.
5. See Kusbini 1976; Harmunah 1987; Soeharto 1995; Kuntoro 2001; Ariff 2001; Ganap 2011; Prakosa 2012; Riasetyani 2013; Setiawan 2014; Wibya 2015; Suadi 2017.
6. McGraw and I had worked together since 2001 when he was conducting dissertation research on *musik kontemporer* and was a visiting member in the Sono Seni ensemble, then directed by I Wayan Sadra. After our Sono Seni rehearsals, McGraw would often join me for late night *keroncong* rehearsals in Surakarta.
7. When I was active in the group, their membership included Andy McGraw, Hannah Standiford, Jessica Zike, Natalie Quick, Paul Willson, Brandon Simmons, Brian Larson, John Priestley, Kyle Dosier, and Zachary Cain. Artists associated with the group included Greyson Goodenow, Beth Reid, and Edward Brietner.
8. This scheme is based on the Javanese *wetonan* calendrical cycle, a thirty-five-day superposition of the seven-day week cycle and the *pasaran* five-day week cycle.

WORKS CITED

Any, Andjar. 1983. "Musik kroncong, musik Nusantara." In *Perjalanan musik di Indonesia*, 79–87. Jakarta: Panitia Penyelenggara PENSI'83.

Ariff, Ahmad. 2001. *Seni Muzik Kroncong* [The Art of Kroncong Music]. Bangi: Penerbit Universiti Kebangsaan Malaysia.

Becker, Judith. 1975. "Kroncong, Indonesian Popular Music." *Asian Music* 15 (1): 14–19.

Cohen, Matthew Isaac. 2006. *Komedie Stamboel: Popular Theater in Colonial Indonesia, 1891–1903*. Athens: Ohio University Press.

Ganap, Victor. 2011. *Krontjong Toegoe*. Yogyakarta: Badan Penerbit Institut Seni Indonesia Yogyakarta.

Ganap, Victor. 2019. "Kroncong Orchestration of Millennial Generation." *Harmonia* 19 (2): 117–25.

Harmunah. 1987. *Musik Kroncong: Sejarah, Gaya dan Perkembangan* [Kroncong Music: History, Style and Development]. Yogyakarta: Pusat Liturgi Yogyakarta.

Hatch, Martin. 1985. "Popular Music in Indonesia." *Popular Music Perspectives* 2: 210–12.

Heins, Ernst. 1975. "Kroncong and Tanjidor: Two Cases of Urban Folk Music in Jakarta." *Asian Music* 7 (2): 20–32.

Kartomi, Margaret J. 1998. "From Kroncong to Dangdut: The Development of Popular Music in Indonesia." In *Ethnologische, historische und systematische Musikwissenschaft: Oskar Elschek zum 65. Geburtstag*, edited by Franz Födermayr and Ladislav Burlas, 145–66. Bratislava: ASCO Art & Science.

Kornhauser, Bronia. 1978. "In Defence of Kroncong." In *Studies in Indonesian Music*, edited by Margaret Kartomi, 104–83. Monash Papers on Southeast Asia, no. 7. Clayton, Australia: Centre of Southeast Asian Studies, Monash University.

Kuntoro, Edhi. 2001. *Analisis Lagu Kroncong Tanah Airku Karya Kelly Puspita* [Analysis of the Kroncong Melody Tanah Airku by Kelly Puspita]. Thesis, Universitas Negeri Semarang.

Kusbini. 1976. *Sejarah Kehidupan-Perkembangan dan Asal-Usul Seni Musik Kroncong Indonesia: Kata Nada dan Rupa* [History of the Life Development and Origins of Indonesian Kroncong Music: Words Notes and Forms]. Yogyakarta: CR.

McGraw, Andy. 2022. "Feeling Time in Indonesian *Langgam Jawa*." *Asian Music* 53 (2): 110–38

Mutsaers, Lutgard. 2014. "'Barat Ketemu Timur': Cross-Cultural Encounters and the Making of Early Kroncong." In *Recollecting Resonances: Indonesian-Dutch Musical Encounters*, edited by Bart A. Barendregt and Els Bogaerts, 259–80. Leiden: Brill.

Pasaribu, Amir. 1986 [1955]. *Analisis Musik Indonesia* [Analysis of Indonesian Music]. Jakarta: PT Pantja Simpati.

Prakosa, Gilang Ryand. 2012. "Improvisasi Permainan Cello Pada Permainan Irama Jenis Langgam Jawa Group Orkes Kroncong Harmoni Semarang" [Cello Improvisations in the Langgam Jawa Style in the Ensemble Orkes Kroncong Harmoni Semarang]. *Jurnal Seni Musik* 1: 68–76.

Riasetyani, Septia Marga. 2013. *Analisis Teknik Permainan Cello dalam Langgam Jawa Yen Ing Tawang Ana Lintang. Karya Tulis* [Analysis of Cello Performance Technique in the Langgam Jawa Yen Ing Tawang Ana Lintang]. Yogyakarta: Jurusan Musik Fakultas Seni Pertunjukan Institut Seni Indonesia Jogjakarta.

Setiawan, Suryono Budi. 2014. *Permainan Cello Kroncong Pada Langgam Jawa* [Performance of Kroncong Cello in Langgam Jawa]. Master's thesis, Universitas Negri Yogyakarta.

Skelchy, Russell. 2015. "If There Are Stars in the Sky: Waldjinah and Keroncong in Postcolonial Indonesia." PhD diss., University of California, Riverside.

Soeharto, A. H., Achmad Soenardi, and Samidi Sunupratomo. 1995. *Serba-serbi Kroncong* [Kroncong Variations]. Jakarta: Penerbit Musika.

Suadi, Haryadi. 2017. *Djiwa Manis Indoeng Disajang*, vol. 1. Bandung: Kiblat Buku Utama.

Tan, Sooi Beng. 1993. *Bangsawan: A Social and Stylistic History of Popular Malay Opera*. Singapore: Oxford University Press.

Tan, Sooi Beng. 2004. "The Musical Life of the Penang Baba: Cultural Mixing and Flexibility in a Multi-Ethnic Society." In *37th World Conference of the International Council for Traditional Music: Conference Contributions— Abstracts*, edited by Don Niles et al. Fuzhou: Chinese National Committee of the International Council for Traditional Music.

Taylor, Jean Gelman. 1983. *The Social World of Batavia: European and Eurasian in Dutch Asia*. Madison: University of Wisconsin Press.

Wibya, Andana Prima. 2015. *Analisis Pola Permainan Cak Dalam Lagu Langgam Jawa Pada Orkes Kroncong Prima Nada Banjarnegara* [Analysis of Langgam Jawa Cak Performance Practice in Orkes Kroncong Prima Nada Banjarnegara]. Master's thesis, Universitas Negeri, Yogyakarta.

Yampolsky, Philip. 1991. Liner notes to *Indonesian Popular Music: Kroncong, Dangdut and Langgam Jawa*, vol. 2 of *Music of Indonesia*. Audio CD, Smithsonian Folkways SF 40056.

Yampolsky, Philip. 2010. "Kroncong Revisited: New Evidence from Old Sources." *Archipel* 79: 7–56.

Yampolsky, Philip. 2013. "Three Genres of Indonesian Popular Music: Their Trajectories in the Colonial Era and After." *Asian Music* 44 (2): 24–80.

10

REFORMASI-ERA POPULAR MUSIC STUDIES

Reflections of an Anti-Anti-Essentialist

Jeremy Wallach

In this chapter I aim to do two things. The first is to discuss some of the burgeoning literature on Indonesian popular music and politics from the 1980s to the present. Additionally, I explore the "could-have-been" of Indonesian popular music studies had it not been so dominated by Indonesia's momentous 1998 political transition and instead was more coextensive with the concerns of culturalist ethnomusicology, of the sort that coalesced around gamelan traditions during the late New Order period. While said approach, which privileges the emic, synchronic, structural, and musicological (and allegedly elides the political and historical), has been critiqued from a number of angles over the years (see Pemberton 1987; Sumarsam 1995; Wallach 2004), the research approaches that replaced it have, I will argue, themselves passed their expiration dates, and the time has come to consider anew the ethnomusicology of Indonesian popular music and work toward new, more illuminating, perspectives.[1]

Following a steady accumulation of pioneering studies by (among others) Judith Becker (1975), William Frederick (1982), Martin Hatch (1989), Craig Lockard (1998), Peter Manuel (1988), and especially Philip Yampolsky (1987a, 1987b, 1989, 1991), the upswing of academic interest in Indonesian mass-mediated popular musics was hardly unwelcome among the gamelan and other traditional music specialists who dominated Indonesian ethnomusicology at the time.[2] On the contrary, prominent voices in the "old guard" contributed pioneering works to the field in the 1990s and 2000s, including Michael Bodden (2005), David Harnish (2005), Margaret Kartomi (2002), René T. A. Lysloff (Wong and

Lysloff 1998), Marc Perlman (1999), R. Anderson Sutton (1996, 2004), Andrew Weintraub (2006), and Sean Williams (1989/1990). Weintraub in particular has emerged as an advocate for Indonesian popular music studies (2014) as well as an authority on *dangdut* and its offshoots (2010, 2013, 2018).[3]

Emma Baulch (2007) and I were among the first Indonesia researchers to focus entirely on popular music, rather than popular music in addition to folk and/or traditional genres. Despite the growing acceptability of Indonesian popular music as a subject of academic study, in graduate school my research interests were mostly met with incomprehension and scorn. My dissertation adviser, a linguistic anthropologist, well-meaningly suggested that I play the different Indonesian popular music genres I wanted to study into a computer in order to highlight the specific formal features that differentiated them (because to him they all sounded alike). Meanwhile, music colleagues told me I would never obtain a teaching appointment if I could not run a gamelan. In the end I caught a lucky break: a position opened up for a music specialist in the only Department of Popular Culture in the United States, and my greatest drawback as a job candidate (studying popular rather than traditional music) suddenly became a strength. Thanks to my appointment at Bowling Green State University I have been able to make a living as a scholar and publish my research.

When I first visited Indonesia in the fall of 1997, I fully expected to become known as a *dangdut* scholar. In fact, that's the genre I overwhelmingly write about in *Modern Noise, Fluid Genres* (2008). I never suspected there would be much scholarly interest in Indonesia's underground rock scene, but the dramatic downfall of the Suharto regime the following year changed all that.

Enter Reformasi

Donald Emmerson (2014), following Benedict Anderson (1982), divides Indonesianist scholarship into "formats" that respond to momentous events in modern Indonesian history.[4] The third of these, associated primarily with Anderson and his students, and developed in response to previous, more optimistic and pro-Western approaches, viewed Suharto's New Order regime (1966–98) as neocolonial and irrevocably tainted by its blood-soaked origins, venal corruption, and brutal suppression of dissent (Emmerson 2014, 277–78). This was the Indonesian studies format that I absorbed as a graduate student.

It seems to me that scholars around my age (fifty) and younger work within a fourth "format," to use Emmerson's terminology, one that draws inspiration from Indonesia's spectacular break from the New Order and subsequent transition to democracy.[5] Certainly there are diverse practitioners within this post-authoritarian format, some (such as Emma Baulch, described below) who emphasize the persistence of rampant corruption, unjust structures of domination, and social inequality in the new Indonesia, and others more inclined to emphasize how extraordinary it is that a sprawling, gigantic multiethnic archipelago nation has maintained its pre-1975 territorial integrity and also remained a functioning democracy for the past twenty-two consecutive years.[6] I am not ashamed to say that I tend toward the latter of these emphases, though later in this chapter I suggest that the time is nigh for a *fifth*, post-Reformasi format that leaves behind the preoccupation with democratization and totalitarianism that we inherited from mentors accustomed to the New Order's heavy-handed dominion.

Emma Baulch's work grapples with the relationship between Indonesian popular music and political change from a skeptical angle without discounting the agency of musicians, scene mediators, and fans; I would argue that she is still working within the post-Suharto format, albeit one strongly influenced by previous frameworks. A former student of political scientist Edward Aspinall, Baulch examines the structural antecedents that made Suharto's downfall less the result of a spontaneous popular uprising than the consequence of large-scale political and economic forces, especially media deregulation and the large-scale entry of multinational corporations into Indonesia's mass media environment (Baulch 2007, 2020).[7]

The collapse of the New Order and the onset of the Reformasi era gave a boost to studies of Indonesian underground music. Wider developments in music scholarship also contributed to a dramatic increase of scholarly activity on this subject, including the rapid rise of punk studies and metal studies in the Western academy.[8] Thus, over the last decade scholars from Europe, North America, Australia, New Zealand, and Asia (including Indonesia itself) have written and presented innovative research on Indonesian underground/indie music employing a variety of theoretical frameworks, from Islamic studies (Saefullah 2017) to commodity fetishism (Martin-Iverson 2011) to musical analysis (Cellini 2017) to subcultural theory (Lukisworo and Sutopo 2017) to gender studies (Agung Daryana et al. 2020). They are a diverse and dynamic group of mostly younger scholars, and I have enjoyed getting to know them at conferences and through cyberspace.[9] They represent the vanguard of a new microdiscipline of Indonesian underground music studies I would have thought most improbable less than ten years ago.

Rethinking Musical Politics

During a return visit to Indonesia in 2017, I began to suspect that the historical cycle that began with Suharto's downfall in 1998 had concluded with the election of reformer Joko Widodo as Indonesia's president in 2014. At the time, Jokowi—a Javanese commoner and heavy metal fan known for effective, pragmatic leadership—seemed to fulfill the promise of Indonesian democracy. But another election loomed, and many feared that Indonesia would follow Poland, Hungary, Brazil, the Philippines, and the United States into a period of increasing totalitarianism. Would Indonesia succumb to what Jean-François Revel termed the "totalitarian temptation" (1978) and choose to elect Jokowi's opponent, Prabowo Subianto, a would-be autocrat who was too brutal even for the dictator Suharto?

Many politicians (and some scholars, e.g., Hatch 2014) seem to believe popular music has a negligible effect on "real" politics. Jokowi's political enemies seemed to think otherwise. In early February 2019 the Indonesian public first heard about RUU Permusikan (Draft Bill Music Law), though it had actually been drafted several months before. The draft bill, ostensibly seeking to "professionalize" Indonesian music, proposed the vetting of all Indonesian performers and the purging of "negative foreign influences." Its numerous, often vaguely worded provisions also included a decree that banned musical performances by nonprofessionals lacking prior government certification, which of course would have dealt a death blow to the thriving Indonesian underground music scene, almost entirely composed of amateurs (as such scenes always are). The bill seemed designed expressly to muzzle Jokowi's most vocal supporters during the run-up to a national election. On June 17, 2019, two months after Jokowi trounced Prabowo to win a second term, RUU Permusikan was permanently shelved by the Indonesian House of Representatives.[10] Underground musicians in Indonesia had once again defeated a challenge to their freedom of expression.

The study of politically engaged, progressive Indonesian music will doubtless continue as it develops beyond denunciations of authoritarianism to address myriad issues from LGBTQ rights to environmentalism.[11] Two brief examples illustrate this. In July 2017 Rebekah Moore (at the time managing the US Embassy's Cultural Center in Jakarta and a gender equality activist) invited me to a low-budget video shoot in South Jakarta featuring an Indonesian feminist hip hop artist. The artist in question, Yacko Oktaviana, was creating a clip for a song in English against street harassment. Harassment of women in public places in urban Indonesia had become so dire that the *New York Times* printed a story about the problem and the grassroots efforts by Indonesian woman to fight back (Cochrane 2017). The lyrics to Yacko's song, "Hands Off," are, in part:

> I don't ask for it, and they don't ask for it,
> So stop staring at me and mind your own fuckin' biz!
> Catcall, is that what you're good at,
> Is dat how you make some fun,

I tell your mama, she be mad, your life must be so sad.
Got smart car, smartphone, but why you ain't so smart?
Oh I forgot you buy your degree in the minimart.[12]

The second example is from the most recent album *Seperti Api* (Like Fire) by Indonesian heavy metal stalwarts Seringai (2018). The album, the band's third full-length release, contains songs decrying racism, hypocrisy, sexual harassment, and political corruption. The fifth track, titled "Enam Lima" (Six Five), refers to the year 1965, when Indonesia began its descent into chaos and the military and anti-communist civilian groups massacred hundreds of thousands. After refrains describing victims of the slaughter reddening the rivers with their blood (a grisly sight well documented in contemporaneous accounts) as General Suharto surveys the carnage, it contains the words: "History is written by those who win / But recorded by those who feel / The truth will win."[13] This is the only song in Indonesian (as far as I am aware) that addresses head-on the 1965–66 killings, which are still a taboo subject in the country. I hope it will not be the last and that, in the end, the truth really shall prevail.[14] Certainly there appears to be little limitation on the political and social issues brave Indonesian popular musicians can tackle with their hard-won expressive freedoms, and the future seems quite open.

Noisy Interruptions

Within the context of highly politicized popular musics, why advocate for a return to the "cultural" ethnomusicology I described at the beginning? There are a multitude of reasons. Chief among them is a development I did not foresee in my turn-of-the-century research, the rise and flourishing of the Indonesian avant-garde/experimental/noise scene. This scene not only boasts strong transnational ties to experimental musicians around the globe (particularly East and Southeast Asia, North America, and Europe), it benefits from ties to Indonesian *musik kontemporer*, a decades-old tradition of avant-garde composition that encompasses both gamelan and Western-oriented work.[15] Moreover, unlike the better-documented noise scenes in wealthier countries, the Indonesian noise scene appears to be well integrated at the grassroots level, with entire families making their own noisy electronics and organizing concerts. American DIY filmmaker John Yingling interviewed prominent Indonesian avant-garde musician Rully Shabara Herman (of ZOO and Senyawa) in 2015:

> When I asked him about what people need to know about Indonesia from a musical standpoint, his eyes widened. "People need to know that we have everything here. What we consider as traditional or primitive

here, may be viewed in the West as avant-garde, or experimental. To us this is just traditional." He laughs. "There are so many types. In West Indonesia, you have more melodic styles, more notes and more singing, Arabic influence. To the center, you have Gamelan, this abstract, sort of spacey sound. That's avant-garde." More laughter. "Toward East Indonesia you have percussion, more fast, tribal. There are so many things on so many islands in between. Things we've never even heard of." (Yingling [2015])

The above remarks exhibit a self-consciousness and cosmopolitanism that defies Western neo-imperialist portrayals of Indonesians as mere producers of kitschy exotica suitable for appropriation by Western composers (the attitude of, say, the Sublime Frequencies record label; see McGraw 2016). As a whole, the published evidence from the last decade strongly suggests that grassroots music making in Indonesia has developed beyond what can be convincingly encompassed by theoretical frameworks emphasizing political resistance, identity, globalization, or nationalism, let alone outmoded positivist assumptions (see Lysloff 2016).

What Is an Anti-Anti-Essentialist?

Clifford Geertz scandalized some when he first referred to himself as an "anti-anti-relativist" (1984) in a published address to the American Anthropological Association. Paul Gilroy (1993) proposes the term "anti-anti-essentialism" for a position that rejects both the ethnonationalist's racial essentialism and the dogmatic postmodernist's bottomless deconstruction of stable identity. In Geertz's and Gilroy's cautious yet mischievous spirit, I propose that Indonesia specialists who regard the cultural distinctiveness of their research foci as analytically important embrace anti-anti-essentialism.

But is the idea of "Indonesia studies" useful (or even defensible) anymore? Critical approaches that take a dim view of "culturalist" explanatory frameworks have inundated the humanities and social sciences, and in a concomitant development, some have called for an end to conventional area studies specializations, based as they are around old-fashioned notions of cultural coherence and consistency based on geographic propinquity. Christopher Miller (2014, 285) astutely points out that Indonesia is actually one of the few area studies topics that still is used as a panel-organizing rubric at the annual meetings of the Society for Ethnomusicology.[16] Like Miller, I maintain that this persistent solidarity in the face of general disciplinary fragmentation can actually be a good thing. (Valuing group cohesion is also very Indonesian, but making such an essentialist statement in writing is precisely the sort of thing that gets one in trouble these days.)

To be clear, the notion that cultures are monolithic, static, rigidly bounded entities that possess an unchanging, identifying "essence" is utterly unsatisfactory and misguided (what's *not* clear to me is if anyone ever actually believed they were, or whether this stance was always just a convenient rhetorical strawperson). Moreover, accounts of social life should never rely on cultural explanations to the exclusion of economic, historical, and institutional factors. Likewise, critical approaches that acknowledge that people within a specific culture vary considerably are ubiquitous in the social sciences. Certainly it is true that culture is not destiny. But this criticism can be taken too far, leaving anthropologists and others unwilling to talk about culture at all. I have yet to meet an Indonesia specialist who denies the existence of cultural difference or doubts its salience. It is certainly dangerous to overgeneralize (i.e., essentialize) cultural differences, but as Marshall Sahlins (2002) points out, the refusal to admit the possibility of cultural coherence would also preclude ideological structures of coercion and domination from exercising their intersubjective effects, since they also depend on a systematic organizational logic larger than an individual consciousness.

Crossing Swords

Yet there is one respect in which cultural relativity is problematic in popular music studies. On February 26, 2009, Benedict Anderson replied to an emailed query I had sent asking if he had received the book I'd sent him. He replied that he had indeed and enjoyed its "mix of anthro, sociology and *joie de vivre*, which rarely go together." He concluded thusly: "My only mild, and unwarranted, reservation is that sometimes your warmth and curiosity leave the reader thinking: There must be a lot of lousy music being created, as in every other place—lazy, imitative, clunky, saccharine, etc. Here is where music and anthropology inevitably cross swords." He has a point. As Joseph Kerman pointed out decades ago, to analyze music is to engage in music criticism, that is, to make value judgments on what you are studying (1986). There can be no such thing as purely "objective" formal analysis, as though musical compositions were naturally occurring phenomena; to choose to write about a given music is to pass judgment on its value. Moreover, the often-unmarked value system underlying music studies tends to be derived from canonical Western elitist principles of artistic originality and "greatness" (see Sheinbaum 2019). This aesthetic value system implies a derisive attitude toward popular forms, and scholars interested in such phenomena often end up crouched in a defensive posture as a result. This is indeed where music scholarship "crosses swords" with the ethnographic relativism of the cultural anthropologist, as the question of artistic value intrudes on the analysis of vernacular, noncanonical musics.

Ethnomusicological research, for its part, is not immune from this aesthetic bias. In a chapter of *The Study of Ethnomusicology* titled (somewhat facetiously) "We Never Heard a Bad Tune," Bruno Nettl poses the question: "What, by an ethnomusicological standard, is good music?" (1983, 350; see also Taylor 2004). Theoretically, any kind of music can be subjected to ethnomusicological analysis. In practice, whether or not a type of music (in Indonesia or elsewhere) receives the attention of ethnomusicologists is related to values encouraged by the discipline and academic culture more generally. But can there be an ethically responsible way to evaluate the music of other peoples? Nettl concludes his discussion of ethnomusicology and aesthetics with the observation, "Ethnomusicology attracts people who are committed to the principles of human, cultural, musical equality. But their selection of subject matter and approach have not always reflected this commitment" (1983, 322). Aesthetics again rears its head! Perhaps, then, it is time to reevaluate how we evaluate Indonesian popular music.

My suggestion is to confront musical judgment head-on rather than seek to dodge it. One might protest that our resulting scholarship might seem less dispassionate and therefore less scholarly and objective. I would counter that readers are smart enough to detect the aesthetic biases of authors no matter how they try to conceal them, so we may as well be up front about them. "A man watches a movie, and the critic must acknowledge that he is that man," wrote Robert Warshow in 1954 (2001, 27). Stripped of its dated sexist language and modified to fit the present context, we might (awkwardly) render the passage: "A person listens to a song (or watches a video or attends a concert) and the ethnomusicologist should show that she/he/they are that person." In other words, we are part of the stories we tell, as listeners in a social relationship with both the musics we study and with the people who play and value those musics.

As for my own subjective feelings about Indonesian popular music, I admit they are hard to write about. I am inspired by K-pop scholar Suk-Young Kim, who is unafraid to add her own personal reactions to the music she researches. About a performance by Taemin (Lee Tae-min) from the group SHINee she writes:

> There he was. A luminous phantom and a real human at once, standing in front of you, drawing in the same air that filled your lungs. The splendor of this moment was unreal, yet it was a part of reality. His

> voice spread and instantly lifted me up from the particularities of that moment, from my jaded skepticism and fatigue, and landed me in the field of memories—memories of lively youth that felt as if it would never come to an end and memories of a strong desire to live a life of dreams. . . . Feeling alive at every beat of a song, at every glimpse of beauty—life goes on because of this. (Kim 2018, 208)

Of course I do not feel as rapturously about the vast majority of Indonesian popular music. But such music is not the reason I travel halfway around the world. There is, however, a minority that makes my trips there worthwhile (although my subjective experience is rather different than that described by Kim). I also try to write about music I do not like, though in my view if ethnomusicologists still don't like *any* of the music they are studying at the conclusion of the research, they're doing it wrong. (Besides, then there really is no solution to the "crossing swords" problem.)

Music Analysis and Indonesian Rock

Throughout this chapter I have suggested that the political is an inadequate framework moving forward with Indonesian popular music studies. Discussions of music and politics tend to circle back to the agonizing question of whether music can encourage progressive social change. As usually posed, this question is divorced from any consideration of the music's specific aesthetic properties.[17] Yet as Barry Shank reminds us, music's political agency is dependent on its aesthetic efficacy (2014).

Even Indonesian heavy metal can be analyzed as Indonesian music. When I presented a version of this chapter at Cornell, I played three songs from Bali and Java that I thought illustrated my point: "The Truth of Imagination" by Eternal Madness (2011), "Singgasana Tuhan" (The Throne of God) by Pas (2003), and "School Revolution" by Voice of Baceprot (2017). All three rock songs had colotomic rhythmic cycles,[18] and the final example even contained a floating vocal line in the chorus that evoked (I thought) the *pesindhèn*. I realized that my examples had failed to be persuasive for everyone when Sumarsam, one of the foremost gamelan experts in the world, asked afterward why, pray tell, I would suggest that they had anything to do with gamelan music.

Despite this setback, I persist in my conviction that there is something musically distinctive about the songs I played that can be linked to the broader musical context in which they operate, for as Rebekah Moore (2013) has pointed out, rock music in Indonesia shares public space with traditional and popular sounds of all kinds. The challenge is creating an analytical language that can access that distinctiveness. In doing so, one does not need to surrender to older paradigms of aesthetic value. Formal analysis and state-of-the-art social theory can be compatible, as illustrated by Katherine In-Young Lee's work on the South Korean performance genre *samul-nori* (K. Lee 2018), a study where music and anthropology avoid entirely the crossing of swords. This approach has also been taken closer to home, so to speak.

In an excellent study of Indonesian death metal (the most popular subgenre of heavy metal in Indonesia) that is both ethnographically grounded and analytically rich, Dennis Lee argues that while death metal as a global subgenre tends to be a bounded, rather purist subgenre, prominent Indonesian death metal bands like Siksakubur and DeadSquad introduce musical elements from an eclectic array of sources, from progressive rock instrumental solos to Middle Eastern micromodal inflections. He concludes, "By hybridizing non-death metal influences in a way that is distinctly Indonesian, these bands reference local cultural practices not only through the inclusion of distinctive musical material . . . but in terms of the incorporative approach itself" (D. Lee 2018, 539). This passage suggests that culturally specific aesthetic strategies can be located at the level of praxis as well as notes, and indeed, this is precisely the kind of analysis that we need: *an ethnographically grounded exploration of how musical structures and practices signify in the cultural lifeworlds of the people who create and understand those structures and practices.*

Indonesian Popular Music as Indonesian Music

In my view, the study of Indonesian popular music should be reintegrated with the study of Indonesian music in general. Indonesians themselves are quite willing to combine folk, classical, and popular idioms in music and other cultural endeavors on a regular basis, after all. It is this need for a holistic understanding of music in Indonesia that makes me an anti-anti-essentialist. I have long argued that Indonesian popular music can reveal much about modern Indonesia, and modern Indonesia can teach much to the world. In the preface to the 2017 Indonesian-language edition of *Modern Noise* published by Komunitas Bambu, I wrote that the book was worthwhile for an Indonesian readership because it had stumbled on a key beneficial aspect of the archipelago's popular culture.

I suggested that Indonesia's national culture was strong because it embraced diversity, using hybrid popular musics as an example. This boded well for democracy, I said, because in Indonesia the urge for inclusiveness was stronger than the urge for fragmentation, because Indonesian life was lived in a state of togetherness and fundamentally social. These arguments were tentative, and full of the usual caveats and qualifiers of academic discourse, as I was and remain fully aware of the real limitations of my research. Yet the past sixteen years, despite terrorist attacks, natural disasters, and economic vicissitudes, had proven that I was onto something: amid the dire forecasts at the time by political scientists and economists that a post-authoritarian Indonesia would descend into civil war and chaos, my optimism was valid (Wallach 2017, xv–xvi).[19]

Most of all we need to proceed modestly with little fanfare. There is always a temptation toward self-congratulation in the popular music studies literature, which could perhaps be justified were it an inoculation against attacks on its legitimacy. (Alas, it is not.) I do not take for granted that the field of Indonesian popular music studies, such as it is, has not descended into insularity or elitism. We in Indonesian popular music studies have been fortunate to have been welcomed by traditional gamelan specialists. In addition, they themselves have sought to embrace ethnomusicology's ascendant social and critical approaches (Berger and Stone 2019; Perlman 2014), including theories of postcoloniality and globalization (Sumarsam 2013; Wallach and Clinton 2019). Now these once-novel approaches have become shopworn and ethnomusicologists are once again searching for new research guides (see Rice 2010). I certainly do not pretend to know what the next important research paradigm will be, but I do want to close with a few words of common sense that some will no doubt still regard as scandalous.[20] First, Indonesian popular music needs to be taken seriously not only as a harbinger of social change but *as* Indonesian music, that is, as a meaningful intervention in Indonesian social and cultural life with important, analytically abstractable, aesthetic properties.

Second, I want to suggest that if our work is to be of use to future generations of Indonesian scholars and musicians and we are to advocate for a country whose monumental accomplishments in politics, music, and culture remain unsung on the global stage, we must also never shrink from the assertion that *Indonesian popular music is good music*. Simple, no?

NOTES

The author thanks Andrew Weintraub for comments on an earlier draft of this chapter. Thank you, Esther Clinton, for your invaluable help with multiple drafts. The author also wishes to thank the symposium organizers, Andrew McGraw and Christopher Miller, and all his fellow participants at the SOSIM conference. A special thanks goes to keynote speaker Philip Yampolsky for his inspiring example over four decades.

1. For a useful overview of the changes the discipline of ethnomusicology has undergone since its inception, see Berger and Stone 2019.

2. There is really no need to reinvent the wheel here. The emergence of Indonesian popular music studies is an oft-narrated tale, and both Perlman 2014 and Weintraub 2014

contain excellent reviews of the relevant literature. Crucial to my own intellectual development were Hatch 1989 and Yampolsky 1987b, 1989, 1991.

3. The 2018 SOSIM conference provided for me the most decisive proof of the institutional legitimacy of Indonesian popular music studies. I was both honored and pleasantly surprised to be included in such a gathering.

4. He concludes his essay with the admonishment, "What a scholar can and should do is to be and remain aware that *any* format, however cherished, both clarifies *and* distorts reality. Introspective awareness of these contrary effects is critical to a scholar's ability to learn from [John Maynard] Keynes's deceptively simple question: 'When the facts change, I change my mind. What do you do, sir?'" (Emmerson 2014, 280, emphasis in original). For a spirited defense of more traditional political science research on Indonesian society that rejects totalizing theoretical frameworks, see Liddle 2014.

5. See van Dijk 2001 for a comprehensive, if dour, political history of this crucial transitional period.

6. Whether one's specific take is anxious or celebratory, I maintain that the dominant narrative of the last twenty years of Indonesia studies has been one of political transition.

7. See also Baulch's important work with the 1970s rock periodical *Aktuil*, which uncovers the long history of rock music as a form of class distinction and masculinist self-expression for Indonesian men (2016). While underground rock music has become more gender-balanced since the late 1990s, it remains heavily male-dominated, consistent with international trends (Berkers and Schaap 2018) and, interestingly, a marked contrast to *dangdut*, where woman singers outnumber men and are essential to articulating *dangdut*'s distinctive melancholy sensuality (David 2014). The gender politics of Indonesian popular music (particularly beyond *dangdut*) is just one of many understudied areas in the field. Later I introduce the reader to the music of hip hop artist Yacko, one of the country's few outspoken feminist musicians.

8. For influential catalysts of these developments, see McClary 1994 and Walser 1993. In the late twentieth century the symbolic importance of esteemed classical music specialists extolling fellow scholars to take pop and rock music seriously should not be underestimated, even if now such exhortations seem nearly banal. Parallel to this development was the "classicalization" of non-Western sounds (marketed as "world music") as record companies became aware of their appeal to well-heeled consumers (Taylor 2012). An overview of academic punk studies can be found in Furness 2012; for a valuable history of twenty-first-century heavy metal scholarship, see Hickam 2015. Indonesia's massive punk and metal scenes have caused it to loom large in both fields whenever researchers have set their sights on the genres' audiences outside the Western world. See, for example, Donaghey 2017; Duncombe and Tremblay 2011; Dunn 2016; Wallach 2020; Wallach et al. 2011.

9. Others in this group include Jim Donaghey, Kevin Dunn, Yulianus Febriarko, Marco Ferrarese, Oliver Hahn, Erik Hannerz, I Putu Tangkas Adi Hiranmayena, Felencia Hutabarat, Kieran James, Marjaana Jauhola, Kimung, Dennis Lee, Brent Luvaas, Rex Marsh, Luigi Monteanni, Steve Moog, Rebekah Moore, Yuka Narendra, Élise Imray Papineau, Frans Ari Prasetyo, Fakhran Ramadhan, Rizky Sasono, Russ Skelchy, Oki Rahadianto Sutopo, Matias Tammiala, Ian Wilson, and William Yanko.

10. *Jakarta Post* 2019; see also Ferrarese 2019.

11. See Sarahtika 2017 and Wallach 2003, 2005, 2008 for discussions of political rock music during the democratic transition. The veteran Balinese band Navicula is the best-known rock group with a strong environmentalist message; see Rebekah Moore's chapter in this book.

12. The clip can be viewed at https://www.youtube.com/watch?v=Q5aoFTzfMuI. As of November 24, 2021, the page had 165,981 views. For more on the video clip and the song, see Gurung 2017.

13. *Sejarah ditulis oleh mereka yang menang / Tapi direkam oleh mereka yang merasakan / Kebenaran akan menang.* Translation by the author. See Pipit Rochijat's 1985 essay in *Indonesia* for an especially vivid and disturbing narrative of the 1965–66 mass murders; see also Cribb 1990. More recently, two provocative films by American Joshua Oppenheimer and the translation of John Roosa's 2006 *Pretext for Mass Murder* have stirred up a great deal of discussion and debate in Indonesia over the tragic events of this period.

14. Worth noting here is the Australian band High Tension, for whom the 1965–66 Indonesian killings are a dominant theme, as in the song "Red White Shame" from their 2018 album *Purge*. The band's singer, Karina Utomo, is of Indonesian descent.

15. For a comprehensive study of the contemporary Southeast Asian noise scene, see Fermont and della Faille 2016, as well as their chapter in this book. For more on *musik kontemporer* and contemporary Indonesian performance art, see Lysloff 2016; McGraw 2013; Miller 2015.

16. In fact, this was quite conspicuously the case at the November 2018 Society for Ethnomusicology Annual Meeting in Albuquerque where an enjoyable panel on "Music, Dance, and Identity in Indonesia" featured papers by David Harnish, Gillian Irwin, and Maho Ishiguro. Henry Spiller chaired the session.

17. See Born 2013 for nuanced discussions of this issue centered around the different "publics" that can result from musical performance. To be absolutely clear, I am not advocating a kind of Neoplatonic search for pure tones and their precultural effects on human consciousness. Aesthetic sensibilities are always "culturized," to use Robert Plant Armstrong's term (1971, 29), and musical devices only acquire meaning and potency to concrete addressees in specific interpretive contexts informed by culture and history.

18. Layered, interlocking instrumental parts moving at different speeds, converging at the beginning of rhythmic cycles, with lower-pitched instruments moving at a slower pace than higher-pitched ones. This is a sonic texture characteristic of gamelan music.

19. This is the original English text. The text in the Komunitas Bambu edition is translated into Indonesian. For more on the inclusive character of Indonesian social life, see Clinton and Wallach 2016.

20. Another bit of common sense: I have argued elsewhere (2019) that ethnomusicologists of popular music should first and foremost *be* ethnomusicologists and take our interlocutors' points of view. Obviously this applies to the Indonesian case, since Indonesian musical tastes (their unironic enthusiasm for smooth jazz, for instance) often differ markedly from the metropolitan, anti-middlebrow aesthetic biases of Western ethnomusicologists, and this must not become a research impediment.

WORKS CITED

Agung Daryana, Hinhin, Aquarini Priyatna, and Raden Muhammad Mulyadi. 2020. "The New Metal Men: Exploring Model of Alternative Masculinity in the Bandung Metal Scene." *Masculinities and Social Change* 9 (2): 148–73.

Anderson, Benedict R. O'G. 1982. "Perspective and Method in American Research on Indonesia." In *Interpreting Indonesian Politics: Thirteen Contributions to the Debate*, edited by Benedict R. O'G. Anderson and Audrey Kahin, 69–83. Ithaca, NY: Cornell Southeast Asia Program Publications.

Armstrong, Robert Plant. 1971. *The Affecting Presence: An Essay in Humanistic Anthropology*. Urbana: University of Illinois Press.

Baulch, Emma. 2007. *Making Scenes: Reggae, Punk, and Death Metal in 1990s Bali*. Durham, NC: Duke University Press.

Baulch, Emma. 2016. "Genre Publics: *Aktuil* Magazine and Middle-Class Youth in 1970s Indonesia." *Indonesia* 102: 85–113.

Baulch, Emma. 2020. *Genre Publics: Technologies, Pop Music and Class in Indonesia.* Middletown, CT: Wesleyan University Press.

Becker, Judith. 1975. "Kroncong, Indonesian Popular Music." *Asian Music* 7 (1): 14–19.

Berger, Harris M., and Ruth Stone, eds. 2019. *Theory for Ethnomusicology: Histories, Conversations, Insights.* 2nd ed. Upper Saddle River, NJ: Prentice Hall.

Berkers, Pauwke, and Julian Schaap. 2018. *Gender Inequality in Metal Music Production.* Bingley, UK: Emerald.

Bodden, Michael. 2005. "Rap in Indonesian Youth Music of the 1990s: 'Globalization,' 'Outlaw Genres,' and Social Protest." *Asian Music* 36 (2): 1–26.

Born, Georgina, ed. 2013. *Music, Sound and Space: Transformations of Public and Private Experience.* Cambridge: Cambridge University Press.

Cellini, Gianluca. 2017. "Some Analytical Consideration on Indonesian Metal Music." *International Journal of Creative and Arts Studies* 4 (1): 71–78.

Clinton, Esther, and Jeremy Wallach. 2016. "Talking Metal: A Social Phenomenology of Hanging Out in Metal Culture." In *Heavy Metal Music and the Communal Experience*, edited by Nelson Varas-Díaz and Niall W. R. Scott, 37–55. Lanham, MD: Lexington Books.

Cochrane, Joe. 2017. "In Indonesia, Women Begin to Fight 'Epidemic' of Street Harassment." *New York Times*, December 9.

Cribb, Robert, ed. 1990. *The Indonesian Killings, 1965–1966: Studies from Java and Bali.* Clayton, Australia: Monash University, Centre of Southeast Asian Studies, Monash Papers on Southeast Asia, No. 21.

David, Bettina. 2014. "Seductive Pleasures, Eluding Subjectivities: Some Thoughts on Dangdut's Ambiguous Identity." In *Sonic Modernities in the Malay World: A History of Popular Music, Social Distinction and Novel Lifestyles (1930s–2000s)*, edited by Bart Barendregt, 249–68. Leiden: Brill.

Donaghey, Jim, ed. 2017. "Indonesia," special issue, *Punk and Postpunk* 6 (2).

Duncombe, Stephen, and Maxwell Tremblay, eds. 2011. *White Riot: Punk Rock and the Politics of Race.* London: Verso.

Dunn, Kevin. 2016. *Global Punk: Resistance and Rebellion in Everyday Life.* New York: Bloomsbury Academic.

Emmerson, Donald K. 2014. "Facts, Minds, and Formats: Scholarship and Political Change in Indonesia." In Tagliacozzo 2014, 267–82.

Fermont, Cedrik, and Dimitri della Faille. 2016. *Not Your World Music: Noise in South East Asia.* Berlin: Syrphe / Ottawa: Hushush.

Ferrarese, Marco. 2019. "Indonesia's 'Dangerous' Moves on Music Strike Discord." *Nikkei Asian Review*, February 27. https://asia.nikkei.com/Life-Arts/Arts/Indonesia-s-dangerous-moves-on-music-strike-discord2.

Frederick, William. 1982. "Rhoma Irama and the Dangdut Style: Aspects of Contemporary Indonesian Popular Culture." *Indonesia* 34: 103–30.

Furness, Zack. 2012. *Punkademics: The Basement Show in the Ivory Tower.* Chico, CA: Minor Compositions/AK Press.

Geertz, Clifford. 1984. "Distinguished Lecture: Anti-Anti-Relativism." *American Anthropologist* 86 (2): 263–78.

Gilroy, Paul. 1993. *The Black Atlantic: Modernity and Double Consciousness.* Cambridge, MA: Harvard University Press.

Gurung, Tsering. 2017. "'I Want to Encourage Women to Fight Back': Yacko Tells Us about the Inspiration Behind 'Hands Off.'" *Vice* (Indonesia), July 25. https://www.vice.com/en_asia/article/9kw7da/i-want-to-encourage-women-to-fight-back-yacko-tells-us-about-the-inspiration-behind-hands-off.

Harnish, David. 2005. "Teletubbies in Paradise: Tourism, Indonesianisation, and Modernisation in Balinese Music." *Yearbook for Traditional Music* 37: 103–23.

Hatch, Martin. 1989. "Popular Music in Indonesia." In *World Music, Politics, and Social Change*, edited by Simon Frith, 47–68. Manchester: Manchester University Press.

Hatch, Martin. 2014. "(Ke)maju(an) ke Belakang: Some Thoughts about the Future of Indonesianist Ethnomusicology." In Tagliacozzo 2014, 287–92.

Hickam, Brian. 2015. "Amalgamated Anecdotes: Perspectives on the History of Metal Music and Culture Studies." *Metal Music Studies* 1: 5–23.

High Tension. 2018. *Purge*. Australia: Cooking Vinyl, limited edition 12" disc and digital album.

Jakarta Post. 2019. "Musicians Welcome Cancelation of Draft Music Bill." June 19, 2019. https://www.thejakartapost.com/life/2019/06/19/musicians-welcome-cancelation-of-draft-music-bill.html.

Kartomi, Margaret. 2002. "Debates and Impressions of Change and Continuity in Indonesia's Musical Arts since the Fall of Suharto, 1998–2002." *Wacana Seni* 1: 109–49.

Kerman, Joseph. 1986. *Contemplating Music: Challenges to Musicology*. Cambridge, MA: Harvard University Press.

Kim, Suk-Young. 2018. *K-Pop Live: Fans, Idols, and Multimedia Performance*. Stanford, CA: Stanford University Press.

Lee, Dennis W. 2018. "'Negeri Seribu Bangsa': Musical Hybridization in Contemporary Indonesian Death Metal." *Metal Music Studies* 4 (3): 531–48.

Lee, Katherine In-Young. 2018. *Dynamic Korea and Rhythmic Form*. Middletown, CT: Wesleyan University Press.

Liddle, R. William. 2014. "Political Science Scholarship on Indonesia: Revived but Constrained." In Tagliacozzo 2014, 253–66.

Lockard, Craig. 1998. *Dance of Life: Popular Music and Politics in Southeast Asia*. Honolulu: University of Hawai'i Press.

Lukisworo, A. Aryo, and Oki Rahadianto Sutopo. 2017. "Metal DIY: Dominasi, Strategi, dan Resistensi." *Jurnal Studi Pemuda* 6 (2): 578–89.

Lysloff, René T. A. 2016. "Worlding Music in Jogjakarta: Tales of the Global Postmodern." *Ethnomusicology* 60 (3): 484–507.

Manuel, Peter. 1988. *Popular Musics of the Non-Western World: An Introductory Survey*. New York: Oxford University Press.

Martin-Iverson, Sean. 2011. "The Politics of Cultural Production in the DIY Hardcore Scene in Bandung, Indonesia." PhD diss., University of Western Australia.

McClary, Susan. 1994. "Same As It Ever Was: Youth Culture and Music." In *Microphone Fiends: Youth Music and Youth Culture*, edited by Andrew Ross and Tricia Rose, 29–40. New York: Routledge.

McGraw, Andrew Clay. 2013. *Radical Traditions: Reimagining Culture in Balinese Contemporary Music*. New York: Oxford University Press.

McGraw, Andrew Clay. 2016. "Radio Java." In *Punk Ethnography: Artists and Scholars Listen to Sublime Frequencies*, edited by Michael Veal and E. Tammy Kim, 323–39. Middletown, CT: Wesleyan University Press.

Miller, Christopher J. 2014. "Of Arcs and De-/Re-Centerings: Charting Indonesian Music Studies." In Tagliacozzo 2014, 283–86.

Miller, Christopher J. 2015. "Cosmopolitan, Nativist, Eclectic: Cultural Dynamics in Indonesian *Musik Kontemporer*." PhD diss., Wesleyan University.

Moore, Rebekah. 2013. "Elevating the Underground: Claiming a Space for Indie Music among Bali's Many Soundworlds." *Asian Music* 44 (2): 135–59.

Nettl, Bruno. 1983. *The Study of Ethnomusicology: Twenty-Nine Issues and Concepts.* Urbana: University of Illinois Press.

Pemberton, John. 1987. "Musical Politics in Central Java (or How Not to Listen to a Javanese Gamelan)." *Indonesia* 44: 17–29.

Perlman, Marc. 1999. "The Traditional Javanese Performing Arts in the Twilight of the New Order: Two Letters from Solo." *Indonesia* 68: 1–37.

Perlman, Marc. 2014. "The Ethnomusicology of Indonesian Performing Arts: The Last Thirty Years." In Tagliacozzo 2014, 293–326.

Revel, Jean-François. 1978. *The Totalitarian Temptation.* Translated by David Hapgood. New York: Penguin.

Rice, Timothy. 2010. "Disciplining *Ethnomusicology*: A Call for a New Approach." *Ethnomusicology* 54 (2): 318–25.

Rochijat Pipit. 1985. "Am I PKI or Non-PKI?" *Indonesia* 40: 37–56.

Roosa, John. 2006. *Pretext for Mass Murder: The September 30th Movement and Suharto's Coup d'État in Indonesia.* Madison: University of Wisconsin Press.

Saefullah, Hikmawan. 2017. "'Nevermind the *Jahiliyyah*, Here's the *Hijrahs*': Punk and the Religious Turn in the Contemporary Indonesian Underground Scene." *Punk and Postpunk* 6 (2): 263–89.

Sahlins, Marshall. 2002. *Waiting for Foucault, Still.* 4th ed. Chicago: Prickly Paradigm Press.

Sarahtika, Dhania. 2017. "How Indonesia's Underground Music Scene Helps Bring Down a Dictator." *Jakarta Globe*, July 12. http://jakartaglobe.id/features/indonesias-underground-music-scene-helps-bring-dictator/.

Seringai, 2018. *Seperti Api.* High Octane Productions. CD.

Shank, Barry. 2014. *The Political Force of Musical Beauty.* Durham, NC: Duke University Press.

Sheinbaum, John. 2019. *Good Music: What It Is and Who Gets to Decide.* Chicago: University of Chicago Press.

Siegel, James. 2011. *Objects and Objections of Ethnography.* New York: Fordham University Press.

Sumarsam. 1995. *Gamelan: Cultural Interaction and Musical Development in Central Java.* Chicago: University of Chicago Press.

Sumarsam. 2013. *Javanese Gamelan and the West.* Rochester, NY: University of Rochester Press.

Sutton, R. Anderson. 1996. "Interpreting Electronic Sound Technology in the Contemporary Javanese Soundscape." *Ethnomusicology* 40 (2): 249–68.

Sutton, R. Anderson. 2004. "'Reform Arts'? Performance Live and Mediated in Post-Soeharto Indonesia." *Ethnomusicology* 48 (2): 203–28.

Tagliacozzo, Eric, ed. 2014. *Producing Indonesia: The State of the Field of Indonesian Studies.* Ithaca, NY: Cornell Southeast Asia Program Publications.

Taylor, Timothy. 2004. "Bad World Music." In *Bad Music: The Music We Love to Hate,* edited by Christopher Washburne and Maiken Derno, 83–103. New York: Routledge.

Taylor, Timothy. 2012. "World Music Today." In *Music and Globalization: Critical Encounters,* edited by Bob W. White, 172–88. Bloomington: Indiana University Press.

Van Dijk, Kees. 2001. *A Country in Despair: Indonesia between 1997 and 2000.* Verhandelingen van het Koninklijk Instituut voor Taal-, Land- en Volkenkunde, 186. Leiden: KITLV Press.

Wallach, Jeremy. 2003. "'Goodbye My Blind Majesty': Music, Language, and Politics in the Indonesian Underground." In *Global Pop, Local Language*, edited by

Harris M. Berger and Michael T. Carroll, 53–86. Jackson: University Press of Mississippi.

Wallach, Jeremy. 2004. "Of Gongs and Cannons: Music and Power in Island Southeast Asia." *Wacana Seni Journal of Arts Discourse* 3: 1–28.

Wallach, Jeremy. 2005. "Underground Rock Music and Democratization in Indonesia." *World Literature Today* 79 (3–4): 16–20.

Wallach, Jeremy. 2008. *Modern Noise, Fluid Genres: Popular Music in Indonesia, 1997–2001*. Madison: University of Wisconsin Press.

Wallach, Jeremy. 2017. *Musik Popular Indonesia 1997–2001: Kebisingan dan Keberagaman Aliran Lagu* [Indonesian-Language Edition of *Modern Noise, Fluid Genres*]. Depok: Komunitas Bambu.

Wallach, Jeremy. 2019. "Rainforest to Raves: Ethnomusicological Forays into Popular Music." *Journal of World Popular Music* 6 (2): 223–27.

Wallach, Jeremy. 2020. "Global Rock as Postcolonial Soundtrack." In *The Bloomsbury Handbook of Rock Music Research*, edited by Allan Moore and Paul Carr, 469–85. New York: Bloomsbury.

Wallach, Jeremy, Harris M. Berger, and Paul D. Greene. 2011. "Affective Overdrive, Scene Dynamics, and Identity in the Global Metal Scene." In *Metal Rules the Globe: Heavy Metal Music around the World*, edited by Jeremy Wallach, Harris M. Berger, and Paul D. Greene, 3–33. Durham, NC: Duke University Press.

Wallach, Jeremy, and Esther Clinton. 2019. "Theories of the Post-Colonial and Globalization: Ethnomusicologists Grapple with Power, History, Media, and Mobility." In *Theory for Ethnomusicology: Histories, Conversations, Insights*, 2nd ed., edited by Harris M. Berger and Ruth Stone, 114–139. Upper Saddle River, NJ: Prentice Hall.

Walser, Robert. 1993. *Running with the Devil: Power, Gender, and Madness in Heavy Metal Music*. Middletown, CT: Wesleyan University Press.

Warshow, Robert. 2001 (1954). *The Immediate Experience: Movies, Comics, Theatre and Other Aspects of Popular Culture*. Enlarged ed. Cambridge, MA: Harvard University Press.

Weintraub, Andrew N. 2006. "Dangdut Soul: Who Are 'the People' in Indonesian Popular Music?" *Asian Journal of Communication* 16 (4): 411–31.

Weintraub, Andrew N. 2010. *Dangdut Stories: A Social and Musical History of Indonesia's Most Popular Music*. New York: Oxford University Press.

Weintraub, Andrew N. 2013. "The Sound and Spectacle of *Dangdut Koplo*: Genre and Counter-genre in East Java, Indonesia." *Asian Music* 44 (2): 160–94.

Weintraub, Andrew N. 2014. "Decentering Ethnomusicology: Indonesian Popular Music Studies." In Tagliacozzo 2014, 345–66.

Weintraub, Andrew N. 2018. "Soundtracks for the Masses: Transmediating India in *Dangdut* Films of Indonesia." In *Making Waves: Traveling Musics in Hawai'i, Asia, and the Pacific*, edited by Frederick Lau and Christine R. Yano, 39–64. Honolulu: University of Hawai'i Press.

Williams, Sean. 1989/1990. "Current Developments in Sundanese Popular Music." *Asian Music* 21 (1): 105–36.

Wong, Deborah, and René T. A. Lysloff. 1998. "Popular Music and Cultural Politics." In *The Garland Encyclopedia of World Music*, vol. 4: *Southeast Asia*, edited by Terry Miller and Sean Williams, 95–112. New York: Garland.

Yampolsky, Philip. 1987a. Liner notes to Idjah Hadidjah's album *Tonggeret*. Icon Records 79173.

Yampolsky, Philip. 1987b. *Lokananta: A Discography of the National Recording Company of Indonesia, 1957–1985*. Madison: Center for Southeast Asian Studies, University of Wisconsin.

Yampolsky, Philip. 1989. "'Hati Yang Luka,' an Indonesian Hit." *Indonesia* 47: 1–17.

Yampolsky, Philip. 1991. Liner notes to *Music of Indonesia*, vol. 2: *Indonesian Popular Music: Kroncong, Dangdut, and Langgam Jawa*. Smithsonian/Folkways SF 40056.

Yingling, John. N.d. [2015]. "The Astounding Underground of Indonesia." *Impose*. http://www.imposemagazine.com/features/the-astounding-underground-of-indonesia. Accessed December 23, 2018.

11

INDONESIAN REGIONAL MUSIC ON VCD

Inclusion, Exclusion, Fusion

Philip Yampolsky

The representation of regional music and theater in Indonesian commercial media has been one of the main topics of my research since the early 1980s. After working on LPs, audio cassettes, and 78-rpm records, I have since 2003 concentrated on the predominant format in the first two decades of the twenty-first century, the video compact disc or VCD.[1] In this research, I aim to see what *is* published on VCD and what is *not*, and to what extent regional genres on VCD are adapted to national conventions and standards, both musical and aesthetic. In the present chapter, my approach is for the most part objective, seeking simply to describe the categories and trends of VCD production. In an extended coda, however, I discuss an example of the kind of traditional rural genre that is excluded from VCDs because it has no commercial appeal. Here my stance becomes critical—not of Indonesians or of Indonesian media, but of ethnomusicology, which, fascinated by popular music and the global, allows such rich rural micro-genres to vanish (as they almost certainly will) undocumented.

VCD History

The VCD was introduced in Indonesia in the second half of the 1990s.[2] Initially it was the medium for pornography and pirated foreign movies, and later for pirated foreign music. VCDs of Indonesian musical and theatrical content began to be produced (in both legitimate and pirated versions) circa 2000. The VCD medium followed on from audio cassettes, which had been introduced at the end of the 1960s. Unlike *their* predecessor medium, LPs, cassettes were cheap to produce, were sold at comparatively low prices, needed only inexpensive playback equipment, and could be recorded anywhere: not only in studios, but also outdoors, in villages, at public performances, and in private homes. Cassette producers sprang up everywhere, and highly localized genres were recorded and sold in regional micro-markets. (In the 1980s I found local cassette production in places as small as Sigli in Aceh and Kraksaan in East Java.) Production of VCDs, on the other hand, is more complicated and expensive than for audio cassettes, so the VCD producers were not as many nor as widespread. Nevertheless they too served many small markets, as you will see later on.[3]

Nowadays the VCD medium is in steep decline, largely as a result of piracy. Pirated VCDs are sold for less than legitimate VCDs or audio cassettes, which discourages legitimate production; but in addition to full-album piracy, there is now, more fatally, widespread unauthorized uploading of the most popular songs of published VCDs to YouTube, where they are viewed for free or downloaded to computers and smartphones.[4] Often just the audio is downloaded in MP3 format to USB flash drives and mobile phones. (An audio download is useful for playback in cars and buses, or just through your TV to ensure a lively, noisy atmosphere in the home.) Many VCD producers have given up, saying they cannot sell enough copies to make a profit. Some markets, however, do continue to produce many titles, or at least to distribute titles produced earlier. The principal remaining production centers for VCDs are Jakarta, North Sumatra (Medan, Kabanjahe), West Sumatra (Padang, Bukittinggi), East Java (Surabaya, Nganjuk, Ngawi), Bali, and Makassar. But even in those still active markets, the authorities cannot do anything to halt uploading to YouTube or downloading to mobile phones. The medium is definitely on the way out.[5]

Two Sectors of the VCD Industry

With regard to music and theater (which I will from here on just call "music"), the VCD industry has two vast sectors: national music and regional music.

National music is aimed at Indonesian audiences and consumers *as Indonesians, without regard to their ethnicity or where they live*. Now, it is a fact of Indonesian society, with its three-hundred-plus ethnic groups,[6] that no localized symbol—no symbol associated with a single ethnic group or region—can be accepted as representing any *other* ethnic group or region; it follows that no regional symbol can serve as a symbol of the nation to the myriad groups and regions. (Imagine the uproar if the national *merah-putih* flag were replaced with one showing a batik pattern, or a Dayak *hudoq* mask.) But without such a symbolic justification—without a recognition of "horizontal" community across regions, as distinct from "vertical" connection to the overarching nation—there is little motivation (except, in rare instances, individual taste) for people in one region to accept (listen to, enjoy, purchase recordings of) the music of any other region, especially if it is sung in a different language. The entertainment industry—television, radio, commercial recording—applies this logic to product marketing: it is generally assumed that no one in region X will be *interested* in the distinctively regional music of region Y.

The result of all this is that no regional music is accepted outside its region (except by emigrants from that region, or again for reasons of individual taste). This means that the only national musics—musics accepted all across the country—are foreign in origin.

The principal categories of national music are secular popular music, Islamic devotional music, and Christian hymns.[7] With the exception of some Islamic music, sung in Arabic, all of this national music is sung in Indonesian,[8] or, to a much lesser extent, in English. (Purely instrumental music, with no singing, is a negligible category of national music.) Of these principal types, the most important and most widely disseminated—the one category crossing all of the geographic, ethnic, linguistic, class, and religious lines—is popular music.[9]

The pervasiveness and commercial appeal of popular music has led to the emergence of religious music in pop idioms: *pop rohani* and *religi*, with lyrics on, respectively, Christian and Islamic themes. There are also popularized versions of older religious genres, such as a combination of *dakwah* and *campursari* (example 1), and *takbiran* with synthesized "house" percussion underneath (example 2).

Indonesian popular music is vibrant, engaging, and diverse, with stars and melodic hooks and intriguing arrangements.[10] It is no disparagement to say that—like many forms of popular music around the world—it is essentially Euro-American (Western, for short) in its major/minor scales, its use of harmony, its instrumentation, idioms, and manner of performance, and also in many of its song forms. There may be other elements mixed in: Middle Eastern and Indian music elements figure in *dangdut* and in the popular Islamic genres. But even so, to a large extent, Western elements predominate in these genres as well. This is not a fault, it is simply a fact: the language and cultural matrix are Indonesian, while the musical idiom is for the most part Western in origin.

The national character of popular music gives it access to national print media and, most importantly, television; its foreign associations link popular music strongly to other powerful and desirable attributes that are similarly perceived to have their locus outside regional areas and ultimately outside Indonesia: modernity, wealth, technology, consumer goods, glamour. And because, within Indonesia, those attributes—and the media that depict and extol them—are concentrated in a handful of large cities, popular music is also inevitably associated with urban centers, primarily, of course, Jakarta.

Regional music, the other principal sector of VCD production, is music closely associated with, and in most cases identified on the VCD insert as coming from, a specific region. If the music has singers (as most music on VCDs does), one definitive marker of its regionality is the language or languages they are singing in.[11] And to the extent that the use of a regional language denotes an ethnic or ethnolinguistic group, then regional music is *closely linked to the ethnic*, whereas the national has no explicit ethnicity. Regional music targets only the inhabitants of its own ethnolinguistic region, as well as people who have migrated out but are nostalgic for their homeland.

In music, and in other arts as well, the national pervades the regional, but the regional does not have national presence.[12] There is no regional music that has national scope, except in the rare case of the borrowing and, so to speak, nationalizing of a regional musical trait. Examples of this are *jaipongan* drumming in the 1980s or *koplo* drumming now (Manuel and Baier 1986; Weintraub 2013). (These nationalizable traits are necessarily instrumental rather than vocal, because a regional language is by definition not national.) In such cases, the musical trait crosses language lines, becoming incorporated either into Indonesian-language music or other regional-language music.

The Traditional and the Regional

A central topic in this paper is the position of traditional music in regional VCDs, so I need to provide a working definition of this key word. I shall use it in a narrow sense here, defining *traditional genres* as ones that do not show *in their music* the influence of the national genres of popular music. The wording "in their music" leaves open the possibility of influence from the national presentational *aesthetic* in their manner of performance. Specifying "national genres" also leaves open the possibility of influence from Western music before the waves of Western popular styles that have inundated Indonesia since the 1950s.

On the basis of this narrow definition, here is a theorem: *all traditional music is regional, but not all regional music is traditional.*

And here is another basic observation: *much of regional music is heavily influenced by two features of national music*, namely, (1) the hegemonic styles of national popular music (*pop, dangdut*, etc.), and (2) the mode of presentation—the aesthetic—characteristic of performances on television, on stage, or in formal settings. I call this, for short, the *pentas* (staged performance) aesthetic or mode. Frequent elements of the *pentas* mode—*separable* elements, not necessarily occurring all at once—include multiple dancers, synchronized movement, polished performance, lively tempo, upbeat mood, spectacle, virtuosity, gigantism, child performers, and comic dialogue (*lawakan*). The more a *traditional* genre on VCD is influenced by these features of national music, the farther it moves, in my terms, away from the wholly traditional toward the category I call *fusion*.

Regional Music on VCD: Inclusions

Here are the principal categories of regional music in the VCD industry:

- regional popular music (forms of pop, rock, and *dangdut* in regional languages);
- traditional genres;
- fusions of traditional music with popular music or the television aesthetic;
- theater;
- new creations, which mostly feature dance.

I will only deal with the first three of these in this chapter.

Regional Popular Music

First comes regional popular music. It is rather astonishing how much of this there is. In appendix 1 I list the markets I know of that have been targeted by VCD manufacturers of popular genres. By "market" I mean an ethnic group or a geographic region or subregion.

Regional popular music is popular music sung in regional languages. (It is almost always sung.) The language is the essential regional feature. Sometimes a local instrument is included in the band, and a local melody may be included in the repertoire; but basically the music of regional popular music is the same as that of the national forms, and thus it is Western in musical vocabulary and idiom. But this is not to say that it is *the same* across all regions: some varieties are indeed distinctive. Sundanese popular music, for example, often uses minor scales approximating the *pelog*-type scales (i.e., those with structural semitones) of Sundanese gamelan music. Toba Batak popular music often features male or female vocal trios. Minangkabau popular music often uses a recognizably Minang melodic idiom.[13] The popular music of Tetun-speakers in Indonesian Timor has been influenced by American country music and by the popular music of neighboring Timor-Leste, which itself has been influenced by Portuguese and Brazilian popular music. And all of these regional forms (and others) can be distinguished from Jakarta *pop*—not only in language but also in affect. Jakarta *pop* is cool and polished, and it is often slow and sad (*galau*, "broken-hearted"—this is the current term for what used to be called *lagu cengeng*, "weepy songs"), whereas, for example, *pop Tetun* is up-tempo, with relentless offbeat chording. But all the regional styles, as well as Jakarta *pop*, use Western instrumentation and the conventional Western harmonic framework, and so does *dangdut*, albeit with more Indian/Middle Eastern touches and with little vocal harmony.[14]

Here are a few examples of regional popular music on VCD; the headings note the genre, followed by the ethnic group that practices it or the region where it is found (or both), and then the title of the track.

REGIONAL POPULAR MUSIC: *POP SUMBAWA* (SUMBAWA BESAR), "TAMPAR EMPAN" (EXAMPLE 3)

The video shows young people in casual clothing arriving at an oceanside beach on motorcycles and playing in the water. There are also six young dancers (three men, three women) from a dance studio (*sanggar tari*) on Pulau Moyo. They dance vigorously in what appears to be traditional Samawa costume or an adaptation of it. Video passages of the dancing are intercut with clips of other young women, wearing different traditional or quasi-traditional costumes, sitting on the sand and lip-synching the words of the song. The instrumentation includes an electronic keyboard producing string and saxophone sounds, along with trap drums. The language is local, but I hear nothing in the music that seems characteristic of Sumbawa (or any other region). The video exemplifies both regional *pop* and the energetic, synchronized, *kreasi baru* dances characteristic of *sanggar*.[15] Here the choreography gives contrasting movements to the men's and women's groups. I don't know whether this is based on a traditional Sumbawa dance, but in any case it has been worked up according to the *pentas* aesthetic.

REGIONAL POPULAR MUSIC: *KENDANG KEMPUL* (BANYUWANGI, EAST JAVA), "TURU NANG DADANE" (EXAMPLE 4)

As is typical of *kendang kempul*, this track incorporates some distinctively Banyuwangi percussion instruments (a triangle, a pair of horizontal gong-kettles, and what sounds like a subdued imitation of Banyuwangi drum sound) into a half-rock, half-*dangdut* arrangement with synthesized strings and electric guitar. *Kendang kempul* melodies use Western minor scales, in a nod to traditional Banyuwangi genres like *gandrung*. Four young women dance in synchronized, *sanggar*-style movements and matching sarong-and-top costumes, while a fifth dances on her own, switching back and forth between two close-fitting modern outfits.

REGIONAL POPULAR MUSIC: *DANGDUT BANJAR* (BANJARMASIN, SOUTH KALIMANTAN), "SI BUNGAS HATI" (EXAMPLE 5)

Musically this is straight *dangdut*, nothing Banjar about it. A young couple stroll along the boardwalk of what appears to be a lakeside restaurant. They rent a romantic pedal boat, with an unromantic staff person sitting behind them to be sure they don't fall out or wreck the boat.

Fusions

I am going to defer discussion of traditional genres until later in this chapter. Instead let's turn to the fusions of traditional and popular music. I have assembled some examples juxtaposing the traditional form and its fusion with popular music.

TRADITIONAL: *RABAB PASISIA SELATAN* (MINANGKABAU, WEST SUMATRA), "BANCANO ALAM DI PESISIR SELATAN" (EXAMPLE 6A)

This example is an excerpt from a sung disaster narrative, similar to those Jennifer Fraser described in a 2013 article. The genre *rabab pasisia selatan* involves a singer (here Isal Melayu) accompanying himself on violin. Dressed traditionally, he sits cross-legged throughout, his torso swaying slightly with the movement of his bow arm.

FUSION: *RABAB DHUT MIX* (MINANGKABAU, WEST SUMATRA): "KIJOK MANGIJOK" (EXAMPLE 6B)

Here is the same singer-violinist, paired with his regular female singing partner, Erni Kas, in a VCD called *Rabab Dhut Mix*. (*Dhut* is an abbreviation of *dangdut*.) Clips of Isal playing and singing in street clothes, swaying with abandon, are intercut with clips of Erni and Isal (without violin) dancing in free-form club style. Isal makes flying motions, with his arms extended. Often the video images of the dancers are doubled, giving us two Isals and two Ernis. The arrangement mixes violin with digital trap drums, bass, and offbeat chords.

FUSION: *RABAB ASOY MIX* (MINANGKABAU, WEST SUMATRA), "RATOK PANGAMEN" (EXAMPLE 6C)

This example features different singers. A frenzied *sanggar* dance, quite untraditional in style for Minangkabau, intercut with the main singers playing violin, singing, and dancing beside a river. The melody is Minang in idiom, aside from the insertion of a phrase from a national *pop anak-anak* song for children. The arrangement is digital disco. This up-tempo song is, surprisingly, identified as a *ratok*, which is ordinarily a slow lament.

In 1995, in East Kalimantan, I recorded a group of Kenyah villagers singing a choral song of the type known as *kendau kancet* (among other names). Gini Gorlinski, who has done extensive research in Kalimantan and Malaysian Borneo, says the genre apparently emerged among the Kenyah in the 1940s and probably derives from Protestant congregational singing promoted by missionaries (Gorlinski 2016). Nevertheless, this has a secular text, and harmonically it has moved far from hymn singing.

TRADITIONAL: *KENDAU KANCET* (KENYAH, EAST KALIMANTAN), "LELENG" (EXAMPLE 7A)

In this example a soloist performs with an unaccompanied mixed homophonic chorus, singing with some thirds but many open fourths and fifths.

I did not shoot video when I recorded "Leleng," and I could not find this or any other *kendau kancet* online. But I did find a VCD version of a song with the same title:

FUSION: *LAGU-LAGU KALIMANTAN TIMUR* (KENYAH, EAST KALIMANTAN), "LELENG" (EXAMPLE 7B)

The melody in this track takes and extends one distinctive phrase of the *kendau kancet* melody "Leleng" but situates it within an arrangement featuring two electric *sape'* (a large plucked lute of the Kenyah), bass, a string wash (from an electronic keyboard), generic traditional-sounding drums (not a trap set), and a male chorus joining at intervals with a repeating phrase in fourths. The main melody is sung (in lip-synch) by a girl about ten years old, in Kenyah costume, holding feathers in both hands, dancing on her own in a forest. The *sape'* give a Kenyah feel to the arrangement. At two minutes in, there is a grand pause, then rock drumming brings the ensemble back in. From there on, it's a rock arrangement with *sape'*, synthesizer, drums, and vocals. If you grew up with rock and roll, as I did, there is something compelling about the break-fill-resume device, but it's not Kenyah.

How about fusions of gamelan and popular music?

FUSION: *CAMPURSARI* (SEMARANG, CENTRAL JAVA), "TERTIMBUN MASA LALU" (EXAMPLE 8)

The song, sung in Javanese, is known in *koplo* and simple rock-*dangdut* versions, always, as here, with rap segments. This lively *campursari* version, by the Semarang group CJDW, has a female singer, two electronic keyboards, a drum set, a tambourine, two electric guitars, and a partial gamelan consisting of three *saron demung* tuned more or less diatonically, plus an augmented (West Javanese?) set of gamelan drums.[16] (There are three other players in the gamelan who don't seem to be doing anything; if they are playing instruments they do so inaudibly.) The point to notice is that this is neither a full gamelan nor a partial set of instruments functioning as they would in a gamelan. It is, aside from the drums, a trio of metallophones playing the tones of a Western natural minor scale. None of the organizational features of traditional gamelan music—gong punctuation, stratification, melodic elaboration—is present. The gamelan instruments contribute only their timbre.

Here is one more pair of examples. Round dances, where the dancers sing while dancing, were traditionally found in many parts of eastern Indonesia. I know them from various regions of Sulawesi and from all over the southeastern islands (Nusa Tenggara Timur), and I suspect they are also common in southern Maluku. In rural communities they may still be done in the old way for important ritual purposes, but, in my observation, for lighter ceremonies and for secular celebrations the dancers no longer sing. Instead, pop music is broadcast through loudspeakers, and the people dance to that—still in a circle, and still with great enjoyment. The dance is homegrown, but the music is imported.

In October 1998 the Pusat Musik Liturgi (PML), a Catholic institute in Yogyakarta dedicated to developing new liturgical music in traditional styles, documented with video the annual *Gawi* ceremonial round dance of the Lio people in central Flores. (The PML first documents traditional performances, then it holds workshops to explore how that music can be adapted and developed for liturgical purposes.)

TRADITIONAL: *GAWI* ROUND DANCE (LIO, FLORES) (EXAMPLE 9A)

A male song leader stands in the center of an inner circle of men and an outer circle of women. The male dancers stamp in a steady beat. The song leader sings rapid-fire words, and all the dancers, male and female, answer with brief sung interjections. There are no instruments.

FUSION: *POP GAWI* (LIO, FLORES), "GAWI" (EXAMPLE 9B)

The composer of this and other *pop Gawi* songs, Moses Wara, told me he incorporates the characteristic *irama Gawi* (the *Gawi* "beat") into pop arrangements.[17] This one has a male soloist, other singers to make a trio or quartet for choruses, an electronic keyboard, and trap drums. The dancing, on the other hand, looks to be traditional—so the fusion here is between the pop music and the traditional dance.

When I first saw this video, I couldn't figure out what was going on: the danc-ers were in traditional costume and formation, but clearly they were singing the words of the pop song on the soundtrack. When I asked Moses Wara about this, he said the soundtrack was a *pop Gawi* song he had recorded in the studio and first published on audio cassette. People in the village knew the song from the cassette, so later, when he wanted video to go with the sound, he took a boom box to the village and set it outside the camera's frame and played the studio recording while the people danced in traditional *Gawi* fashion and lip-synched the words. I asked Moses Wara's publisher why not simply use traditional *Gawi* songs as the soundtrack? He replied unequivocally that such a recording would not sell. The traditional music is too stiff and unorganized, he said; it sounds like a speech (by which I assume he referred to the song leader's word-dominated delivery).

An article from 2011 about Eman Bata Dede, another composer of *pop Gawi*, remarks admiringly that he has helped preserve the traditional *Gawi* ritual event by making it easier to perform. "In the past," the article says, "Gawi was exhaust-ing, because people had to dance and sing from night until morning. Now they don't have to do this anymore. Since the emergence of *lagu Gawi* [Gawi songs], all the people have to do is dance" (Anwar and Oktora 2011, 213). Pop as a labor-saving device.

Another trait of fusion genres is the gigantism I mentioned earlier. This is a trait promoted mainly by the tourist industry and by local governments hoping to attract tourists. Consider the genre *gandrung Banyuwangi*. In its tra-ditional form, this involves a female singer-dancer (the *gandrung*), accompa-nied by a small ensemble of two violins and percussion. The *gandrung* dances sometimes alone and sometimes flirtatiously with men who come forward from the audience to join her. More recently, the number of dancers has been increased to four or six, while an older woman (normally an experienced *gandrung* considered too old to dance) sits behind them and does the sing-ing. Very recently, the regional government of Banyuwangi has mounted a colossal performance called *gandrung sewu*—like Mahler's "Symphony of a Thousand," but with *gandrung*. Literally, one thousand schoolgirls and young women dance the formerly solo *gandrung* dance outdoors. The music is still provided by a singer and a small ensemble, now broadcast through huge loud-speakers (example 10, where the number of dancers is announced at the end as twelve hundred).

There has been a similar development for the *likurai* dance of Timor, per-formed by a file of women who hold small drums under their left arms and drum as they dance. The regional government in Atambua boasts it has achieved a national record by mounting a *likurai* with six thousand dancer-drummers (example 11). I have also heard rumors of colossal performances of the Acehnese sitting dances.

I've strayed from the VCDs here, since these gigantesque forms are not yet on VCD. They are, however, examples of fusions of the traditional with aspects of the *pentas* aesthetic. Other fusion traits that *are* seen on VCD are a shift away from a genre's older repertoire, which may feature large compositional forms, slow tempo, and sometimes somber mood, to newer, shorter, lighter pieces. We see this in the gamelan-*campursari* fusions, and we can see it in another form in the greatly increased proportion of comic dialogue in theater forms on VCD (and in live performance). There is also a tendency to add dances in *sanggar*-style choreography to genres formerly carried by music alone. We could regard this simply as an accommodation to the ineluctably visual nature of the VCD medium, but I suggest it is also an indication of the ascendancy of television in mass entertainment. So also are the wordless playlets that often illustrate the situations described in the songs on a VCD.

The fusion forms present a solution to the perennial Indonesian problem of how to reconcile the regional and its putative opposite, the "modern." Symbols of modernity, typically Western—instrumentation, scales, harmonic system, formal structure, choreographic style, and performance aesthetic—are mixed with regional elements (language, costume, possibly melody, possibly local instrumental timbres; one or some or all of these at once). It must be acknowledged that the results are widely accepted as convincingly representative. I have never, for example, heard people complain that modernized "regional songs" (*lagu daerah*) are insufficiently regional because they lack regional instruments or a distinctive regional "sound."[18]

Traditional Genres

What about the traditional genres, the ones that do not show obvious efforts at fusion? Indeed, there are many traditional genres on VCD. The Balinese VCD industry in particular is full of traditional genres represented with traditional repertoire, traditional instrumentation, and apparently traditional performance practice. The traditional sector of the Minang industry is almost as rich, or at least it was in the first decade of this century, when one could find VCDs of many traditional genres (Suryadi 2003, 2010). (I found fewer when I visited in 2016.) In other parts of the country, the number of such genres on VCD has sharply declined. Appendix 2 gives a list, definitely not exhaustive, of traditional genres still available on VCD.[19]

Something to note in appendix 2 is that—with the exception of the Balinese genres and Javanese *tayuban*—every genre listed is either *professionalized* or *spectacularized*, and most are presented in the *pentas* mode, as staged performances (often in unrealistic contexts, such as in a field or on the steps of a building). These apparently are the criteria that normally qualify a traditional genre for representation on VCD.

It is telling that the two exceptions I just noted are the only VCD genres that regularly *locate* their content, indicating on the cover insert the home village of the performers (in the case of Balinese genres) or the place of performance (for *tayuban*). The reasons are related but different. In Bali, I propose, many villages support gamelans to perform for temple festivals, and all such groups aspire to a high degree of coordination and polish. Those that appear on VCD are acknowledged to be excellent, but unlike the stars of popular music, they are not elevated beyond the reach of the viewer, nor do they exhibit, like some *dangdut* or *koplo* performers, socially extreme behavior that ordinary people would be afraid to imitate. Nor does the professionalism of these groups set them apart: VCDs serve not as epitomes of unattainable artistry (or glamour) but as models to aspire to. Someday, it could be your own village named on the VCD cover.

With Javanese *tayuban* VCDs, the professionals (the female singers and the gamelan musicians) share the frame with the local men who come forward to dance. The men demonstrate confidence and self-control by dancing—indeed, to me the most notable element of *tayuban* VCDs is the imperturbability of the male dancers, their apparent indifference to the female singers (and vice versa) (example 12). The *tayuban* is a ceremony asserting social hierarchy at the local level; the professionals are a group invited from outside to provide an occasion for that assertion. This is why most VCDs of popular *tayuban* groups are identified as performing in this village or that village. In both the Balinese and Javanese cases, the location is a selling point for the VCD. People buy the VCD to compare their own local practice with practices elsewhere. Neither spectacle nor professionalism is needed to legitimate the appearance of these genres on VCD.

Exclusions

What traditional music is *not* on commercial VCD? I see four main categories:

- communal genres without elements of the spectacular
- sung narratives
- older repertoire of traditional genres
- genres embarrassing to the authorities

Communal genres not lending themselves to spectacular presentation include:

- singing at wakes and funerals and other communal occasions[20]
- other kinds of unaccompanied singing (*mocoan* in East Java; *dhalang jemblung* in Central Java)
- music for *adat* occasions[21]

- music featuring rustic, handmade, or old-fashioned instruments[22]
- self-delectative genres (Jew's harps, solo flutes, leg xylophones)
- any kind of unpolished—especially rural—music, unless the performers can be presented as comic bumpkins (as in West Javanese *calung* VCDs and some Madurese *saronen* VCDs)

Most forms of sung narrative in Indonesia—*sinrilli'* and *massureq* from South Sulawesi; *dendang Pauah* and *sijobang* from West Sumatra; *nyanyi panjang* from mainland Riau; *turi-turin* from North Sumatra; *hoho* from Nias; *kentrung* and *pantun Sunda* from Java; *tekna'* from West Kalimantan, to name just a few—have no presence on VCD. (Two important sung-narrative genres in Bali, *kidung* and *kakawin*, are marketed as audio CDs but not as VCDs.) Two exceptions are the Minangkabau genre *rabab pasisia selatan* (described earlier in connection with example 6a) and the Buginese genre of narratives (*cerita*) accompanied by *kacapi* (plucked lute) (example 13).[23]

As I observed earlier, traditional genres that have adapted to Western aesthetics or commercial demands (in what I describe as a form of fusion) tend to minimize or abandon their older repertoire if it is characterized by large compositional forms, slow tempos, or somber or contemplative moods. In Central Javanese gamelan music, for example, the extended *gendhing* forms of the classical repertoire, which still dominated audio cassettes of gamelan music in the 1970s and 1980s, have given way on VCD to shorter, faster forms (often in flashy, contrastive loud-and-soft arrangements) or to gamelan versions of melodies from the *langgam* genre of popular song.[24] The mostly slow, unmetered violin and vocal pieces of the Bimanese *biola rawa Mbojo* repertoire are not found on VCD;[25] instead one hears up-tempo, fixed-meter pieces, usually supplemented by a *dangdut* drum (example 14). The late and much-missed anthropologist Mary Steedly, who worked in Karo communities in North Sumatra, told me that the old standard repertoire of the Karo *gendang lima sedalanen* ensemble (which we recorded together in the 1980s) has fallen away; instead the patriotic songs of Djaga Depari (1922–63), from the time of the Indonesian Revolution in the late 1940s, are now considered the classical repertoire. Today they are played, both on VCD and in live events, on a keyboard (with programmed Karo drumming and synthesized imitations of the other Karo instruments), along with more modern *pop Karo* songs. An exception to this trend to abandon older repertoire is again found in Minangkabau VCDs, in the often mournful songs of *saluang jo dendang*. (But remember the un-*ratok*-like *ratok* example of fusion in example 6c.) Bali offers another exception: the constant demand there for musical (and marketing) variety has encouraged the production of a small number of VCDs of older, now-rare genres (*gong gede*, seven-tone *Semar pegulingan*, *selonding*).[26]

My final category of what is not on VCD is disreputable genres, ones that the government or religious authorities try to ban or restrict. Chief among these are erotic dancing and the singing of bawdy lyrics.[27] Jennifer Fraser reported at our conference on ribald singing late at night in *saluang jo dendang* performances (see her chapter in this book). You will not find these on openly published VCDs, though perhaps underground videos circulate. Nor will you find the Balinese performances of *joged bumbung* and *genjek* that are labeled as *joged porno, joged hot*, or *joged maut*, in which a woman (the *joged*) dances with men from the audience. *Joged* is a Balinese version of the *ronggeng* tradition found in many parts of Indonesia (other examples, mentioned earlier, being *gandrung Banyuwangi* and old-style *tayuban*). There is an uncontroversial form of *joged bumbung*, in which the women dance flirtatiously but continually evade the stylized advances of the men, who pretend to be overcome with passion. But typically, in *joged hot*, the women abandon evasion and rub up against the men with quick pelvic thrusts, or push them to the ground and briefly climb on top. It should be said that these performances, though lewd, are not menacing (the women are in command throughout), and there is uproarious laughter from men, women, and children in the audience. The music is simple and repetitive, but it is wholly Balinese in idiom.

TRADITIONAL: *JOGED MAUT* (BALI) (EXAMPLE 15)

I know of one published VCD of this kind of performance, titled *Joged Maut*. Example 15 gives a mild excerpt from it, in which the young *joged* was very much in control of the event and did not allow it to get too raunchy. A young man came out of the crowd to dance with her. Whenever he tried to get too close, she held him off with her long fingernails. Then he bent over backward, displaying the crotch of his pants to her, whereupon, with a swift sideways jolt of her hip, she knocked him right over. Other episodes on the VCD featured older *joged* who were considerably more permissive and aggressive. This VCD did make it to market, but it was soon banned and withdrawn.[28]

I have recently learned that something similar to *joged hot* takes place late at night during *tayuban* events in Java. As I said above, these events involve local amateur men and professional female singer-dancers. In the old days they could turn into rowdy drunken affairs, with the men kissing and grabbing the women at the end of each statement of the gamelan melody. On VCD there is none of this: the men and women seem utterly indifferent to each other, dancing in proximity but without interaction, as in example 12. However, Amrih Widodo, who has studied *tayuban* for years, told me in 2019 that *tayuban* can still turn rowdy in the later stages, after the video cameras are turned off.

Regional VCDs convey a message about what is valuable and what is not in regional music, a message consonant with national trends toward commodification of arts and the hegemony of urban, presentational, television-based aesthetics. While popular music in regional languages is clearly very strong in the VCDs, as are the fusions combining elements of regional and national music, including the pervasive *pentas* aesthetic, traditional music is in a more liminal state.

I am not claiming that traditional music in Indonesia is dying or has already died: the existence of the genres listed in appendix 2 disproves such a claim. Nor can we assume that what we see in VCDs is what people are doing on the ground, in real life. They may still be performing traditional genres in more or less the traditional manner, and young people may be learning the repertoire and acquiring the technical skills necessary to take over when the older performers withdraw. (We cannot know for sure without ethnographic and ethnomusicological accounts from the various regions.)

But, actually, I don't believe it. My sense from my own observations (since 2011 mainly in Nusa Tenggara Timur [NTT], the southeastern islands) and reports from other researchers is that the number of people able and willing to perform the old genres *in the old way* is rapidly diminishing as those people age, and younger generations are not coming forward to take their place. (I know this for a fact in Timor.) Traditions may indeed survive, but many will do so in a reduced, tokenized, *representative* form, self-consciously demonstrating ethnic or regional identity. Genres that formerly entertained performers and onlookers for hours on end will become (have already become, in many cases) seven-minute items in *malam kesenian*, stage potpourris of ethnic music and dance.

Here the study of the VCDs becomes particularly significant, because in them we see the *image* of traditional music, the *representation* of traditional music that is disseminated to Indonesian audiences. This representation emphasizes professionalism and spectacle, and in so doing it devalues precisely the kinds of music I listed as "exclusions" (aside from the disreputable genres, which are valued or devalued for other reasons). It also devalues local performance for local audiences, promoting instead the *pentas* mode: neater, cleaner, impersonal performances directed outward toward a broader audience with less intimate involvement. The VCDs replace the contextual (a dance at a wedding, a song at a gathering) with the dislocated (performers on a stage, in front of a government building, in a field); they valorize the hypertrophy of forces (six dancers instead of one or two; six thousand *likurai* drummers). Ultimately, they contribute to the marginalization—the erasure—of the rural in favor of the urban, the localized and specific in favor of the diffuse and generic, in Indonesian popular culture and public discourse.

Coda: Singing in Timor

I'm going to step outside the VCD framework again and close with something from my current fieldwork among Southern Tetun in Indonesian Timor, close to the border with Timor-Leste. This is a vanishing, rural, communal music, and a good example of what I'm calling "excluded" genres. It is group singing without instruments, requiring complex skills to perform and drawing on a great store of oral literature and local knowledge, but it is locked in its highly localized language, Tetun Terik,[29] and it has no spectacular or virtuosic features to attract uninitiated outsiders, or even to inspire young people from within the culture to take it up.

The song I offer here is sung at wakes by the relatives, friends, and neighbors of the deceased. Other melodies are sung for other occasions: corn tying after the harvest, sago pounding, and ceremonies connected with clan houses (*uma lulik*).

A Tetun melody, once initiated in a singing episode, is repeated over and over until the singers take a break, usually twenty or thirty or forty-five minutes later. The lyrics, in contrast, change constantly. They consist for the most part of fixed, preexisting two-line poems, called *kananuk*, which are strung together spontaneously in performance. Continuity of topic and appositeness of a verse to the one before are valued. Commonly, two groups of singers—men in one group, women in the other—alternate, and while one group is singing the other confers to decide on a verse to respond with.[30] *Kananuk* are not attached to melodies; there are many melodies and countless *kananuk*, and in theory any *kananuk* may be sung to any melody, though both must suit the occasion.

Nowadays, the singers are almost all in their sixties and seventies. They learned the art of singing (the melodies, the verses, and how to combine them) when they were teenagers, but no teenagers are learning it now to carry it on. In the old days, wakes and other community observances with singing were among the few occasions when boys and girls could meet and flirt and perhaps find partners. And singing well was a way to shine, to attract admiring eyes, to earn the respect of the community in which one could expect to live out one's life. So there was a strong incentive for young people to learn to sing. Nowadays the horizons of people's lives have expanded beyond the village network, and there are many new opportunities for young people to connect—in school, on the internet, via mobile phones. They no longer need to put in the effort to learn to sing. So the singing is left to the old.

My research in Indonesian Timor, aside from straightforward recording and ethnographic documentation of the singing, is largely focused on the way *kananuk* lyrics are fitted to melodies. Since the melodies are longer than the poetic lines, the *kananuk* must be extended. This is done by inserting words and vocables that are *extrinsic to the poem* and do not contribute to its meaning. Each melody has what I call its own unique *melodic text*, a fixed template of these extrinsic syllables, into which the words of the preexisting couplet (the *poetic text*) must be fitted. The aim is unison enunciation by the chorus of both the poetic and the melodic text (though in practice there is often variation among the singers, particularly in vocables).[31] So what is required of the singers is (1) to know the melody, (2) to know the words and vocables of the melodic text and where to sing them in the course of the melody, (3) to know (or be able to pick up from an initial solo or a hurried conference) the text of the *kananuk* to be sung, and then (4) to fit that poetic text, in segments according to a fixed pattern, into the gaps in the melodic text. They must also (5) observe required repetitions of words of the *kananuk* text falling at certain points in the melody.[32]

Here are three two-line *kananuk* that were sung in sequence in the village of Builaran to a wake melody there called "Ailakna'it." (In some other communities it is called "Tua Lekik.") First, I give the plain text and a rough translation:[33]

1a. Naruka oa kiak, ko'a tua dalan.	Send an orphan to tap palm wine from a tree at the side of the road.
1b. Tua turu nakdulik, nakdu[lik] turu.	The sap drips without stopping [this is an image of weeping].
2a. Naruka oa kiak, baa taa tali.	Send an orphan to cut a vine for a rope.
2b. Taa tali la kotu, tanis tuur nein.	The vine can't be cut. He sits and waits, weeping.
3a. Wee lele manu kiak, nalo kadomi.	An orphan chicken is swept along on the current, making me remember with sadness.
3b. Liras taba tabasar, nalo kadomi.	It beats its wings, making me remember with sadness.

Table 11.1 shows the intercalation of these poetic texts into the unchanging melodic text belonging to "Ailakna'it." The words of the *kananuk* are given in boldface italics, and the structural words and vocables of the melodic text are in regular roman. The interweaving of these two texts is complex, requiring the singers to interrupt the discursive poetic text with vocables and words from the melodic text at prescribed moments. Moreover, the syntactic breaks in the poetic text do not always match pauses in the melody (indicated by the vertical lines in table 11.1). For example, a strong cadence and long pause come *before* the last word of the poetic line, although the second syntactic unit is incomplete

TABLE 11.1 Three two-line *kananuk* (1a/1b, 2a/2b, 3a/3b), as sung in sequence in Desa Builaran to the melody known there as "Ailakna'it"

A. BEFORE CAESURA

	1	2	3	4	5	6	7	8	9	10	11
1a. Naruka oa kiak, . . .	ae	*Naruka*	lo oho lo ho	ado oho	*oa kiak*	*oa*	ele ae	*oa kiak*			
1b. Tua turu nakdulik, . . .	ae	*Tua turu*	lo oho lo ho	ado oho	*na-*la-*kdulik*	*na-*	ele ae	*nakdulik*			
2a. Naruka oa kiak, . . .	ae	*Naruka*	lo oho lo ho	ado oho	*oa kiak*	*na-*	ele ae	*Naruka*			
2b. Taa tali la kotu, . . .	ae	*Taa tali*	lo oho lo ho	ado oho	*la kotu*	*la*	ele ae	*la kotu*			
3a. Wee lele manu kiak, . . .	ae	*Wee lele*	lo oho lo ho	ado oho	*manu kiak*	*manu*	ele ae	*manu kiak*			
3b. Liras taba tabasar, . . .	ae	*Liras taba*	lo oho lo ho	ado oho	*ta*-la-*basar*	e* *ta-*	ele ae	*Tabasar*			

B. AFTER CAESURA

	1	2	3	4	5
1a. . . . ko'a tua . . .	*ko'a*	e	*ko'a*	*tu[a]*	lo oho lo ho o
1b. . . . nakdu[lik] . . .	*na-*	e	*nak-*	*-du[lik]*	lo oho lo ho o
2a. . . . baa taa . . .	*oa*	e	*baa*	*taa*	lo oho lo ho o
2b. . . . tanis tuur . . .	*tanis*	o*	*tanis*	*tuur*	lo oho lo ho o
3a. . . . nalo ka- . . .	*nalo*	e	*nalo*	*ka-*	lo oho lo ho o
3b. . . . nalo ka- . . .	*nalo*	e	*nalo*	*ka-*	lo oho lo ho o

C. FINAL WORD

	1	2	3	4	5	6	7	8	9	10	11
1a. . . . dalan	ae ae	*dalan*	ele a ele ala	*dalan*	tebes	ele ala	*dalan*	*dalan*	ele he	*dalan*	olo ho o
1b. . . . turu	ae ae	*turu*	ele a ele ala	*turu*	tebes	ele ala	*turu*	*Turu*	ele he	*tu[ru]*	olo ho o
2a. . . . tali	ae ae	*tali*	ele a ele ala	*tali*	tebes	ele ala	*tali*	*Tali*	ele he	*ta[li]*	olo ho o
2b. . . . nein	ae ae	*nein*	ele a ele ala	*nein*	tebes	ele ala	*nein* e* *nein**	*Nein*	ele ae	*nein*	olo ho o
3a. . . . domi	ae ae	*-domi*	ele a ele ala	*-domi*	tebes	ele ala	*-domi*	*-domi*	ele hae	*-domi*	olo ho o
3b. . . . domi	ae ae	*-domi*	ele a ele ala	*-domi*	tebes	ele ala	*-domi*	*-domi*	ele ae	*-domi*	olo ho o

Note: Following the source text of the *kananuk* at left, the text as sung is set in numbered columns, with "poetic text" in bold italics, "melodic text" in regular roman. The three segments (A, B, C) of the first line of a *kananuk* are sung consecutively, then the three segments of the second line, and so forth. Not shown here: an initial stanza of syllables without discursive meaning, sung before each two-line *kananuk*, and a single such phrase, much shorter, sung afterward. Vertical lines indicate pauses in the melody. * marks anomalous insertions.

without that final word. These patterns of insertion, repetition, and enjambment across melodic cadences are applied to every *kananuk* sung to this melody. Audio excerpts from my recording of "Ailakna'it" are in example 16.

This music has no hope of entering the world of the VCD, or its likely successors, YouTube and your mobile phone. The language is obscure, the tempo is slow, the scale and melody are weird by pop standards, the singers are old and wrinkly, and they don't do anything but sit there and sing. You can't put drums or a keyboard or harmony on it. You can't dance to it, you can't make a spectacle out of it. It's of no use to the industry.

But it is of use to the Tetun-speakers, or at least it was. For that reason alone—not to mention for the formal devices just described, which may or may not be peculiar to the southeastern islands, or to Timor alone, I don't yet know[34]—it should be studied and documented before it is lost. And this is true for all of the musics that fall outside the sphere of interest of commercial entertainment. I am not at all saying we should not *also* study the musics that *are* present in commercial media. But precisely because those musics are mediatized, they leave evidence of themselves in the historical record. The rural genres I'm speaking of here, unsuited to and invisible in the media, *leave no trace* unless they are documented. They are chapters in the record of human creativity, but the chapters are written in disappearing ink. The whole of that record, regardless of its presence in or absence from the media, should be systematically documented and annotated. And for the rural genres, there is no one to do it but researchers, indigenous or foreign. My core audience at Cornell was ethnomusicologists, but really anyone—academically trained or not, and emphatically including Indonesians as well as outsiders—can do the necessary work, by applying the commonsense methods of careful documentation. Still, I will close by looking straight at the ethnomusicologists. Media are fickle and driven by commerce. We should not be.

Appendix 1: Regional Pop/Rock/*Dangdut* VCDs—Targeted Markets

Each name of a place or ethnic group below appears as a descriptor on one or more VCDs of regional popular music (as I define the term in this paper). The descriptors are typically of the form "*Pop* [x]," "*Lagu* [or *Lagu-lagu*] *Daerah* [x]," or "*Dangdut* [x]." In such a formula, I understand the descriptor to be targeting the place or group as a market for the VCD. "Kab." stands for *kabupaten*, the largest administrative unit below the level of the province. This list is certainly incomplete with regard to Kalimantan, Sulawesi, Maluku, and Papua.

Sumatra

Nias, Toba, Karo, Pakpak, Simalungun, Tapanuli Selatan ("Tapsel"), Kab. Mandailing Natal ("Madina"), Melayu, Pasaman, Minangkabau, Pesisir Selatan, Mentawai, Ocu, Rejang, Kerinci, Jambi [unspecified], Bangka, Semende, Muara Enim, Palembang, Lampung Pesisir, Abung, Menggala

Java

Sunda, Java [i.e., Central and East], Cirebon, Banyuwangi, Madura

Kalimantan

Bidayuh, Kanayatn, Iban, Kab. Sanggau, Kab. Sintang, Kab. Landak, Kab. Ketapang, Kalimantan Tengah [unspecified], Banjarmasin

Bali & Nusa Tenggara Barat (NTB)

Bali, Sasak, Sumbawa Besar, Taliwang, Bima-Dompu

Nusa Tenggara Timur (NTT)

Sumba, Flores, Manggarai, Ngada, Nage-Keo, Ende, Lio, Sikka, Larantuka, Lamaholot, Lembata, Alor, Rote, Sabu, Belu, Malaka, Meto, NTT [unspecified]

Sulawesi

Bugis, Makassar, Toraja, Mandar, Poso, Pamona, Banggai, Buton, Muna, Tolaki, Gorontalo, Manado, Minahasa, Sangihe

Maluku

Halmahera, Maluku Utara, Maluku Tenggara, Banda Naira, Sula, Obi, Ambon, Tanimbar, Ternate

Papua

Papua [unspecified], Maibrat, Kaimana

Appendix 2: Traditional Music Genres on Commercial VCD

TABLE 11.2 Partial list of traditional music genres on commercial VCD (2000–2018)

Traditional genres	Fusion versions
gondang sabangunan (Toba Batak)	
uning-uningan / lagu opera (Toba Batak)	pop instruments added
saluang klasik (Minang)	*saluang disco, saluang dangdut*
rabab pasisia (Minang)	*rabab dhut* mix, etc.
kecapi (Minang)	
selawat dulang (Minang)	
indang / randai (Minang)	
calempong (Riau)	pop instruments and idiom added
randai (Kuantan, Riau)	
zapin (Riau)	
gitar tunggal (South Sumatra and Lampung)	
gitar tunggal Semende (South Sumatra)	
gambus (Lampung)	
gambang kromong (Jakarta/Banten)	*gambang kromong pop*
tembang Cianjuran / kacapi suling (West Java)	
degung (West Java)	
calung (West Java)	
kliningan (West Java)	
ketuk tilu (West Java)	
jaipongan (West Java)	*dangdut jaipong*
Banyumas genres with gamelan	*campursari*
dolalak (Purworejo)	
Central Javanese genres with gamelan	*campursari, langgam*
tayuban (East and Central Java)	*tayub moderen, tayub campursari*
ngremo (East Java)	
jula-juli (East Java)	
wayang forms (throughout Java, Bali, Lombok)	wayang with *lawak* emphasis

(Continued)

TABLE 11.2 (CONTINUED)

hadrah (East Java)	spectacular, virtuoso
sandur (Madura)	
saronen (Madura)	added *lawak*
gandrung Banyuwangi	*kendang kempul*
angklung Banyuwangi	
kuntulan (Banyuwangi)	spectacular, virtuoso
Balinese gamelan/theater/vocal	theater with *lawak* emphasis
kelentangan (Lombok)	dance added
gendang beleq (Lombok)	
joget, jangger (Lombok)	
sape (Kenyah, East Kalimantan)	
dance with gong-row (Kanayatn, West Kalimantan)	
karungut (Ngaju, Central Kalimantan)	
kacapi Makasar (South Sulawesi)	
kacapi Bugis (South Sulawesi)	
gambus (South Sulawesi)	
sakeco (Sumbawa Besar, only one track on one pop VCD)	
biola rawa Mbojo (Bima, Sumbawa)	
gambo enke (Bima, Sumbawa)	
biola gambus (Bima, Sumbawa)	
togal, tide-tide, and similar dances (North Maluku)	

Two traditional genres represented only in their fusion versions:

gonrang Simalungun	pop instruments and idiom added
gendang lima sadalanen (Karo)	*gendang keyboard/lagu perkolong-kolong*

Notes: (1) No information on the quantity of VCDs for each genre is implied here. In some cases only one or two VCDs of a genre were encountered. (2) No traditional genres from Nusa Tenggara Timur were found on commercial VCD. (3) Current data (after ca. 2006) are lacking for some parts of Kalimantan, Sulawesi, Maluku, and Papua. (4) Genres where music is incidental and the focus is on trance, costumes, or theater (e.g. *reyog, jaranan, ebeg, debus, tong-tong*) are omitted from the list.

NOTES

The audio, video, and visual examples discussed in this chapter are available on its companion webpage, https://blogs.cornell.edu/soundingoutindonesianmusic/volume/yampolsky/. Also on the page is an additional selection of VCD covers, representing regional popular musics, fusion genres, and traditional genres, and a postscript with additional thoughts on supporting vanishing traditions.

1. This is a written-up version of my keynote talk at the SOSIM conference. I have tried to retain the informal tone of the presentation, though I've expanded on some of the points, attached some notes, and inserted some things I ought to have said. I thank Andrew Weintraub, Lorraine Aragon, and the editors and reviewers of this book for comments on draft versions.

2. For the technical characteristics of the VCD medium, see https://en.wikipedia.org/wiki/Video_CD.

3. For a case study of a VCD production house in Pati, on the North Coast of Java, see Kusno 2012. Thanks to Andrew Weintraub for bringing this *skripsi* to my attention.

4. On YouTube, the commercial videos are posted alongside amateur videos made on mobile phones.

5. With it goes a valuable source of information about musical practice in our era. There are trade-offs here: mobile phones are portable and accessible anywhere there is a signal, whereas the VCD needs an emplacement; the selection available on the internet is seemingly unlimited, but the quality of video and audio on a mobile phone or on You-Tube is generally inferior to that of a VCD; viewers may get one song from a group but rarely a whole album, so the group's style and artistry is conveyed only in a minimal unit (the "greatest hits" syndrome reduced to a single vacuum-packed hit). Also, and not to be sneered at by researchers, the VCD can be easily archived.

6. This figure (from Wikipedia, September 29, 2018) is the most conservative I have found. In contrast, Suryadinata et al. (2003, 10) point out that the Biro Pusat Statistik, in its publications concerning Indonesia's 2000 census, assigns codes to 1,072 "ethnic and sub-ethnic groups."

7. Some of the national (albeit niche) genres discussed in our conference—such as metal, punk, and avant-garde composition—do not appear in this list because they are not generally sold as commercial VCDs, being disseminated instead through the internet or hand to hand.

8. Excluding the markedly regional dialects of Indonesian, such as Kupang Malay or Bahasa Betawi. These do not have national currency.

9. Popular music is of course subdivided into many genres and styles. By far the most important and commercially successful are *pop Indonesia* and *dangdut*. (For *dangdut*, a key source is Weintraub 2010. There is as yet no solid history of *pop Indonesia*.) Some of the styles of *pop Indonesia* are *reggae, rap, country, bossa, lounge,* and *rohani. Metal* and *jazz* are on their own, subdivisions of popular music but not of *pop Indonesia*.

10. Like any popular music anywhere, it also has its share of vapid, sentimental, and musically uninspired songs.

11. In contrast to the national music category, there are also regional music VCDs that are instrumental only, such as VCDs of Balinese gamelan, of certain repertoires of Central Javanese gamelan, and of Sundanese *kecapi-suling*. Here the regional association is established by the language of the pieces' titles or by a locating descriptor on the VCD insert ("Gambus Selayar"), or the publishers may assume that the genre name itself sufficiently communicates the music's regionality.

12. This holds for all elements of regional culture except, interestingly, cuisine—which raises the question: Why are people willing, in fact eager, to sample cuisines from other ethnic groups, but not to sample other kinds of music? Two other elements of regional

culture that can, in certain cases and to a limited degree, travel outside their region are textiles and handicrafts, but here—with the exception of cheap mass-produced batik, which is sold everywhere and has lost much or all of its Javanese connotation—the traffic flows predominantly from the regions to wealthy cosmopolitan elites, who view such regional productions as exotica.

13. It thus comes close to the *fusion* category I describe below. The difference is that *pop Minang* is not advertised as combining pop with any specific genre of Minangkabau traditional music.

14. For a somewhat different take on regional popular music, with emphasis mainly on Minangkabau, see "The Ethnic Modern," chapter 3 in Barendregt et al. 2017. See also Barendregt 2002.

15. Although I am not skilled in the analysis of dance, I will venture an impressionistic observation: in addition to synchronized movement, uniform costumes, and the *pentas* aesthetic, *sanggar* dances seem often to emphasize the dancers' arms, extended straight out from the body (up, down, front, to the sides) or waved about. For more on *sanggar,* see Nyoman Catra's chapter in this book.

16. For more on the CJDW group, see Widyastuti 2011.

17. *Pop Gawi* is my term for these songs, not Moses Wara's.

18. Returning briefly to the Pusat Musik Liturgi's harmonized and organ-accompanied arrangements of traditional regional melodies (or new melodies composed in accordance with PML's analysis of regional idiom): congregations are proud, I was told, when music they perceive to be theirs is arranged in European style; they see it as a gesture of respect from the outside world. Indeed, some people told me that until they heard the PML arrangements, "we never knew our music could sound so beautiful [*indah*]."

19. In 2016–18 I traveled in Sumatra, Bangka-Belitung, Java, Madura, South and Southeast Sulawesi, Bali, and the main islands of NTB and NTT, updating those segments of the survey of Indonesian VCD production I began in the early 2000s. Consequently, the information in appendix 2 is fresher for those regions than it is for the ones I have not yet revisited: Kalimantan, Sulawesi (aside from the south and southeast), Maluku, and Papua.

20. Rural group singing is the focus of my current research in Indonesian Timor and Timor-Leste.

21. *Adat* may be cursorily defined as a set of conventions and customs governing ceremonial and ritual behavior. *Adat* rules are often specific to one locality or ethnic group.

22. Localized instruments of this sort are often featured by Palmer Keen in his interesting and eclectic Aural Archipelago videos at http://www.auralarchipelago.com/. You do not see these in commercial VCDs.

23. Lorraine Aragon suggested to me that these genres may retain their presence on VCD because there are so many out-migrants from both of these groups, nostalgic for the language and sounds of home.

24. See Darsono and Ishiguro's contribution in this book for a discussion.

25. Such as *Lopi Penge* on volume 16 of the *Music of Indonesia* series, Smithsonian Folkways SFW 40443.

26. Two of the older genres most remote from contemporary tastes are *gambuh* and *gambang*. Neither appears on VCD.

27. Some people consider *dangdut* and *koplo* dancing to be unacceptably erotic (see Weintraub 2011), but these genres are too popular, with too wide a national audience, to suppress—and they are mild in comparison with the *joged hot* described here, or the explicitly sexual stage dancing (too much even for VCD) for which Perbaungan in North Sumatra is notorious.

28. This VCD is not online, but a search for *joged porno* or *joged hot* will turn up many similar videos, apparently shot on mobile phones but not published as VCDs.

29. This is the rural form of Tetun spoken in the eastern part of Indonesian Timor and in some southern regions of Timor-Leste. Tetun Terik is to be distinguished from the Portuguese-influenced Tetun known as Tetun Dili or Tetun Praça, one of the two official languages of the Republic of Timor-Leste (the other being Portuguese). Tetun Terik differs markedly from Tetun Dili in vocabulary and in certain grammatical features.

30. In the recording from Builaran discussed below, the singers had decided on the *kananuk* beforehand, to guard against mistakes or falters, so no conference was needed.

31. There may also be unison deviation from regularity (i.e., from the "fixed template") in the insertion of elements. I have marked deviations in table 11.1 with asterisks. The norms and limits of deviation and variation are a topic of my continuing research.

32. In table 11.1, for example, the first one or two syllables of column 5 of the A segment of every line are repeated in column 6, and the whole of column 5 is repeated in column 8. (Column 6 in line A.2b is anomalous, for reasons I do not yet understand.) Column 1 of the B segment is repeated in column 3. And the final word of the poetic text, first stated in column 2 of the C segment, is repeated in columns 4, 7, 8, and 10 of that segment.

33. The initial transcription of the Tetun Terik poems from my field recordings was done by Erwin Tae in Betun, Kabupaten Malaka, NTT. We then worked together to add the words and vocables of the melodic text. Erwin Tae also provided an Indonesian summary of the meaning, which I have here put approximately into English.

34. A similar, though not identical, system is found in the *vaihoho* singing of Fataluku speakers at the eastern tip of the island of Timor (in the Republic of Timor-Leste). For more on Tetun and Fataluku text setting, see Yampolsky 2022.

WORKS CITED

Anwar, Khaerul, and Samuel Oktora. 2011. "Eman Bata Dede: Mengangkat Gawi Jadi Lagu Pop Daerah." In *Ekspedisi Jejak Peradaban NTT: Laporan Jurnalistik Kompas*, edited by Atika Walujani Moedjiono, 210–13. Jakarta: Kompas.

Barendregt, Bart. 2002. "The Sound of 'Longing for Home': Redefining a Sense of Community through Minang Popular Music." *Bijdragen tot de Taal-, Land- en Volkenkunde* 158 (3): 411–50.

Barendregt, Bart, Peter Keppy, and Henk Schulte Nordholt. 2017. *Popular Music in Southeast Asia: Banal Beats, Muted Histories*. Amsterdam: Amsterdam University Press, 2017.

Fraser, Jennifer. 2013. "The Art of Grieving: West Sumatra's Worst Earthquake in Music Videos." *Ethnomusicology Forum* 22 (2): 129–59.

Gorlinski, Gini. 2016. "Kenyah *Kendau Kancet* Choral Singing of Indonesian and Malaysian Borneo: Reflections on a Triptych." In *Performing Indonesia*, edited by Andy McGraw and Sumarsam. Washington, DC: Freer & Sackler Galleries, Smithsonian Institution. https://asia.si.edu/essays/article-gorlinski/.

Kusno, Timoteus Anggawan. 2012. "Proses Produksi *VCD* Dangdut Lokal di Wilayah Pesisir Utara Jawa (Studi Kota Pati)." B.A. skripsi, Jurusan Ilmu Komunikasi, Fakultas Ilmu Sosial dan Politik. Yogyakarta: Gadjah Mada University.

Manuel, Peter, and Randal Baier. 1986. "Jaipongan: Indigenous Popular Music of West Java." *Asian Music* 18 (1): 91–110.

Suryadi. 2003. "Minangkabau Commercial Cassettes and the Cultural Impact of the Recording Industry in West Sumatra." *Asian Music* 34 (2): 51–89.

Suryadi. 2010. "The Impact of the West Sumatran Regional Recording Industry on Minangkabau Oral Literature." *Wacana: Jurnal Ilmu Pengetahuan Budaya* [Fakultas Ilmu Pengetahuan Budaya, Universitas Indonesia] 12 (1): 35–69.

Suryadinata, Leo, Evi Nurvidya Arifin, and Aris Ananta. 2003. *Indonesia's Population: Ethnicity and Religion in a Changing Political Landscape*. Singapore: Institute of Southeast Asian Studies.

Weintraub, Andrew N. 2010. *Dangdut Stories: A Social and Musical History of Indonesia's Most Popular Music*. New York: Oxford University Press.

Weintraub, Andrew N. 2011. "Morality and Its (Dis)contents: *Dangdut* and Islam in Indonesia." In *Divine Inspirations: Music and Islam in Indonesia*, edited by David D. Harnish and Anne K. Rasmussen, 318–36. New York: Oxford University Press.

Weintraub, Andrew N. 2013. "The Sound and Spectacle of *Dangdut Koplo*: Genre and Counter-Genre in East Java, Indonesia." *Asian Music* 44 (2): 160–94.

Widyastuti, Ika Maulid. 2011. "Keberadaan Paguyuban Campursari 'CJDW' sebagai Sarana Hiburan: Studi Kasus Paguyuban Campursari CJDW di Desa Mukiran Kecamatan Kaliwungu Kabupaten Semarang." Skripsi (sarjana). Semarang: Jurusan Sosiologi dan Antropologi, Fakultas Ilmu Sosial, Universitas Negeri Semarang.

Yampolsky, Philip. 2022. "Poetic Text and Melodic Text: Text-Setting in Two Song Traditions of Timor." *Asian Music* 53 (1): 80–126.

Part IV

SOUND BEYOND AND AS MUSIC

12

A RADICAL STORY OF NOISE MUSIC FROM INDONESIA

Dimitri della Faille and Cedrik Fermont

Noise music in and from Indonesia has recently been receiving shy but growing global exposure in specialized magazines and online resources and at art events. It is, without a doubt, the largest and most active scene in experimental extreme music in Southeast Asia. Emerging in the early 2000s, later than many of their European or North American counterparts, it is now, we dare to say, among the most stimulating and thriving noise scenes in the world. Understanding the trajectory and current characteristics of noise music in Indonesia is particularly interesting, not only because it contributes to the understanding of a little-documented art and music scene in the country but also because it can help compare and contrast with other local artistic practices.

In this chapter we propose to introduce the reader to some historical and social aspects relating to noise music in Indonesia. A book we published in 2016 contains a section expanding on that topic (Fermont and della Faille 2016, 83–97). Here, we would like to focus specifically on an outline of contemporary noise music in Indonesia by presenting some artists, organizations, and labels and also emphasizing commonalities between Indonesia and the rest of Southeast Asia as well as highlighting the unique characteristics of noise music in Indonesia. This chapter has a special emphasis on the harsh noise and the more academic or electroacoustic scenes, as we have found them to be interconnected despite differences in their aesthetics and organizational structures. As such, this research focuses mostly on individuals and collective actors making noise music possible rather than studying the audience or analyzing the aesthetics. However, this would be a totally different research that would undoubtedly garner fascinating results.

Research for this chapter is mostly based on our many conversations and observations and on the time spent with musicians from Indonesia, in the country and abroad. We have traveled to Indonesia on several occasions in the past fifteen years and have continuously interacted with the local noise communities. We also base our research on the collection and analysis of many documents (fanzines, blogs, music reviews, etc.), oral sources, and interviews.[1] In our research we are often confronted with the issue of the lack of archives. Most artists and organizations in Indonesia keep little documentation, either by design, by carelessness, or simply by lack of understanding the importance of it. Hopefully, pieces like this one can help foster better documentation practices, if it is something the art communities wish for.

As such, we are recounting a partial story of contemporary noise music in Indonesia, oriented toward two strong ideas. First, we are attempting to show that such art movements from Indonesia partake in the global history of art and music. They are not isolated cultural developments whose specificities would make them essentially, inherently, and exclusively Indonesian. We contend that because of ethnocentric storytelling, their significance is more often than not obliterated from global historical accounts of the development of arts and music. Second, we are attempting to emphasize the role of women in such developments. In Indonesia and elsewhere, women have little encouragement to participate in the artistic scenes. We contend that when they are active, their role is downplayed or even silenced. Our goal here is not to debate the "how" and "why" of these exclusion processes; our goal is to offer, when possible, detailed information that could foster counternarratives.

A Short Introduction to Noise Music

Let us begin with a short introduction to noise music as it relates to Indonesia. Noise music encompasses a wide variety of genres of music created by composers and experimentalists close to the European and North American academia and also from performance art, underground music, and avant-garde rock experiments. In this chapter, we are using "noise music" as a loose label to describe different sonic practices that may be considered "extreme" or at least unusual to the untrained ear.

One of its characteristics is its tendency to be transgressive and criticize social order or the status quo. Indeed, often, but certainly not always, noise music carries in its aesthetics a discourse critical of political, social, and economic institutions.

It is perhaps more visible for the harsher noise subgenres than it is for the more ambient incarnations of noise music. In Indonesia noise music is maybe less politicized than the punk, oi, and metal scenes. The noise community tends to be more focused on the performance itself, as artist Indra Menus told us in June 2019, "making noise just for the sake of loudness and aggressiveness." However, several noise projects from Indonesia have included subversive or political lyrics in their music, such as the artists Liwoth and Direct Action Group.[2] Even if the noise scenes do not react to social, political, or economic conditions in a direct political way, the sense of building and sharing together and the resourcefulness inside the community to organize tours, shows, workshops; share knowledge and education; and often find innovative approaches to producing its own tools to create noise music in spite of the economic adversities proves that there is a certain form of sociopolitical involvement inside the community.

As the practice of noise music in Indonesia demonstrates, there are various ways to perform and record noise music. The tools range from the most current digital tools to vintage analog or do-it-yourself (DIY) instruments. When performed digitally, noise music is using, for the most part, the same software for music composition and performances that are popular in other electronic music genres and elsewhere in the world. When performed analogically, many noise musicians are using mostly vintage and recent analog synthesizers to produce a rich and thick sound, or various types of microphones. Other noise musicians often use some of the equipment familiar to rock musicians such as mixers, guitar pedal effects, and guitar amplifiers. However, it is very common in the noise scenes to use this equipment in ways different than intended by the manufacturers or to build one's own instruments. Wukir Suryadi (Bambu Wukir of the band Senyawa from Java) is known to transform bamboo and agricultural tools into stringed instruments that can produce a wide range of high- and low-pitched sounds.[3] The Javanese collectives Lifepatch and House of Natural Fiber (see below) have produced sound art from biological material by using, for instance, molecular reactions to create sound.

Contemporary Classical and Electroacoustic Music

Part of the explanation for the specificities of noise music from Indonesia lies perhaps in the influential early experimentations in electronic music in the country. Indeed, among the countries of Southeast Asia, Indonesia has one of the most vibrant contemporary classical music scenes, with a pronounced experimentalist character. Though it only emerged relatively recently, in the 1970s, it grew quickly thanks to European, Japanese, and North American cultural influ-ences and cultural exchanges. Notable Indonesian contemporary composers like Slamet Abdul Sjukur (1935–2015), Harry Roesli (1951–2004), or Otto Sidharta (born in 1955) are among the musicians who have benefited from the largest global outreach, contributing to promoting contemporary music from Indone-sia abroad as well as strengthening a local community of contemporary musical research and performance.[4]

Many noise musicians in Indonesia have had various encounters with the aforementioned composers—or their students—and have been influenced by national contemporary classic or electroacoustic music. Beyond some obvious aesthetic resemblances, there are several intersections between the two scenes. We have encountered many noise artists citing contemporary classical or elec-troacoustic music as elements of references for the development of their aesthet-ics. We are under the impression that contemporary or electroacoustic music has provided exposure to unusual sounds and has generated enough curiosity. Perhaps, also, the reputation of such famous composers, with whom many have interacted, has provided more legitimacy for the otherwise "difficult" sound experimentations. But an understanding of contemporary noise music, as it emerged in Indonesia in the early 2000s, lies equally in the analysis of the more "popular" genres of metal and punk music.

The Current State of Noise Music in Indonesia

Let us outline briefly the social and material conditions of the emergence of noise music in Indonesia around 2000 as we understand them. During the 1990s, punk, oi, hardcore, and metal bands in Indonesia developed DIY networks similar to those already in place in many other parts of the world. Local bands started to release their own cassettes and magazines and to host independent concerts.[5] Interestingly, in Indonesia these music scenes were united beyond their aesthetic differences. To a large extent, they still are united against common enemies: pov-erty, corruption, police abuse, dictatorship, and capitalism praised by the regime. As far as we understand, it seems that those movements in the 1990s—at the end of *Orde Baru*, the "New Order," or the Suharto era—mostly emerged from the (often impoverished) youth and was facilitated by increased internet access. This is how cultural studies scholar Nuraini Juliastuti describes that era:

> This is the generation who were born in the glorious time of the New Order era and started their university life when *Reformasi*—the last few years of the 20th century, which saw the destruction of

the military-backed New Order—has already passed.... There is also the dynamic growth of personal websites, easily invented through blog technology. All these media activities indicate the strong need of the youth to showcase their personal things, and the new technology is a free way to express and do things. The new media has opened up explorations on freedom, which focus on ourselves—the youth. (Juliastuti 2006, 142)

The Indonesian government and local authorities did not seem to see that youth movement as a threat. This music was deemed to be entertainment for the masses. And this view probably facilitated the growth of punk and metal beyond major cities like Bandung, Jakarta, or Denpasar, and in small towns and villages in many parts of the archipelago. Huge concerts and festivals hosted foreign artists like Metallica (in 1993), Sonic Youth (1996), and Napalm Death (2004).[6]

Concurrently, one of the earliest noise bands to emerge in Indonesia is perhaps Hubologist. The project seems to have published a noise cassette in 1995, about which little is known outside a review in the punk fanzine from Bandung, Tigabelas, published by musician Arian13 (Arian Ariffin).[7] In 1998 Jeffray Arwadi of the metal bands Armageddon Holocaust and Kekal started an industrial and noise project called Worldhate. Some of their tracks were published on various international cassette compilations, among them *Tape Heads One—Tape Heads Stand Up*, published on famous American tape label Hal-Tapes. Worldhate published a cassette on the Slovakian tape label Black Orchid Productions in 2001.[8]

The early times of harsh noise music in Indonesia are subject to debates and some myths (Dunlea 2015). But it is documented and generally agreed that most developments in noise music from Indonesia have occurred after 2000 (Hardyanto 2013, 39–41). This is true for the noise music coming from the more popular scenes of metal and punk as well as those grounded in the more academic electroacoustic music and sound art. From the outbreak of noise music in Indonesia, punk, metal, and noise have been interconnected aesthetically and organizationally. And it also built on the distinct artistic influences and networks of electroacoustic music and sound art.

What we know about the reasons for the emergence of the Indonesian noise scenes is still a bit elusive; more extensive research needs to be done in order to fill the gaps. For what we understand, as surveyed in interviews with active members of the scenes, we comprehend that some musicians wanted to explore new paths and push social boundaries, due to their disappointment with the punk or metal scenes getting "too mainstream." For instance, British seminal hardcore band Napalm Death's Indonesian concerts have attracted more audience than North American pop superstar Avril Lavigne, to the point that the current president

Joko "Jokowi" Widodo is known to be a fan of Napalm Death and other extreme metal bands.[9] In that context it seems that some artists had been looking for means of engaging in more radical ways outside of capitalist business. If some bands looked at the roots of old-school punk music, others experimented with new sounds inspired by the punk ethics that allow anyone to pick up an instrument or microphone and perform. Noise musicians have pushed that freedom further. When one does not need to write a melody, noise is totally free, and it is not rare to see noise musicians creating their own instruments or tools to produce music.

Some musicians discovered noise music thanks to fanzines or file-sharing networks on the internet. For instance, Dirga, a noise musician active in the duo Shoah, explains in the *BISING* documentary film on noise in Indonesia that he discovered the seminal Japanese act Merzbow thanks to the defunct free peer-to-peer network Audiogalaxy, active between 1998 and 2002 (Rizaldi and Utama 2014). It appears that another peer-to-peer community, Soulseek, undoubtedly helped bring noise music to Indonesia, as it did all over the world.

If the alternative scenes connected to metal, grindcore, hardcore, and punk music substantially became the biggest in Asia if not the world, it is perhaps no surprise that in the past twenty years or so, the Indonesian noise communities have also become the most active in Southeast Asia.[10]

There is an understandable perceived dichotomy between the electroacoustic community and the DIY, noise, experimental, and free improvisation communities. But in Indonesia, the distance is not that great, and both communities are not isolated from one another. Beyond punk and metal, noise musicians come from a variety of backgrounds, including art school and academy graduate. Some have studied under the guidance of pioneers in academic and electroacoustic music. Artists like Kalimayat, Individual Distortion, To Die, Sodadosa (all from Yogyakarta), Bertanduk! (Jakarta), and Aneka Digital Safari (Bandung) are important acts who, among many others, laid the foundations of the Indonesian noise scene. They are also important musicians who are not afraid to cross boundaries and mix various genres. Some noise musicians in Indonesia are referring to Sonic Youth or Incapacitants or the feedback noise in garage rock such as mentioned by Wednes Mandra (Asangata, Bangkai Angsa) in the documentary film *BISING* (Rizaldi and Utama 2014)—the word *bising* means "noise" in Indonesian. Some others, like Gembira Putra Agam (Pemuda Elektrik/Sungsang Lebam Telak), mention modern music composer, experimentalist, and theorist John Cage in reference to why or how they compose noise music (Rizaldi and Utama 2014). More generally, noise musicians with a training in contemporary academic electronic or electroacoustic music are abundant.[11]

Diversity in the Profiles of Noise Musicians

The diversity of profiles of noise artists prevents us from establishing a typical path into noise music. Furthermore, we can perhaps think that the diversity of careers is a defining characteristic of noise in and from Indonesia. In this section, we are presenting some highlights in the career of four currently active artists who identify broadly with the genre. This section attempts to illustrate that noise music in Indonesia operates at the intersection of various artistic communities, from punk to metal and from sound art to academic music.

Indra Menus

Indra Menus (Martinus Indra Hermawan, born in 1982) is one of the most important figures in the Indonesian noise scene. He has been actively bridging local noise and experimental scenes with the punk scene.[12] He is certainly one of the artists who has successfully explored that connection while also maintaining contacts with academia. In a conversation we had with him in June 2019, he declared that there is a certain culture in Indonesia that allows bridging arts and academia, and that, as someone who is very active in the arts scene, he shares some of the research interest with academia. Active from Yogyakarta, Indra is a multifaceted person. He is involved at many levels of playing, distributing, or reflecting about noise music in Indonesia. Being part of the punk hardcore band To Die, founded as early as 1998, he has been active for over two decades. To Die is now run by Indra as a solo noise project with various influences from ambient drone to punk and more.

Indra is active in the seminal Jogja Noise Bombing (JNB) collective of harsh noise music created in 2009 (see below). He is also connected with the more academic music scenes and people like pioneer Otto Sidartha, who have opened doors for noise and experimental synth musicians. He has also maintained connections with Irfan R. Darajat, a prominent member of Kajian Musik LARAS, an academic group dedicated to research in sound.

Indra actively organizes tour and concerts. For instance, he now co-runs an underground collective booking agency, YK Booking, using a network of venues and contemporary art galleries in Yogyakarta. JNB, of which Indra is a founding member, has organized concerts in various styles of noise music. For instance, they have, on a couple of occasions, invited Patrick Gunawan Hartono (see below), who has an academic background. Indra is also behind Relamati Records, an independent label founded in 2002 that has been publishing extreme music on cassettes.

In various conversations we had with Indra, he mentioned that punk and noise attitudes are very similar. If the musical output is different, they share analogies in the DIY attitude, he claims. In 2015, in an effort to document and distribute noise music from Indonesia to a global audience, he released an anthology covering twenty years (1995–2015) of noise and experimental music.[13] It was first released as an eighteen-track compilation cassette on a label in New Zealand and was subsequently expended to a 123-audio track DVD.

Indra used to write for the Malaysian/Southeast Asian *Shock&Awe!* magazine focused on the DIY punk culture.[14] He is involved with the annual event Jogjakarta Zine Attack and has published various DIY music zines. Recently he wrote *Pekak! Skena Eksperimental Noise di Asia Tenggara dan Jepang* [Deaf! Experimental Noise Scenes in Southeast Asia and Japan] (Menus 2017), a book in which he documents his trips to other Asian countries and shares his subsequent reflections.

Patrick Gunawan Hartono

Patrick Gunawan Hartono (born in 1988) studied electronic music at the Pelita Harapan Conservatory of Music with Otto Sidartha, someone whom he considers a mentor. He is from the younger generation of experimental musicians with a strong academic background. He is one of the few Indonesian experimental composers who lives abroad.

Originally from Makassar in South Sulawesi, he is now based in the Netherlands. In 2007–8 he returned to Indonesia, where he studied at the Institut Seni Indonesia (Indonesian Institute of the Arts, ISI) before studying electronic music composition at the Institute of Sonology (Netherlands), IRCAM (France), and Sonic Arts at Goldsmiths University (United Kingdom).

Patrick is actively bridging the noisier experimental music with academia. In a conversation we had in June 2019, he told us that beyond differences in approach with that of JNB, for instance, he is also an active promoter of noise music. But his approach to noise music is strongly rooted in electroacoustic and acousmatic experimentations. And for that matter, even if he does not often collaborate with the DIY and harsh noise scenes, he is well acquainted with them. He sometimes shares the stage with them at events or festivals and has served as a technical adviser.

Patrick has a strong interest in sound spatialization, the technique of locating sounds via various audio channels.[15] He is also known for his use of the generative software technique known as granular synthesis, which creates grain and makes various noises seem like they collide in cascades of pitches and fast variations of speed.

Vincensius Christiawan

Vincensius Christiawan (born in 1975), or Venzha Christ, is a sound artist who also creates noise and other forms of electronic music under the name Electrocore

(Lysloff 2016, 491–94). Trained as a designer, he is known for his field recordings, sound art, and technological experimentations. He has extensively performed and researched internationally. During residences in Europe, North America, the Middle East, and across Asia, he has explored ways to relate space science and exploration with new media art. For instance, in 2018, as an artist, he participated in a simulation of life on Mars in the Utah desert (Maharani 2018). His participation as an artist results from common interests expressed by people from the scientific project Mars Society after their visit at the ARTjog, Yogyakarta's art fair in 2016. In 2013 a project called Area 51 interpreted sounds recorded with an ultrasonic frequency receiver around the infamous US Air Force base. With his 2016 project "Indonesia Space Science Society," Venzha has worked with various scientists and engineers to achieve an art installation that translates visually and audibly signals from space.

A pioneer in Indonesia, he started to focus on the field of new media art in 1999, through the House of Natural Fiber (HONF), a new media art laboratory he cofounded with Irene "Ira" Agrivina, Istasius "Itaz," and Tommy "Imot" Surya (Jurriëns 2013, 51). HONF includes people from various backgrounds: interior design, experimental music, fashion design, poetry, and VJing.[16] With its longevity, this collective project is said to have played an important role in the sustainability of new media art in Indonesia (Jurriëns 2016).

Around the year 2000, with new media artist Jompet Kuswidananto, Venzha cofounded the short-lived experimental music group Garden of the Blind. They are known to have used found objects, bicycles, repurposed musical instruments, and various technologies in their harsh sonic live performances.

Venzha is the founder of the Education Focus Program (EFP), which builds connections and interactions between the local creative community, researchers, and artists. He aims to create more connections between academia and the music scenes, especially when it comes to using technology in experimental ways. For instance, with his project Electrocore, Venzha reinterprets radio waves and sonic environments through the use of medical devices.

He is also director of Yogyakarta International Videowork Festival (YIVF) and Cellsbutton, a yearly international festival of media arts held in Yogyakarta since 2007.

Gema Swaratyagita

Gema Swaratyagita (born in 1984) is a contemporary classical and electroacoustic music composer. Originally from Jakarta but living in Surabaya, she got her undergraduate and graduate education in literature, arts, and cultural education at various institutions in Surabaya. She has been selected at various national competitions, including earning a fellowship from the Empowering Women Artists program in 2012 and 2013 and a fellowship of the Kelola Foundation Art Grants program in 2018. She performs and presents her compositions internationally.

Among various musicians and composers with whom she has studied, she has received education from Slamet Abdul Sjukur (Rosalia 2020). She is the director of the not-for-profit organization Pertemuan Musik Surabaya, founded by Sujkur in 1957. With activities in Surabaya, Jakarta, and Pekanbaru, Pertemuan Musik holds discussions, community meetings, and workshops on a variety of genres of contemporary music.

A trained pianist, she also experiments with voice and gamelan. For her composition work, she was selected to compose for the prestigious German chamber group Ensemble Modern, for which she provided a contemporary piece for voice, ensemble, and *suling*, an Indonesian bamboo flute, which was premiered in 2015 for the Indonesia Lab in Frankfurt.[17] In her experimentations she is known for her soundscapes, a genre of contemporary music often associated with the more academic noise music, as well as her sound collages.[18] In 2012 she collaborated with Dutch sonologist Piet Hein van de Poel on the City Soundscapes project.

Gema has a varied professional career; on top of directing Pertemuan Musik, she is a music teacher at the Sjuman School of Music and a radio journalist. She is a very active organizer who collaborates beyond genre boundaries with a variety of artists and musicians, including Otto Sidharta, Indra Menus, and Patrick Gunawan Hartono.

Organizations and Events

One's understanding of noise music in and from Indonesia would only be partial if solely focused on individual trajectories. Indeed, a defining characteristic of the genre in Indonesia lies perhaps in the fact that it is a highly collaborative and collective art scene. We have noticed a unique culture of sharing and being together. Here are some examples of the work of the several organizations, venues, and events that make noise music in Indonesia possible.

Jogja Noise Bombing (JNB) is a collective created in 2009 that organizes mostly noise and harsh noise public invasive shows, some in spaces like parks and streets (Menus and Stellfox 2019). They differentiate themselves from *pengamen* (itinerant street musicians) who do it for a living. JNB musicians enjoy creating noise performances without being limited by space, money, and permits.

In a feature article on the collective, musician and journalist Gisela Swaragita describes the beginnings of JNB as follows.

> Tired of playing noise sets at punk and metal shows, they wanted to play at shows dedicated to noise music. The cost of putting on shows was prohibitive, however, especially since noise wasn't popular enough to draw paying crowds. So they decided to take the noise out on the streets and use public locations as their venues.
>
> And so, on a sunny afternoon in early 2010, seven of these kids dragged their equipment out onto the streets and played all across town, hitting up locations such as the front yard of a public live house, a street intersection and a university gym. (Swaragita 2016)

This sometimes leads to outstanding situations including their 2013 performance at the Taman Kuliner, an outdoor food court and park in central Yogyakarta. During that performance a dumbstruck and eventually annoyed security guard interfered to put an end to the event.[19] JNB also gives noise concerts in unusual places like restaurants and bars, not always accustomed to this kind of sonic violence. The group runs a one-week event whose goal is to introduce their activities to the public: noise actions, basic synthesizer-building workshops, and Pure Data software programming. People who have been involved with JNB include Indra Menus, Arie Bowo, Krisna Widiatham, Woro, Adit, Akbar, Hilman, Wednes Mandra, Rio Nurkholis, Yogi, and Pandu Hidayat.

Lifepatch is a citizen collective project based in Yogyakarta. It has about a dozen active members, including Agus Tri Budiarto, Andreas Siagian, Adhari Donora, and Ferial Afiff, some of whom are former members of HONF. It also has a couple of active female members. It operates in various fields of sound and digital arts, from creating a sound generator called Atari Punk Console Tiger 0.1 to biological art, hacking, and environmental and other scientific projects.[20] For many years they have been active internationally, mostly in Europe and Japan (Fong 2017). In 2014 they received an honorary mention at the prestigious Prix Ars Electronica.

Created in 1988 as an exhibition event, Biennale Jogja has now become one of the most important events dedicated to visual art in Indonesia. The Biennale also present concerts, audiovisual installations, and dance performances. During its three decades of existence, Biennale Jogja set up many other events connected to the sound art and experimental scene, including the extreme experimental music of Senyawa.

New events that attempt to integrate artists from Southeast Asia at the regional level have been emerging. In October 2018 the inauguration of Nunasonic took place in Yogyakarta.[21] Nunasonic is a collaborative project involving Yes No Klub (Yogyakarta), WSK Festival of the Recently Possible (Manila), Playfreely/Black-Kaji (Singapore), and CTM Festival for Adventurous Music and Art (Berlin). Following the kickoff in Yogyakarta and supported by the German Goethe Institute, Nusasonic has taken different shapes and formats. It has visited Manila for the WSK Festival in 2019 and Singapore for the BlackKaji festival the same year. It has facilitated a focus on Indonesia and Southeast Asia at the Berlin CTM festival in 2019 and 2020.

Labels

A lot of music enthusiasts in Indonesia use the internet to listen to or discover music, as many cannot afford imported recordings or manage the complex logistics of importing physical media. Before having access to internet resources, Indonesian alternative artists had been publishing on cassette tape and CD-R for the most part. A very limited number of labels had printed music on CD and vinyl. Today, internet-based distribution through sites such as Archive.org, Bandcamp, Soundclick, or Soundcloud makes it easier to access and release music. This also creates a convergence between the release and additional information about activities and scene building (Putra and Irwansyah 2020). Before the growth of Bandcamp, currently the most popular internet-based platform to release Indonesian music, Archive.org was popular, and to this day countless hours of noise music from Indonesian labels and artists are still available on that platform.[22] There are lots of labels in Indonesia who publish and/or distribute noise and experimental music; some are exclusively dedicated to this genre, while others are more eclectic. They are often based online but also sometimes produce and distribute CD-R and tapes.[23]

Sharing and the sense of community are parts of culture in Indonesia as clearly reflected in the way labels, organizers, and artists work. Observing the scene, one can easily notice how collaborations are part of the daily activities of artists and labels. The noise music communities are built on ideas of sharing, gifts, donations, and helping each other. The ideas of *koneksi* (connection, or access to a network of people) and *kolaborasi* (collaboration) seem to be driving methods of production in the music scenes (Juliastuti 2018, 97). Based on such material and social interconnection, a collective movement of Indonesian netlabels called the Indonesian Netlabel Union emerged in Surabaya in 2012.[24] One of the objectives of this union is to propagate an understanding of fair use and free culture. Anitha Silvia is an administrator of the Indonesian Netlabel Union and a cultural activist who also works at the c2o Library, a small media library and collaborative space in Surabaya. Founded in 2008 by Kathleen Azali, c2o is also a venue for performance art.

Based in Yogyakarta, Yes No Wave Music is one of the most important Indonesian netlabels in the genre. It has been active since 2007 and is run by Wok the Rock, Bagus Jalang, and Adya Mahardhika. Their catalog includes artists from various alternative scenes from folk to punk hardcore, noise, black metal, and so on. Since 2010 the collective has been organizing monthly events where local and international artists can perform diverse genres of music, including techno, noise, surf rock, hip hop, and punk.

Women and Noise Music in Indonesia

We regret that the Indonesian noise scene is not as diverse in gender representation as in some other countries in Southeast Asia.[25] In an online 2020 interview, Sabrina from the collective Sarana declares, "Even if noise comes to existence as a response to the phallocentric idea of the lead-guitarist (one male with his big phallus on the stage showing his virtuosity), there are some elements in noise that remained quite patriarchal" (von Rosa 2020). For instance, women are still very much a minority in the community. Indonesia is a very patriarchal society, and even though the situation of women is improving, the place of women in the Indonesian arts scene does not equal that of men. In order to explain the situation of women in contemporary Indonesian noise music, it would be difficult to separate cultural influences from religious influences. If religion can be an explanatory factor, there are also cultural elements that prevail to explain the current situation, which is not unique to noise music. Indeed, as far as we understand, the situation is or has been similar in the punk and metal scenes.

In an interview in January 2021, Rega, a female musician, told us that traditionally, Indonesia has different understandings of gender identities.[26] She regrets that throughout its modern history, Indonesia has developed a binary gender hierarchy, based in part on conservative Muslim interpretations. According to her, this created unhealthy standards for women and a toxic masculinity that is visible at events where sexual harassment is a reality. In an interview in January 2021, Dea, another female musician, told us that because of the patriarchal structure of society, women feel that they are neither heard nor supported when they want to denounce harassment. In this case, women tend to leave the community and pursue other activities. Dea tells us that what makes the noise community interesting is the touring and bonding activities, which often happen at night. Women do not want to send a signal of sexual promiscuity, she says, and therefore they keep missing out on connecting opportunities for their own protection. Recently, however, women in the underground music scene in Indonesia have taken to social media to denounce harassment, as reported by Rega.

The punk and metal scenes, which have been around longer than the noise scene, have seen a remarkable shift since their first male-dominated concerts of the 1990s. As we have observed, today's noise concerts are clearly more mixed in gender, and extreme music scenes are aware of gender issues. This led to workshops and events such as the Lady Fast 2016, a festival of punk music, art, and discussions for people in Indonesia who identify as women. This festival was unfortunately interrupted by hard-line Islamists and the police (Unite Asia 2016). The problem of gender equality has also been raised inside the noise community, which acknowledges the work of some female composers and organizers who wish to increase the presence of women beyond members of the audience. As we showed, the situation of women in the noise scene in Indonesia may or may not be a result of religious patriarchy. But, as Dea points out, there are other explanations beyond Indonesia's culture, religion, and social fabric. She regrets that historically there is no female role model in the global noise community to look up to.

Currently in Indonesia female artists such as Dyah "Woro" Isaka Parameswara (Menstrual Synthdrone) or Rega Ayundya Putri (of the noise duo Mati Gabah Jasus) are getting more visibility. The collective Sarana (Anissa Maharani, Istanara Julia Saputri, Sabrina Eka Felisiana) has been the first all-female collective performing noise in Indonesia, starting their activities in 2015. They are also behind the Samarinda Noise Fest, the first international noise festival ever to happen in Samarinda, Kalimantan. In 2017 artists from across Indonesia, Singapore, and the United States converged on the festival.[27] In 2018 members of Sarana were involved in Sonic Wilderness, a program initiated by European artist Antye Greie-Ripatti (AGF) during the Nusasonic festival, which emphasizes interaction and collaboration, and explores any sound that can be found in nature or various public places. But as Dea told us in January 2021, there is an understandable fear among female artists that they would only serve as tokens of superficial integration to appeal to international feminist movements. She fears that the feeling of tokenism—a disingenuous promotion geared toward international funders, organizers, and festivals—could negatively affect the participation of women in noise music in Indonesia.

Indonesia as an Integral and Exceptional Part of Southeast Asia

In this chapter we wanted to outline how Indonesia partakes in a global artistic movement, as an equal member, no different than most countries outside Southeast Asia. Even if the Indonesian noise communities are by far the largest in the region, we have noticed several traits in common with the rest of Southeast Asia. For that reason, we affirm that noise music in Indonesia is part of a global movement that was not born in the region, a movement that transcends, for the most part, local cultural specificities. Most of the influence of the aesthetics and the organization of the noise scenes from Indonesia originates in Europe and the United States. As with many countries in the region, the influence of Australia and Japan is also heavily felt. It would be a bit presumptuous to be able to identify Indonesian noise music based solely on aesthetic criteria. At the same time, it would be incorrect to state that noise music contributes to the "Westernization" of Southeast Asian culture. Indeed, the influence of Japan noise music is very important in Indonesia and the rest of Southeast Asia. Some artists there also choose to integrate identifiable national cultural markers. The sense of territorial belonging is strong in noise music in Indonesia and in other countries of the region.

Another common trait shared with the rest of Southeast Asia is the minimal connection and firsthand experience artists from Indonesia have with the rest of the region. This was particularly true early on in our research in Indonesia. Until a couple of years ago, most of the artists in Indonesia had little if any contact with other countries in Southeast Asia. When they traveled abroad to perform or connect with other artists, they would go to Australia, Europe, Japan, or, to a lesser extent, the United States. Since around 2015–16, contacts and travel between Indonesia and Southeast Asia have increased due to several factors. First, the Japan Foundation has helped supporting artists, organizers, and curators in and around the region (Lippit 2016; Menus 2017).[28] Second, a general economic growth in most countries of Southeast Asia has raised disposable income and further integrated Southeast Asian societies through a globalized economy.

Another factor contributing to recent changes is perhaps the wide online circulation of ideas and information and the development of English reading proficiency. If artists and music aficionados in Indonesia had access to shared files on peer-to-peer networks, now blogs and platforms such as Facebook help build a stronger understanding of the social context of that music and better knowledge of its trajectory at the global and regional levels. On top of the widespread availability of electronic communications through Facebook, Whatsapp, and LINE, we have also noticed that the increase of regional artistic connections is facilitated by more affordable and more efficient air travel between countries in Southeast Asia.

Acknowledging the participation of Indonesia in a global artistic movement does not negate any specificities. Indeed, the noise communities from Indonesia have distinctive characteristics setting them apart from communities in other countries in the region and perhaps at the global level.[29]

Self-Built and Local Instruments

Indonesia is a unique case in Southeast Asia, where many independent noise musicians build their instruments or buy locally produced electronic gear. One of the reasons is economic; many local musicians cannot afford imported electronic gear. About 11 percent of the population lives under the poverty line, but the gap between rich and poor people can be enormous, especially in rural areas where almost half of the population still lives (World Bank 2016). Additionally, we can say that DIY hacking, circuit bending, and instrument building allow for certain social ethics that resonate with some cultural traits of Indonesia, such as collaboration (*kolaborasi*).[30] Some independent instrument makers from various cities (Bandung, Surabaya, Depok, or Yogyakarta) produce their own low-cost DIY synthesizers, sound generators, and effects.[31] Workshops are being given as well as concerts organized by the DIY electronic music community (Sarahtika and Muchtar 2018). It has to be noted that those synthesizers are greatly used by noise musicians (Szumer 2015). Until recently, the DIY electronic music gear community had its own blog, titled Synthesia.id, run by Lintang Radittya (under the alias Kenalirangkai Pakai).[32] The blog contained plenty of references to synthesizers and workshop announcements. Most of that has now moved to Facebook.

Territoriality

All over Java, and now more than ever on other islands, various organizations, events, or festivals are facilitating noise and experimental music. Contrary to what anthropologist Brent Luvaas (2009) observed about indie pop in Indonesia, noise music is very territorialized and identifies as such. Artists, bands, labels, and organizations claim their connection with the territory, either their cities or their larger area. While creating links with global music communities, they remain very conscious and affirmative of their territorial origins with a sense of *terroir*.

Recently we have noticed increased connection between cities and islands in Indonesia through national tours. Artists from Indonesia are traveling more inside the country, and at the same time, we see increased numbers of foreign artists traveling and touring in Indonesia, a phenomenon almost unheard of only just a few years ago. Organizations such as Biennale Jojga, HONF, and the recent Nusasonic festival have contributed to building international connections between the country and the rest of the world. If Yogyakarta seems a cultural hub in Indonesia, it is clearly not the only city with a vibrant noise and art scene. The capital Jakarta and Bandung also host vivid scenes and a great number of concerts.

In addition to some of the aforementioned groups, we can name organizations and events active throughout Indonesia such as Kolektif Hysteria and their Kotak Listrik events (Semarang), Electrowork (Surabaya), Main-Main Musik (Surakarta), Jakarta Noise Fest (Jakarta), Bukan Musik Bukan Seni Rupa (Yogyakarta), More Brutality Less Harmony (Bandung), RRRec Fest (Sukabumi), and Yogyakarta Contemporary Music Festival (Yogyakarta). There are noise musicians and concerts in Java, Bali, Kalimantan, Sulawesi, and Sumatra.[33] In our observations, we have not seen other countries in Southeast Asia with a noise community so well distributed over the whole country. Considering the fragmented nature of the Indonesian territory and the variety of local cultures and languages, this is unique in the region.

Relation to the City

Jogja Noise Bombing (JNB) and Melawan Kebisingan Kota are two initiatives unique to Indonesia. They are groups of people who are taking over public space to perform, without permits, noise music in an occupied space. It requires a public administration that is open to "unruly" acts and a relatively transparent application of municipal bylaw through law enforcement as well as a population that is generally open to nonconventional artistic expressions. This is the case for most cities in Western and Central Java. The concept developed by JNB in 2009 has not fallen on deaf ears and is slowly spreading to other parts of the country. Melawan Kebisingan Kota (literally, "Against City Noise") in Surabaya has been active since 2012, doing street noise performances, workshops to build noise and experimental instruments, and concerts. Another collective based in Kalimantan, Samarinda Noise Bombing, is now also offering similar events.

JNB created a buzz in the music scene when they were featured in an article in the Indonesian edition of *Rolling Stone* magazine (Triantoro 2016). Annamira Sophia Latuconsina wrote her undergraduate thesis in ethnomusicology about them (2014). Their concept even reached the Philippines, where Noisebath PH organized Dead Nation Noise Bombing in the Tarlac city of Luzon. But initiatives like that remain largely unheard of elsewhere in Southeast Asia.

Social Class

In Indonesia we have observed a social phenomenon almost unique in Southeast Asia. Underground cultures in Indonesia also tend to be cross-class cultures. This is something also observed by anthropologist Sean Martin-Iverson in his study of the underground music youth in Bandung in the 2000s (Martin-Iverson 2012). The noise scenes or communities not only tend to erase some social and gender-specific issues but also appear to distance themselves from strongly codified popular audio cultures, for example, *pop Indonesia* (mostly favored by the middle to upper classes) and *pop melankolis* and *dangdut* (mostly favored by "lower" social classes) (Wallach 2008, 73–74). From our observations and interviews, it seems that artists, organizers, and fans in the noise music scenes of Indonesia represent a wide variety of social classes. According to our observations, they are probably the most socioeconomically diverse communities in Southeast Asia.

Musicians from Indonesia have regrettably been little documented, even if their scenes are some of the largest and most active in the world. While women in these communities are faced with some challenges and their participation has been discreet until recently, there are some initiatives to facilitate some changes. Artists from Indonesia have been increasingly traveling abroad and also exposed to other communities in Southeast Asia.

Looking at the various noise communities in Indonesia allows us to examine both the artists' agency and the diverse influences unique to the social fabric of Indonesia. The noise music communities from Indonesia have a relatively recent history emerging mostly after 2000; in many instances they began in relative isolation from each other. But it was never a spontaneous phenomenon that happened by chance in various places of the country. Noise musicians are building on the heritage of national academic music, global noise, and art rock. The emergence and strengthening of noise music are also a reaction to the perceived mainstreaming of the punk and metal scenes specific to Indonesia. As a social organization, it is influenced by the many years of scene building from the said extreme music scenes and has also benefited from the work of seminal contemporary art music composers. The noise music scenes in Indonesia are uniquely defined by their refusal to be pigeonholed, marked by hybrid or fluid aesthetics and organizational cross-overs. They are also characterized by their culture of collaboration and sharing.

It is our belief that the global history of noise music remains incomplete as long as it does not mainstream such art movements as they exist in Southeast Asia, and Indonesian artists are some of the foremost contributors to the diversity and current dynamism of the genre at the global level.

NOTES

1. Over the years, since we first visited Indonesia in 2004, we have discussed the Indonesian noise music scenes with Annisa Maharani, Dholy Husada, Gema Swaratyagita, Ika Vantiani, Indra Menus, Julian "Togar" Abraham, Riar Rizaldi, Ricky Ravasia, Rully Shabara, Theo Nugraha, Woto "Wok the Rock" Wibowo, and Wukir Suryadi, to name only

but a few. This does not include some of the artists mentioned in this chapter, nor many of the artists and organizers with whom we have shared a stage, a meal, and accommodations in Indonesia or elsewhere. For more information about our backgrounds, intentions, and *modus operandi*, see Nawfal 2020.

2. See for instance, Liwoth's 2010 performance "Next Trash," featuring Asangata, in which a male performer is dressed up as a female Muslim wearing a full-coverage *jilbab*: https://youtu.be/3WNscylAI30; or Direct Action Group's 2009 performance "Live," where the performance is centered around a criticism of mass media communication: https://youtu.be/MiFF5iHeVnE. See also the interview with Ican Harem from Liwoth in Rizaldi and Utama's 2014 documentary film *BISING*.

3. For more information on Wukir Suryadi and his band Senyawa, see Novak 2018.

4. For more information on Sjukur and Sidharta and the history of *musik kontemporer*, see Miller 2014. For a profile of Harry Roesli, see Tyson 2011.

5. See Baulch 2007 for a study of such networks in Bali, and Luvaas 2012 for a similar phenomenon in indie scenes.

6. For a discussion of such concerts, including the riot surrounding Metallica's 1993 concert at the Lebak Bulus Stadium, south of the capital Jakarta, which resulted in about a hundred people being arrested and about that many being hurt, see Baulch 2007, chap. 1.

7. For more information on Tigabelas, sometimes also spelled Tiga Belas, see Prasetyo 2017, 208–9.

8. Around 1999–2000, a noise musician from Indonesia sent us a CD-R demo in our capacity as a record label manager, which sadly we misplaced, and along with it any subsequent information about the artist.

9. President Joko Widodo's interest in heavy metal has been widely documented in mainstream media. For more details, including pictures of him in metal T-shirts, see Bachelard 2014.

10. On the regional and global significance of the metal and punk scenes in Indonesia, see Darmawan 2019; Lawson 2020; Munn 2014; Tedjasukmana 2007; Warner 2014.

11. Some of the artists with training in academic or electroacoustic music that are involved with the contemporary noise and experimental scenes are Patrick Gunawan Hartono, Philemon Mukarno, Gema Swaratyagita, Verita Shalavita Koapaha, and Andreas Arianto Yanuar.

12. For one example of Indra Menus's work, see the 2017 concert at https://youtu.be/CwNp1A2RB_c. In the background is a banner signaling opposition to the controversial new Yogyakarta International Airport (NYIA).

13. The compilation is available for online streaming at https://endofthealphabetrecords.bandcamp.com/album/pekak-indonesian-noise-1995-2015-20-years-of-experimental-music-from-indonesia.

14. The magazine was published between 2010 and 2015. There are no online archives for the articles, but more information about the fanzine can be found at https://shockawemedia.wordpress.com/.

15. For an example of how Hartono uses grain, sound generation, and spatialization, see https://youtu.be/De3GL2_5Xkk.

16. For a sense of HONF and its goals, see the video of a presentation by Venzha at the Innovative City Forum in Japan in 2015, an event supported by the Japan Foundation: https://youtu.be/E4GqETiVagk.

17. The following video presents one of Swaratyagita's composition "Da-Dha-Dah," performed by Ensemble Modern in Amsterdam, Netherlands, in 2015: https://youtu.be/8OS9mwQNpqQ.

18. For an example of Swaratyagita's involvement with the sonic art and performance scenes, see a video of her collaboration performance in Surabaya in 2015: https://youtu.be/MmBXZEjS2qs.

19. The interaction between performing artists during a 2013 event at a park and a member of the security team has been documented here: https://youtu.be/W7gmsB-HoUKs. This had no consequences for the performers other than amusement. The news of the unfortunate event quickly went viral online.

20. For an overview of Lifepatch's hacking workshops, see this video presenting their work in Medellín, Colombia, in 2018: https://youtu.be/AUkpsAwhMNE.

21. The first event in the Nunasonic series assembled "43 artists from Thailand, Singapore, the Philippines, Malaysia, and Indonesia" in "a multi-day lab where new artist pairings, a hacklab, and a sonic wilderness group play together and create new musical works, ideas, and possibilities." For the full description see https://www.goethe.de/prj/nus/en/art/niy.html.

22. See, for instance, music released by the netlabel Mindblasting on Archive.org: https://mindblasting.wordpress.com/.

23. Some of the most prominent netlabels are Death Tiwikrama Productions, Mindblasting Netlabel, Spasm Records, Ear Alert Records, and Relamati Records.

24. See http://web.archive.org/web/20210301192614/http://indonesiannetlabelunion.net/.

25 Despite historical recognition of gender diversity and nonbinary/trans identities in Indonesia, the presence of individuals who identify as such is not evident in the Indonesian noise circuit. Some trans or gender-nonconforming artists are visible in other Southeast Asian countries. This does not necessarily indicate a lack of such artists in Indonesia, only that we have not yet interacted with any individual who publicly identifies as such.

26. Here, Rega refers to Javanese *reog*, a pre-Islamic traditional dance performance that transcends the gender binary and male-female normative sexuality.

27. A video compilation of the performances by the most notable acts at the Samardina Noise Fest 2017 is available here: https://youtu.be/I1BJv2tDWGY.

28. The Japan Foundation is a soft power extension of Japan's foreign policy. Several projects supported by the foundation have heightened the integration of noise musicians from Indonesia in Southeast Asia: the Asian Music Festival (2014–17), which gathered artists from Japan and East/Southeast Asia; a pan-Asian research project titled Asian Sounds Research (2014–16), under the coordination of Japanese experimental musician Sachiko M; and a fellowship program allowing artists to take arts residences throughout Southeast Asia. Indra Menus is a former fellow of that program.

29. For more context about the DIY and academic noise music scenes in Southeast Asia, see Fermont and della Faille 2016; for a comparison between Southeast Asia and East Asia with an emphasis on sound art, see Fermont and della Faille 2020.

30. DIY instruments and hacking are seldom found in punk and metal scenes, and are seemingly unique to noise music. Sarah Benhaïm, in her 2019 survey of the DIY (European) noise scene, sees it as embedded in nonhierarchical social models and criticism of education and economics, allowing for very local modes of action. We believe that her findings apply to the Indonesian DIY noise scene.

31. Kenalirangkaipakai (KRP), Störn, Vascolabs, SURA, Uncle Twist, METH, VCONT, and Adios are some noticeable examples.

32. The following websites contain some archives of that blog: http://synthesia-ind.blogspot.com/, https://synthesiaid.wordpress.com/, and http://kenalirangkaipakai.blogspot.com/.

33. Chaos Non Musica is a noise and experimental music festival from Bali. Grintabachan and Insitu Recordings are record labels also from the island. In Kalimantan, the Samarinda Noise Fest is a relevant festival and Hirang a notable record label. Some artists from Kalimantan include Nugraha, Sarana, Sabrina, Bent, Jeliwan Tok Hudoq, Jeritan, Melpomene At Orgasms, and Atmospheric Iqbal. The Frozen Grapes label is active from Sulawesi. Some artists from the same region include Busukyangbernanah and Satan Loves Nintendo. Some artists active from Sumatra include Artmosf, Microtron Sumatra, Semestha, and Wan Is The Bastard.

WORKS CITED

Bachelard, Michael. 2014. "Indonesia's Likely New President Joko Is a Megadeth Fan but This Is No Cause for Alarm." *Sydney Morning Herald*, July 9. https://www. smh.com.au/world/indonesias-likely-new-president-joko-is-a-megadeth-fan-but-this-is-no-cause-for-alarm-20140710-zt1r7.html.

Baulch, Emma. 2007. *Making Scenes: Reggae, Punk, and Death Metal in 1990s Bali*. Durham, NC: Duke University Press.

Benhaïm, Sarah. 2019. "DIY et hacking dans la musique noise. Une expérimentation bricoleuse du dispositif de jeu." *Volume!* 16 (1): 17–35.

Darmawan, Hikmat. 2019. "Indonesia, the World's Metal Nation." Indonesia National Book Committee. http://web.archive.org/web/20210421192129/ islandsofimagination.id/web/articles/indonesia-world%E2%80%99s-metal-nation. Accessed 5 February 2021.

Dunlea, Reed. 2015. "Look into Indonesia's Insane Noise Scene." *Noisey*, July 20. https://www.vice.com/en/article/rze3k9/indonesias-insane-noise-scene.

Fermont, Cedrik, and Dimitri della Faille. 2016. *Not Your World Music: Noise in South East Asia*. Berlin: Syrphe / Ottawa: Hushush.

Fermont, Cedrik, and Dimitri della Faille. 2020. "Sound Art in East and Southeast Asia: Historical and Political Considerations." In *The Bloomsbury Handbook of Sound Art*, edited by Sanne Krogh Groth and Holger Schulze, 175–83. London: Bloomsbury.

Fong, Cherise. 2017. "Lifepatch, the Indonesian Lab That Rejects the Maker Label." *Makery*, March 7. https://www.makery.info/en/2017/03/07/ lifepatch-le-lab-indonesien-qui-refuse-letiquette-maker/.

Hardyanto, Deswin. 2013. "Ekspresi Personal Krisna 'Sodadosa' dalam Membangun Citra Estetikmusik." Undergraduate thesis, Etnomusikologi Fakultas, Institut Seni Indonesia Surakarta.

Juliastuti, Nuraini. 2006. "Whatever I Want: Media and Youth in Indonesia Before and After 1998." *Inter-Asia Cultural Studies* 7 (1): 139–43.

Juliastuti, Nuraini. 2018. "Limits of Sharing and Materialization of Support: Indonesian Net Label Union." *Inter-Asia Cultural Studies* 19 (1): 87–102.

Jurriëns, Edwin. 2013. "Between Utopia and Real World." *Indonesia and the Malay World* 41 (119): 48–75.

Jurriëns, Edwin. 2016. "The Rise of Indonesian Digital Art: Indonesia's Avant-Garde New Media Art." Asia and the Pacific Policy Society Policy Forum, April 28. http://www.policyforum.net/rise-indonesian-digital-art/.

Latuconsina, Annamira Sophia. 2014. "Jogja Noise Bombing: Komunitas Experimental-Noise di Jogjakarta." Undergraduate thesis, Etnomusikologi Fakultas, Institut Seni Indonesia Yogyakarta.

Lawson, Dom. 2020. "How Indonesia Built the World's Most Exciting Underground Metal Scene." *Metal Hammer*, July 2. https://www.loudersound.com/features/ how-indonesia-has-built-the-worlds-most-exciting-underground-metal-scene.

Lippit, Takuro Mizuta. 2016. "Ensembles Asia: Mapping Experimental Practices in Music in Asia." *Organised Sound* 21 (1): 72–82.

Luvaas, Brent. 2009. "Dislocating Sounds: The Deterritorialization of Indonesian Indie Pop." *Cultural Anthropology* 24 (2): 246–79.

Luvaas, Brent. 2012. *DIY Style: Fashion, Music and Global Digital Cultures*. London: Berg.

Lysloff, René T. A. 2016. "Worlding Music in Jogjakarta: Tales of the Global Postmodern." *Ethnomusicology* 60 (3): 484–507.

Maharani, Shinta. 2018. "10 Pertanyaan Buat Satu-Satunya Orang Indonesia yang Ikut Simulasi Hidup di Mars." *Vice Indonesia*, September 7. https://www.vice.com/id/ article/9kv9ap/10-pertanyaan-buat-satu-satunya-orang-indonesia-yang-ikut- simulasi-hidup-di-mars.

Martin-Iverson, Sean. 2012. "Autonomous Youth? Independence and Precariousness in the Indonesian Underground Music Scene." *Asia Pacific Journal of Anthropology* 13 (4): 382–97.

Menus, Indra. 2017. *Pekak! Skena Eksperimental Noise di Asia Tenggara dan Jepang.* Yogyakarta: Warning Books.

Menus, Indra, and Sean Stellfox. 2019. *Jogja Noise Bombing: From the Street to the Stage*. Yogyakarta: Warning Books.

Miller, Christopher J. 2014. "Cosmopolitan, Nativist, Eclectic: Cultural Dynamics in Indonesian Musik Kontemporer." PhD diss., Wesleyan University.

Munn, Karli Kk. 2014. "Indonesia's Radical Underground Punk Scene." *Radio National*, November 28. https://www.abc.net.au/radionational/programs/archived/360/ indonesias-radical-underground-punk-scene/5919506.

Nawfal, Ziad. 2020. "The Global Neighbourhood." *Wire* 440: 28–31.

Novak, David. 2018. "Down on the Street." *Wire* 412: 30–35.

Prasetyo, Frans Ari. 2017. "Punk and the City: A History of Punk in Bandung." *Punk and Post-Punk* 6 (2): 189–211.

Putra, Rizky Ramandhika, and Irwansyah. 2020. "Increasing Awareness of the Scene on Indonesian Independent Music. Study of Media Convergence and Do It Yourself by Subnoise Music Collective." *International Journal of Multicultural and Multireligious Understanding* 7 (11): 523–33.

Rizaldi, Riar, and Adythia Utama. 2014. *BISING: Noise and Experimental Music in Indonesia*. Video documentary, Indonesia, 67 minutes.

Rosalia, Pramita Dikariani. 2020. "Pertemuan Musik Surabaya (PMS) tahun 1957– 2006." *Terob* 10 (2): 61–71.

Sarahtika, Dhania, and Joy Muchtar. 2018. "Plug It In: Indonesia's Growing Mod Synth Scene." *Jakarta Globe*, August 13. https://jakartaglobe.id/culture/ plug-indonesias-growing-mod-synth-scene/.

Swaragita, Gisela. 2016. "A Brief History of Jogja Noise Bombing." *The Wknd*, August 12. http://www.the-wknd.com/v3/features/ articles/a-brief-history-of-jogja-noise-bombing/.

Szumer, Zacharias. 2015. "Synth-Building Culture in Indonesia: An Interview with Lintang Radittya." *Cyclic Defrost*, June 21. http://www.cyclicdefrost. com/2015/06/synth-building-culture-in-indonesia-an-interview-with-lintang- radittnya-by-zacharias-szumer/.

Tedjasukmana, Jason. 2007. "Best Alternative-Music Scene." *Time*, Best of Asia. http://content.time.com/time/specials/2007/best_of_asia/ article/0,28804,1614524_1614477_1614463,00.html. Accessed 5 February 2021.

Triantoro, Oleh Soni. 2016. "Jogja Noise Bombing Fest 2016." *Rolling Stone Indonesia*, January 29. http://www.rollingstone.co.id/article/read/2016/01/29/140506131/1108/jogja-noise-bombing-fest-2016.

Tyson, Adam D. 2011. "Titik Api: Harry Roesli, and Music, and Politics in Bandung, Indonesia." *Indonesia* 91: 1–34.

Unite Asia. 2016. "Shit Went Down at Lady Fast Event in Yogyakarta Indonesia Last Night . . ." *Unite Asia*, April 3. https://uniteasia.org/shit-went-down-at-lady-fast-event-in-yogyakarta-indonesia-last-night/.

Von Rosa, Ferner. 2020. "The Non-Mimetism of Noise: Interview with Sabrina from Sarana." *Forum Nepantla*, April 6. https://forum-nepantla.org/the-non-mimetism-of-noise-interview-to-sabrina-from-sarana/.

Wallach, Jeremy. 2008. *Modern Noise, Fluid Genres: Popular Music in Indonesia, 1997–2001*. Madison: University of Wisconsin Press.

Warner, Sarah. 2014. "Backstage at Indonesia's Biggest Metal Festival." *The Music*, October 23. https://themusic.com.au/features/backstage-at-indonesias-biggest-metal-festival/HK4PDjEwMzI/23-10-14/.

World Bank. 2016. *Global Monitoring Report 2015–2016*. Washington, DC: World Bank. http://pubdocs.worldbank.org/pubdocs/publicdoc/2015/10/503001444058224597/Global-Monitoring-Report-2015.pdf (no longer available).

13

AUDIBLE KNOWLEDGE

Exploring Sound in Indonesian *Musik Kontemporer*

Christopher J. Miller

The past decade has witnessed a remarkable amount of activity in the burgeoning field of sound studies. But wait—is it a field . . . yet? At what point does an area of interest or a topic of study become a field? With researchers of sound, or as Jonathan Sterne dubs them, "sound students" (2012, 3), coming from so many disciplines—musicology, ethnomusicology, anthropology, science and technology studies, art history, film studies, psychology, and cognitive science, to name just a few—it is perhaps more apt to characterize sound studies, in its field-in-formation state, as a crossroads. I'm picturing highways, somewhere remote. There's enough traffic for a few prospectors (scholars), with the support of some larger commercial entities (publishers), to see fit to erect structures like a reader (Sterne 2012), a handbook (Pinch and Bijsterveld 2012), an anthology (Bull 2013), a companion (Bull 2018), and a collection of keyword essays (Novak and Sakakeeny 2015). But so far, the land remains unincorporated. There are, as of yet, no Departments of Sound Studies. Instead, most who pass through carry on down their own respective disciplinary routes, focused on their own particular concerns, employing their familiar methodologies.

Most relevant for my present purposes is how little traffic there is between sound studies and the intersection represented by this book, between music and Indonesia.[1] This is generally the case with music scholarship on most parts of the world beyond the West—which, as Sterne acknowledges, remains the "epistemic center" for much of sound studies (2015, 73). But the more fundamental reason for the lack of connection, it seems to me, is that music is not just sound, and not all sound is music. Ethnomusicologists have long regarded music expansively, venturing far and wide for new insights and theories. But for the most part they have been less concerned with music's sonic nature, or with the broader realm of sound and sound making within which music as sound exists, than with the social and cultural dimensions of forms readily recognized as music.

One notable Indonesia-focused exception, from before sound studies became a thing, is R. Anderson Sutton's provocative interpretation of how electronic sound technology reinforces the Javanese ideal of *ramé*. Translating the word as "busy, noisy, congested, tangled—but in a positive sense" (1996, 258), Sutton mostly grounds his own take in the substantial literature by fellow ethnographically oriented Indonesianists. He turns his attention to the "Javanese soundscape," using a term coined by R. Murray Schafer in the sense that has become commonplace, to designate "the larger environment of sound in which people live" (Sutton 1996, 251). But rather than engaging in the project of acoustic ecology that Schafer initiated, with its emphasis on documentation and evaluation, distinguishing between high- and low-fidelity soundscapes (Schafer 1994),[2] Sutton's analysis hews more closely to the conjoining of acoustics and epistemology that Steven Feld captured with his own neologism, "acoustemology," a term that remains specialized.[3]

The fullness of Indonesian soundscapes, and the particular "knowing-with and knowing-through the audible" (Feld 2015, 12) that goes with it, is directly relevant to the case I focus on in this chapter: a seemingly exceptional approach to composition pioneered at ASKI Surakarta in the 1970s that takes as its starting point the exploration of sound. But with this case, I am concerned first and foremost with music proper, and with music's own turn toward sound— especially, though not exclusively, within the realm of contemporary art music. This turn anticipated and fed into the scholarly one that has come to be known as sound studies. So I too am carrying on down my own disciplinary route— though my hope, having picked up a few new tools to triangulate between sound exploration, sound studies, and the broader trend of sound as music, is to shed some light on each of these, and what examining one offers to the others. After describing a representative example of sound exploration, I raise the question of its relationship to the now substantial history of similar innovations in a still mostly Western avant-garde, and to the broader changes wrought by new technologies, itself a significant focus for sound studies. Finally, I explore the cultural basis of sound exploration specific to Indonesia, in distinctive practices of listening and sound making, prevailing conditions of hearing, and the status of the concept of noise, all of which raise questions as to what is fairly regarded as exceptional—a hallmark of the avant-garde—and what is actually commonplace.

An Example

July 11, 2004. I've made my way up to the campus of ISI Surakarta, the performing arts institute some distance from the center of the city more familiarly known
as Solo. It's the first meeting of Sekar Anu, a group of eight composers from
Indonesia and the United States that I co-convened with Nick Brooke.[4] Things
aren't quite going as planned. Only five of the eight participants are present. Nick
himself is in New York for the premiere of his opera at Lincoln Center's summer
festival. Andy McGraw is stuck in Thailand waiting for a visa. AL Suwardi has
some personal matters to attend to.

We're also without the gamelan instruments we were hoping to use and had
tried to arrange for in advance. Sitting in a mostly empty room, with only the
few instruments that Andrew Raffo Dewar and I Dewa Nyoman Supenida have
brought with them, we start by discussing our ideas for the piece we will perform
in just a week at the Yogyakarta Gamelan Festival.[5] Pande Made Sukerta, the
most senior member present, presides. In that role, he's about to allow the rest to
speak first, but unable to contain himself, he shares what he's imagining: chickens. Specifically, young chickens, with an instrument playing a plaintive melody
to express the feeling of being separated from one's mother.

The weirdness bar set high, the rest of us introduce our ideas, and then we
move to trying things out with what we have at our disposal (which does not yet
include chickens). Some of these things will make it into the piece we perform at
the festival. We swish flutes through the air to produce a whistling sound—in the
performance we also use bows. We slap hands on the top of a desk, riffing on the
tendency some musicians have to absentmindedly play drum patterns on their
thighs. Sukerta at one point starts rubbing his fingers on windowpanes; this does
not make the cut. Dewar, taking out his soprano saxophone, asks, "What about
this?" and proceeds to play a continuous stream of seemingly random notes, à
la Evan Parker. Supenida immediately responds with a similar peal on a large
sarunai he's brought with him from Padang Panjang.[6]

The next day Suwardi is back. He doubles our resources by making available a number of instruments of his own design and construction—Suwardi has
long distinguished himself as an instrument inventor and builder. These bear
more or less resemblance to existing instruments. His *dan bau* is basically similar to the Vietnamese original, and like current models it includes a pickup and
a speaker—though in his case, the speaker is separate from the body, allowing
Suwardi to produce wailing feedback after initially serenading the chickens. An
older instrument from the 1980s is a *gendèr* outfitted with the long resonators
and mechanized revolving vanes of a vibraphone. I'm the one who mostly plays
this, in both an idiomatic fashion with mallets and by bowing it, a technique

I borrowed from Suwardi for use in my own pieces. A more recent invention is modeled after the rack-mounted *angklung*, with pairs of cowbells tuned to *slendro* in place of the bamboo rattles now most often tuned to a Western chromatic scale. This instrument becomes the vehicle for Ida Bagus Widnyana's signature contribution of a Balinese lullaby. Least conventional are three single-string zithers of Suwardi's own design, each with thick wire strung over a small bossless gong, using a piece of tile as a bridge. Sukerta takes a *suling* and tries bouncing it on the string, and rubbing one end on the gong. In the end we mostly stick to bowing, which produces no shortage of timbres, from low, growly fundamentals to whistling higher partials. This blends well with the slow glissandi generated by a SuperCollider patch that Dewar plays on his laptop over a borrowed sound system.

When McGraw makes it to Solo, on day three, he hooks up a contact microphone I had brought to a water bottle, to amplify the noisy crackling of the plastic as he squeezes it. I suggest using the sound as one of several elements—along with Dewar's saxophone, Supenida's *sarunai*, Suwardi's *dan bau*, and McGraw and Widnyana playing *reyong*-type figuration on Minangkabau *talempong*—in an improvisational game that becomes the final section of the piece. In this game, which we later refer to as "ping pong," we take turns playing steady streams of sound until passing the "ball" (the turn to play) with a nod to another player. Later, once Sukerta has procured the chickens, we attach the mic to the bottom of their cage, to transform their scratching and pecking into violent bursts of static. I'm at the mixer, bringing the sound in and out as I receive and give cues. On the day of the festival, Sukerta deliberately withholds their food so that they peck with extra urgency and force when he finally feeds them during the performance.

In both material and process, the piece we created—titled "Maya," a loanword from Sanskrit meaning "illusion or hallucination," but also *ayam* (chicken) backward—is representative of an experimentalist approach to composition developed in the 1980s at ISI Surakarta, or ASKI, as it was then called.[7] This approach, in which the exploration of sound plays a central role, was pioneered in the late 1970s by Sukerta, Suwardi, and other students who would then go on to become faculty. As Sukerta wrote in a statement about his first piece in this vein, from 1979: "In my composition Malam I began with the assumption that any object can be a potential source of many sounds with a wide range of characteristics. The objects I have used here are not only gamelan instruments, but anything that can be considered a source of sound, for example, drinking glasses, fabric, bicycles, mallets, sheets of tin, etc. as well as food like crisp chips (*krupuk*) that are chewed or crushed. A musical composition expresses something with sounds—and that something is what I experience and am able to express" (Sukerta, quoted in Sadra 1991, 22). Summing up this new approach,

Sukerta's and Suwardi's colleague I Wayan Sadra identifies "exploration (*penjelajahan* or *eksplorasi*)" at its "heart." In some cases, this involved "a redefining of the traditional musical vocabulary," but as often it "focuses on the structure and anatomy of the gamelan, based on the principle that every instrument can be the source of many sounds if played in an unconventional manner" (Sadra 1991, 21). Many composers, like Sukerta, looked for other sources of sound, such as bicycles, *krupuk*, or chickens. Others, most notably Suwardi, created new instruments. In all cases, the goal is to "accumulate and accommodate a wide range of possibilities to create a wealth of choices and variables" (Sadra 1991, 21). These discoveries are then combined, connected, and developed into episodes, which in turn are arranged into a sequence that is further refined and rehearsed. In most cases, key decisions are made by a designated composer, but the process as a whole is deeply collaborative. Notation may be used to communicate some ideas, but mostly players learn, develop, and perform their parts with a similar level of individual latitude as that found in traditional Indonesian musics.[8]

Though it was rare, even in the 1980s, for entire compositions to consist exclusively of the sounds found through exploration, it was common for lengthy sections to do so. And the way in which conventional material was interwoven or otherwise incorporated typically maintained an emphasis on distinctive sonic gestures and textural clouds of sound. Again, "Maya" is representative. The long introduction lingered in the drones of the gong-zithers, bowed *gendèr*, and electronics for a good five minutes before Sukerta and McGraw began drumming almost imperceptibly on the table. Only after another two minutes, after Supenida and Widnyana joined in, did the drumming grow more animated and prominent, the energy heightened further when Supenida began to sing *kekawin*, and then to play *sarunai*. Still, the overall effect was more a layering of textures than melody and accompaniment. The single instance in "Maya" of a coordinated presentation of a metered melody was when Widnyana played the lullaby on the cowbell-*angklung*, accompanied by myself on vibraphone-*gendèr* and Suwardi on *dan bau*. Even here, however, there was only one straightforward iteration, lasting less than two minutes. This followed an abstract and unmetered rendition in the style of a *pathetan*, with the *dan bau* first playing alone (serenading the chickens under the veil draped over their cage), then joined by *gendèr* and isolated punctuating notes on the *angklung*. The melody in meter was repeated, but quickly overtaken by multiple slow glissandi on several *suling* and feedback on the *dan bau*, and eventually Dewar's and Supenida's Evan Parkeresque flurries on saxophone and *sarunai*, as a transition to the closing "ping-pong" section—which concluded with Sukerta releasing the chickens.

Music's Sonic Turn

The sound exploration undertaken by composers at ASKI Surakarta, far from unique, is one of many instances of a widespread shift in music toward sound—toward the full range of sounds and the particularity of those sounds, as opposed to the circumscribed set of "musical" sounds, of interest less in themselves and more for the syntactical structures in which they may be organized (notes from a scale, arranged to form melodies and/or harmonies, in regular rhythmic patterns). Within narratives centered on experimental or avant-garde music—here referring specifically to the various groupings (Piekut 2011, 6) of mostly American and European composers with foundations in and affiliations with the Western art music tradition—this shift is often cast in terms of an expansion of resources.[9] As American composer John Cage proclaimed in a "credo" originally published in 1937: "I believe that the use of noise . . . to make music . . . will continue and increase until we reach a music produced through the aid of electrical instruments . . . which will make available for musical purposes any and all sounds that can be heard" (Cage 1961, 3–4). More than two decades earlier, Italian futurist Luigi Russolo penned a manifesto calling for an "art of noises," realizing his vision through the invention of mechanical noisemakers he called *intonarumori*. In between, in the 1920s, the French expatriate Edgard Varèse made his mark with the liberal use of sirens and indefinitely pitched percussion instruments. In 1948 French radio engineer Pierre Schaefer pioneered what he would call *musique concrète*, realizing Cage's prophecy by creating compositions exclusively from recorded sound (Collins et al. 2013, 46–47). Cage followed suit in 1952 with his "Williams Mix," for which he and his assistants laboriously assembled "minutely and obliquely cut pieces of magnetic audiotape . . . from a stock of 500 to 600 recorded sounds" (Kahn 1999, 113).

Cage most pointedly questioned the relationship between music and sound in another piece from 1952, the infamous "silent piece," *4'33"*. The work was not an abnegation of music and sound; on the contrary, it aimed to direct the audience's attention to the sounds that are all around them. In this respect, it was the ultimate realization of Cage's new dictum, to "let sounds be themselves" (Cage 1961, 10). But it was not the last word. Far from settling the matter, it opened up new possibilities. As Morton Feldman exclaimed to Cage, "Now that things are so simple, there's so much to do" (Cage 1961, 72). Indeed, in the decades since, there has been a proliferation of what Piekut calls "advanced sonic practices" such as "field recording, noise, open improvisation, installation, graphic notation, text scores, dub remixing, live signal processing, drone, turntablism, electro-acoustic improvisation, sound art, minimalisms, orchestral pop, sampling, new instruments, live coding, glitch, tape collage, new primitivisms, and biomusics" (2017, 439).

The Question of Influence

It is tempting to relate the sound exploration of ASKI composers to the story I've sketched above. English composer Alec Roth, in the most extensive and technically analytic study of composition at ASKI, suggested that young composers there "seem to have discovered an Indonesian equivalent of Ligeti's world of 'clocks and clouds'" (1987, 119). I had similar thoughts when I first heard their music in 1991, but thinking now about their approach, I find it more akin to that of German composer Helmut Lachenmann, in its systematic and exhaustive exploration of all possible means of eliciting sound from instruments, and to that of the free improvisation group AMM, in the strength of its orientation toward sound, in starting first with sounds and following their lead in the process of combining them to create episodes, and out of those episodes pieces.[10] Jakarta-based composer Franki Raden once hailed Suwardi's "Sebuah Proses"—a piece from 1984 that presented the process of sound exploration itself "as a composition" (notes by Suwardi, reproduced in Hardjana 1986, 311)—as the realization of Cage's ideal of eliminating "the boundary between art events and everyday reality" (review by Raden, reproduced in Hardjana 1986, 346).

Such similarities cannot, however, themselves be taken as proof of kinship. As I have argued elsewhere (2011, 2014), direct influence from the predominantly Western avant-garde, of the sort theorized by Harold Bloom, in which artists create themselves in relationship to their precursors (1997), played practically no role in the emergence of sound exploration at ASKI. Suwardi only heard Cage's music two years after "Sebuah Proses," when he sought it out while at the University of Michigan in 1986 to teach gamelan, his curiosity piqued by Raden's review (Suwardi, personal communication, September 8, 2004). Similarly, drummer Eddie Prévost reports having "only the vaguest idea" who Cage was when he cofounded AMM in 1965, recounting how when he was asked by a journalist about the composer's influence, he assumed Cage "was a drummer I hadn't heard of" (Prévost 1995, 13). The issue is not merely one of exposure, or lack thereof—though to be sure, in Suwardi's case there were next to no opportunities to learn about Cage or other avant-garde composers in his immediate environment.[11] More fundamentally, it has to do with the operative frame of reference. For Prévost and his AMM cofounders, this was jazz. For Suwardi and his colleagues, it was *karawitan*. Pushing them beyond that frame were the experimentalist aesthetics and practices promoted by ASKI's director, Gendhon Humardani, and modeled by dancers Sardono W. Kusuma and Suprapto Suryadarma, with whom they collaborated.

Zooming out from these cases, a no-less-significant driving factor behind the broader shift toward sound is the development of new technologies. While a good number of the "advanced sonic practices" in the above-quoted list from Piekut were pioneered by artists who took Cage's classes at the New School for Social Research and then went on to found movements such as Fluxus, or to create the Happening as an alternative intermedia performance form (Kahn 1999, chap. 8–10), others represent a "vernacular avant-garde" (Piekut 2017, 439). In some cases these may have picked up on stimulus from Cage et al., but more fundamentally they stemmed from the possibilities afforded by sound recording and amplification. Engineers in Jamaica pushing the limits of their studio equipment in their dub remixes (Veal 2007) and Japanese musicians creating impenetrable walls of noise (Novak 2013) stand respectively as exceptionally acute examples of engagement with the malleability of recorded sound and the sheer power of amplified sound. They are vernacular in the ways they have picked up on, and in turn fed back to, practices central to what has become the musical mainstream. Studio production, responsible for the majority of music one encounters today, in Indonesia no less than anywhere else, itself represents a significant turn toward the quality of sound, in the many decisions made at every step of the process, from microphone choice and placement to the final mastering. The harsh character of noise merely takes to an extreme a commonly desired outcome with amplification: to not simply ensure sound's audibility but to maximize its impact, whatever that sound may be.

Sukerta, Suwardi, and their colleagues were not working in a vernacular context but in the "hothouse atmosphere" of a government-funded institution (Roth 1987, 429). Nor did they engage with electronics in any substantial way.[12] Nevertheless, the changes wrought by sound technology made their mark on the soundscape they experienced, and thus as background to their explorations it must have played some role. But how do we assess its impact?

Perspectives from Sound Studies

In a signature contribution to sound studies, Jonathan Sterne complicates the stories told about our modern-day relationship to sound, with their focus on the irrevocable changes wrought by newly invented sound reproduction technologies, by examining how those technologies are themselves "artifacts of vast transformations in the fundamental nature of sound, the human ear, the faculty of hearing, and practices of listening that occurred over the long nineteenth century." Sterne thus presents sound itself as something with a history, as bound up with "capitalism, rationalism, science, colonialism" and other factors behind "the 'maelstrom' of modernity" (Sterne 2003, 2). Sound is also culturally contingent. Sterne argues this too, but he admits, in his keyword entry in Novak and Sakakeeny's collection, that his own work, like most of sound studies, remains Eurocentric (Sterne 2015, 74n3).

The soundscape most Indonesians experience today shares with that which prevails in the West two fundamentally modern features: the ubiquity of recorded sound, and the noise of traffic, appliances, industry, and other "chaotic" and "incoherent" elements of what bio-acoustician Bernie Krause terms the "anthropophony."[13] It includes, to be sure, significantly distinctive features: those deriving from fauna specific to Indonesia's tropical ecosystem along other environmental sounds; humanly produced sounds that are intentionally meaningful, such as the dominant, or domineering, Islamic call to prayer (Henley 2019), or the diverse sounds used by wandering vendors; and particular differences in the technosphere, such as the greater prevalence of small-engine motorcycles. Also significantly different is how the modern Indonesian soundscape assumed its current form. Focusing for the moment on recording, playback, and broadcasting technologies, while these have had some presence in Indonesia since soon after they were invented—a mere five years after, in the case of Edison's phonograph (Yampolsky 2013, 66)—their patterns of diffusion were circumscribed. They seem to have been concentrated in urban areas, if the report of Suwardi and Sukerta's younger colleague Sukamso is more broadly applicable: even as late as 1971, in the village of Karanganyar, less than an hour's drive from Surakarta, there was only one single radio receiver.[14]

Most fundamental is the fact that sound recording technologies were not invented in Indonesia but imported. This is not to suggest that Indonesians were merely passive and powerless recipients of technology, or other facets of modernity, though asymmetries in power that prevailed under colonial rule and persisted in its shadow must be acknowledged. When and where radios, gramophones, microphones, and loudspeakers were taken up, it was with great enthusiasm, as Rudolf Mrázek so vividly recounts (2002, especially chap. 5, "Let Us Become Radio Mechanics"). They were adopted in a colonial context with its own patterns of profound transformation, which undoubtedly included transformations not just in the soundscape but in sound more broadly conceived. These transformations were not, however, the same as those instigated by the physicists, inventors, capitalists, medical practitioners, and telegraph operators through their work with telephones, radios, record players, and their technological antecedents (Sterne 2003), or those arising from the efforts of acousticians, architects, and engineers who transformed the spaces in which Americans heard music and other sounds, and in doing so transformed their culture of listening (Thompson 2004). Neither the native inhabitants in the Dutch East Indies nor, for that matter, the European colonizers would have participated in the deliberations of otologists, philosophers, physiologists, and music theorists in Europe between 1633 and 1928 that Erlmann posits as the origins of modern aurality (2010). If we accept Latour's contention that we have never been modern (1993), we also need to recognize the diverse conceptions of sound and forms of sound knowledge that pertain, and persist, in other parts of the world, such as Indonesia.

The Roots of Sound Exploration

How, then, if not from a specific model, or as a vernacular response to mediated sound, did the practice of sound exploration emerge as a central and most distinctive aspect of the compositional approach developed at ASKI? That sound exploration was taken up so readily suggests a deeper cultural basis.

In general terms, it seems that there is in Indonesia a heightened level of attentiveness to and appreciation, or at least tolerance and acceptance, of all manner of sound. There are numerous examples of this. There is the abundance of onomatopoeic words in Indonesian languages—150 starting with the letter K alone in one Indonesian-English dictionary (Echols and Shadily 1998). Many of these are extremely specific: *kelepak*, the "sound of a hand slapping s.t.," *keletak*, the "sound of a pebble striking wood," *keletang*, the "sound of jingling or tinkling (of silver coins)," and *keletuk*, the "sound of rapping on a hollow wooden surface, table, etc." or "sound of creaking (of wooden furniture, floor, etc.)." There is a myriad of sounds and calls identifying specific wares and foods used by mobile street vendors. I learned from my time in Solo that a small gong signals ice cream; swishing high-pitched bells signal chicken *saté*; a series of open and closed knocks on a small woodblock signals fried noodles; a drawn-out "teeeee" in a high-pitched falsetto—the second syllable of *roti*—signals bread. There is an abundance of sound-making toys. Some, like whistles and flutes, resemble simple musical instruments. Others are more distinct, like humming tops that sound like low-pitched sirens, descending gradually as they slow down, or clay frogs with a reed to produce a buzzing sound.

Where I find sound studies most helpful in thinking more precisely about the kinds of sound and sound making I've described so far is the focus many scholars bring to conditions of hearing and practices of listening—which as Sterne has most cogently argued are historically and culturally specific (2003, 2012)—and to the ways of "knowing-with and knowing-through the audible" so elegantly conveyed by Feld's term "acoustemology." Feld also points out how "sounding" is "simultaneously social and material" (2015, 12). Acoustemology is especially helpful in starting to understand what Sadra had in mind when, after a nearby mosque started blaring Islamic music at a fairly loud volume during one of our conversations, he brought up the notion of "sound cosmology." In that instance, he focused on the differences between the response of a hypothetical newly arrived American, who would find loud music and sound disturbing, and that of Indonesians, who are not bothered by them, understanding them as signals, or codes.[15] He offered as another example the use of car and motorcycle horns besides alerting other drivers, relaying how Sukerta would honk his horn from some distance to let his family know he was returning home (Sadra, personal communication, July 23, 2004). The examples might seem to have mostly to do with how inhabitants in one of the most densely populated parts of the world cope with the resulting abundance of sound. Sadra's evocation of "sound cosmology," however, grounds these attitudes and practices in conceptions of the power of sound that for him are presumably associated with Balinese Hinduism—conceptions that are parallel but distinct from those associated with Christianity, which, as Sterne points out, undergird what he calls the "audiovisual litany" of differences between hearing and seeing developed by Walter Ong and Marshal McLuhan in their theorizing of "orality" and "secondary orality" (Sterne 2012, 66–67; 2003, 15–17). The dynamics of orality are most certainly relevant in an Indonesian context, though one would want to take into account not just Hinduism but also Islam—whose central text, the Qur'an, is believed to have been revealed orally, and is conventionally recited, rather than read silently.

For the time being, I will focus on worldly matters, such as the relationship between musical and extramusical sound. The example of sound-making toys points to a continuity rather than a hard distinction between the two. Take the energy and time Suwardi put into inventing and building instruments: some elaborate, like the vibraphone-*gendèr* Sekar Anu used for "Maya," or a "water *suling*" where air passes via tubes through water in a small canister on its way to a standard *suling*; some simple, like a short piece of bamboo with rubber covering each end and a single blowhole. On the one hand, they were a response to the push from ASKI director Gendhon Humardani to break free from traditional conventions. On the other, they represent an outgrowth of activity Suwardi has engaged in since childhood. At an early age, inspired by the toys he bought from vendors at wayang performances or *sekaten*, he tried his hand at making his own. Like other children, he would play with scraps of bamboo left over from newly built houses, going a step further than most by cutting pieces and arranging them into a scale. He continued with this kind of "experimentation" after returning from a tour to Europe with the choreographer Sardono, using "glasses filled with water." He "still used a lot of traditional material"—his thinking "was still tied" to the *pelog* and *slendro* scales. But gradually he turned more to "just sound." He tried to find sounds, improvising by himself as he was not yet sure how to put them together. "Finally, after some time, I was opened by all kinds of sounds," and he realized that they "can be arranged as one likes, can become a composition" (Suwardi, personal communication, September 8, 2004).

To be sure, there was for Suwardi, Sukerta, and Sadra a conceptual shift that accompanied the shift in practice to using all manner of sounds. Sukerta and Sadra recounted their initial difficulty accepting Sardono's experiments when they first worked with him in 1972, both asking themselves "What *is* this?" (*apa ini?*). Sadra relayed having this reaction to a dancer repeatedly ripping a cloth, which he chalked up to the "superiority complex" he subscribed to at the time, in which "anything other than *gong kebyar* wasn't any good." Later, he understood "what was sought was a connection between the sound and the visual" (Sadra, personal communication, July 23, 2004). Discussing both this cloth and the metal puppets sculptor Hajar Satoto created for Wayang Budha, a project led by Suprapto Suryadarma, Sukerta granted that such elements were "mischievous" (*nakal*), but the cloth was "for dance, not music," and the sound of the puppets was "not yet regarded as music." "Mischievousness in music," as far as Sukerta knew, "started in 1978, with me." He then went on to describe "gathering" sounds. Some of these he searched for deliberately, such as shaking a flexible sheet of plywood, while others he happened upon, such as *krupuk* or the sound of air passing over the end of a *suling* he was carrying while riding on a motorcycle. After finding these sounds, he played around with them. I commented that such a "broad awareness of sound" was interesting—that on the one hand, it's "an extremely simple idea," but on the other, there "has to be a significant change in thinking." Sukerta immediately pointed to his head and said "it must be opened" (Sukerta, personal communication, July 8, 2005).

Sound exploration was in many respects exceptional, but in others less so. It involved the opening of minds, but those minds were perhaps not so tightly closed to begin with, at least with respect to the admissibility of other sounds. In no small part, this was a function of the openness of built space. As part of Humardani's larger project of creating a contemporary existence for traditional Indonesian performing arts, the efforts of ASKI composers contributed to a vision of art shaped by Humardani's study of modern dance in the United States and his reading of Western aesthetic philosophy. In this vision, art was effectively treated as an independent realm, an ideology that in the Western world led, among a host of social, cultural, and institutional changes, to the construction of concert halls—the acoustics of which are the focus of Thompson's study of the "soundscape of modernity" (2004). Eventually, after ASKI had become ISI, and a good while after it had relocated to the outskirts of Solo, it erected its own *teater tutup* (closed theater). But the principal performance space they first put up on the new campus was a grand *pendhapa*. And indeed it was the smaller *pendhapa* of Sasanamulya, the complex within the Sunan of Surakarta's palace that previously housed ASKI, where Suwardi, Sukerta, Sadra, and their peers carried out their initial experiments.

Pendhapa, and the related Balinese *balé*, are pavilion-like structures, with vaulted roofs supported not by walls but by columns. They thus provide shade and shelter from rain but are otherwise open to the surrounding environment. The sound of the gamelan these structures house thus blends with the sounds of birds twittering during the day—often as they fly about inside the structure—and of insects and frogs at night. Not surprisingly, musical references to frogs abound in both Java and Bali. They are identified as a model for *kotekan*, the interlocking figuration in Balinese music (Gold 2005, 58–59), and referenced in the name of the archaic Javanese gamelan *kodhok ngorek*, which means "croaking frogs." A particularly exceptional example is a traditional Javanese gamelan piece that could be seen as a precedent for ASKI-style sound exploration: *Gendhing Bonang* "Kodhokan," a piece with a section in which most of the musicians stop playing their regular parts and instead imitate the sounds of frogs.

Exceptional/Unexceptional

The keyword that gets to the heart of what distinguishes the acoustemology behind ASKI-style sound exploration from other instances of music about sound is noise. This is not because the concept is central. On the contrary, it is mostly absent. It doesn't translate—at least not directly.

The dominant sense of noise in European-language discourse around music crystalized in the writings of physiologist and physicist Hermann von Helmholtz, who established a "formal categorical division" between "periodic" and "nonperiodic" waveforms—between musical sounds, defined as those having a clear pitch, and nonmusical noise (Novak 2015, 127). Pitches of this sort, organized into structures such as scales, may not be truly universal to all music making; long before their adoption by the likes of Cage, there have been traditions using only percussion and other indefinitely pitched sources of sound. But they are ubiquitous. But then so is noise. As Novak points out, "nonperiodic noise is inherent in most instrumental sounds, such as the puff of air that precedes a flute tone, or the bowing sound on a violin" (127). Yet the overwhelming focus on pitch in Western traditions of music theory, with its privileging of "tonal consonance and harmonic development over timbre, rhythm, and texture," marginalized noise, turning it into music's other. The "resident noises" within music thus required liberation by twentieth-century experimental composers, in defiance of the dominant Helmholtzian order (Kahn 1999, 79–83).

My argument here is that noise, resident and otherwise, did not need liberating in Indonesia. Indonesian languages are among those that "do not distinguish noise as a general category of sound" (Novak 2015, 125). Instead, there are more specific adjectives. *Bising* describes sounds that are grating, shrill, or deafening, or the sensation of ringing in one's ears after exposure to such sounds; this is the word used by Indonesian practitioners of "extreme" forms elsewhere termed noise (della Faille and Fermont, in this book). Then there is *ramé*, discussed by Sutton (1996) and glossed by Novak as "the clamorous noisiness of social life in festivals and marketplaces [that implies] a healthy and lively atmosphere" (Novak 2015, 125). *Ramé* is a quality sought deliberately in the "simultaneity of soundings" in the "Balinese ceremonial soundscape" (Gold 2005, 1). The atmosphere when gamelan play in Javanese courts may be more subdued, but it too admits other sounds. There, the idealized mode of listening is not the "focused listening" at a "Western concert" (Becker 1997, 46), and certainly not the "structural listening" argued for by Schoenberg and Adorno (Subotnik 1996), but rather one consistent with Javanese mystical practice, in which "one is enjoined to relax one's perceptions, to be open to a wider, broader set of sensual input" (Becker 1997, 46).

Pitch is unquestionably significant in traditional conceptions of music, as evident in Suwardi's retrospection about his thinking being tied to *pelog* and *slendro*, and also, in a more mystical vein, in the symbolic meaning attributed to specific tones by court musician Sastrapustaka in his exegesis on the names of the keys of gamelan instruments (Sastrapustaka 1984; Becker 1997). But physically, and perhaps metaphysically also, rather than existing in opposition to nonmusical noise, pitch lies at one end of a continuum, as a particularly important point of focus within a broader field of sound. Consonance, an all-important quality in Western art music that enables its richly developed harmonic language, is by no means completely absent in gamelan. But there is much more in the way of complexity, with the rich inharmonic spectra of struck bronze, and ambiguity, arising from the multiplicity of intonations between players and instruments.[16] There are rather more noises—resident and copresent; intentional and incidental; musical, environmental, and social. In addition to those already mentioned, there is the pronounced scratch in *rebab* bowing, the buzzing of metal keys against metal posts on *saron*, the rattling of resonators. There is also the occasional knocking to fine-tune *kendhang*, the clinking of glass and ceramic when food and drink are passed around, the stylized cries and clapping of the male chorus, and the nearly omnipresent background of chatting, by listeners and sometimes also by players.

None of this is to minimize the boldness of the work of Suwardi, Sukerta, and their colleagues. Sound exploration did not develop organically out of traditional gamelan practice. It took the prodding of Humardani within the hothouse atmosphere he helped foster at ASKI, as well as interactions with artists such as Sardono, to open their minds and push them beyond the familiar and conventional. But once that happened, sound exploration was the logical alternative. The music they then created is exceptional, and extraordinary, in its radical shift in emphasis away from traditional structures to that which was incidental. It is rather less exceptional when viewed alongside the widespread shift toward sound in the mostly Western avant-garde, as ASKI sound explorers did not have to contend with the pervasive and restrictive Helmholtzian notion of what sound counts as musical. From an even broader perspective, it is perhaps this notion itself that is most exceptional. With the loosening of its grip on musical imagination, thanks not only to the avant-garde, vernacular or otherwise, but to practices of sound making and conditions of hearing that have become common across the board, the "West" seems to be joining "the rest" in a more happily noisy, or rather sonorous, future. Indonesia was already there.

NOTES

1. Two recent examples are Rasmussen 2017 and McGraw 2019.

2. See Kelman 2010 for a critical review of the uses and (mis-)applications of the term "soundscape." For what it's worth, from the course "Acoustic Communications" I took at Simon Fraser University—part of the curricular legacy of the World Soundscape Project Schafer founded there in the 1960s—I understand the term to refer to the totality of sounds encountered in a given location. This meaning holds throughout this chapter. A subcommittee of the International Organization for Standardization saw fit to distinguish between the "acoustic environment," as "sound at the receiver from all sound sources as modified by the environment . . . actual or simulated, outdoor or indoor, as experienced or in memory," and "soundscape" as "acoustic environment as perceived or experienced and/or understood by a person or people, in context." "Acoustics—Soundscape—Part 1: Definition and Conceptual Framework," 2014, https://www.iso.org/obp/ui/#iso:std:iso:12913:-1:ed-1:v1:en. I took "Acoustic Communications" with Susan Frykberg in the fall of 1991, the same semester I first heard the music of composers from ISI Surakarta discussed in this chapter.

3. Feld notes that he coined "acoustemology" in 1992 (2015, 12). He used it in a 1994 essay that also plays with the alternate formulation "echo-muse-ecology," published in the newsletter of the World Soundscape Project. How more widely the term will be taken up after appearing as a keyword in Novak and Sakakeeny's volume (Feld 2015) remains to be seen, but conceptually it reflects the shift in perspective that much of sound studies is bringing about.

4. Brooke and I decided on Andrew Raffo Dewar and Andy McGraw as the participants from the United States, and then the four of us suggested Indonesian composers to invite, settling on Pande Made Sukerta, I Dewa Nyoman Supenida, AL Suwardi, and Ida Bagus Widnyana.

5. The Yogyakarta Gamelan Festival, pitching itself as an international gathering of "gamelan lovers," has aptly been characterized as "more a celebration of musical syncretism and experimentation than of tradition" (Perlman 1999, 2). See my dissertation for a profile of the festival and its founder, Sapto Raharjo (Miller 2014, 466–86).

6. Born in Bali, Supenida took a position at the arts college in Padang Panjang, West Sumatra, after graduating from the parallel institution in Denpasar.

7. For a video recording of "Maya," see https://youtu.be/XPZe3AWoRio?t=799.

8. See Roth 1987 for a more thorough discussion of this compositional process, as well as analysis of selected pieces. See also the handbook prepared by Sukerta—who was for many years the primary teacher of composition at ASKI—a reproduction of which was published by Jody Diamond in *Balungan* in 2017, as well as the profiles of Suwardi and Sukerta in Diamond's 1990 documentary.

9. Cope 1993 and Griffiths 2010 are two representative surveys focused exclusively on art music. Sound art, like sound studies, concerns itself with sound "beyond music," as Licht signals in the title of his 2007 survey, yet many of the composers in my thumbnail history here figure prominently in his attempt to define the term. These composers, especially John Cage, loom large in most books on the topic, such as Lander and Lexier 1990 and LaBelle 2006. Goddard et al. 2013 focuses squarely on the vernacular avant-garde I bring up in the next section of this chapter, while Cox and Warner 2004 and a number of book-length studies (including Demers 2010; Kelly 2009; Kim-Cohen 2009; Rodgers 2010; Voegelin 2010) look across the spectrum of academic, popular, and avant-garde music and sound art. Makis Solomos's 2020 monograph *From Music to Sound* explores most explicitly the idea I propose here, of a sonic turn within music. None of these studies, however wide-ranging, ventures beyond art worlds rooted in the West.

10. György Ligeti's compositions represent a trend with European contemporary art music of creating music from colorful sonorities and masses of sound, rather than from conventional melodies, harmonies, and rhythms, for which the Polish music theorist Józef Chomiński, focusing on the work of his compatriots, coined the term "sonorism" in the 1960s (Harley 1998). Lachenmann is best known for works employing what, borrowing Pierre Schaefer's term, he calls *musique concrète instrumentale*. This approach developed out of a prioritizing of sonorities and "sound structures," inspired by Ligeti's "Atmospheres" as a "principle exemplar of sonorism," but which he also identified in the music of Chopin and Debussy (Williams 2013, 75–77). AMM had a connection to this continental avant-garde through former member Cornelius Cardew, who "for a short and uncomfortable time" worked as an assistant to Karlheinz Stockhausen (Prevost 1995, 9), though as explained below, its primary members came out of England's jazz scene.

11. Suwardi did acknowledge receiving a cassette with the music of Boulez from Raden sometime in the 1970s, but this was an isolated exchange, in contrast to Raden and his Jakarta-based colleagues seeking out recordings from European embassies, cultural centers, and a local flea market. Suwardi, personal communication, 8 September 2004; Tony Prabowo, personal communication, August 7, 2005; Otto Sidharta, personal communication, June 6, 2005.

12. I Wayan Sadra experimented with both live electronics and studio production while in residence at Dartmouth College in 1991; his 1992 reflection on his "first experiences" conveys just how out of his element he felt. The studio piece, "Mimpinya Salju," was released on a 1993 album of Sadra's compositions. This work is truly exceptional; amplified and electronically produced sounds occasionally found their way into the works of ASKI composers—such as the motorcycle horns that blast at the end of Sukerta's "Mungkin," the first piece I heard by him, on a 1991 North American tour by a group from ASKI—but for the most part, they worked with acoustic resources.

13 Bernie Krause interviewed by Tim Hinman in "The Sound of Life Itself," the inaugural episode of the podcast *Sound Matters*, produced by Bang and Olufsen. https://www.bang-olufsen.com/en/story/sound-matters-episode-1, accessed July 17, 2019.

14 This came up after Sukamso revealed, after asking him what music he liked in his youth, that there wasn't anything other than gamelan. When I asked about radio, and he told me that in 1971 there was only one, I assumed he meant one station. He then clarified he meant one receiver, owned by the richest person in the village. Sukamso, personal communication, August 4, 2004.

15 Sadra's generalizations about differing attitudes toward sounds made by others brings to mind an anecdote relayed by Sutton, though their explanations differ; Sutton interprets the "violent reaction" of the Javanese man to being asked to turn down his radio as stemming in part from "the desirability of sound to combat emptiness" (1996, 260).

16 The topic of tuning has become somewhat arcane within Anglophone ethnomusicology, Indonesianist or otherwise, and more the province of composers and theorists. For a detailed examination of the spectra of gamelan instruments, with tentative suggestions on implications for tuning, see Sethares 2005, chap. 10. See Perlman 1994, 534–41, for a more emic consideration of Javanese conceptions of intonation, or *embat*, in conjunction with an examination of the interest in gamelan on the part of American devotees of just intonation.

WORKS CITED

Becker, Judith. 1997. "Tantrism, Rasa, and Javanese Gamelan Music." In *Enchanting Powers: Music in the World's Religions*, edited by Lawrence Eugene Sullivan, 15–59. Cambridge, MA: Harvard University Center for the Study of World Religions.

Bloom, Harold. 1997. *The Anxiety of Influence: A Theory of Poetry*. 2nd ed. New York: Oxford University Press.

Bull, Michael, ed. 2013. *Sound Studies: Critical Concepts in Media and Cultural Studies*. Milton Park, UK: Routledge.

Bull, Michael. 2018. *The Routledge Companion to Sound Studies*. Milton Park, UK: Routledge.

Cage, John. 1961. *Silence*. Middletown, CT: Wesleyan University Press.

Collins, Nick, Margaret Schedel, and Scott Wilson. 2013. *Electronic Music*. Cambridge: Cambridge University Press.

Cope, David. 1993. *New Directions in Music*. 6th ed. Madison, WI: Brown & Benchmark.

Cox, Christoph, and Daniel Warner, eds. 2004. *Audio Culture: Readings in Modern Music*. New York: Continuum.

Demers, Joanna Teresa. 2010. *Listening through the Noise: The Aesthetics of Experimental Electronic Music*. New York: Oxford University Press.

Diamond, Jody. 1990. *Karya: Portraits of Contemporary Indonesian Composers*. Videocassette (VHS). Hanover, NH: American Gamelan Institute. Also available via https://youtu.be/Jre0k-tldfQ.

Echols, John M., and Hassan Shadily. 1998. *Kamus Indonesia-Inggris: An Indonesian-English Dictionary*. 3rd ed. Revised and edited by John U. Wolff and James T. Collins in cooperation with Hassan Shadily. Jakarta: Gramedia.

Erlmann, Veit. 2010. *Reason and Resonance: A History of Modern Aurality*. New York: Zone Books.

Feld, Steven. 1994. "From Ethnomusicology to Echo-Muse-Ecology: Reading R. Murray Schafer in the Papua New Guinea Rainforest." *Soundscape Newsletter* 8: 4–6.

Feld, Steven. 2015. "Acoustemology." In Novak and Sakakeeny 2015, 12–21.

Goddard, Michael, Benjamin Halligan, and Nicola Spelman, eds. 2013. *Resonances: Noise and Contemporary Music.* New York: Bloomsbury Academic.

Gold, Lisa. 2005. *Music in Bali.* Oxford: Oxford University Press.

Griffiths, Paul. 2010. *Modern Music and After.* 3rd ed. New York: Oxford University Press.

Hardjana, Suka. 1986. *Enam Tahun Pekan Komponis Muda, Dewan Kesenian Jakarta, 1979-1985: Sebuah Alternatif.* Jakarta: Dewan Kesenian Jakarta.

Harley, Maria Anna. 1998. "The Polish School of Sonorism and Its European Context." In *Crosscurrents and Counterpoints: Offerings in Honor of Bengt Hambræus at 70,* edited by Per F. Broman, Nora Engebretsen, and Bo Alphonce, 62–77. Göteborg, Sweden: Göteborgs Universitet.

Henley, David. 2019. "Sound Wars: Piety, Civility, and the Battle for Indonesian Ears." In Porath 2019, 228–53.

Kahn, Douglas. 1999. *Noise, Water, Meat: A History of Sound in the Arts.* Cambridge, MA: MIT Press.

Kelly, Caleb. 2009. *Cracked Media: The Sound of Malfunction.* Cambridge, MA: MIT Press.

Kelman, Ari Y. 2010. "Rethinking the Soundscape." *Senses and Society* 5 (2): 212–34.

Kim-Cohen, Seth. 2009. *In the Blink of an Ear: Toward a Non-Cochlear Sonic Art.* New York: Continuum.

LaBelle, Brandon. 2006. *Background Noise: Perspectives on Sound Art.* New York: Continuum.

Lander, Dan, and Micah Lexier, eds. 1990. *Sound by Artists.* Toronto: Art Metropole.

Latour, Bruno. 1993. *We Have Never Been Modern.* Cambridge, MA: Harvard University Press.

Licht, Alan. 2007. *Sound Art: Beyond Music, Between Categories.* New York: Rizzoli.

McGraw, Andy. 2019. "Resounding Power: Balinese Perspectives on the *Gong Agung*." In Porath 2019, 254–82.

Miller, Christopher J. 2011. "Indonesian Experimentalisms, the Question of Western Influence, and the Cartography of Aesthetic Authority." In proceedings of *Beyond the Centres: Musical Avant Gardes since 1950.* Aristotle University of Thessaloniki, Greece. http://btc.web.auth.gr/proceedings.html.

Miller, Christopher J. 2014. "Cosmopolitan, Nativist, Eclectic: Cultural Dynamics in Indonesian *Musik Kontemporer*." PhD diss., Wesleyan University.

Mrázek, Rudolf. 2002. *Engineers of Happy Land: Technology and Nationalism in a Colony.* Princeton, NJ: Princeton University Press.

Novak, David. 2013. *Japanoise: Music at the Edge of Circulation.* Durham, NC: Duke University Press.

Novak, David, and Matt Sakakeeny, eds. 2015. *Keywords in Sound.* Durham, NC: Duke University Press.

Perlman, Marc. 1994. "American Gamelan in the Garden of Eden: Intonation in a Cross-Cultural Encounter." *Musical Quarterly* 78: 510–55.

Perlman, Marc. 1999. "The Traditional Javanese Performing Arts in the Twilight of the New Order: Two Letters from Solo." *Indonesia* 68: 1–37.

Piekut, Benjamin. 2011. *Experimentalism Otherwise: The New York Avant-Garde and Its Limits.* Berkeley: University of California Press.

Piekut, Benjamin. 2017. "Post-War Music and Sound." Contribution to the forum "Defining Twentieth- and Twenty-First-Century Music," convened and edited by David Clarke. *Twentieth-Century Music* 14 (3): 439–42.

Pinch, T. J. and Karin Bijsterveld. 2012. *The Oxford Handbook of Sound Studies.* New York: Oxford University Press.

Porath, Nathan, ed. 2019. *Hearing Southeast Asia: Sounds of Hierarchy and Power in Context.* Copenhagen: Nordic Institute of Asian Studies.

Prévost, Eddie. 1995. *No Sound Is Innocent: AMM and the Practice of Self-Invention, Meta-Musical Narratives, Essays.* Matching Tye, UK: Copula.

Rasmussen, Anne K. 2017. "Women Out Loud: Religious Performance in Islamic Indonesia." In *Theorizing Sound Writing,* edited by Deborah A. Kapchan, 191–215. Middletown, CT: Wesleyan University Press.

Rodgers, Tara. 2010. *Pink Noises: Women on Electronic Music and Sound.* Durham, NC: Duke University Press.

Roth, Alec R. 1987. "New Composition for Javanese Gamelan." PhD diss., University of Durham.

Sadra, I Wayan. 1991. "Komposisi Baru: On Contemporary Composition in Indonesia." *Leonardo Music Journal* 1 (1): 19–24.

Sadra, I Wayan. 1992. "Reflections on a First Experience in Electronic Music." *Leonardo Music Journal* 2 (1): 105.

Sadra, I Wayan. 1993. *Karya: Compositions by I Wayan Sadra. New Music Indonesia,* vol. 3. CD. New York: Lyrichord.

Sastrapustaka, B. Y. H. 1984. "Wedha Pradangga Kawedhar" (Knowledge of Gamelan Revealed). Translated by R. Anderson Sutton. In *Karawitan: Source Readings in Javanese Gamelan and Vocal Music,* edited by Judith Becker and Alan Feinstein, vol. 1: 305–33. Ann Arbor: Center for South and Southeast Asian Studies, University of Michigan.

Schafer, R. Murray. 1994. *The Soundscape: Our Sonic Environment and the Tuning of the World.* Rochester, VT: Destiny Books.

Sethares, William A. 2005. *Tuning, Timbre, Spectrum, Scale.* 2nd ed. London: Springer.

Solomos, Makis. 2020. *From Music to Sound: The Emergence of Sound in 20th- and 21st-Century Music.* Milton Park, UK: Routledge.

Sterne, Jonathan. 2003. *The Audible Past: Cultural Origins of Sound Reproduction.* Durham, NC: Duke University Press.

Sterne, Jonathan. 2012. *The Sound Studies Reader.* New York: Routledge.

Sterne, Jonathan. 2015. "Hearing." In Novak and Sakakeeny 2015, 65–77.

Subotnik, Rose Rosengard. 1996. "Toward a Deconstruction of Structural Listening: A Critique of Schoenberg, Adorno, and Stravinsky." In *Deconstructive Variations: Music and Reason in Western Society,* 197–225. Minneapolis: University of Minnesota Press.

Sukerta, Pande Made. 2017. "Alternative Methods in Composition of New Karawitan." *Balungan* 12: 3–16.

Sutton, R. Anderson. 1996. "Interpreting Electronic Sound Technology in the Contemporary Javanese Soundscape." *Ethnomusicology* 40 (2): 249–68.

Thompson, Emily Ann. 2004. *The Soundscape of Modernity: Architectural Acoustics and the Culture of Listening in America, 1900–1933.* Cambridge, MA: MIT Press.

Veal, Michael E. 2007. *Dub: Soundscapes and Shattered Songs in Jamaican Reggae.* Middletown, CT: Wesleyan University Press.

Voegelin, Salomé. 2010. *Listening to Noise and Silence: Towards a Philosophy of Sound Art.* New York: Continuum.

Williams, Alastair. 2013. *Music in Germany since 1968*. Cambridge: Cambridge
    University Press.
Yampolsky, Philip. 2013. "Music and Media in the Dutch East Indies: Gramophone
    Records and Radio in the Late Colonial Era, 1903–1942." PhD diss., University
    of Washington.

Part V

MUSIC, GENDER, AND SEXUALITY

14

"EVEN STRONGER YET!"

Gender and Embodiment in Balinese Youth *Arja*

Bethany J. Collier

Featuring a nearly seamless relationship between music, dance, and theater, the operatic dance-drama *arja* has long been a popular form of entertainment for local audiences in Bali. *Arja* unites poetic song (*tembang*) and instrumental music (traditionally *gamelan gaguntangan*) with danced depictions of stock characters in a storytelling process that unfolds over the course of several hours. Often performed at village celebrations, temple ceremonies, and cultural festivals, *arja* performances follow a formulaic structure and draw on a variety of story types, including Balinese legends, historical narratives, and modern dramatic tales. While audience interest in traditional performance genres like *arja* has fluctuated over time in response to a range of historical and cultural developments, the past fifteen years have seen an especially notable resurgence in the development of new children's and youth *arja* groups, called *arja anak-anak* or *arja cilik* and *arja remaja* (Sumatika 2007; Sutiawan 2012; *Pos Bali Online* 2016).

While doing fieldwork in Bali in 2012, I arrived at the weekly rehearsal for an *arja remaja* group I had been following for several years. On this particular day, the director had called in only a few students to practice, so I observed as one of the longest-standing members thrust her BlackBerry forward to record the teacher's rendition of her *tembang*. My own digital devices in hand, I documented the rehearsal process: the director moved on to help a second student begin learning a new role, and it was clear from the start that this typically buoyant, gregarious teenager was nervous, reluctant, and perhaps even displeased with the new assignment. Instead of sitting attentively like her peers and following the teacher's physical and vocal gestures, this girl slumped her shoulders and folded her arms around her body. Her singing was barely audible. "Aduh . . . tolong!" the director begged the surprisingly withdrawn student. "Kerasin biin bedik!"

Kerasin biin bedik. This encouraging yet impatient prodding, spoken that day in common Balinese, can be understood to mean "A little louder still" or "Even stronger yet." On the surface, the director's request can be understood as a simple appeal for the uncharacteristically subdued girl to sing more loudly, or with more confidence. But placing this outburst in a broader context—one where seasoned female performers devote countless hours to training a new generation of young and adolescent girls for *arja* performance—allows its deeper implications to come into view. Extending our analysis to encompass the pedagogical landscape of *arja remaja* reveals an embodied process that is marked by both intimacy and initiative, throughout which revered female performers sculpt and prod the young voices and bodies of their aspiring student artists.

In this chapter, I suggest that the pedagogical and performance processes tied to *arja remaja* have the potential to disrupt the ostensible endurance of conventional gender ideals as iterated and reinforced by Indonesian national and Balinese local ideologies. Examining how these ideologies participate in configuring and distributing social power in traditional Balinese contexts uncovers a dynamic that tends to sustain men's authority in public spheres while it mutes women's voices in those same arenas. This self-reinforcing structure is paralleled in traditional domestic contexts and extends forcefully into the performing arts, a generally male-dominated realm within which Balinese discourses on power circulate ubiquitously.

As I will show, *arja* stands as an exception to this tendency, not only because its casts comprise mostly female performers, but more importantly because *arja*'s privileging of vocal music generates an embodied pedagogical process. In the context of *arja remaja*, this process is usually presided over by older, accomplished female performers, and a teacher's effort to situate embodiment as the nucleus of their pedagogy yields a multidimensional set of results: first, it exposes students to an expansive range of possible expressions of the feminine and facilitates safe exploration of these roles; second, it cultivates the formation of tightly integrated relationships between students' voices and their bodies, regardless of what elements of identity become visible as that relationship coheres; and third, it secures a public arena for the projection of these newly embodied roles, a step that amplifies young female voices in ways that other performance contexts in Bali do not. As the opening vignette reveals, a call to "Kerasin biin bedik" is inflected by its own structures of power, by challenges related to human development and coming of age, and by the omnipresent force of media-based technology in contemporary Balinese life. In the context of this pedagogical process, though, *Kerasin biin bedik* echoes further as a rallying cry, urging girls to probe their routine experiences as young Balinese women and invest more fully in bringing their voices into the public realm.

Ideologies That Mute

The opportunity for Balinese women to project their voices in ordinary contexts is constrained by a number of forces, including Indonesian national ideology and Balinese customary practice (*adat*).[1] During the New Order, the hierarchy of the state was mapped onto the family, in part through discourse related to *kodrat wanita* (I: the "intrinsic nature of woman" [Tiwon 1996, 48]) and the *Panca Dharma Wanita* (I: Women's Five Duties). These five principles position "women as appendages and companions to their husbands, as procreators of the nation, as mothers and educators of children, as housekeepers, and as members of Indonesian society—in that order" (Suryakusuma 1996, 101). These tenets underlie the dominant system that Suryakusuma famously called "State Ibuism" (derived from the Indonesian word for "mother" or "matron"), a collection of practices, actions, and policies that "aimed to domesticate, depoliticize and segregate women in the development process" (Ledda 2010).[2] Official government endorsement of this doctrine ensured that gender roles were strictly defined in both the public and domestic spheres, with women's primary duties binding her to the household realm over which her husband presides as head.

Indonesian national ideology on gender aligns in many ways with local *adat*'s directives. Balinese *adat* is often cited as closely connected to Balinese Hindu religious practice and is the central prescriptive force in Balinese community life.[3] As a set of cultural norms and practices related to ethics (I: *etika*), morality (I: *susila*), and ceremony (I: *upacara*), *adat* guides adult behavior and shapes how children imagine their futures. *Adat* apportions responsibilities, sets limitations, and yields benefits to men and women both differently and unequally, especially in matters related to inheritance and family law (Sukerti et al. 2016).[4] Within domestic life, for example, *adat* assigns women the daily responsibility for preparing and making offerings at various sites inside the home, in the family temple, and around the extended family compound. *Adat* also regulates residency and parental rights by prescribing virilocality for most families and paternal custody in cases of separation or divorce (Parker 2001, 181–82).[5]

Balinese *adat* acts on the female body from a young age and in ways that it does not act on the male body.[6] For example, as young Balinese women mature, they are forced to reckon with the tension between fertility and purity, both of which are lauded in Balinese *adat* but which clash with each other in contemporary culture.[7] While many communities maintain the expectation that a woman should remain a virgin until marriage, because the fertile female body is the vessel where religious discourse around ancestry, reincarnation, and descendancy plays out, many Balinese couples will not formally plan a wedding until the woman has demonstrated that her fertility is intact by successfully carrying a pregnancy through the first trimester.[8] These ideals implicate each other, and if they are upset—by the loss of an early pregnancy, or when infertility issues plague a premarriage relationship—a resulting breakup typically has much more serious implications for the female partner than for the male. In such cases, speculation may swirl that she has surrendered her purity, which makes her a less desirable marriage partner for another man, or that her body is inadequate as a reproductive vessel (Parker 2001, 179–81).

As these examples show, there are various sites around which tensions play out in Balinese women's daily lives, and the issues only become heightened when viewed in realms that are typically male-dominated, like the performing arts. In such contexts, the asymmetrical control that religious guidelines and cultural norms exert over female bodies as compared to male bodies is even more apparent than in everyday experience. For example, one children's ensemble I encountered in my research had come into being as the result of a clash between these same two competing ideals, fertility and purity. In this village's rare, distinctive tradition, the sacred group's female performers must all be "pure" girls who "do not yet know men," and group membership is mandated to be both exclusive and stable.[9] The selected children are therefore bound together as a unit to perform in temple contexts: if any member falls away or quits, or if a female member becomes "impure," the whole group must disband and a new one be established.[10] The formation and consecration of this particular children's group as their village's ritual ensemble transpired in haste, when a teenage member of the then-active ritual ensemble became pregnant, forcing the end to that generation's activities and initiating a series of ritual purifications in their village. The essential point here is not that this single performer's choice impacted her entire troupe, although it was clear that other group members indeed felt some disappointment, even resentment, that their friend's actions led to the group's dissolution. Rather, the central issue lies in the tension that plays out on these young women's bodies: activating the reproductive capacity of their fertility makes public the surrender of their purity, which in turn (in this village's practice) leads directly to both the demise of their group's status as a consecrated community body and a concomitant loss of their agency as ritual performers.

These examples provide a view of how, in traditional Balinese contexts, gender ideologies indeed "[distribute] social power differently among women and men, affecting them differently" (Cusick 1999, 474). So while many Balinese women do not have decision-making power at the local community (*banjar*) level, they are still subject to its rulings (Parker 2001, 190), a norm that constitutes a "structural exclusion from positions of civic and ritual authority" (Jennaway 2002, 33).[11] This marks Balinese women as "socially 'muted'" (33), an act that "not only signifies women's exclusion from formal levels of discourse, that is, from the domain of public power, but also indicates a parallel constraint upon their sexuality" (34). Viewing this through the lens of *arja* performance, however, has the potential to disrupt some of these seemingly rigid structures. By beginning with the voice—very commonly the female voice, trained by an experienced female artist, sounding from within the female body[12]—*arja*'s processes invert this dynamic and bring women's voices into the public sphere where they can be projected outward from the stage, at least temporarily unmuted.[13]

Projecting Female Voices

Arja is one of the few arenas of Balinese performance where women truly predominate.[14] In sharp contrast to the many male-centered Balinese art forms such as instrumental music, shadow puppetry, and masked performance, where women's participation is an exception, a new development, or in some cases controversial, *arja* relies on casts of women—indeed, on their voices and bodies—to convey its messages.[15] These messages are delivered via an ensemble of (typically) twelve performers, with roles ranging from male to female, refined to coarse, and servant to nobility (see table 14.1).[16] With nearly two-thirds of these roles played by women who have mastered and integrated a daunting range of artistic skills, *arja* provides a unique opportunity for female performers to embody and collaboratively display a range of gender, class, and status identities.

Exploring the stories of remarkable female performers who challenge boundaries has been one useful avenue for scholars to initiate questions about gender, power, and ideology in the Balinese arts.[17] Indeed, when female *arja* performers adopt and present their various roles on public stages, the influence of their voices extends over their audience and their fellow artists: their labor draws viewers in to consider that there may be many possible ways of "doing gender" (West and Zimmerman 1987).[18] One actress, for example, portrays a discerning prince whose restraint and nuance convey stability, refinement, and power. On the same stage, another actress plays an eccentric and unruly princess who races madly around the stage, dancing provocatively and impulsively blurting out her thoughts. Integrating their bodies and voices to depict this broad range of stock characters, female performers bring compelling stories to life for audience members of all ages. When these performances successfully entice audiences

TABLE 14.1 *Arja's* stock roles, attributes, and sex for each character, and the typical sex of the role's performer

STOCK ROLE	DESCRIPTION	PERSONALITY ATTRIBUTES	CHARACTER'S SEX	PERFORMER'S SEX
Condong	Maidservant to Galuh	Wise, bossy	Female	Female
Galuh	Princess	Sweet, refined	Female	Female
Limbur	Mother of Galuh	Wise, maternal	Female	Female
Desak Rai	Maidservant to Liku	Eccentric, funny	Female	Female
Liku	Princess	Bawdy, unrefined	Female	Female
Penasar	Servant to Mantri Manis	Refined	Male	Male
Kartala	Servant to Mantri Manis	Wise	Male	Male
Mantri Manis	Prince	Refined, wise	Male	Female
Punta	Servant to Mantri Buduh	Unrefined	Male	Male
Wijil	Servant to Mantri Buduh	Funny	Male	Male
Mantri Buduh	Prince	Unrefined, arrogant	Male	Female

to become entangled in the narrative reality of the stage, *arja* serves—at least temporarily—to destabilize the presumed endurance of traditional cultural values like gender ideals.[19] Examining, then, what is at stake for the individual women who execute this labor and how their past experiences have shaped the landscape of women's performance today are but two of the valuable contributions that a biographical approach can offer.

Little scholarly attention has focused, though, on how these same women deploy their expertise in teaching roles in order to effectively and intentionally cultivate a strong, critically minded new generation of young performers.[20] By curating how, what, and whom they teach, the contemporary *arja* teacher extends her influence beyond the geography of her own performance space and gradually emboldens new female performers to raise their voices in the public arena. Viewed in this way, *arja* pedagogy that is developed and enacted by adept female teacher-performers represents a discursive site where social norms and cultural values related to gender and the female body can be inverted and negotiated.[21]

Embodiment is at the core of this pedagogy, aimed at uniting the kinesthetic, intellectual, aesthetic, and spiritual elements of the art form. *Arja's* complex integration of vocal and instrumental music, dance, and theater demands virtuosic performers who are exceptionally well rounded and able to balance requisite competencies. As pedagogues, then, *arja* teachers work to develop training strategies that ensure effective transmission of this complex skillset to their students. Selecting cast members and carefully filling stock roles with the young artists they believe are best suited for each part is an essential starting point. Mindful that each stock character has a particular manner of singing, moving, speaking, and dressing that coincides with his or her set attributes, teachers necessarily seek students whose vocal and physical features match those different characteristics: as much as possible, they typecast while forming their youth troupes. This typecasting is most effective when it replicates in onstage life the Balinese real-life tendency for "bodily behaviors—one's postures and demeanor, the tone of one's voice—[to be] constantly attended to and read as signs of inner moral states" (Errington 1990, 17).[22] For example, *arja*'s Mantri Manis (the refined prince) composes himself in a poised but fluid stance that transforms via smooth, controlled gestures from one pose to the next. Using a thin, nasal timbre and relatively high tessitura, he communicates only through the elevated medium of song, avoiding altogether the mundane act of speech.[23] These refined "bodily behaviors" serve as markers of his ethical qualities: he is a sage and judicious leader, always able to exercise restraint, and a deliberate and reflective counselor. In searching for an actress to play this role, then, *sanggar* directors seek an artist who not only fits the voice and body type but ideally is herself both firm and gentle, and confident enough to garner onstage visual focus while conveying the quiet authority of a courtly prince.

Once assigned their roles, students learn to negotiate the specific combination of refined or coarse, nobility or servant, and male or female along with other aspects of character identification as they work within the conventions of *arja* form and the constraints of their bodies to skillfully represent their character in song, dance, speech, and movement. Because *arja* experts declare the primacy of singing *tembang* over all other elements, most teachers begin by testing, strengthening, and conditioning new students' voices and teaching appropriate poetic meters and texts. For example, famous Singapadu-based *condong* Ni Nyoman Candri ("Bu Candri") sits with her students as they first learn their *tembang*, singing together to memorize its basic melody and pair it with an appropriate text, tasteful phrasing, and idiomatic embellishments (*wilet*).[24] Like Bu Candri, Tjokorda Istri Putri Rukmini models subtle movements of the head, facial features, and neck as she sings with her students, believing that these tiny gestures are crucial to producing the correct melody and projecting a beautiful, nuanced sound. Similarly, the multitalented *arja* performer Desak Made Suarti Laksmi ("Bu Desak") often kneels alongside new students as they attempt to trace the melodic line she demonstrates. While singing, Bu Desak waves her index finger, flicks her wrist, and shifts her head and neck to emphasize her chosen musical contour. These small gestures are set within the larger yet still subtle movements of her legs and torso, rising from and settling back down to her kneeling position, extending and releasing her body to match the rise and fall of the melody.

The primary goal of this first pedagogical step is to help the novice performer learn how to inhabit her voice, and then to establish a clear connection between that voice, the interior space of her body, and her body's visible exterior. This focus on the voice first before the body inverts the priority that *adat* establishes for women in the domestic sphere, where the female body labors while the voice remains muted.[25] Because these gendered values have been inscribed in girls from an early age, it is not surprising that boys generally exhibit self-assurance and risk-taking during these early stages of the vocal training process to a greater extent than their female counterparts do. While many young girls initially hesitate, giggle, and wrap their arms around their bodies when singing in front of a new teacher or among peers for the first time, young boys in the same context typically sit up straight, hold their arms at their sides, and look their teacher in the eye. Additionally, girls and boys manage their struggles and embarrassment differently throughout the pedagogical process. During passages where they falter or make a mistake, the former often cast their eyes downward, let their voices trail off, and cover part of their faces, while the latter often laugh, sing past the error, widen their eyes, or slap their legs in an "Aw, shucks!" gesture.[26] These distinctions suggest that the initial, crucial stage of *arja* pedagogy—when the voice is first being conditioned and basic competencies related to song are being developed—elicits preliminary responses from girls and boys that parallel the way they manage other challenges in their lives and in accordance with their enculturation as gendered members of Balinese society.

For many young students, this step unfolds over days or weeks, in both group and individual contexts, before they gain enough confidence to demonstrate strong, independent command of their *tembang*. Once students are able to confidently project their voices, the pedagogical process works next to strengthen the full integration of the voice and the body by gradually developing other key skills that *arja* demands, including mastery of standard dance combinations, techniques for narrative development, and strategies for group improvisation.[27] Like *adat*, this stage of *arja* pedagogy acts directly on the body. As is common in other Balinese dance pedagogy, teachers stretch, press, mold, and swat their students' body parts into character-specific standing positions, gestural subtleties, and codified choreographic cycles. While most young girls have prior Balinese dance training, *arja* teachers often cite such experience as more problematic than useful: since *tembang* is the focal point of *arja* performance, the dance should manifest as a physical elaboration of the *tembang* rather than the *tembang* serving as decoration for the dance. Typical critiques of amateur *arja* performers point to their overemphasis of danced elements; a lack of subtlety, nuance, or focused power in small gestures; and occasions when overzealous movement eclipses their *tembang*'s sentiment (Collier 2014, 463). For this reason, this key step of the process challenges students to revisit the notion of embodiment and allow the inner-body work of the voice to manifest externally in appropriate movement.

As students gain competence, *arja* pedagogy transitions gradually to a "hands-off" model, but even this part of the process facilitates embodiment. During such rehearsals, teachers dart from one student to another, demonstrating different body positions and vocal inflections, then waiting as the students perform it back convincingly before stepping in front of another student to coach her in the same way. While this approach does not involve any direct physical contact with the students, the young artists closely watch and carefully emulate their teacher in turn, acting as if they have become her shadow, or as if they can emplace themselves in her (figure 14.1). At its surface, this intermediate phase appears to be little more than a logical next step in preparing the student for independent performance. However, the ability to demonstrate her character's song and

FIGURE 14.1 Ni Nyoman Candri (*far left*) adopts a "hands-off" pedagogical approach while coaching members of Sekaa Arja Kirtya Kencana Budaya (Bengkel, Tabanan) at her home in Singapadu, Gianyar, in 2013. Photograph by the author.

dance with appropriate affect does not itself mean that a student has mastered embodiment or characterization. The in-between stage, then, is a crucial transitional moment when the teacher expands the pedagogical sphere beyond tactile experience by literally stepping away from her student. The consequent transition to proximate-distance learning initiates a practice of projection, whereby the student is empowered to see herself in her teacher, the master performer, and begin realizing her own transformation from student to performer.

Even Stronger Yet?

The opportunity to experiment with a range of femininities—defined here as a set of different ways to imagine, experience, and express the feminine—allows a young actress to safely explore intersecting relationships between her body, her voice, and, to some extent, her fellow performers' bodies and voices. In some cases—as with Bu Desak's short, spunky, and chatty candidate for Desak Rai, or Bu Candri's tall, strong-willed, even bossy choice for Mantri Buduh—this cultivates the formation of a tightly integrated connection between the student's voice and her body, allowing her to openly and even proudly display aspects of her personality that may not conform to Balinese society's ideal model of demure, *halus* femininity, but without suffering typical social repercussions for her deviance.[28] There is, however, no single, seamless pathway to the moment of confident public debut. While some girls assuredly embrace their physical and personality traits, quirks and all, others express reluctance, nervousness, or muted disappointment when identified as *cocok* (I: "suitable" or "appropriate") to play characters that are older, "fat," or harsh like Liku or Limbur. For a girl who has been shamed for her body type or chided for being too outspoken, embodying one of these roles requires her to exploit—eventually in front of a large audience—those very aspects of her body, voice, or disposition about which she is already self-conscious. In such a case, the girl's desire to become a successful performer forces her to reckon with her personal insecurities and fully embrace the body she inhabits, a progression that can be awkward and even painful to undertake, especially during adolescence and in a public, social context. Given this, the more private pedagogical space of the youth *arja* rehearsal can serve as a productive site where initial hesitations like the ones highlighted in this chapter can yield to playful experimentation, positive reinforcement, and gradual incorporation of those qualities.

Participating in this type of training process can equip girls with the skills and opportunities they need to develop and execute an alternate professional identity, one that may well follow them publicly throughout their whole life. This is a prospect that female performers, young and seasoned alike, raise unsolicited and frame as a positive outcome of their dedication to *arja*. They note that performing *arja* allows a woman to stay active past her physical "prime," unlike in dance, the one other performing arena where Balinese women have access to power. "If you perform *arja*," one young woman explained, "you're not limited by age. For dancers, once you have a few wrinkles, no one will use you anymore.... For *arja* performers, there are some older ones like *Ninik* who still get used, even at their age. That's a good thing about *arja*" (Aniek Ferdiantini, personal communication, July 2014).[29] This common discourse is seductive, for it advocates purportedly liberating aims related to women's participation in the arts and signals an inspiring level of optimism among young performers as they envision their potentially long future careers. But it is also conflicting, for it exposes the persistence of sexist social mores that privilege the youthful, firm, able body as a public object, suitable for the voyeuristic gaze and, by contrast, cast the aging, increasingly wrinkled body as abject, to be concealed or retired from the stage. Paradoxical circumstances like these complicate efforts to make categorical declarations about gender politics in Bali, but insofar as they reproduce discourse on the physical body in isolation from other aspects of personhood and identity, they are also precisely the contexts that can be most impacted by the more integrated, embodied type of approach that characterizes *arja* pedagogy and performance.

Arja teachers who center embodiment in their pedagogy safeguard an intimate process and setting within which students can avail themselves of the necessary tools and avenues to probe an eclectic set of gender- and identity-related possibilities before ever taking to the stage. Once teachers are confident in their students' preparation, they facilitate the key transition from the privacy and security of the routine rehearsal to the open, public space of the performing arena. Whether that performance takes place in their local village, where the audience might well comprise the cast members' family and neighbors, or at a major festival that attracts viewers from around the island and beyond, recently trained performers are faced with the task of navigating the challenges and exhilaration of their newfound autonomy when they reach the public stage. While first-time actresses may not yet identify this as a liberating moment, other young performers with more stage experience, whose training has prepared them for multiple roles, or who have identified deeply with a particular character over time do have the capacity to recognize, harness, and exercise their agency in performance.

The extent to which a young actress's voice can effectively impact conventionally held ideas related to gender and authority became apparent to me one evening in 2019, as I enjoyed a popular youth *arja* group's appearance at the annual Bali Arts Festival. That night's standing-room-only crowd quickly warmed up to the story and seemed especially awed by the group's newest Galuh, a perfectly cast primary school student who executed a stunning opening sequence. About an hour into the show, the comic male servant Penasar Manis made a forceful entrance, singing and dancing around the stage with his characteristic swagger. Following suit, his slighter counterpart Kartala ambled onstage and the pair took up their lighthearted banter, pushing each other around the stage and tossing jokes back and forth (figure 14.2). The audience clapped with delight and roared with laughter, but soon a low murmur rose up in the outdoor arena. "Are those girls?" Fervent whispers mixed with giggles. "No, no way." Then, wide-eyed uncertainty: "Could they be?"

The rumble that circulated among audience members was a mix of speculation and disbelief, resulting from the convincing nature of the newly trained actresses' *penasar* characterizations and reflecting the extent to which the audience's expectations were interrupted when faced with the prospect of such unorthodox casting. This reaction came as no surprise to the *sanggar* directors, who unapologetically acknowledged that their unprecedented decisions to cast and train young women for these roles might uncomfortably stretch both the genre's conventions and their audience's tolerance: if

FIGURE 14.2 Penasar Manis, performed by Made Ayu Oka Wijayanti, jokes with Kartala, performed by A. A. Made Gitaningtyas Adhi Susila, at the 2019 Bali Arts Festival. Photograph by the author.

men can earn accolades for playing female roles, they reasoned, why shouldn't female performers have a parallel opportunity to try out roles that are typically reserved for men?

Like their teachers, the *penasar* actresses saw the potential for their performance to achieve multiple aims. The Penasar Manis, in particular, was a long-standing group member in her early twenties who already functioned as a strong role model for the *sanggar*'s younger performers-in-training: she routinely led rehearsals and often coached new members when the directors were unavailable, and she had cycled through learning several different *arja* roles over the course of her early career. But the ambitions that motivated her to study the *penasar* role extended beyond a simple desire to inspire younger girls around her: she also sought to disrupt both the general presumption that male actors would be playing those roles and the deeply entrenched view that women lack the physical stamina and commanding charisma needed to convincingly portray the comic servants. While the audience members' stunned mid-scene chatter seemed to confirm that the young women's performance had indeed complicated their assumptions, the path to accomplish this goal was fraught with a double bind. On the one hand, the female performers had to render their own identities as women illegible in order for the audience to take them seriously: "passing" as men was necessary to maintain the integrity of their *penasar* characterizations. On the other hand, fully concealing their identities as women would erase their efforts at the very moment they sought to influence the gendered narrative around *penasar* performance: the audience could only be confronted with the subversive nature of the performance if they became aware that the performers were actually women.

In the weeks following their performance, the young women's social media posts engaged playfully with the tensions embedded in this double bind. Sharing a pair of preperformance photos taken with her counterpart, one caught her followers' attention with the caption, "Handsome, right?" before continuing on to report a smooth performance and extend public thanks to her teacher for the "truly extraordinary experience."[30] Her partner reflected similar sentiments, calling the performance "such a great opportunity to act as. . . 'not the real me'" and expressing relief and delight—punctuating her response with the "tears of joy" emoji—when one follower admitted they truly didn't realize she wasn't a male performer. "*Astungkara* you didn't suspect anything," she wrote, "that's what we were going for."[31]

This context leads to two important conclusions. First, empowering young *arja* performers to publicly project their individual voices strengthens their capacity to contend with aspects of the cultural systems that impact their daily life. This first conclusion compels us to reframe how we interpret the actresses' efforts to conceal their personal identity markers—especially their sex—when they perform as *penasar*. Viewed through this lens, what might initially appear to be an ordinary attempt to stay "in character" can be better understood as a deliberately destabilizing move, intended to incite precisely the type of incredulity that spread through the arts festival audience that evening. By generating an unusual sense of ambiguity related to their sex, the actresses' adept performance successfully converted the stage to a discursive space where the audience was obliged to reconsider the perceived impossibility that girls could be convincing as *penasar*. In providing space where the audience both could and must ask, "Could they be [girls]?" these young actresses initiated a public conversation about the gendered assumptions and paradoxical structures that circulate around them.

Second, it is imperative to expand and nuance existing arguments about the progressive nature of *arja* to better attend to the labor and processes that underlie the cultivation of the genre's predominantly female performers. At its base, this assertion seeks to underscore the transformative role of the *arja* teacher, an overlooked figure whose work is often executed away from public view and—like domestic labor—is thus easily rendered invisible. In tandem with this, it aims to problematize the ways that elevating the public, ephemeral spectacle of performance can overshadow the importance of the intimate, iterative practices of pedagogy and rehearsal. Given that these processual contexts are precisely the ones that both generate young performers' readiness to take to the professional stage and can operate as preliminary spaces for traversing social norms, coming to understand how veteran female performers structure and curate these experiences exposes the multiple levels within which Balinese women's labor has to function in order to begin mediating culturally embedded systems related to gender and power.

Taken together, these conclusions suggest that accessing *arja*'s potential as a productive site for interrogating cultural norms and social values necessitates a shift in critical focus from ostensibly culminating acts like public performance to the iterative practices like training and rehearsal that gradually sculpt novice students into masterful artists. While learning to perform *arja* cannot itself dissolve the complexities that characterize daily life for Balinese women and girls, participating in the intimate, integrative processes discussed here equips young artists with tools and practices that allow them to imagine different futures for themselves and future generations. As girls grapple with some of the constraints that bind Balinese women to established norms and restrict their ability to negotiate for power, undertaking a commitment to *arja* can embolden them to raise their voices and become "even stronger yet," both on and off the stage.

NOTES

All non-English text is Balinese, except for Indonesian text indicated by the abbreviation "I." This chapter is based on research carried out in Bali during various one- to two-month periods between January 2012 and July 2019. I am grateful to Sanggar Makara Dwaja, Sanggar Puri Saraswati, and Sanggar Seni Citta Usadhi for welcoming and allowing me to carry out this research in their communities. In particular, I thank *sanggar* directors Ni Nyoman Candri, Tjokorda Istri Putri Rukmini, and Desak Made Suarti Laksmi, all of whom are extraordinary artists, inspiring teachers, and generous liaisons. I am also grateful to Bucknell University for supporting my research through a semester of untenured faculty leave (spring 2012), a semester of sabbatical (fall 2017), a summer 2019 research grant from Bucknell's Center for the Study of Race, Ethnicity, and Gender (CSREG), and the ongoing commitment of the Ellen Williams Professorship in Music (2016–21).

1. Any view of *adat* that depicts it exclusively as a structural, constraining force fails to take into account the varied, individual ways that humans relate to such systems in circulation. As ethnomusicologist Nicole Reisnour notes in her nuanced 2018 exploration of vocal music, ethics, and religion, "the adat sphere also enables particular forms of self-making and world-making and can thus be thought of as a space of possibility and freedom" (21).

2. Suryakusuma first coined this phrase in her 1988 master's thesis, "State Ibuism: The Social Construction of Womanhood in New Order Indonesia," and later published a dual-language (English and Indonesian) revision by the same name (Suryakusuma 2011). Some have questioned the endurance of her concept in the post-Suharto, post-Reformasi era, a critique she addressed convincingly in a short 2012 piece, "Is State Ibuism Still Relevant?"

3. Literature on Balinese *adat* and its relationship to religion and culture in Bali is abundant. See, for example, Boon 1977, Warren 1993, Picard 1996, Ramstedt 2004, Hauser-Schäublin 2011, Picard and Madinier 2011, and Hauser-Schäublin 2013.

4. Balinese legal scholars have recently turned significant attention to issues related to women's inheritance rights, in part in response to a 2010 decree related to this issue. See, for example, *Udayana Master Law Journal* articles Sadnyini 2016, Ratmini 2016, and Sudantra and Dharma Laksana 2016.

5. This stands in sharp contrast to American and European norms, where rulings about custody and related matters hinge heavily on contributing factors, including some that are prevalent but disregarded in the Balinese context, like domestic violence, substance abuse, infidelity, and polygamy. It is also important to note that exceptions to this virilocal system exist in Bali, such as when a family has no male descendant, so a daughter's husband joins her household and their children are then tied to the wife's lineage. See Geertz 1975, especially 54–55.

6. While aspects of this argument seemingly align with elements of and concepts from American feminism, this is not an attempt to assert the universal applicability of Western feminist ideals or to posit *arja remaja* as a site for the projection of a Balinese feminism. In my view, the right to make such a declaration, if one is even to be made, belongs to those who live the daily realities of *adat* and its proscriptions. I will contend, however, that we can view *arja*'s embodied pedagogical process and the teachers who invest in that process as "doing the work of feminism—that is, creating strategies that enable [one] to perform various identities, often in conjunction with so-called traditional ones, that resist and critique issues of gender within her specific context" (Koskoff 2013, 214).

7. Discourse around menstruation engages with similar tensions. While the biological link between ovulation, menstruation, and fertility is widely understood in Bali, menstruating women are considered spiritually impure and are thus prohibited from entering temples, making offerings, or undertaking other religious tasks.

8. While it may seem redundant to include descendancy as a third prong in the context of Balinese discourse on ancestry and reincarnation, it is important to consider that not all descendants are recognized as reincarnated ancestors, and that male descendants—whether or not they are themselves acknowledged as reincarnated ancestors—are highly valued as the presumed blood link that enables future reincarnations within the family line.

9. This example serves as an important reminder that even when performance is a powerful arena for challenging conventional gender expectations, it can also (sometimes simultaneously) bind women and girls more tightly to traditional gender norms.

10. My inquiries about whether the same standard for purity applied to the group's young boys were met with giggles, shaking heads, or silent eyebrow raisings. While a developing pregnancy is a clear sign that a girl is no longer a virgin, in the case of a boy, one member's parent noted, "How would we ever know?"

11. Some Balinese communities, particularly those known as *Bali Aga* or *Ulu Apad*, exercise different models of social organization, within which the roles and status of women may vary significantly from what I describe here. For discussion of such communities, see Ottino 1994 and Reuter 2002, 2006. For the limited purposes of this chapter, further references to "Balinese women" should be understood as bounded, referring to the majority Hindu Balinese population.

12. There are two distinct reasons that I emphasize the voice as a starting point here, and qualify that these voices are female, sounding from within female bodies. First, cross-gender performance is common in Indonesian dance and theater traditions, so there is ample space for female voices to sound from male bodies. A particularly relevant example in the Balinese context is the all-male *arja muani*. Second, and more importantly, beginning with the voice brings into view a process within which all the pathways—the interior space through which columns of air rush, the physical apparatus of the voice, the material body that contains the interior space and apparatus, and the pedagogical sources that teach embodiment—connect in, on, and through female bodies.

13. This exploration of the female voice, embodiment, and *arja* pedagogy is informed by foundational works on the voice and vocal music in Bali (Wallis 1979; Herbst 1997), influential anthropological studies related to various dimensions of voice and voicing (Keane 1997; Srivastava 2006; Harkness 2014), and ethnographic studies of gesture and embodiment in music and dance (Rahaim 2012; Hahn 2007). Harkness's concept of a "phonosonic nexus" has been particularly impactful, as it "allows us to analyze systematically two important facts: that the voice concerns both sound and body, and that it links speech and song. Furthermore, this concept clarifies the relationship between literal understandings of 'voice' (e.g., a laryngeal setting involving vocal cord adduction, a material locus of human sound production, an instantiation of a speaking or singing individual, etc.) and more tropic understandings of 'voicing' (e.g., a metonym of political position and power, a metaphor for the uniqueness of an authentic self or collective identity, an expression of a typifiable persona, etc.). These two related views consider voice as a ubiquitous medium of communicative interaction and channel of social contact and as the positioning of a perspective within a culturally meaningful framework of semiotic alignments" (12). His work points too to Feld and Fox's similar observation that "one [discourse] is a more phenomenological concern with the voice as the embodiment of spoken and sung performance, and the other is a more metaphoric sense of voice as a key representational trope for social position and power" (Feld and Fox 1994, 26, quoted in Harkness 2014, 234).

14. Women play an essential role within the arena of traditional Balinese dance. While some works in the traditional dance repertoire include a sung component, most focus on

the physically expressive artistry of the female body without engaging the female voice. There are also a few Balinese genres (*janger* and *sandya gita*, for example) in which women's and men's voices and bodies are equally present. Despite this relatively equal balance, the roles and interactions assigned to men and women performing within these genres are clearly circumscribed and typically align with or reinforce the same gender ideals imposed by Balinese *adat*.

15. See Ballinger 2005, Palermo 2009, and Downing 2019. There are versions of *arja* that are exceptions, like the all-male *arja muani*, but that is itself another powerful site for gender discourse and negotiation in Bali. On *arja muani*, see Kellar 2002.

16. See Dibia 1992 and Hobart and Pujawati 2001 for richly descriptive reckonings of each character's personal attributes.

17. See Kellar 2004, Palermo 2005, Goodlander 2012, and Coldiron et al. 2015 for examples of this approach.

18. In their seminal article, West and Zimmerman declare that "the 'doing' of gender is undertaken by women and men whose competence as members of society is hostage to its production. Doing gender involves a complex of socially guided perceptual, interactional, and micropolitical activities that cast particular pursuits as expressions of masculine and feminine 'natures'" (1987, 126).

19. See Kellar 2004 for further discussion of this idea. The interactive nature of the performance-audience dynamic in Balinese theatrical performances is well documented; see, for example, Dibia 1992 and Jenkins 1994.

20. It is true that men also take on teaching roles with *arja* groups, although their involvement is often allied with a female teacher's efforts or dedicated exclusively to male students. More importantly, men already have considerable access to public influence and power in other social and political areas, so the opportunity to project their voices is not unusual. Further, as noted earlier, *arja* is the only realm of Balinese performance where men are in the minority, so women's voices also actually outnumber theirs.

21. The three teachers highlighted in this study range in age from their forties to early seventies, and they represent a variety of family, socioeconomic, and educational backgrounds. For these reasons, among others, their pedagogical strategies and approaches to gender ideologies differ somewhat from each other. Of the three teachers, Desak Made Suarti Laksmi is the most outspoken about her efforts, so it is tempting to identify her extensive experience in the West as the leading contributor to this perspective. While this has indeed been impactful in many ways, she identifies her exceptional experiences studying instrumental music as a young child and her father's support as the primary influences on her ideological framing.

22. Thanks to Andrew McGraw for drawing my attention to the connection between Errington's important work and the discourse commonly referred to as an "ethics of sincerity." Reisnour's (2018) convincing exploration of ethical orientations that operate in the context of post-Suharto Bali, noted earlier, posits the centrality of an "ethics of divine blessing" within Hindu Balinese subjectivity, a suggestion that contrasts with the above example's orientation toward an ethics of sincerity.

23. This contrasts with most of his counterparts, who alternate flexibly between sung passages and spoken segments. The only other *arja* character who exclusively sings is the refined heroine, the princess Galuh.

24. The examples that follow derive from my research in two sites in Singapadu village—observing Bu Candri with her students (from various villages and *sanggar*) and Tjokorda Istri Putri Rukmini ("Cok Pring") with the students of Sanggar Puri Saraswati—and in Mengwitani village, observing Bu Desak with her students (from various villages but all members of Sanggar Seni Citta Usadhi, the *sanggar* she cofounded with her husband, famous *topeng* dancer I Nyoman Catra). See Collier 2014 for a concise artist's

biography of Bu Candri and Bu Desak. While all three of these teachers are deeply invested in training young students because they want to ensure continuity in Bali's *arja* tradition, they also work actively to support their female students and think critically about the likely impact of traditional domestic issues including marriage, pregnancy, relocation, child-rearing, and *banjar* obligations on their futures as performers.

25. I do not mean to imply that Balinese women do not speak in their own homes or engage in dialogue with others on a regular basis. It is indeed commonplace for women to converse and gossip with each other, an occurrence I have heard multiple Balinese men liken to "the clucking of chickens." Such exchanges, however, typically occur in private, domestic, or gendered spaces like kitchens and markets, and among only women. While I believe such conversations are important for the many ways they can impact their participants (for example, by cultivating intimacy among acquaintances, creating empowering partnerships, bringing issues of concern to light, and encouraging empathy), such discussions do not ordinarily cross into typically male-dominated public arenas where crucial decision-making takes place. That these exchanges usually do not (and indeed often cannot) move beyond such domestic/gendered realms reinforces their "muted" nature: they do occur, but they are kept down, unheard outside of the private circle.

26. Deeper analysis of these (and other) differences in pedagogy and response for young women and men in *arja* contexts is the subject of another article currently in progress.

27. See Collier 2014 for a more detailed description of the pedagogical process in contemporary *arja remaja* settings.

28. See Harriot Beazley's 2008 "'I Love *Dugem*': Young Women's Participation in the Indonesian Dance Party Scene" for an account of another (albeit radically different) Balinese space in which young women successfully negotiate and inhabit alternate identities that are otherwise unaccepted in their daily lives.

29. "Ninik" literally means "Grandma" in common Balinese, but in this context its use explicates both the generational separation between student and teacher and the affectionate nature of their relationship.

30. Anak Agung Made Gitaningtyas Adhi Susila (@ajunggit), "Ganteng kan? 😊/ . . . / Akhirnya berjalan lancar pementasan malam ini 💛/ Kirang langkung aksamayang 🙏/ Sukma [*sic*] ibu @desaksuarti pengalamannya sangat luar biasa 😊," Instagram post, June 19, 2019.

31. Ni Made Ayu Oka Wijayanti (@ayuokawijayantii), "Such a great opportunity to act as a [*sic*] 'not the real me,'" Instagram post, July 3, 2019, https://www.instagram.com/p/BzczxIrHrhF/. The original text of the first comment on this post reads, "'Seken' Kaden mb sing dek ne dek dduuhhhh jeg muani ajan ngenah. 😆" The performer's response reads, "wkwk. . astungkara mb sing menduga, itu yg di cari [*sic*] 😂."

WORKS CITED

Ballinger, Rucina. 2005. "Woman Power." *Inside Indonesia* 83. http://www.insideindonesia.org/woman-power.

Beazley, Harriot. 2008. "'I Love *Dugem*': Young Women's Participation in the Indonesian Dance Party Scene." *Intersections: Gender and Sexuality in Asia and the Pacific* 18 (October). http://intersections.anu.edu.au/issue18/beazley.htm.

Boon, James A. 1977. *The Anthropological Romance of Bali 1597–1972: Dynamic Perspectives in Marriage and Caste, Politics and Religion.* Cambridge: Cambridge University Press.

Coldiron, Margaret, Carmencita Palermo, and Tiffany Strawson. 2015. "Women in Balinese Topeng: Voices, Reflections, and Interactions." *Asian Theatre Journal* 32 (2): 464–92.

Collier, Bethany J. 2014. "Looking to the Future: Training a New Generation for Balinese Arja." *Asian Theatre Journal* 31 (2): 457–80.

Cusick, Suzanne. 1999. "Gender, Musicology, and Feminism." In *Rethinking Music*, edited by Nicolas Cook and Mark Everist, 471–98. Oxford: Oxford University Press.

Dibia, I Wayan. 1992. "The Arja Theatre: Vocal and Instrumental." In *Balinese Music in Context: A Sixty-Fifth Birthday Tribute to Hans Oesch*, edited by Danker Schaareman, 277–96. Winterthur, Switzerland: Amadeus.

Downing, Sonja Lynn. 2019. *Gamelan Girls: Gender, Childhood, and Politics in Balinese Music Ensembles*. Urbana: University of Illinois Press.

Errington, Shelly. 1990. "Recasting Sex, Gender, and Power: A Theoretical and Regional Overview." In *Power and Difference: Gender in Island Southeast Asia*, ed. Jane Monnig Atkinson and Shelly Errington, 1–58. Stanford, CA: Stanford University Press.

Feld, Steven, and Aaron A. Fox. 1994. "Music and Language." *Annual Review of Anthropology* 23: 25–53.

Geertz, Hildred, and Clifford Geertz. 1975. *Kinship in Bali*. Chicago: University of Chicago Press.

Goodlander, Jennifer. 2012. "Gender, Power, and Puppets: Two Early Women *Dalangs* in Bali." *Asian Theatre Journal* 29 (1): 54–77.

Hahn, Tomie. 2007. *Sensational Knowledge: Embodying Culture through Japanese Dance*. Middletown, CT: Wesleyan University Press.

Harkness, Nicholas. 2014. *Songs of Seoul: An Ethnography of Voice and Voicing in Christian South Korea*. Berkeley: University of California Press.

Hauser-Schäublin, Brigitta. 2011. "Spiritualized Politics and the Trademark of Culture: Political Actors and Their Use of *Adat* and *Agama* in Post-Suharto Bali." In *The Politics of Religion in Indonesia: Syncretism, Orthodoxy, and Religious Contention in Java and Bali*, edited by Michel Picard and Rémy Madinier, 192–213. New York: Routledge.

Hauser-Schäublin, Brigitta, and David D. Harnish, eds. 2014. *Between Harmony and Discrimination: Negotiating Religious Identities within Majority-Minority Relationships in Bali and Lombok*. Leiden: Koninklijke Brill NV.

Hauser-Schäublin, Brigitta, ed. 2013. Adat *and Indigeneity in Indonesia: Culture and Entitlements between Heteronomy and Self-Ascription*. Göttingen: Universitätsverlag Göttingen.

Herbst, Edward. 1997. *Voices in Bali: Energies and Perceptions in Vocal Music and Dance Theater*. Hanover, NH: University Press of New England.

Hobart, Mark, and Ni Madé Pujawati. 2001. "Arja: Theatre Where Women Rule." *Seleh Notes* 8 (3): 1–10.

Jenkins, Ronald Scott. 1994. *Subversive Laughter: The Liberating Power of Comedy*. New York: Free Press.

Jennaway, Megan. 2002. *Sisters and Lovers: Women and Desire in Bali*. Lanham, MD: Rowman & Littlefield.

Keane, Webb. 1997. *Signs of Recognition: Powers and Hazards of Representation in an Indonesian Society*. Berkeley: University of California Press.

Kellar, Natalie. 2002. "Arja Muani as the Modern-Day Agent of Arja's Liberal Gender Agenda." In *Inequality and Social Change in Indonesia: The Muted Worlds of Bali*, edited by Thomas Reuter, 86–117. London: Curzon Press.

Kellar, Natalie. 2004. "Beyond New Order Gender Politics: Case Studies of Female Performers of the Classical Balinese Dance-Drama *Arja*." *Intersections: Gender, History and Culture in the Asian Context* 10. http://intersections.anu.edu.au/issue10/kellar.html.

Koskoff, Ellen. 2013. "Afterword." In *Women Singers in Global Context: Music, Biography, Identity*, edited by Ruth Hellier, 213–26. Urbana: University of Illinois Press.

Ledda, Elena. 2010. "Meet Julia Suryakusuma." September 16. https://nugenderandexcellence.wordpress.com/2010/09/16/meet-julia-suryakusuma/#more-77.

Ottino, Arlette. 1994. "Origin Myths, Hierarchical Order, and the Negotiation of Status in the Balinese Village of Trunyan." *Bijdragen tot de Taal-, Land en Volkenkunde* 150 (3): 481–517.

Palermo, Carmencita. 2005. "Crossing Male Boundaries." *Inside Indonesia* 83. https://www.insideindonesia.org/crossing-male-boundaries.

Palermo, Carmencita. 2009. "Anak mula keto 'It was always thus': Women Making Progress, Encountering Limits in Characterising the Masks in Balinese Masked Dance-Drama." *Intersections: Gender and Sexuality in Asia and the Pacific* 19. http://intersections.anu.edu.au/issue19/palermo.htm.

Parker, Lynette. 2001. "Fecundity and the Fertility Decline in Bali." In *Borders of Being: Citizenship, Fertility, and Sexuality in Asia and the Pacific*, edited by Margaret Jolly and Kalpana Ram, 178–202. Ann Arbor: University of Michigan Press.

Picard, Michel. 1996. *Bali: Cultural Tourism and Touristic Culture*. Singapore: Archipelago Press.

Picard, Michel. 1999. "The Discourse of Kebalian: Transcultural Constructions of Balinese Identity." In *Staying Local in the Global Village: Bali in the Twentieth Century*, edited by Raechelle Rubinstein and Linda H. Connor, 15–49. Honolulu: University of Hawai'i Press.

Picard, Michel. 2003. "What's in a Name? Agama Hindu Bali in the Making." In *Hinduism in Modern Indonesia*, edited by Martin Ramstedt, 56–75. New York: RoutledgeCurzon.

Picard, Michel, and Rémy Madinier. 2011. *The Politics of Religion in Indonesia: Syncretism, Orthodoxy, and Religious Contention in Java and Bali*. New York: Routledge.

Pos Bali Online. 2016. "Pentas Arja Remaja, Penonton Membludak." July 3. https://www.posbali.id/pentas-arja-remaja-penonton-membludak/ (no longer available).

Rahaim, Matthew. 2012. *Musicking Bodies: Gesture and Voice in Hindustani Music*. Middletown, CT: Wesleyan University Press.

Ramstedt, Martin, ed. 2004. *Hinduism in Modern Indonesia*. New York: RoutledgeCurzon.

Ratmini, Ni Ketut Sri. 2016. "Hak Warisan dan Hubungannya dengan *Daha Tua* Menurut Hukum Adat Bali." *Jurnal Magister Hukum Udayana* 4 (2): 391–408.

Reisnour, Nicole Joanna. 2018. "Voicing Selves: Ethics, Mediation, and the Politics of Religion in Post-Authoritarian Bali." PhD diss., Cornell University.

Reuter, Thomas A. 2002. *Custodians of the Sacred Mountains: Culture and Society in the Highlands of Bali*. Honolulu: University of Hawai'i Press.

Reuter, Thomas, ed. 2006. *Sharing the Earth, Dividing the Land: Land and Territory in the Austronesian World*. Canberra: ANU E Press.

Sadnyini, Ida Ayu. 2016. "Implementasi Keputusan MDP Bali Tahun 2010 ke dalam Awig-Awig Desa Pakraman di Bali." *Jurnal Magister Hukum Udayana* 5 (3): 627–38.

Srivastava, Sanjay. 2006. "The Voice of the Nation and the Five-Year Plan Hero: Speculations on Gender, Space, and Popular Culture." In *Fingerprinting Popular Culture: The Mythic and the Iconic in Indian Cinema*, edited by Vinay Lal and Ashis Nandy, 122–55. New Delhi: Oxford University Press.

Sudantra, I Ketut, and I Gusti Ngurah Dharma Laksana. 2016. "Pengaruh Ideologi Gender Terhadap Perkembangan Hak Waris Perempuan Bali." *Jurnal Magister Hukum Udayana* 5 (4): 818–32.

Sukerti, Ni Nyoman, I Gusti Ayu Agung Ariani, and I Gusti Agung Ayu Ari Krisnawati. 2016. "Implikasi Ideologi Gender Dalam Hukum Adat Bali (Studi di Kota Denpasar)." *Jurnal Magister Hukum Udayana* 5 (4): 805–17.

Sumatika, Wayan. 2007. "Kiprah Anak-anak Bali di PKB -Menggebrak Jagat Seni, Melestarikan Budaya Leluhur." *Bali Post*, June 23. http://www.balipost.com/ BaliPostcetak/2007/6/23/bd2.htm.

Suryakusuma, Julia. 1996. "The State and Sexuality in New Order Indonesia." In *Fantasizing the Feminine in Indonesia*, edited by Laurie J. Sears, 92–119. Durham, NC: Duke University Press.

Suryakusuma, Julia. 2011. *State Ibuism: The Social Construction of Womanhood in New Order Indonesia*. Depok: Komunitas Bambu.

Suryakusuma, Julia. 2012. "Is State Ibuism Still Relevant?" *Inside Indonesia* 109 (July 1). https://www.insideindonesia.org/is-state-ibuism-still-relevant.

Sutiawan, M. D. 2012. "Denpasar Komit Bangkitkan Kesenian Arja." *Metro Bali*, May 2. http://metrobali.com/denpasar-komit-bangkitkan-kesenian-arja/.

Tiwon, Sylvia. 1996. "Models and Maniacs: Articulating the Female in Indonesia." In *Fantasizing the Feminine in Indonesia*, edited by Laurie J. Sears, 47–70. Durham, NC: Duke University Press.

Wallis, Richard Herman. 1979. "The Voice as a Mode of Cultural Expression in Bali." PhD diss., University of Michigan.

Warren, Carol. 1993. Adat *and* Dinas: *Balinese Communities in the Indonesian State*. Kuala Lumpur: Oxford University Press.

West, Candace, and Don H. Zimmerman. 1987. "Doing Gender." *Gender and Society* 1 (2): 125–51.

15

A PROLEGOMENON TO FEMALE *RAMPAK KENDANG* (CHOREOGRAPHED GROUP DRUMMING) IN WEST JAVA

Henry Spiller

In my 2010 book, *Erotic Triangles*, I argued that conventional Sundanese gender ideology in West Java, Indonesia, demands that men dance their masculinity through the mediation of female singer-dancers who also serve as objects of desire, accompanied by a single male drummer, who follows the male dancer's movements with drum patterns that are closely coordinated with the dance gestures. I contended that the interaction between the male dancer and the male drummer models the way men jockey with one another for status, all the while deflecting any tension to their shared masculine relationship to the female performer. It is these three elements—"free" dance, closely coordinated drum accompaniment, and female performers—that constitute the book's titular "erotic triangle." Finally, I made the case that this "free" dancing and the drum playing that accompanies it were thus unassailably masculine; one of my conclusions was that "a female kendang [drum] player would wreak serious havoc" on Sundanese gender ideology (Spiller 2010, 176).

This "erotic triangle" model explained why audiences responded differently to group dances performed in unison depending on whether the dancers were men or women. Men, I asserted, were expected to showcase their individuality—their personal masculinity—in dance. Even when they danced together, they performed individualized, idiosyncratic movements.

In contrast, audiences valued unison dances performed by groups of women, which reinforced the notion that a solo male drummer controlled the movements of the women and thus promoted a gender ideology characterized by hegemonic masculinity. I described the lukewarm reception received by the dance "Tari Baksa" that choreographed men to dance in unison (Spiller 2010, 199–203).

Living culture is rarely so cut and dried, of course, and it didn't take very long to discover some weakness in that last assertion about female drummers—over the past several years I have encountered several instances of women playing *kendang* in various contexts. This chapter focuses on performances by women of *rampak kendang*, which itself is a relatively new genre, probably created in the 1970s, in which groups of (male) drummers combine coordinated, unison, virtuosic drumming with clever, sometimes surprising, and often amusing movements.[1] *Rampak kendang* has been a staple of student groups, professional stage shows, and international tours since its first appearance on the scene; only in recent years, however, have women participated.

In my defense, I didn't specifically account for *rampak kendang* in *Erotic Triangles*. As it turns out, even all-male *rampak kendang* runs afoul of the erotic triangles formulation, because it involves men dancing in a coordinated, choreographed fashion rather than with the freedom that characterizes most Sundanese masculine dance. This "feminine" approach to dancing, however, is mitigated by the men's primary roles as drummers (rather than dancers) and by their exaggeration of other decidedly masculine characteristics, such as establishing an individual identity through virtuosity and clowning. The slippery gender representations in *rampak kendang* demonstrate that the landscape of gender ideology is remarkably fluid in modern Indonesia and supports my contention that the performing arts is an important arena for imagining and normalizing changing values—as well as for bolstering existing entrenched ideologies. The rise of specifically female *rampak kendang* only further illustrates the role of the performing arts in establishing, reinforcing, and challenging the norms of gendered behaviors in West Java. This chapter, after some information about the genesis of *rampak kendang* in general and female *rampak kendang* in particular, presents my initial thoughts about the significance of female *rampak kendang*.

The Rise of *Rampak Kendang*

In Sundanese, the word *rampak* has the sense of a unified group of some sort; it might be applied to the rank and file of a military marching group, for example, or to individuals working together toward a common goal. Perhaps the most evocative English translation would be "crew." In the realm of the performing arts, it has been applied to the combination of notes in a musical chord (*rampak swara* [Soeharto 1978, 122]), as well as to coordinated groups performing in media once associated with soloists. For example, when the music director at

Bandung's Radio Republik Indonesia (RRI) station in the 1950s, Entjar Tjarmedi, wanted to make the long, inscrutable melodies of old *gamelan degung* pieces more accessible to post-independence radio audiences, he and his associates composed words and vocal melodies to go with them. To avoid undignified associations with *pesindhèn* (female solo singers with gamelan groups) and *ronggeng* (female singer-dancers), in keeping with *degung*'s aristocratic roots, they performed the new vocal parts with several female voices in strict unison and called this new style *rampak sekar* ("group song" [Spiller 2006]). The term *rampak* also is applied to group versions of formerly solo dances (e.g., "Tari Kandagan Rampak").

Rampak kendang became popular in the 1980s and is associated with *jaipongan*, a music and dance innovation from around the same time. Since its emergence in the late 1970s, *jaipongan* has insinuated itself into a premier spot in the canon of Sundanese traditional arts. It was originally billed as a combination of so-called classical dance, the Sundanese martial arts *penca silat*, and the wild drumming for men's social dance (usually facilitated by professional female dancers) from the Karawang region, especially as perfected by the drummer Suwanda in the 1970s, and elaborate, often flashy arrangements of gamelan music. The creation of *jaipongan* is traditionally attributed to Gugum Gumbira, a choreographer and musical entrepreneur who widely distributed cassettes of *jaipongan* music (along with other genres) through his record company, Jugala, and popularized the dances with his troupe of performing artists (see Caturwati and Ramlan 2007; Hellwig 1993; Williams 1998).

In hindsight it is clear that Gugum's success was predicated on the work of other artists, including the drummer Suwanda and the scholar/performer Nandang Barmaya, who rarely receive credit in mainstream discourse for their important contributions to *jaipongan*. According to one of my consultants, Nandang Barmaya died with a "broken heart" (I: *sakit hati*) as a result (Otong Rasta, personal communication, January 1, 1999; see also Foley 2015). Suwanda, on the other hand, has taken to claiming full credit for the invention of *jaipongan* in recent years. Suwanda also makes the case that *rampak kendang*, in some form or another, has been a part of the musical landscape in Karawang for decades, and that its association with *jaipongan* in the 1980s only expanded its scope throughout West Java.[2] Regardless of who "created" *jaipongan* or *rampak kendang*, it is clear that Jugala's commercial recordings and live performances helped popularize both new genres throughout West Java—and beyond—in the 1980s.

One important antecedent was the musical accompaniment for Sundanese martial arts—*penca silat*—called *kendang penca*, which is an ensemble that includes a small gong, *tarompet* (shawm), and two sets of *kendang* (see Spiller 2016). The player of the *kendang indung* (mother drum) provides static ostinati, while the other drummer, playing the *kendang anak* (child drum), closely follows the gestures of the martial artist(s). While *rampak kendang* often quotes some of the drumming patterns of *kendang penca*, and the overall approach to organizing gestures in *rampak kendang* is similar to that of *penca silat*, it is profoundly different in that all the drummers play in unison.

Another key element of *rampak kendang* is the fast, loud, virtuosic drumming associated with *jaipongan*. In *jaipongan* the drumming is closely allied with the dance gestures, providing sharp aural echoes of the crisp movement accents that characterize the choreography. As cadres of young, energetic, male musicians learned the style, it was perhaps only a matter of time before the drumming itself came to the foreground. The original *rampak kendang* performances also borrowed from comedic musical traditions that involved group drumming, such as *ogel* and *reog* (Soepandi and Atmadibrata 1976, 48–50; see also Solihin 1986), in which four male comedians performed verbal and physical clowning to the accompaniment they themselves provided with interlocking patterns on *dog-dog* (single-head conical drums).[3] The practice of incorporating their physical comedy into the gestural activities required to play the drums is a key point of departure for *rampak kendang* choreographies. Combining all these influences—*kendang penca*, *jaipongan*, and *reog*—provides a flexible framework for performances that can either emphasize flashy choreography or foreground precise drumming.[4]

While the group dance mentioned earlier—"Tari Baksa"—was not well received by viewers, audiences loved—and continue to love—*rampak kendang*. I suspect, in this case, that the unison is read as highlighting the men's individual virtuosity, rather than suggesting that they are being controlled. Furthermore, the choreographies generally allow each male performer to showcase his own personality and individuality, often involve featured solos for some of the drummers, and even provide a space for competition. And they show their proficiency in a very masculine activity: drumming.

Based primarily on examination of videos, some from my own recent trips to West Java, some from the many relevant videos that Sundanese individuals have posted on YouTube, I've identified several different approaches to female *rampak kendang*. These approaches are differentiated by elements such as the physical arrangement of the drums, playing techniques, the audibility of the drumming, and the participants' costuming. I will argue that while these approaches indeed create a space with considerable potential for troubling and challenging existing gender ideologies, in many ways they also serve to reinforce existing ones.

"Rampak Kendang Jaipong"

Choreographies called "Rampak Kendang Jaipong" typically include three or more women, dressed in matching costumes typical for *jaipongan* dancers. The women combine conventional *jaipongan* dance gestures and phrases with new dance phrases that involve hitting some drums; they may also leave the drums behind at times and perform standard *jaipongan* dancing. Although the women's drums themselves are ordinary Sundanese *kendang*—one large two-head barrel-shaped *kendang indung* and one or more small *kulanter*—they are set up in an unconventional way. Figure 15.1 illustrates both the typical setup for Sundanese *kendang* (as played by the seated men in the photograph) and the altered setup for "Rampak Kendang Jaipong" (as played by the standing women). The typical setup places the *indung* at an approximately forty-five-degree angle to the floor, which provides access to both drum heads, as well as allowing the drummer to alter the tension, and thus the pitch, of the larger head with the heel. Two or more *kulanter* are placed within easy reach. In the altered setup, the *indung* is placed upright, with its small head resting on the floor, and the two *kulanter* are stacked on top of each other. Both the *indung* and the *kulanter* thus present heads at approximately waist height, which the dancers can hit with sticks while maintaining standing dance poses.

Although the movement vocabulary and costumes come from *jaipongan*, it is not *jaipongan* music, which is characterized by a relatively long gong phrase broken into five discrete movement/drumming patterns, ending with a dramatic choreographic accent on—or just before—the gong stroke. Rather, the music follows *rampak kendang*'s usual scheme, mostly derived from *penca silat*, of short, very fast, repeated drum patterns, often with complex syncopations, strung together into an almost continuous wash of drum sounds. Granted, *jaipongan* choreographies typically begin with this sort of fast, loud, boisterous kind of music but usually settle into a cyclical form. The emphasis in *rampak kendang* is on the boisterous, lively, and infectious.[5]

My first experience with "Rampak Kendang Jaipong" was a group from STSI Bandung (now called ISBI Bandung) that combined a trio of women dancer/drummers with a rather standard male *rampak kendang* group (see figure 15.1). My overall impression was that the women were performing a *jaipongan*-style dance to the accompaniment of three male drummers, and the drummers occasionally injected the comical gestures and antics of *rampak kendang* into the act. The women used the drums primarily as a dance prop; their playing did not add noticeably to the sonic texture of the performance.

Some versions of "Rampak Kendang Jaipong" include a section where the female dancers hide briefly behind the drums and reemerge wearing either masks or sunglasses. The masks are those of female-gendered clowns, who generally perform routines that highlight nonfeminine behaviors. The sunglasses might be a reference to *sintren*, a well-known trance dance from the North Coast performed by adolescent girls. In both cases, the face coverings provide conventional

FIGURE 15.1 Performers from STSI Bandung present "Rampak Kendang Jaipong" at the Sri Baduga Museum, June 5, 2013. The seated men play sets of *kendang* set up in the conventional way, while the women's *kendang* is arranged in a different manner. Photograph by the author.

disavowals of any intentional transgressive behavior on the part of the performers, and perhaps soften any gender-bending implications of women playing drums.

"Rampak Kendang Jaipong" has been incorporated into some versions of the music/dance performance called *upacara adat* (traditional ceremony) that has become a fixture of middle-class Sundanese weddings over the past few decades. A wedding *upacara adat* typically combines a variety of Sundanese music and dance genres to accompany a highly stylized and scripted version of a relatively minor Sundanese wedding custom: the welcoming and escorting of the groom and his party into the grounds and house of the bride's family (see Spiller 2010, 255–61). It is "a pageant that draws upon traditional characters and symbols to cast the newlywed couple as aristocrats for a day and welcome them (and their guests) to the reception" (Spiller 2010, 6; see also Swindells 2004). In the *upacara adat, rampak kendang* appears to replace "Tari Merak" ("Peacock Dance"), a group female dance, which contributed to the fantasy of an aristocratic event by evoking ceremonial female dances (*srimpi* or *bedhaya*) of the Javanese royal courts. In this context, "Rampak Kendang Jaipong" appears to further reinforce, rather than challenge, conventional gender ideology.

Indeed, as I read it, "Rampak Kendang Jaipong" in any context does very little to challenge existing gender ideologies and the way they are performatively

iterated in music and dance. Although the women hit drums, they are not playing them in a conventional manner. They mostly use plain wooden sticks, which
do not produce the round tones produced with Sundanese padded sticks, and
they typically do not play at all with bare hands. In fact, any sound at all is negligible. The drums are not amplified and are mostly inaudible. In other words,
the drums are more visual props than musical instruments. Most significantly:
a "real"—that is, a *male*—drummer, along with other musicians, provides the
actual soundtrack for the dancing.

Rampak Kendang with Seated Female Drummers

Women's conventional clothing and standards of modesty are one barrier to their
playing *kendang*. The usual playing position requires sitting at the *kendang* with
one's legs spread wide to facilitate using one foot to stabilize the *kendang indung*
and the other to press on the *indung*'s head to modulate its pitch. Women's traditional dress includes a tightly wrapped *kain*, which effectively puts her legs into
a sort of straitjacket.

Jaipongan dance costumes, with their relatively loose, long skirts, have long
allowed female dancers more freedom of movement for their legs, to facilitate
the deep pliés and vigorous stepping required by the choreography. So while it is
still nominally transgressive for a woman to sit with her legs spread, at least it's
now physically possible.

I witnessed a version of *rampak kendang* with seated female drummers at
Taman Budaya on June 29, 2013, in which the women played their drums in
the male position. Once again, however, the female drummers were not amplified, and any sounds they made were overpowered by the heavily amplified male
drummer with the accompanying musicians, and at times the "real" drummer
played fast, syncopated patterns that the women didn't attempt to mime. In
short, the women literally "went through the motions" (although they certainly
looked as if they had some basic competence playing *kendang*). They stood and
danced for a while, even repositioning the *kendang indung* in the upright position
associated with "Rampak Kendang Jaipong." This version also included a section
in which the women recited the mnemonic drum syllables that musicians often
use to communicate about drum patterns—another demonstration, presumably,
of their genuine skill as drummers.

A performance troupe from Majalengka features a trio of women who
have developed a rich *rampak kendang* routine. Several videos of the group,
Putri Mayang Cinde, are available on YouTube, including a performance from
July 2016.[6] At the beginning of the performance proper (00:35), the female

performers are seated and appear to be playing their *kendang*, but there's no audible sound until the "real" drummer joins in (00:38), bolstered by the sound system. Later in the performance, the women don comical masks and perform a standup comedy routine (04:08), along the lines of a *reog* performance. Finally, they sit at the drums again and do a genuine version of *rampak kendang* (10:25), although their drumming is not particularly well coordinated or individually accomplished.

In both these examples, the drumming activities once again do more to *reinforce* prevailing gender ideology than to challenge it: we *see* the women drum, but we don't really *hear* them; the female performers cite all of the usual tropes of comedy, such as grotesque masks and frequent stopping for silly commentary, to ensure audiences don't take them too seriously as drummers; and the women are not particularly successful at assuming male roles as drummers—the audience, amused by their ineptness, is more convinced than ever that drumming is men's work.

Equality on Display

Finally, I'd like to highlight a *rampak kendang* performance that might indeed challenge prevailing notions of gender.[7] The YouTube video documents a mixed-gender group formed by members of the West Java branch of the Indonesian National Police Force (POLRI Jabar), in Bandung for the seventy-first anniversary of the force in 2017. According to members of the group quoted in an online news item about the event, they prepared the performance to demonstrate both the quality of their training and their connection to the local community (Wiyono 2017).

The routine starts conventionally enough—the female participants dance, in unison, a *jaipongan* routine to the accompaniment of a recording. Conventional, that is, except for one detail: instead of flashy *jaipongan* costumes, the women wear their police uniforms—trousers (olive drab or camouflage), uniform shirts, and modest *jilbab* (head covering) in some cases, topped for this occasion with a *iket kepala* (traditional headcloth). At the end of their group dance, the women join the group of men (wearing the same uniforms as the women, minus the *jilbab*) that has been waiting by the sets of *kendang* that have been set up (03:05), and the men and women dance together in unison. As they begin their *rampak kendang* routine (03:27), they all perform the same roles—as both drummers and dancers. Their choreography features both "seated" and "standing" drummers, but both the seated and standing groups are mixed-gender—some women play seated, some men play standing.

The personnel—still a mixed-gender group—follow up with a typical *penca silat* demonstration (05:45), beginning with the slow drum ostinato called *tepak paleredan,* in which the groups show off several rehearsed martial routines, followed by *mincid*—stepping or pacing (06:20). At a signal, the drummers accelerate into a different rhythm, called *padungdung* (06:45), in which a few performers show off their sparring skills, as well as their prowess with weapons—in this case the large sword called *golok.*[8] One police officer then takes the floor to show off his break-dancing skills (07:48) before the whole group reassembles for another round of *rampak kendang* (08:10).

Here, the men and women are treated more or less the same—they wear the same clothes, do the same drumming, and dance the same movements. Of course, in their police training, they are already accustomed to a certain gender equity. Additionally, in this choreography, the dissonance of placing female performers on a par with their male counterparts is lessened by citing *penca silat*—a performance genre in which gender equity has a firmer basis after a couple of decades of skilled female movers. However, it is by no means completely equal, of course, and female *kendang* players would still be regarded as unconventional for *penca silat* performances (Spiller 2016, 330–31).

A number of possible inspirations—*penca silat, jaipongan,* and *reog*—for *rampak kendang* have already been mentioned. But what about precursors to specifically *female* versions? One possible inspiration could be the development of group drumming utilizing *bedug* in Banten and other far west parts of Java. *Bedug* are large barrel drums associated with mosques, usually mounted horizontally in frames so they can be beaten while standing. *Adu bedug* (group *bedug* drumming, also called *rampak bedug*) perhaps started in the early twentieth century, as young people passed the time during Ramadan after breaking the fast (Hamid n.d.). Eventually they created ensembles with multiple *bedug* drums; in recent years, the practice has gone coed, with male drummers who sit on top of the horizontally mounted drums, beating them from above, while women stand on the ground and hit the heads at shoulder height. Teams work on complex choreographies that go along with pop music favorites for competitions.

Another inspiration could be female drumming groups from abroad, such as the South Korean Drumcat Seoul Motor Performance, whose aggressive, confident approach to drumming inspired one Indonesian blogger to reconsider her own earlier experiences with *rampak kendang,* which she suggested were not well received by Sundanese audiences because of the consumers' preconceptions about femininity and drumming (Gumilang 2017). These models of strong female drumming help set the stage for new inroads for women's *rampak kendang*—and presumably for changes in prevailing gender ideology.

Regardless of the specific cultural dynamics that created a space for female *rampak kendang* performances, I will draw several tentative conclusions about the versions that I have described. First, although the very notion of a female drummer carries notes of transgression, the choreographies I have described do not necessarily challenge hegemonic ideas about masculinity and femininity; in fact, they often reinforce them. Simply because a woman is playing *kendang* does not mean she wields the same power as a man. As I argued in *Erotic Triangles*, drumming influences the behavior of others by dominating the audible dimension of a performance space—by being heard. Women's drumming, however, is often rendered inaudible in *rampak kendang* performances, emphasizing their unequal access to such power. Male drummers mobilize a variety of conventional tonal/timbral resources, made possible by a rich repertory of Sundanese playing techniques that rely on the way the drums are set up; choreographies that alter this drum setup by standing the drums up to be at waist height severely limit these conventional Sundanese techniques. Male drummers in *rampak kendang* are provided opportunities for individual sonic expressions of masculine display, but female drummers are relegated to a quiet, submissive role in many performances. In the visual dimension, male drummers typically do not dress to attract attention, relying on their sonic expressions to take control, while female drummers wear costumes that concede control to others by inviting an objectifying male gaze.

Despite these hegemonic forces that operate on female *rampak kendang*, versions that verge on providing genuine equity between the sexes—for example, the POLRI performance—look more to *penca silat* for precedents, in which male and female performers (at least those who don't play musical instruments) have a more level playing field, than to traditional music and dance.

It is too soon to speculate about the future of female *rampak kendang*—will it continue to reify conventional gender ideology, or will it eventually open up a space in which to explore new gender roles, or some combination of both? Perhaps we are witnessing the beginnings of a real sea change in musical gender ideology in West Java.

NOTES

All non-English text is Sundanese, except for Indonesian text indicated by the abbreviation "I."

1. For an example, see https://www.youtube.com/watch?v=9oYxpX0Q0Z0.

2. See the extended interview with Suwanda at https://www.youtube.com/watch?v=5u-XOFTFe7U (part one), https://www.youtube.com/watch?v=7H6SJ6-8U6k (part two), and https://www.youtube.com/watch?v=VW-LCmtyvTA (part three).

3. See https://www.youtube.com/watch?v=FLBd4844pxY for an example of *reog*.

4. For an example of a version that emphasizes choreography, see https://www.youtube.com/watch?v=9oYxpX0Q0Z0, which features ten drummers who stand up and

dance, move from one set of drums to another, and even throw their drums into the air on a number of occasions. For an example of a version that emphasizes drumming virtuosity, see https://www.youtube.com/watch?v=AVQ7BdhaWbQ, in which each drummer remains seated at his own set of drums but enhances the drumming with coordinated hand, arm, and head gestures.

5. e.g., https://www.youtube.com/watch?v=goWJkwmSZ-Q, https://www.youtube.com/watch?v=lZhaaoyd4iY, https://www.youtube.com/watch?v=I-bm26JXCgU.

6. Available at https://www.youtube.com/watch?v=9rMoCXvmruE.

7. Video available at https://www.youtube.com/watch?v=E8xuseNG9Pg.

8. See Spiller 2016 for more information on the musical accompaniment for *penca silat*.

WORKS CITED

Caturwati, Endang, and Lalan Ramlan, eds. 2007. *Gugum Gumbira: Dari ChaCha ke Jaipongan*. Bandung: Sunan Ambu Press, STSI Bandung.

Foley, Kathy. 2015. "The Ronggeng, the Wayang, the Wali, and Islam: Female or Transvestite Male Dancers-Singers-Performers and Evolving Islam in West Java." *Asian Theatre Journal* 32 (2): 356–86.

Gumilang, Sekar. 2017. "Feministik di Balik Perlawanan Gender" (blog post), October 10. http://sekargumilang.blogspot.com/2017/10/feministik-di-balik-perlawanan-gender.html.

Hamid, D. H. Nurendah. n.d. "Adu Bedug di Banten," *Kawit* 1 (1–2): 23–25.

Hellwig, Jean. 1993. "Jaipongan: The Making of a New Tradition." In *Performance in Java and Bali: Studies of Narrative, Theatre, Music, and Dance*, edited by Bernard Arps, 47–58. London: School of Oriental and African Studies, University of London.

Soeharto, M. 1978. *Kamus Musik Indonesia*. Jakarta: PT Gramedia.

Soepandi, Atik, and Enoch Atmadibrata. 1976. *Khasanah Kesenian Daerah Jawa Barat*. Bandung: Pelita Masa.

Solihin, Asep. 1986. *Perbendaharaan Tabuh Reog Buhun pada Perkumpulan Seni Reog Mitra Siliwangi Bandung*. Bandung: ASTI.

Spiller, Henry. 2006. *Rampak Sekar*, liner notes for CD ACD 018. Surakarta: Lokananta.

Spiller, Henry. 2010. *Erotic Triangles: Sundanese Dance and Masculinity in West Java*. Chicago: University of Chicago Press.

Spiller, Henry. 2016. "Sundanese *Penca Silat* and Dance Drumming in West Java." In *The Malay Fighting Art of Pencak Silat: From Southeast Asian Village to Global Movement*, edited by Uwe U. Pätzold and Paul H. Mason, 317–34. Leiden: Brill.

Swindells, Rachel. 2004. "Klasik, Kawih, Kreasi: Musical Transformation and the Gamelan Degung of Bandung, West Java, Indonesia." PhD diss., City University, London.

Williams, Sean. 1998. "Java: Sunda." In *The Garland Encyclopedia of World Music*, vol. 4: *Southeast Asia*, edited by T. E. Miller and S. Williams, 699–725. New York: Garland.

Wiyono, Andrian Salam. 2017. "Rampak Kendang TNI-Polri meriahkan HUT Bhayangkara 71 di Bandung." Merdeka.com, July 10. https://www.merdeka.com/peristiwa/rampak-kendang-tni-polri-meriahkan-hut-bhayangkara-71-di-bandung.html.

16

APPROACHING THE MAGNETIC POWER OF FEMALENESS THROUGH CROSS-GENDER DANCE PERFORMANCE IN MALANG, EAST JAVA

Christina Sunardi

This chapter draws from my book *Stunning Males and Powerful Females: Gender and Tradition in East Javanese Dance* (2015) and other prior work to present some of the ways performers have expressed and embodied female power in the regency of Malang, East Java, through dance and its accompanying gamelan music. My book explored different manifestations of female power in Javanese history and society—including spiritual, sexual, martial, and economic—and various social and political pressures, particularly since the declaration of independence in 1945, that have attempted to control and contain female power by separating maleness from femaleness, by mapping femininity to female bodies and masculinity to male bodies, and by privileging heterosexuality (Blackwood 2005). Drawing on ethnographic fieldwork in Malang conducted from 2005 to 2007 and several follow-up trips, I contended that in accessing and embodying female power through dance and its accompanying gamelan music, men, women, and *waria* (males who dress and live as female) performers were maintaining cultural and social space for female power despite the pressures attempting to control and contain it.[1] This led to the main argument of my book, which was that through the continuous transformations performers have made to tradition, they have been negotiating culturally constructed boundaries of gender and sex—sometimes reinforcing these boundaries, sometimes transgressing them, sometimes doing both simultaneously (2015, 1). This chapter focuses on one aspect of that argument—that magnetic spiritual power gendered female was at the heart of the cross-gender dance performances I encountered—as a means to reflect on studies of Javanese gamelan music, dance, and culture in relation to gender and to bring one of the more abstract ideas of my book into sharper focus.

Selected Work on Javanese Gamelan Music and Dance in Relation to Gender

Scholars have explored a variety of topics and issues in the rich literature on Javanese gamelan music. Given that the music has been and continues to be dominated by male musicians, it is not surprising that many studies (my work included) have focused on the practices and ideas of as well as materials produced primarily by males. Some examples include Jaap Kunst's survey of music in Java (1949), Mantle Hood's analysis of mode (1954), Becker and Feinstein's edited compilation of translations of writings by Javanese musicians and theorists (1984, 1987), and many articles on theoretical concepts and performance practice.[2] Other significant monographs since the 1990s include R. Anderson Sutton's analysis of regional gamelan traditions (1991), Benjamin Brinner's study of competence and interaction (1995), Sumarsam's research into gamelan history and the politics of the development of gamelan music theory (1995), Marc Perlman's investigation of implicit melody concepts (2004), and Marc Benamou's examination of the concept of *rasa* (feeling) through musicians' verbal and musical discourse (2010). All of this work has pushed the study of gamelan (and the discipline of ethnomusicology) into fruitful directions.

Javanese gamelan scholarship also has been a fascinating site in which analysts have explored issues pertaining to gender. A number of scholars have intentionally centered women's roles and contributions as musicians. R. Anderson Sutton (1984, 1987), Susan Walton (1996), and Nancy Cooper (2000) highlight not only the importance of women's roles as featured singers in Javanese gamelan ensembles but also their agency and creativity as artists and as women. Women have also played important roles as instrumentalists in Javanese gamelan history, which Sarah Weiss (1993, 2002, 2006) and Marc Perlman (1998) explore through examinations of *gendèr* (a type of metallophone) playing styles that are associated historically with women musicians and gendered female.

Studies of Javanese dance have also offered important insights into issues of gender, providing further foundation for the analysis of gender concepts, roles, relationships, and negotiations through performance, and providing lenses through which to probe senses of masculinity and femininity. Felicia Hughes-Freeland considers women's roles as dancers, the power of femaleness in dance, and ways the New Order state has reconstructed female-style dance to conform to its notions of art for nation-building purposes (1993, 1995, 1997, 2006,

2008b, 2008c). R. Anderson Sutton and Paul Wolbers examine dance forms in Banyuwangi, at the eastern tip of Java, noting that in the nineteenth century, males dressed as females performed a type of ritual dance called *seblang* (Sutton 1993, 136; Wolbers 1989, 8) and a type of social dance called *gandrung* (Wolbers 1986, 79; 1989, 8; 1993, 35; Sutton 1993, 136; see also Yampolsky 1991). In his work in East Java on *ludruk* theater in 1960s Surabaya, James Peacock (1987) analyzes the complex roles played by male performers who specialize in female roles, including performing the female-style welcoming dance *Ngremo Putri*. Peacock shows how the male performers specializing in female roles both challenge and reinforce concepts of refinement and ideal womanhood, and, writing to cultural constructions of masculinity, pressures that they face to live as men in their offstage lives. Drawing further attention to cross-gender performance, Jan Mrázek (2005), Laurie Margot Ross (2005), and Felicia Hughes-Freeland (2008a) have written about the work of the acclaimed Central Javanese dancer Didik Nini Thowok, a male artist who specializes in female-style dances. Henry Spiller delves into the cultural construction of maleness and masculinity through his investigation of masculinity in Sundanese dance performance, the relationships between dance and music, and the relationships between dancers and drummers (2010).[3]

This body of literature, as well as many other works in addition to those listed above, has provided a foundation on which I have built in my own studies of gender, dance performance, and gamelan in Malang. I have been particularly interested in concepts of femininity and masculinity; the experiences of women, men, and *waria* artists; intersections between artists' on- and offstage lives; religion and spirituality; interactions between musicians and dancers; senses of tradition, history, and local identity; cultural politics; and the impact of the Indonesian state (Sunardi 2009, 2010, 2011, 2013, 2015, 2020). Below I turn to a slice of that work, further reflecting on scholarly literature by showing some of the ways I have built from it.

The Impact of Femaleness in Cross-Gender Dance Performance

The dances at the center of my research included *Beskalan, Ngremo,* and masked dances in female and male styles. In general, female styles feature smaller movements and narrower stances than male styles. Most of the dances that I studied and observed, whether in a male or female style, could be performed by males or females, although some dances, such as *Ngremo Tayub*—a male-style dance almost inevitably performed by women—and *Ngremo Putri*—a female-style

dance that in Malang was typically performed by males—were customarily performed as cross-gender dances.[4]

Judith Butler (1990, 1993, 1999) has inspired me to view sex and gender as
unstable constructs that are continuously constituted by and through what people do with their bodies, including dancing, singing, playing instruments, and
talking about dancing and playing music. Performers captivated me through
cross-gender dance and their bodily expressions of complex senses of gender,
including female masculinity—masculinity that is expressed, embodied, and
owned by females (Halberstam 1998, 1–2, 15)—and male femininity—femininity that is expressed, embodied, and owned by males (Boellstorff 2004; 2005,
169, 171, 175; 2007, 82, 99, 108). Strikingly, an underlying femaleness characterized most cross-gender dance performances that I observed and discussed with
my interlocuters. One of my teachers articulated a sentiment that was consistent
with what many other performers and audience members had been indicating in
various ways: when he sees a woman performing male-style dance, her femaleness is still apparent and he is drawn to her femininity; when he sees a man
perform female-style dance, he is affected by the femininity of the dance and the
dancer, not the dancer's maleness (Stefanus Yacobus Suryantono, personal communication, July 31, 2006; Sunardi 2009, 476, 479, 481; 2015, 45, 85). This led
me to question why the femaleness had such a strong impact, and I posited some
answers by exploring spiritual power.

Like many analysts of Javanese culture, I have found Benedict Anderson's discussion of spiritual power (*kasektèn*) in Java very influential. According to him,
spiritual power is "that intangible, mysterious, and divine energy which animates
the universe" (Anderson 1990, 22). It is able to be accumulated, and the more of
this divine energy a person or object has, the more spiritually powerful a person
or an object is (22–27). Spiritual power may be acquired in a number of ways,
such as through ascetic practices and through the possession of spiritually powerful objects (Anderson 1990, 23–27; see also Keeler 1987, 41–48). This spiritual
power affects others in a number of ways, but seemingly without effort on the
part of the spiritually potent person (Anderson 1990, 54). One manifestation
of a person's spiritual power is that others are "magnetically attracted" to them
(Anderson 1990, 53; Sunardi 2015, 2–3).

Calling attention to the fact that Anderson based his analysis on the ways
males expressed and embodied spiritual power and highlighting that he ultimately outlined a dominant, male-centered, and aristocratic ideology of spiritual power, feminist scholars such as Sarah Weiss (2006, 55–56), Nancy Cooper
(2000), and others have enriched understandings of spiritual power in Java and
different ways it is expressed, embodied, negotiated, and connected to social status by examining women's roles and experiences.[5] In Nancy Cooper's analysis

of the power that women vocalists in Central Javanese gamelan wield and exert, she productively distinguishes the "pure state" of power, which may be accessed by males and females, from "the gendered uses of power," identifying a type of "attracting power" that she associates specifically with women as "centripetality" (Cooper 2000, 613). I have expanded Cooper's notion of centripetality to refer to spiritual power associated with femaleness more broadly in Javanese society— that is, femaleness connected to female bodies and/or to behavior or demeanor commonly accepted as feminine—in order to explore ways this attracting female power has been accessed, embodied, and expressed by women, men, and *waria*. Building from both Anderson's (1990, 33, 53) and Cooper's (2000, 614) meta- phor of a magnet to describe the attracting force of spiritually powerful people, I refer to spiritual power gendered female as "the magnetic power of femaleness" or "magnetic female power" (Sunardi 2015, 4).

Historical precedent for magnetic female power exists in Java in the centuries- old concept of *shakti* (Becker 1988, 385). Judith Becker explains that *shakti* as well as the importance of the unification of female and male forces were important components of Tantric philosophy; this philosophy was originally from India and was present in Java during medieval times, which spanned the eighth to sixteenth centuries (1993, 3, 8). Drawing from both Judith Becker (1988, 388) and Felicia Hughes-Freeland (1995, 198), I have come to understand the modern Javanese concepts of *sekti* and *kasektèn* (*sakti* and *kesaktian* in Indonesian)— spiritual power—as derived from the Indic concept but no longer necessarily gendered female. Indic senses of *shakti* as female energy and its importance to male potency, however, do survive, as Becker and Hughes-Freeland have shown in their studies of Central Javanese female style court dance (Becker 1991, 116; 1993, 128; Hughes-Freeland 1995, 201). I believe that these senses of *shakti* also survive and are manifest in cross-gender dance performance in Malang (Sunardi 2015, 3).

Females Performing Male-Style Dance

Female dancers, as well as the mostly male musicians who accompanied them, maintained and made cultural space for the expression of magnetic female power through women's performance of male-style dance (Sunardi 2015, 33–62). In per- forming male-style dance, women articulated senses of female masculinity that entailed keeping their femaleness visible and audible. Building on Halberstam, I view this as a form of "layering," a theatrical strategy in which a performed gendered role is noticeably superimposed—layered—onto an actor's own gendered self (Halberstam 1998, 260–61). One form of layering occurs "when a drag king performs as a recognizable male persona" and intentionally permits "her femaleness to peek through" (260). Similarly, female dancers in Malang "layered" masculinity onto their female bodies when performing the recognizable male personas portrayed through male-style dances, allowing their femaleness to "peek through" a male veneer.

The dance *Ngremo Tayub*, an adaptation of the male-style dance *Ngremo Lanang* that is almost inevitably performed by women, offers one of the most obvious examples of the ways women layered maleness onto their femaleness through movements. Movements associated with masculinity included those drawn from various male-style dances and from a form of martial arts called *pencak silat*. While higher arm positions, wider leg stances, and larger head movements were utilized, females tended to articulate such "masculine" movements in what performers identified as a suppler manner than males did for male-style dances, imbuing *Ngremo Tayub* with a certain grace and fluidity that performers associated with female-style dances and femaleness more broadly. Other movements were associated more directly with femaleness, such as movements drawn from aerobics—typically a woman's activity—and from "pat-a-cake" hand games—movements associated with children's activities. In *Ngremo Tayub*, then, a male-style dance performed by female bodies, movements associated with femaleness were juxtaposed with movements associated with maleness but executed in a suppler manner, thereby contributing to the production of a type of female masculinity (Sunardi 2015, 43).

Dancers highlighted their femininity through the costume and makeup for *Ngremo Tayub* as well. The dancer and vocalist Karen Elizabeth Sekararum explained that the womanhood of the dancer is emphasized through the costume, jewelry, and makeup, despite the mustache that is penciled on and the maleness of the dance style (personal communication, November 29, 2005). As seen in figure 16.1, the dancer Sri Handayani (b. 1982) does not look like a man but like a woman trying to look sort of like a man. Sri's costume, with its strapless top and vest, differs from the long-sleeved shirts that male dancers typically wear for performances of *Ngremo Lanang*. Furthermore, her female figure is enhanced through the cut of the top and the way she has fastened it. Sri's bare arms reinforce her womanliness and are rather erotic in a Muslim context in which many women cover their shoulders and the top part of their arms, if not most of or all of their arms, in public. She has on a wig of short hair, and a male-style headcloth. Sri also used cosmetics to make her femaleness apparent. The false eyelashes, the pink and purple colors of the eye shadow, the shape of the eyebrows, and the soft application of blush are recognizably feminine according to conventions of East Javanese dance makeup (Sunardi 2009, 485–86; 2013, 149; 2015, 46–48).

FIGURE 16.1   The female dancer Sri Handayani poses in a costume for the male-style dance *Ngremo Tayub*, 2006. Photograph by the author.

Performers also negotiated sonic boundaries of gender through musical conventions. In *Ngremo Tayub* the voices of the dancers further complicate the maleness of the dance as their voices make it obvious that the dancers are female. In short, their voices layered their femaleness over the maleness of the dance style

(Sunardi 2013, 150–51; 2015, 52). Moreover, male musicians as well as female dancers were agents in the production of female masculinity and contributed to the process of sonic layering. For example, musicians contributed to the production of female masculinity through their drumming. Dennis Suwarno (1957–2021) said that the character and feeling of *Ngremo Tayub* was still coquettish even though women were wearing a male costume. For this reason, he explained, he would play the drum "coquettishly" by making the strokes sound higher and lighter, and by playing relatively sparsely (personal communication, August 8, 2006; Sunardi 2009, 481; 2015, 55). Through the articulations of female masculinity, performers were maintaining the dancers' impact and power as women despite the male veneer, thereby expressing and producing the magnetic power of femaleness.

Males Performing Female-Style Dance

Male dancers who performed female-style dance expressed, embodied, and represented male femininity in diverse ways, maintaining cultural space for males to access, embody, and make visible the magnetic power of femaleness as well. In the *ludruk* theater performances I observed in Malang—performances that featured mostly all-male casts—I could not help but notice that the male artists who specialized in female roles, called *tandhak ludruk*, worked quite hard to look convincingly feminine (figure 16.2). Some of these artists lived as men in their daily lives while others lived as *waria*. Regardless, most wore figure-enhancing undergarments such as corsets. Some wore spandex or spandex-like shorts that gave their buttocks a shapelier, more feminine silhouette. Some males, likely those who lived as *waria*, had full breasts, perhaps from hormone therapy or silicone injections (Boellstorff 2007, 94). Most spent a considerable amount of time doing their makeup, expertly softening and smoothing their complexions with foundation and powder; enhancing their eyes with layers of eye shadow, with eyeliner, and with false eyelashes; highlighting the bone structure of their faces with blush; and defining their lips with lipstick. To sound feminine, male *tandhak* cultivated their falsetto range in order to sing in the same high register as females. For the female-style dance *Ngremo Putri* they also sang melodies that exploited higher pitches and used vocal ornamentation to make the lines sound more feminine (Sunardi 2015, 81).

Performers and audiences valued male *tandhak*'s abilities to realistically look like women, pointing to their expectations that *tandhak* pass or virtually pass. As one artist and I watched footage from a *ludruk* performance that I had videotaped, I remarked that the *tandhak* were very coquettish. He replied that the

FIGURE 16.2 An artist, likely assigned male at birth, performs the female-style dance *Ngremo Putri* as an opening dance for a *ludruk* performance, 2009. Photograph by the author.

tandhak used to be too coquettish and so looked like cross-dressers; their director told them to tone it down a bit, and now they were good (personal communication, 2005). Musicians reported that although they know most *tandhak ludruk* are male, the way they play and feel can be affected by *tandhak* who are particularly believable as women. The drummer Kusnadi (1944–2016) explained that because *tandhak ludruk* can embody the soul of a woman and are coquettish, he did not feel like he was drumming for a man (personal communication, August 12, 2006). Expecting and allowing themselves to be convinced, many audience members were taken in by the *tandhak*'s feminine beauty, relishing their own confusion. I frequently overheard men and women commenting with a bit of awe that a particular *tandhak* looked just like a "real" or "authentic" woman (*perempuan asli*), or wondering whether one was a "real" woman. I did not hear similar comments from those watching female performers performing male-style dance, suggesting that viewers had different expectations for males performing female-style dance than for females performing male-style dance. Some people, however, such as the dancer Luluk Ratna Herawati (1967–2021), said that no matter how good *tandhak ludruk* are, they do not look like women even though they can be more beautiful than women (personal communication, January 4, 2006; Sunardi 2009, 473, 476; 2015, 77–79, 84–85).

Some male dancers, including those who lived as men, attributed their abilities to perform convincingly as women to their abilities to locate and draw on their feminine qualities—that is, the male femininity they identified in their own selves. For example, Kadam (1939–2014), who lived as a man, said that he naturally had a high voice, so he was suitable for female roles. Generalizing that male *tandhak*'s ability to perform female roles stemmed from their own feminine attributes, he explained that most males who perform female roles are able to do so because they have "women's blood" or "women's hearts" (personal communication, May 23, 2006; Sunardi 2009, 465; 2015, 89). Some *tandhak* reinforced their female roles onstage and their feminine tendencies in general by referring to themselves and other male *tandhak* as *seniwati*, the feminine form of the word *seniman*, or artist (Lestari, personal communication, April 30, 2006; Kadam, personal communication, May 23, 2006). In this manner, they linked their temporary transformations to womanhood to their identities as professional, gendered performers (Sunardi 2009, 478; 2013, 152; 2015, 90). As mentioned above, others lived as *waria* and thus visibly presented their femininity both on- and offstage.

While I observed and spoke with *waria* dancers, *waria* were not the main focus of my research, and much remains to be explored about their experiences, creativity, artistic sensibilities, gender identities, and life histories. Further analysis of *waria* performers also has the potential to contribute to discussions of terminology that work to recognize and normalize the plurality of gender subjectivity and expression in diverse cultural contexts, while also acknowledging the difficulties of translation. Tom Boellstorff discusses the challenges of using English terms for *waria*, finding that "transgender" and "transsexual" do not quite capture how the *waria* he consulted see themselves. While he recognizes drawbacks, he explains his own preference for using "'male transvestites' as an overall term because 'transvestite' captures how warias usually see themselves as originating from the category 'man' and as remaining men in some fashion" (2007, 82). Additional challenges of using English terms for *waria* include the continuous emergence of new vocabulary in transgender studies, the array of terms transgender people use to identify themselves in English-speaking contexts such as the United States, and differing attitudes among transgender people about the same terms; what one person may find respectable another may find dehumanizing (Green et al. 2018, 100, 106). Terminology is also subject to change in Indonesia. Drawing on more recent research in Yogyakarta and Jakarta in 2014 and 2015, places frequented by foreign researchers and journalists, Benjamin Hegarty found that *waria* understand the English term "transgender" and that some use it (2017, 78–79). A line of inquiry for further research in Malang would be to see whether *waria* performers use the English terms "transgender" or "trans*" (or "cisgender," for that matter), and if so, how, why, and to what extent the usage of these terms might speak to the magnetic power of femaleness.

The gloss that I have used for *waria*—males who dress and live as female—is meant to communicate the male femininity that is a key part of *waria* identity and to allow for the recognition of *waria* as a gender subjectivity that is distinct from that of "woman" (Boellstorff 2004, 2005, 2007; Oetomo 2000, 50; Sunardi 2015, 63–93). At the same time, I do not mean to imply that there is any one way of living as female or identifying as a woman, that all males who live as female necessarily identify as *waria* rather than as women, or that identifying as a *waria* and as a woman is mutually exclusive. Hegarty analyzes an interview with a group of *waria* in which one does refer to herself as a woman (2017, 86). More research in Malang among *waria* performers may reveal a multiplicity of *waria* gender subjectivities as well as updated analyses of their activities, cultural work, and activism as performers.

The Magnetic Power of Femaleness

The scholarship cited in this chapter—a small sampling of the rich work that is available—points to the complex negotiation of gender in a variety of gamelan cultures on the island of Java, such as the roles, power, and creativity of women in Central Java as *gendèr* players (Weiss 1993, 2002, 2006; Perlman 1998) and vocalists (Sutton 1984, 1987; Walton 1996; Cooper 2000); the significance of cross-dressing practices in nineteenth-century dance forms in Banyuwangi in which males performed as females (Sutton 1993; Wolbers 1986, 1989, 1993; Yampolsky 1991); and the ways women and men are essential in the construction of masculinity in Sundanese dance forms (Spiller 2010). I have perhaps been drawn to the literature on gender in gamelan cultures that somehow draws attention to the important place that femaleness—articulations of femininity, bodies perceived as female or feminine, women-identifying performers, males taking on femaleness, and so on—occupies, despite the majority of professional gamelan musicians being male. In short, I have been drawn to the magnetic power of femaleness.

This chapter has presented some of the ways the magnetic power of femaleness was manifest through cross-gender dance performance in Malang as a means of reflecting on studies of Javanese gamelan music, dance, and culture in relation to gender and showing some of the ways men, women, and *waria* have expressed and produced complex senses of gender, including female masculinity and male femininity. The presentation of female masculinity and male femininity through the cross-gender dance performances I observed were not necessarily analogous as the impact and expression of femaleness was stronger in both. This femaleness that so powerfully affected audiences and other performers, I believe, is a manifestation of the centuries-old Indic concept of *shakti*. While my book explores this and other aspects of magnetic female power in more detail, future studies might draw more from queer and transgender studies to further analyze the ways artists, especially *waria* and other gender nonconforming performers, negotiate conventions of performance, senses of gender, and their own identities as they express their creativity and continue to transform gamelan music and dance traditions in the twenty-first century.

NOTES

Research in Indonesia was funded at various stages by a Fulbright-Hays Doctoral Dissertation Research Abroad Program Fellowship; a University of California Office of the President Pacific Rim Mini Grant; UC Berkeley Center for Southeast Asia Studies Grant-in-Aid Scholarships; and a UC Berkeley Graduate Division Travel Award. I thank Didik Nini Thowok and LPK Tari Natya Lakshita, M. Soleh Adi Pramono and the Mangun Dharma Art Center (Padepokan Seni Mangun Dharma), and the Indonesian Institute of Sciences (Lembaga Ilmu Pengetahuan Indonesia) for sponsoring me in Indonesia. I thank Andy McGraw and Chris Miller for organizing and inviting me to participate in the engaging SOSIM conference held at Cornell University in March 2018, and to Divya Sriram for handling many of its logistical details. All of the other conference participants inspire me with their scholarship and artistry, and I thank everyone for their support. I am grateful to Cornell University and an Adelaide D. Currie Cole Endowed Professorship in the School of Music at the University of Washington for funding my travel expenses. My Cole Professorship also supported the writing of this chapter. Thank you to Andy McGraw, Chris Miller, and the anonymous reviewers for reading my work and providing helpful feedback. Any shortcomings or errors that remain are my own.

1. The culturally sensitive term *waria*, a composite of the Indonesian words *wanita* (woman) and *pria* (man), was developed by the Indonesian government in 1978 (Boellstorff 2007, 83).

2. For example, McDermott and Sumarsam 1975; Sutton 1978; 1979; 1998; Vetter 1981; Brinner 1993; Sunardi 2017.

3. Other studies of gender and performance in Sundanese arts include Williams 1998 and Weintraub 2004.

4. For more on cross-gender performance traditions in Central, East, and West Java, see Sunardi 2015, 20–21.

5. See also Madelon Djajadiningrat-Nieuwenhuis 1987, 46; Brenner 1995, 25–29; 1998, 148; Sears 2007, 54–58.

WORKS CITED

Anderson, Benedict. 1990. "The Idea of Power in Javanese Culture." In *Language and Power: Exploring Political Cultures in Indonesia*, 17–77. Ithaca, NY: Cornell University Press.

Becker, Judith. 1988. "Earth, Fire, *Sakti*, and the Javanese Gamelan." *Ethnomusicology* 32 (3): 385–91.

Becker, Judith. 1991. "The Javanese Court Bedhaya Dance as a Tantric Analogy." In *Metaphor: A Musical Dimension*, edited by Jamie C. Kassler, 109–20. Sydney: Currency Press.

Becker, Judith. 1993. *Gamelan Stories: Tantrism, Islam, and Aesthetics in Central Java*. Tempe: Program for Southeast Asian Studies, Arizona State University.

Becker, Judith, and Alan H. Feinstein, eds. 1984. *Karawitan: Source Readings in Javanese Gamelan and Vocal Music*, vol. 1. Ann Arbor: Center for South and Southeast Asia Studies, University of Michigan.

Becker, Judith, and Alan H. Feinstein, eds. 1987. *Karawitan: Source Readings in Javanese Gamelan and Vocal Music*, vol. 2. Ann Arbor: Center for South and Southeast Asian Studies, University of Michigan.

Benamou, Marc. 2010. *Rasa: Affect and Intuition in Javanese Musical Aesthetics*. Oxford: Oxford University Press.

Blackwood, Evelyn. 2005. "Gender Transgression in Colonial and Postcolonial Indonesia." *Journal of Asian Studies* 64 (4): 849–79.

Boellstorff, Tom. 2004. "Playing Back the Nation: *Waria*, Indonesian Transvestites." *Cultural Anthropology* 19 (2): 159–95.

Boellstorff, Tom. 2005. *The Gay Archipelago: Sexuality and Nation in Indonesia*. Princeton, NJ: Princeton University Press.

Boellstorff, Tom. 2007. *A Coincidence of Desires: Anthropology, Queer Studies, Indonesia*. Durham, NC: Duke University Press.

Brenner, Suzanne A. 1995. "Why Women Rule the Roost: Rethinking Javanese Ideologies of Gender and Self-Control." In *Bewitching Women, Pious Men: Gender and Body Politics in Southeast Asia*, edited by Aihwa Ong and Michael G. Peletz, 19–50. Berkeley: University of California Press.

Brenner, Suzanne A. 1998. *The Domestication of Desire: Women, Wealth, and Modernity in Java*. Princeton, NJ: Princeton University Press.

Brinner, Benjamin. 1993. "Freedom and Formulaity in the Suling Playing of Bapak Tarnopangrawit." *Asian Music* 24 (2): 1–38.

Brinner, Benjamin. 1995. *Knowing Music, Making Music: Javanese Gamelan and the Theory of Musical Competence and Interaction*. Chicago: University of Chicago Press.

Butler, Judith. 1990. "Performative Acts and Gender Constitution: An Essay in Phenomenology and Feminist Theory." In *Performing Feminisms: Feminist Critical Theory and Theatre*, edited by Sue-Ellen Case, 270–82. Baltimore: Johns Hopkins University Press.

Butler, Judith. 1993. *Bodies That Matter: On the Discursive Limits of "Sex."* New York: Routledge.

Butler, Judith. 1999. *Gender Trouble: Feminism and the Subversion of Identity*. New York: Routledge.

Cooper, Nancy I. 2000. "Singing and Silences: Transformations of Power through Javanese Seduction Scenarios." *American Ethnologist* 27 (3): 609–44.

Djajadiningrat-Nieuwenhuis, Madelon. 1987. "Ibuism and Priyayization: Path to Power?" In *Indonesian Women in Focus: Past and Present Notions*, edited by Elsbeth Locher-Scholten and Anke Niehof, 43–51. Dordrecht: Foris Publications.

Green, Jamison, Dallas Denny, and Jason Cromwell. 2018. "'What Do You Want Us to Call You?' Respectful Language." *TSG: Transgender Studies Quarterly* 5 (1): 100–110.

Halberstam, Judith. 1998. *Female Masculinity*. Durham, NC: Duke University Press.

Hegarty, Benjamin. 2017. "The Value of Transgender: *Waria* Affective Labor for Transnational Media Markets in Indonesia." *TSG: Transgender Studies Quarterly* 4 (1): 78–95.

Hood, Mantle. 1954. *The Nuclear Theme as a Determinant of Patet in Javanese Music*. Groningen: J. B. Wolters.

Hughes-Freeland, Felicia. 1993. "*Golék Ménak* and *Tayuban*: Patronage and Professionalism in Two Spheres of Central Javanese Culture." In *Performance in Java and Bali: Studies of Narrative, Theatre, Music, and Dance*, edited by Bernard Arps, 88–120. London: School of Oriental and African Studies, University of London.

Hughes-Freeland, Felicia. 1995. "Performance and Gender in Javanese Palace Tradition." In *'Male' and 'Female' in Developing Southeast Asia*, edited by Wazir Jahan Karim, 181–206. Oxford: Berg.

Hughes-Freeland, Felicia. 1997. "Art and Politics: From Javanese Court Dance to Indonesian Art." *Journal of the Royal Anthropological Institute* 3 (3): 473–95.

Hughes-Freeland, Felicia. 2006. "Constructing a Classical Tradition: Javanese Court Dance in Indonesia." In *Dancing from Past to Present: Nation, Culture, Identities*, edited by Theresa Jill Buckland, 52–74. Madison: University of Wisconsin Press.

Hughes-Freeland, Felicia. 2008a. "Cross-Dressing across Cultures: Genre and Gender in the Dances of *Didik Nini Thowok*." Asia Research Institute Working Paper Series No. 108, https://ssrn.com/abstract=1317146. Accessed December 21, 2021.

Hughes-Freeland, Felicia. 2008b. *Embodied Communities: Dance Traditions and Change in Java*. New York: Berghahn.

Hughes-Freeland, Felicia. 2008c. "Gender, Representation, Experience: The Case of Village Performers in Java." *Dance Research* 26 (2): 140–67.

Keeler, Ward. 1987. *Javanese Shadow Plays, Javanese Selves*. Princeton, NJ: Princeton University Press.

Kunst, Jaap. 1949. *Music in Java: Its History, Its Theory and Its Technique*. Vols. 1 and 2. The Hague: Martinus Nijhoff.

McDermott, Vincent, and Sumarsam. 1975. "Central Javanese Music: The Patet of Laras Sléndro and the Gendèr Barung." *Ethnomusicology* 19 (2): 233–44.

Mrázek, Jan. 2005. "Masks and Selves in Contemporary Java: The Dances of Didik Nini Thowok." *Journal of Southeast Asian Studies* 36 (2): 249–79.

Oetomo, Dédé. 2000. "Masculinity in Indonesia: Genders, Sexualities, and Identities in a Changing Society." In *Framing the Sexual Subject: The Politics of Gender,*

Sexuality, and Power, edited by Richard Parker, Regina Maria Barbosa, and Peter Aggleton, 46–59. Berkeley: University of California Press.

Peacock, James L. 1987. *Rites of Modernization: Symbolic and Social Aspects of Indonesian Proletarian Drama*. Chicago: University of Chicago Press.

Perlman, Marc. 1998. "The Social Meanings of Modal Practices: Status, Gender, History, and *Pathet* in Central Javanese Music." *Ethnomusicology* 42 (1): 45–80.

Perlman, Marc. 2004. *Unplayed Melodies: Javanese Gamelan and the Genesis of Music Theory*. Berkeley: University of California Press.

Ross, Laurie Margot. 2005. "Mask, Gender, and Performance in Indonesia: An Interview with Didik Nini Thowok." *Asian Theatre Journal* 22 (2): 214–26.

Sears, Laurie J. 2007. "Postcolonial Identities, Feminist Criticism, and Southeast Asian Studies." In *Knowing Southeast Asian Subjects*, edited by Laurie J. Sears, 35–74. Seattle: University of Washington Press / Singapore: NUS Press.

Spiller, Henry. 2010. *Erotic Triangles: Sundanese Dance and Masculinity in West Java*. Chicago: University of Chicago Press.

Sumarsam. 1995. *Gamelan: Cultural Interaction and Musical Development in Central Java*. Chicago: University of Chicago Press.

Sunardi, Christina. 2009. "Pushing at the Boundaries of the Body: Cultural Politics and Cross-Gender Dance in East Java." *Bijdragen tot de Taal-, Land- en Volkenkunde* 165 (4): 459–92.

Sunardi, Christina. 2010. "Making Sense and Senses of Locale through Perceptions of Music and Dance in Malang, East Java." *Asian Music* 41 (1): 89–126.

Sunardi, Christina. 2011. "Negotiating Authority and Articulating Gender: Performer Interaction in Malang, East Java." *Ethnomusicology* 55 (1): 31–54.

Sunardi, Christina. 2013. "Complicating Senses of Masculinity, Femininity, and Islam through the Performing Arts in Malang, East Java." In *Performance, Popular Culture, and Piety in Muslim Southeast Asia*, edited by Timothy P. Daniels, 135–60. New York: Palgrave Macmillan.

Sunardi, Christina. 2015. *Stunning Males and Powerful Females: Gender and Tradition in East Javanese Dance*. Urbana: University of Illinois Press.

Sunardi, Christina. 2017. "Talking about Mode in Malang, East Java." *Asian Music* 48 (2): 62–89.

Sunardi, Christina. 2020. "A Mythical Medieval Hero in Modern East Java: The Masked Dance *Gunung Sari* as an Alternative Model of Masculinity." *Ethnomusicology* 64 (3): 447–72.

Sutton, R. Anderson. 1978. "Notes Toward a Grammar of Variation in Javanese Gender Playing." *Ethnomusicology* 22 (2): 275–96.

Sutton, R. Anderson. 1979. "Concept and Treatment in Javanese Gamelan Music with Reference to the Gambang." *Asian Music* 11 (1): 59–79.

Sutton, R. Anderson. 1984. "Who Is the *Pesindhèn*? Notes on the Female Singing Tradition in Java." *Indonesia* 37: 118–33.

Sutton, R. Anderson. 1987. "Identity and Individuality in an Ensemble Tradition: The Female Vocalist in Java." In *Women and Music in Cross-Cultural Perspective*, edited by Ellen Koskoff, 111–30. New York: Greenwood.

Sutton, R. Anderson. 1991. *Traditions of Gamelan Music in Java: Musical Pluralism and Regional Identity*. Cambridge: Cambridge University Press.

Sutton, R. Anderson. 1993. "*Semang* and *Seblang*: Thoughts on Music, Dance, and the Sacred in Central and East Java." In *Performance in Java and Bali: Studies of Narrative, Theatre, Music, and Dance*, edited by Bernard Arps, 121–43. London: School of Oriental and African Studies, University of London.

Sutton, R. Anderson. 1998. "Do Javanese Gamelan Musicians Really Improvise?" In *In the Course of Performance: Studies in the World of Musical Improvisation*, edited by Bruno Nettl with Melinda Russell, 69–92. Chicago: University of Chicago Press.

Vetter, Roger. 1981. "Flexibility in the Performance Practice of Central Javanese Music." *Ethnomusicology* 25 (2): 199–214.

Walton, Susan Pratt. 1996. *Heavenly Nymphs and Earthly Delights: Javanese Female Singers, Their Music and Their Lives*. PhD diss., University of Michigan, Ann Arbor.

Weintraub, Andrew N. 2004. "The 'Crisis of the *Sinden*': Gender, Politics, and Memory in the Performing Arts of West Java, 1959–1964." *Indonesia* 77: 57–78.

Weiss, Sarah. 1993. "Gender and *Gender*: Gender Ideology and the Female *Gender* Player in Central Java." In *Rediscovering the Muses: Women's Musical Traditions*, edited by Kimberly Marshall, 21–48. Boston: Northeastern University Press.

Weiss, Sarah. 2002. "Gender(ed) Aesthetics: Domains of Knowledge and 'Inherent' Dichotomies in Central Javanese Wayang Accompaniment." In *Puppet Theater in Contemporary Indonesia: New Approaches to Performance Events*, edited by Jan Mrázek, 296–314. Ann Arbor: Centers for South and Southeast Asian Studies, University of Michigan.

Weiss, Sarah. 2006. *Listening to an Earlier Java: Aesthetics, Gender, and the Music of Wayang in Central Java*. Leiden: KITLV Press.

Williams, Sean. 1998. "Constructing Gender in Sundanese Music." *Yearbook for Traditional Music* 30: 74–84.

Wolbers, Paul Arthur. 1986. "Gandrung and Angklung from Banyuwangi: Remnants of a Past Shared with Bali." *Asian Music* 18 (1): 71–90.

Wolbers, Paul Arthur. 1989. "Transvestism, Eroticism, and Religion: In Search of a Contextual Background for the Gandrung and Seblang Traditions of Banyuwangi, East Java." *Progress Reports in Ethnomusicology* 2 (6): 1–21.

Wolbers, Paul Arthur. 1993. "The *Seblang* and Its Music: Aspects of an East Javanese Fertility Rite." In *Performance in Java and Bali: Studies of Narrative, Theatre, Music, and Dance*, edited by Bernard Arps, 34–46. London: School of Oriental and African Studies, University of London.

Yampolsky, Philip. 1991. "Songs Before Dawn." Liner notes to *Music of Indonesia 1: Songs before Dawn: Gandrung Banyuwangi*. Smithsonian/Folkways Recordings CD SF40055.

Part VI
PERSPECTIVES FROM PRACTICE

NINES ON TEACHING BEGINNING GAMELAN*

Jody Diamond

G ong plays first, and sounds in the last place.

A ll parts are made of relationships.

M elody is in contour, not pitch.

E very contribution has value.

L istening is of prime importance.

A wareness grows of drums leading time.

N o worries, the music's your teacher.

* "Nines . . ." has nine syllables on each line.

"FIX YOUR FACE"

Performing Attitudes between Mathcore and *Beleganjur*

Putu Tangkas Adi Hiranmayena

In 2012, on the way to Gamelan Tunas Mekar's rehearsal, I played a song by Dillinger Escape Plan called "Fix Your Face" for my father. I cranked up the volume on the mathcore tune and sure enough, his response, in Balinese, was, "Apa ng'redek ne . . . Pak sing demen" (What's all this commotion . . . I don't like it).[1] Mission accomplished! I successfully annoyed him, and yet, at the back of my mind, I was seeking a bit of approval for this music that I thoroughly enjoy. Fast-forward five years to 2017. I played the same song, again with the intention to rile him up. This time his response was "Tu, ne lu'ung anggo beleganjur" (Tu, this song is great for *beleganjur*). I was quite surprised as it was not the reaction I expected, and quite frankly, it was confusing. Although this time, his reaction did not necessarily denote approval or joy, he recognized it as being valuable enough for cross-cultural hybridity. What exactly happened in five years that could have changed his mind about the song? Whatever the reason, it was enough of a push for me to undergo a musical transposition project: one between mathcore and *gamelan beleganjur*; one between juxtaposing cultures; one that is intergenerational.

This chapter centers around my arrangement of Dillinger Escape Plan's "Fix Your Face" for Gamelan Tunas Mekar, a Denver-based Balinese gamelan ensemble under the direction of I Made Lasmawan—whom I know as my father. I transcribed this piece for *gamelan beleganjur* (Balinese processional music) and recorded it with Gamelan Tunas Mekar as an artistic endeavor that problematizes performance in creating the musical faces that I present as an Indonesian American musician.[2] The project was not a hybridization created to justify the music I am interested in performing but rather a re-fusion: that which heavy metal scholar Jeremy Wallach describes as a refusal to stay boxed in the categories prescribed by ethnomusicological assumptions. Wallach suggested the term in a response to my presentation at the SOSIM conference on which this chapter is based: "Putu, ever since the version of 'Silver Dagger' last night,[3] *langgam Jawa*–style, I've been thinking of what to call performances like that one and the performance you just played. I think they are re-fusions. They are taking something and doing it in a different style. It's a product of multiple back-and-forth motions in music. And it's a refus-ion, it's also a refusal to stay boxed in to any particular genre category." The piece re-fuses my role of gamelan educator with musical ideologies that adhere to my own positionality as an artist-scholar. As an extension of this stance, this chapter is structured by my experiences in ethnomusicology and conversations with gamelan practitioners, and supplemented by scholars' theories that I view as inseparable from my worldview. It critiques and frustrates genre categories, director identities, and clashing temporal ideologies by an auto-ethnographic inquiry into my own role as an Indonesian American artist-scholar. I begin with an autobiographical description of the musical and intellectual world that leads to my understanding of intercultural identity as it relates to a gamelan. I include critiques into emic and etic perspectives, Colorado sound ecologies, and dynamic embodiments of first- and second-generation Indonesian artists—all of which highlight the nuances of performing attitudes, and the performance of attitude, especially that conveyed by the Balinese term *benen mua*. I then describe my aesthetic decisions in transposing a mathcore piece to *gamelan beleganjur* in order to sound *benen mua* and critique societal intellectualism. Then I discuss the spectrum between cultural appropriation and cultural appreciation, as musical hybridities tend to teeter between the two in their refusal to be confined to one identity or another and evade labels. I highlight intercultural sensibilities and the contributions to what will later be my own study on neocolonial music making (that which largely lives within the realm of post-colonialism). I then conclude with an understanding of a human being's positionalities as it relates to diverse hybridities and practices that is navigable for peoples' complex musical (cultural) desires, with an emphasis on the enactment of intercultural identities. The questions proposed in this study are the seeds of what I intend to be a larger project on the colonized mind of gamelan practitioners and their bypassing of critiques of cultural appropriation. I hope to highlight the complications of a cultural mediator by framing my own creative intentions in relation to community identities and attitudes. In doing so, I use *benen mua* as a vehicle for artistic expression; a self-reflection of intercultural identity and a problematization of pedagogical methodologies as an artist-scholar.

Benen Mua

The title of my arrangement, "Benen Mua," is a Balinese translation of Dillinger's "Fix Your Face" and an extension of the concepts presented in this chapter. I conceive this performance as one that caters to a social "Other," one that reveals the embodied and artistic tensions inherent in constantly having to "fix my face" during the performance of intercultural identity. *Benen mua* is neither formal nor colloquial. It is a phrase—employed primarily by Balinese parents to their children—used to describe the performance of attitudes in contexts that require a momentary reshaping of identity: an attitude that resembles the passive aggressiveness of cultural mediation, a comfort found in the frustrations of social relations, and affects created in generational shifts.[4] I've chosen to stay vague, employing the passive voice, to invite readers to locate these ideas within their own personal experiences. Imagine when guests are invited to a family gathering and children are asked to alter their behavior for the sake of politeness. It has to do with not being too exuberant, and thus disruptive, as kids often are, thus instilling social awareness and sensitivity. In adulthood, people tend to bite their tongue when what one wants to say would be hurtful or counterproductive, or would cause someone to react angrily. *Benen mua* has specifically to do with speech and impulse control. In either case, *benen mua* is a means to acclimate momentarily to the external situation. I use the related English-language metaphor "biting the tongue" to highlight the constraints faced by highly esteemed Indonesian artists in community building. This frame is also relevant to my interpretation of Dillinger Escape Plan's lyrics for "Fix Your Face."[5] Although Dillinger Escape Plan has described the lyrics in terms of romantic relationships, I have often felt similar affects with my relationship to the myriad of gamelan ensembles I've been a part of and even taught. When they say, "You want a vision you can't have, a line that you can't walk," or "No way you and I will ever be done," I relate these lyrical lines to the way compromise of artistic vision is always at the forefront of artistic relationships for native *gamelan* teachers in the United States. It implies a legacy of relationships that are inextricably linked to personal philosophies of diasporic artists. *Benen mua* encapsulates the embodied complexities of these pedagogues who have found residency outside of Indonesia. I conceptualize *benen mua* to problematize the performance of attitudes in Indonesian expressive arts. Are Indonesian artists truly afforded a chance to practice music according to their own artistic outlook? The presence of gamelan teachers in the United States would imply that they do. But is this a façade or perhaps indirect coercion by an institution (academic or otherwise)? How might they enact the role of a cultural mediator and cultural ambassador through a co-optation of musical performance? Where and how might a gamelan teacher find home in a place that is distant from their geographical roots? These questions arise from my own interactions with gamelan families between Indonesia and the United States in their feeling of acceptance when a performance is "just fine." This practice of "tongue biting" may support sustainable ensemble practices, efficient pedagogical methods, or demonstrate awareness of cultural privilege. It is in favor of the community, which in this case is largely American; it is a performance that is cultivated to safeguard the outsider's sensibility: it is survival. To *benen mua* is to "bite the tongue," which eventually manifests as a performance of attitude in intercultural identity.

Indonesian American

I was born in the town of Surakarta on the island of Java, Indonesia, in March 1989. Shortly after (roughly nine months), my family moved to San Diego, California, where my father took an adjunct teaching position at San Diego State University. When my family first arrived in the United States, we were already integrated within the processes of one of ethnomusicology's ideologies of reciprocity: bring a native practitioner to the locale of new gamelan communities as an opportunity for building a different, more diverse cultural economy, and in order to give American students a chance to practice fieldwork "at home."[6] My family then moved to Colorado in 1993, and we have been here ever since. I eventually received a BA in visual and performing arts with an emphasis on music and theater from the University of Colorado, Colorado Springs; an MA in integrative studies with an emphasis on ethnomusicology and systems inquiry from the University of California, San Diego; and I am currently working on a PhD in ethnomusicology from the University of Illinois at Urbana-Champaign. As a first-generation Indonesian person in the United States, I share this role with a handful of others whose families have also found residence somewhere across the country. A small number are Balinese gamelan pedagogues.[7] Although our identities and interests vary, we share the weight of Balinese artists in the United States: a quaint community that carries a heavy load as culture bearers. Thus, the term "ethnomusicology" has been in my vernacular for a long time because it was primarily within the realm of music that our interactions were most meaningful. But as the discourse of ethnomusicology is inherently pan-idiomatic—changing identity based on what theories or methodologies are currently idiomatic—so too was my understanding of it. I often asked myself, "Will my definition of ethnomusicology be adequate enough not to trivialize, but concise enough not to bore?" As Bruno Nettl has argued, it is a term and field that is subject to constant re-identification and re-formation.[8]

Being the son of a renowned gamelan artist has inadvertently positioned me in the thick of ethnomusicological interest, either as secondhand observer or direct subject. It put me in the position of an insider prior to any understanding of binary oppositions, as I was able to traverse the spectrum of emicness and eticness. This contributed to my personal worldview, which framed an amalgam of artistic ideas and refused complacency. I would often have difficulties compartmentalizing differences in artistic sensibilities, which stemmed from experiencing Indonesian music, dance, and visual art simultaneously, it was difficult to separate artistic modalities and sensibilities, even as they relate to various social theories.

Growing up, my days were spent in a public school, followed by rehearsals at one of the universities where my father taught, and the occasional performance at social events, a common schedule shared with my first- and second-generation Balinese co-patriots. As my father traveled around the United States, the car became my preferred place to sleep, and so a comfortable place. This became standard practice for my family and me, with summers reserved for traveling back to Indonesia. The academic institutions in which my father worked afforded Western educational opportunities all while being able to stay connected with Indonesia.[9] But there was one caveat: although returning to Bali every summer may seem like a luxurious vacation to others, we were always busy hosting study abroad programs for university students, or people interested in learning about Bali. Going home to Bali without a batch of twenty rowdy college students was rare. The trips were necessary and important for familial connectivity and the dissemination of knowledge, but we rarely had true leisure time. Even with Indonesia's practices of *jam karet* (literally "rubber time") and a sense of *nongkrong* (hanging out), we had to disperse our time to accommodate not only foreign visitors but the sociocultural structures of Bali—primarily partaking in constant ritual ceremonies and their events. The "island of one thousand temples" did not rest to accommodate our desired vacation from American academic life.

Traveling back and forth between the United States and Indonesia often meant that people in America and Indonesia asked me questions such as, "Which one do you like better?" or "Which one do you call home?" These questions were monotonous and strange; they were questions I constantly struggled to answer because it meant that my identity was always in question. To give a specific answer was to neglect one place or the other, deny my intercultural persona, or suggest a lack of gratitude. It related to social power differentials in both places that shaped my worldview, as I actively silenced myself in dominating conversations. I often share these experiences with other children of immigrant parents and I associate it with a constant state of liminality—a feeling that didn't provide any foundational identity. Music became for me a grounding force—unfortunately, however, associated with a large degree of cynicism.

It has been a struggle to find a comfortable place in the world, including the musical world. But with much silence (and noise), I have come to accept it. Playing gamelan for the majority of my life made me rebellious against it for a period of time. But in this time of criticizing my musical heritage, I found heavy metal and experimental music—which eventually led me back to being actively interested in gamelan. I took up drum set as an instrument that was loud and individualistic yet had the potential for community and nuance. Certain branches of heavy metal and experimentalism tend to be very niche, which confirmed my position on the periphery; my cosmology resembled living on the edge of prescribed assumptions. Many people said, "Oh, you're Pak Made's son, you must be good at gamelan," or "Oh, you like American experimental music, you must have thrown away tradition," or "You're an academic that studies noise and metal?" Then there would be the sound of crickets (silence), followed by laughter, which would cap off with an awkward, "Uhhh . . . that's cool." In a life unnecessarily defined by others, I found the margins of heavy metal and experimentalism to be an entry point into what my priorities are as an academic and an artist. It was a place of solace shared by my band of musickers at the edge of communities that were already marginalized.

Between Heavy Metal and *Beleganjur*: "Fix Your Face" to "Benen Mua"

The hybridization of gamelan with other musical idioms is not a groundbreaking avenue, but it has certainly not been exhausted, especially as a community-generating endeavor.[10] Works that feature gamelan in new, hybrid musical contexts continue to emerge with gamelan's dispersal across the globe (Steele 2013). Even in Indonesia, gamelan is fused with foreign artistic expressions and finds new sonic sensibilities. Ethnomusicologists such as Rebekah E. Moore, Jeremy Wallach, and Elizabeth Macy have done extensive studies on these sound worlds and their relation to popular musics.[11] For many of these ensembles, the way to stay in conversation with the global music world is to hybridize in some way. The circulation of ideas afforded by social media platforms and YouTube has provided educational and even pedagogical methods in which to diversify worldviews. Covers of American Top 40 popular music on gamelan are becoming popular, especially for some Javanese gamelan ensembles. This practice is becoming niche and has even created more genres of music.[12] They are fun and lighthearted, but they also serve as an exercise in globalization: performing foreign songs on local instruments. What it also offers is a chance to experience new musics via popular idioms. Someone from America who knows of Bruno Mars but not of *karawitan* can move through the gateway of diversity via musical hybridity.

American mathcore and Balinese *beleganjur* are two loud musics that challenge social order through complex musicalities, malleable communal priorities, and an embodied *benen mua*. When gamelan performances—outside of Indonesia—are enacted within these contexts, the ensemble shapes itself to justify, while also contesting, the attitudes of the practitioners. How is local community established in tandem with conversations across oceans through *beleganjur*? What kind of trust is needed in order to traverse parallel attitudes of performance? Who is in conversation when an American metal piece is performed on *beleganjur* that drastically departs from traditional performance contexts and musical styles? What are the results of performing gamelan when Colorado-based gamelan musicians are told to enact a Balinese-embodied script for performance without knowledge or understanding of Balinese gestures in situ? What shortcomings emerge when practitioners' attitudes are formed independent of Balinese cultural context? I do not propose answers to these questions but rather highlight the complexities through musical composition and self-reflexivity.

One of *beleganjur*'s primary codifications of performance has to do with endurance and physical dexterity. Both in competitions and religious ceremonial processionals—a distinction I will make between the spectrum of secular and sacred in Balinese expressive arts—physicality is at the forefront of an embodied realization of *beleganjur*'s social functions, which manifests as a music of the youth and perpetuation of community legacies. Just before one of the *beleganjur* competitions at the 2018 Pesta Kesenian Bali (Bali Arts Festival) I met up with my friend, Agoes Thana, from the village of Uma Poh, Tabanan. He is the composer for the Tabanan regency and is gaining recognition as one of the top *beleganjur* pedagogues of the decade. By the time I had met up with him, the group had already finished sound check and were changing into their costumes for the evening. I had a chance to speak to some of the members, most of whom, although very excited and prideful, were already showing exhaustion, though this was an affect that was frequently felt. In more religious-ceremonial contexts such as *ngaben* (cremations), *beleganjur* is performed for a majority of the day and processed for many kilometers. In the village of Bangah in the mountains of the Tabanan regency, where my family is from, these processions take place through ravines and over hillsides. Rarely are there any flat surfaces. Studies on *beleganjur* often describe the enactment as getting rid of evil spirits and creating music that dispels dark energy. Many composers I have spoken to, such as Thana, describe composing *beleganjur* music to entice evil spirits so they do not disrupt the primary ceremony. The physical and cosmological dexterity for *beleganjur* is specific to its social functions and tied to endurance in a way that is malleable across generations.

Mathcore, on the other hand, is a music that requires a different kind of performative affect. Its emergence is within the histories of North American metalcore and hardcore genres with bands such as Botch, Converge, Dillinger Escape Plan, and many more. The music is abrasive and employs many arrhythmic structures along with through-composed chord structures. All of this occurs within a short temporal frame; most songs hover around one to three minutes. Dillinger Escape Plan has one of the most aggressive and alarming stage presences of any live music group. They are often seen hanging from rafters, jumping off amplification systems, diving into crowds with their instruments, or even inviting the whole audience onto the stage. When asking about Dillinger Escape Plan's stage presence, many interviewers are curious about their abrasiveness and the consistency of performance for twenty years. The band often responds that they are unable to play the music any other way.[13] This musico-physiological phenomena is a testament to the exigency required in performing attitudes. Both *beleganjur* and mathcore require a particular kind of physical exertion that contributes to the temporal affect of the performance. Their similar musical sensibilities sometimes differ in ideology as one appropriates ideas of darkness and the other appreciates it by cleansing sacred space, but this is a juxtaposition of priorities in practice.

The instrumentation for "Benen Mua" consists entirely of a *beleganjur* ensemble with the addition of some supplemental instruments: eleven *ceng-ceng kopyak*, one gong *ageng*, one gong *lanang*, one *kempur*, one *kajar*, one *tawa-tawa*, a pair of *ponggang*, one set of *reyong*, and one *kendang bebarongan*. The decision for this instrumentation was based on which gamelan instruments are available (in accordance with performer competency) that could best emulate the energy of amplified metal instrumentation. The primary intention for this musical realization was transferring the rhythmic complexity of "Fix Your Face," along with arranging a portion of the piece to include improvisational noise. In each section of the piece at least one of the instruments had an improvisatory role. This artistic element is unusual for *beleganjur* sensibilities because this type of gamelan is known for its hyperprecision in its rhythms and choreography. It is also seldom used in mathcore because of the genre's tendency to enact arhythmic structures.

The structure of the piece followed the original mathcore tune. Attempting to adhere to traditional Balinese form, I framed "Benen Mua" as having a head, body, and feet with colotomic structures as rhythmic foundations. The main motif (which became the *kawitan* or head) is in a gong cycle of twenty-four beats; the *pengawak* (the main body) is in a twenty-six beat cycle; and the *pekaad* (the feet or departure) is in a six beat cycle. Ironically, the cyclical parameters in each section had very little relevance to my teaching of the piece. I refrained from using any numerical markers because I see that as a post-performance analytical inquiry. It is a hindrance in my pedagogical process but useful to analyze later for the purposes of musical theory.

In between the *pengawak* and *pekaad* is the collective improvisation section where the instructions were "Make as much noise as fast as you can and watch each other for hard cutoffs." I emphasized the necessity for full body movement. This is also the only section of the piece where the human voice is used, and two of our members screamed as a transitional marker. For myself, this was also the most important section. I wanted to create a particular sense of exhaustion I have personally felt in traditional Balinese *beleganjur* contexts, which include processing through villages for many hours and moving as a unit. In the United States, no *beleganjur* performance will ever evoke this same affect because it is not a necessary component to local performance practice.[14] Practices involving cross-cultural hybridity fall short and are potentially offensive due to their lack of sensitivity to traditional context. Here I am not proposing that experimentation is a deterrent but that practitioners should have context for what is being experimented on.

Cultural Appropriation and Cultural Appreciation

The conflation of cultural appropriation and cultural appreciation are understandable, but it is not a topic that should be taken lightly, especially for practitioners of gamelan. With the growing number of gamelan finding residence outside of Indonesia, we must do work to decolonize our social interactions through practices and attitudes, not only within the performing ensemble itself but also in performance. Otherwise, we are susceptible to "all-for-the-taking" neocolonial movements. I suggest that cultural appropriation and cultural appreciation are not isolated categories but rather a spectrum of performance in dialogical relationships with native practitioners. I follow many ethnomusicologists' view that cultural appropriation of artistic expression often disempowers native practitioners and creates unethical relationships.[15] I have often seen this in gamelan ensembles where people sample instruments and integrate the recordings into idioms such as electronic music, with no intention of learning about the source or paying homage to Indonesian culture. A cultural appreciation in performance, on the other hand, would be to sample the gamelan after gaining permission from native practitioners and having studied the music in some capacity.

In many artistic expressions, especially collaborative works, a certain kind of attitude is required to provide a basis of understanding to fit within local social frameworks. In most cases, expressive arts afford practitioners and listeners a frame that forms the parameters of social ethics. Certain attitudes are performative in the context of gamelan performances as they tend to involve audience members' initial experience with Indonesian arts.[16] The group bears the responsibility of knowing that they will be changing worldviews and they act accordingly. For many people in the United States, these performances serve as first impressions that leave an embodied impact due to their overwhelming sonic properties. They change the way a person listens and experiences sound cultures, if ever so slightly. While the internal politics of an ensemble are as diverse as the identity of the practitioners, what is performed in front of an audience is a conglomeration of attitudes into a unified event. How then is appropriation or appreciation interpreted and by whom? What value does this question have? I employ this binary to discuss the complexities and continuum of performing a music that "is not yours." Is this a mere matter of definition, or are there stringent constraints that bind each perspective ontologically? My initial response is that the line between appropriation and appreciation is thick, in the Geertzian sense. What makes it confounding and ostensibly conflating are the sociopolitical nuances that are embedded within each.

The gamelan teachers I have worked with in the United States understand this to a great degree.[17] It is embedded in the Balinese concept of *desa, kala, patra*: the ability to adapt to your surroundings and bring a sense of home wherever it is necessary.[18] This does not mean that there is no longing or homesickness for Indonesia. In fact, it is quite the contrary; it is their way of dealing with their longings for the native land within every community they enter and with every individual they meet. My re-fusion of *beleganjur* and mathcore was indeed a refusal to be boxed in. But my agenda also included a desire to open artistic doors to disparate and marginalized communities. In this way, it is still an educational endeavor, but it is one that was on my own terms with subsets of music that I personally identified with. My concern is not simply to change peoples' worldviews through exposure to different musics; it is a way to find comfort in a web of complex identity networks.

We can continue to problematize the spectrum between appropriation and appreciation on the grounds of performing attitudes, or more specifically *benen mua*. To collectively hybridize and foster subjective artistic discovery requires an awareness of personal biases when necessary and recognizing their potential hindrance to cultural synthesis. There are particular sociopolitical realities grounded in the historicity of gamelan that has let foreign practitioners get away with capitalizing on Indonesian musics and avoid scrutiny in the name of musical enjoyment.[19] My concern here is that without accountability from scholars, artists, and pedagogues, musics such as gamelan are subject to losing their functions and will progress in a way that is unethical. This has been explored extensively in the book *Performing Ethnomusicology: Teaching and Representation in World Music* (Solís 2004), but where it falls short is a call to action. This line of appropriation and appreciation falls into the realm of performing attitudes and how one effectively enacts *benen mua*. Ostensibly, there is nothing inherently wrong with people enjoying artistic expressions, movements, and idioms, but a lack of sensitivity to adaptation or of reciprocity of knowledge sharing is problematic. A slight anecdotal tangent: recently a colleague of mine asked if I ever felt like I was appropriating heavy metal, because it is not technically "my music." This was an alarming question and, quite frankly, an insensitive one. Its implications were that because of my Indonesian origin, I do not have the capacity to use other musics with which I may have grown up. Ironically, heavy metal is in fact a music that contributes to my upbringing. This superficial conversation is one example in which actively enacting *benen mua* is necessary, but in a way that also educates people on problems of stereotypes.

My own musical practices—at least in gamelan—have always embodied a different aura. Because teaching gamelan turns pedagogues into cultural ambassadors, every ensemble is an educational meeting, and the artistry is always part of a larger agenda. I and other first- and second-generation Balinese musicians feel the burden of representation much more heavily than others. Balinese people who grew up in Bali perhaps have the sense of "cultural authority" that what they are doing is expanding their own tradition within its own context. Non-Balinese, though often quite careful of representation, have less at stake socially and artistically in doing something nontraditional; it's almost expected. But the dichotomy between these two lies in how Indonesian American artists must first make sure that another party is satisfied before they are. The gray area comes with attempting to find artistic identity when it is always controlled by a social "other." Fortunately for me, one way of finding this identity was in combining gamelan with the musics I have found in my own social milieu: mathcore and experimentalism (which includes certain branches of improvisatory practices). The physicality necessary to enact these kinds of musics made my connections with other humans interpersonal, at times quite directly. Mosh pits, cremation ceremonies, and contact improvisation literally had me shoulder to shoulder with my artistic collaborators.

Every element of "Benen Mua" correlates to the social frustrations I have described in re-fusion and "biting the tongue." This was a way to produce a piece that highlights the refusal to stay in the confines of one idiom not by separating them, but by blurring the lines of musical sensibility. I was interested in the affective response of performers when working with tradition and experimentalism simultaneously. Which aspects of the musical sensibilities were from mathcore and which from *beleganjur*? Are the two parts of the re-fusion separable from one another? Transforming "Fix Your Face" to "Benen Mua" was a project that reprioritized Gamelan Tunas Mekar's artistic intentions, recontextualized their cultural understandings, and re-fused the idiomatic implications of sonic borders. The embodiment of attitudes in performance groups may be analogous with their musical sensibilities, but it certainly does not shape them. What it does offer is an insight into the privileges we all enact when playing any music, especially that of another culture. It then posits the question, "Is there a point where this foreign music becomes my own?" The simple answer is "Yes, of course," but how do we recognize our colonial tendencies and cultural appropriation, that is, the co-opting of musical cultures without an awareness of privilege and negligence in *benen mua*?

These perspectives synthesize the nuances and complexities of "tongue biting" in the enactment of *benen mua*—one that ties directly to the notion of re-fusion. Native practitioners of gamelan exercise this as a way of existing in a foreign place and also creating opportunities in reciprocity. For them, it is true that a great deal of artistic works performed by this community of pedagogues are part of the agenda of a social "other," whether an academic institution, government diversity program, or local communities. It is the inverse of re-fusion in its constraint and confirmation of superficial pigeonholing. We as artist-scholars can become more aware of performing more contextual attitudes where necessary for a less selfish and less colonial transmission of knowledge. This is why academic and public communities have to recognize the superficialities that are afforded by globalization and perform *benen mua* when enacting re-fusion.

NOTES

1. Mathcore is a subgenre of heavy metal. For more about Dillinger Escape Plan, see http://www.dillingerescapeplan.org.

2. See https://www.youtube.com/watch?v=lf1ja_nTFOo and https://www.youtube.com/watch?v=ZNydgX1obPk for two performances by Gamelan Tunas Mekar.

3. "Silver Dagger" is an American folk ballad. Hannah Standiford arranged the song and performed it with Rumput for the event "Kroncong and Kontemporer" as part of the SOSIM conference.

4. In contexts of Balinese social events, kids will sometimes be told "Benen mua" to subdue their demeanor in favor of comforting guests. I experienced this as a child myself and have observed it while conducting fieldwork.

5. Lyrics taken from http://www.darklyrics.com/lyrics/dillingerescapeplan/ireworks.html#1.

6 This was a large component of Mantle Hood's work in the late 1950s and early 1960s. His initial collaboration, bringing the late Hardja Susilo to UCLA, exemplified his activism in bimusicality and a tendency to reciprocate by constructing a proactive world-view, one that engages directly with the subject's way of living.

7 To name just a few with first- or second-generation Indonesian children similar in age to me, the Wenten family in southern California, the Asnawa and Kertayuda families in Illinois, the Saptanyana family in New York, and the Berata family in northern California.

8 In Bruno Nettl's introduction to *Nettl's Elephant* (2010) he describes an interaction in which the standard practice in explaining the field of ethnomusicology includes a fumbling of words in an attempt to synthesize its mission and methodologies, something many ethnomusicologists experience when giving their "elevator speech."

9 The academic institutions in which Pak Made Lasmawan works on a weekly basis are Colorado College, the University of Colorado at Boulder, Metropolitan State University of Denver, and the University of Wyoming at Laramie. In addition, he teaches community gamelan with Gamelan Tunas Mekar and travels all over the United States annually.

10 For examples, see Wallach 2008.

11 Moore 2013 problematizes the role of popular musics in syncretizing with indigenous socialities.

12 Hybridization of musical sensibilities and modalities is inevitable in a world that has become more globalized. Contemporary relationships between people and their experiences do not require the presence of human bodies in close proximity. It is possible to create meaningful relationships via technologies such as the internet. But ironically, these spaces require less *benen mua* but more superficiality, primarily because they do not require the expediency of inhibited socialities or immediate confrontation. Peoples' reaction times can be expanded, or people can simply ignore information on the internet with no social repercussions.

13 See "Exit Interview: The End of the Dillinger Escape Plan," posted by Alternative Press, https://youtu.be/aTlPuVPCy8I.

14 The points of contention I would like to address here are within the realms of different physicalities and temporalities between Bali and the United States, and simultaneously, between mathcore and *beleganjur*. With this transposition, I wanted the performers to feel a particular kind of exhaustion and a combination of affective temporalities. To follow mathcore musicians would mean to partially destroy instruments and bodies, which would be contrary to gamelan cosmologies; to follow *beleganjur* sensibilities was to process for long periods of time or extend the piece and perform choreography, which is against mathcore's anarchist qualities. I mediated the two by playing at a peak performance physicality for a sprint of time. This way it was more of a dash than a trial of endurance.

15 Andrew McGraw, Ben Brinner, Elizabeth Clendinning, Chris Miller, and Henry Spiller have all questioned the ethics in relationships between Balinese peoples and non-native gamelan practitioners during collaborations of Indonesian expressive arts.

16 Audiences in Denver have exclaimed their shift in worldview after a Gamelan Tunas Mekar performance. This dataset comes from three decades of performing in the Colorado gamelan ecology.

17 My Balinese teachers in the United States include Bapak I Nyoman Wenten, Bapak I Ketut Gede Asnawa, Ibu Putu Oka Mardiani, and Bapak I Ngurah Kertayuda, all of whom are a part of the Balinese Allstars collective that I organize.

18 Many Indonesianist scholars have made this point. For a contemporary perspective, see Macy 2010.

19 Various gamelan ensembles out of Indonesia have blurred the lines of cultural appropriation, and there has never been a real inquiry into its ethics.

WORKS CITED

Barz, Gregory, and Timothy Cooley. 2008. *Shadows in the Field: New Perspectives for Fieldwork in Ethnomusicology.* New York: Oxford.

Brinner, Benjamin. 2013. "The Ecology of Musical Transmission between Indonesia and the United States." Paper presented at Performing Indonesia: A Conference and Festival of Music, Dance, and Drama, at the National Museum of Asia Art of the Smithsonian Institution, November 3, 2013. https://asia.si.edu/essays/article-brinner/.

Clendinning, Elizabeth. 2013. *Pedagogy, Performance, and Community in the Transnational Balinese Traditional Performing Arts Scene.* PhD diss., Florida State University.

Farnell, Brenda. 2012. *Dynamic Embodiment for Social Theory: I Move Therefore I Am.* New York: Routledge.

Landis, Kevin, and Suzanne Macaulay. 2017. *Cultural Performance: Ethnographic Approaches to Performance Studies.* London: Palgrave.

Macy, Elizabeth McLean. 2010. *Music Tourism in New Orleans and Bali: A Comparative Study of Cultural Tourism Development.* PhD diss., University of California Los Angeles.

McGraw, Andrew C. 2013. *Radical Traditions: Reimagining Culture in Balinese Contemporary Music.* Oxford: Oxford University Press.

Moore, Rebekah E. 2013. "Elevating the Underground: Claiming a Space for Indie Music among Bali's Many Soundworlds." *Asian Music* 44 (2): 135–59.

Nettl, Bruno. 2010. *Nettl's Elephant: On the History of Ethnomusicology.* Urbana: University of Illinois Press.

Solís, Ted, ed. 2004. *Performing Ethnomusicology: Teaching and Representation in World Music Ensembles.* Berkeley: University of California Press.

Steele, Pete. 2013. *Balinese Hybridities: Balinese Music as Global Phenomena.* PhD diss., Wesleyan University.

Wallach, Jeremy. 2008. *Modern Noise, Fluid Genres: Popular Music in Indonesia, 1997–2001.* Madison: University of Wisconsin Press.

WANBAYANING

Voicing a Transcultural Islamic Feminist Exegesis

Jessika Kenney

بسم الله الرحمن الرحيم

Kanthi Nami Gusti Allah
Kang Maha Welas Asih

This chapter is a kind of musical sketch or *catetan* (note) of a vocal practice, where terms, transliterations, and translations can be repositioned to elicit different meanings, nuances, sonic manifestations, and conceptual dynamics. The key term, *wanbayaning*, is my own, and the focus of the present exegesis. This approach is inspired by, but not limited to, learned aspects of Indonesian aesthetics and approaches to language. This is also a sketch of a method of composition, based in a nonreductive exegetical process that supports experiences of sacredness while reading—"'Iqra!" (Read! [Qur'an 96:1])—and listening (*myarsa*). At the SOSIM conference, I presented these ideas as a talk interspersed with vocalizations; here, a transdisciplinary method of a verbal and visual score is used to invoke similar spaces, by suggesting the recitation of some textual elements given here out loud. I invite you to recite, with your own accents, linguistic knowledge, and melodic memories in areas of tonality, pronunciation, and breath. In this way our collective contemplations may be embedded in these sounds both actively and passively, affirming that what is left out, or what remains silent, still may retain its own space, recognizing the inherent biases of this "oppressor's language."[1] With this transcultural endeavor, we may open some practical and theoretical doorways between Indonesian and other vocal musics and recitation practices, as well as connecting practices of Islamic feminism, sound studies, voice studies, experimental music, anti-racist intersectional feminism, creative liturgy, and exegesis, or *tafsir*. Vocal practice and *tafsir* are here central, although decentralizing, methodologies. The texts included are from the Qur'an, *sastra Jawa* (Javanese poetic literature), and Persian poetry of the twelfth to fifteenth century CE.

On a personal level, I choose these texts to honor the teachers and cultures I have learned from, in twenty years of working involvement in Indonesian cultures locally and in diaspora, beginning in 1996 with the study of Central Javanese *sindhenan* (the solo female vocal element of *karawitan*), as well as studies beginning in 2004 of Persian *radif*, or collections of aurally transmitted melodic patterns coinciding with the recitation of the *ghazal* and other poetic forms. Studying *sindhenan* in Central Java impressed a particularly Indonesian aesthetic of knowledge building, which for me was laid on a foundation of learning jazz improvisation.[2] I specifically credit and honor the transformative powers of Black music and the struggles of Black musicians in America, for opening doors to cultural, political, and spiritual possibilities for the whole world. Through one of these doors I traveled to Indonesia in the late 1990s, a strange moment in history tenuously situated between the extension of the Cold War and what Ronak K. Kapadia calls the "forever war" (2019), or the perpetual militarization of Palestine, Iraq, Syria, and Afghanistan, and the continued colonization of the stolen land I grew up on. My childhood experiences hearing terrible war stories, as one of three children of a 1st Recon Marine in Vietnam, were echoed in witnessing the continued vilification of communism in Indonesia. This intergenerational trauma resonated with the moments around the fall of Suharto in 1998, including the monetary crisis and the riots.

Amid all this, the memorization and listening required for learning *sindhenan* became part of the process of acculturation for me as well as expressions of solidarity with the liberatory efforts of Indonesian artists in many fields. I was welcomed into communities of *karawitan*, visual and performance art, street art, DIY punk and metal subcultures, and community discussion groups, as well as avant-garde theater, dance, and music. More recently, I have been a regular participant at the Women's Mosque of America in Los Angeles (founded in 2015), which I believe carves out sonic and social space for practices of Islamic feminist *tafsir* or exegesis.[3] The following Qur'anic exegesis, as an example of feminist textual and social engagement, offers many possibilities for a rich discussion on the roles of the early women of Islam, the power of the voices of spiritually adept women, and the uses of their knowledge:

يَٰنِسَآءَ ٱلنَّبِىِّ لَسْتُنَّ كَأَحَدٍ مِّنَ ٱلنِّسَآءِ
إِنِ ٱتَّقَيْتُنَّ فَلَا تَخْضَعْنَ بِٱلْقَوْلِ فَيَطْمَعَ ٱلَّذِى
فِى قَلْبِهِۦ مَرَضٌ وَقُلْنَ قَوْلًا مَّعْرُوفًا

O Women Disciples of the Prophet,
Unique among women when you are vigilant,
May you not yield your words
Based on the ambitions of one whose heart is sick
Instead voice wise words.

(Qur'an 33:32)

The Divine Voice may offer instructions in using words that are *ma'rufan* (Arabic: known), here translated as "wise." *Ma'ruf* is linguistically related to *makrifat* (Javanese: enlightenment) and *erfān* (Persian: gnosis). In esoteric traditions, the heart is often associated with knowledge, and *makrifat* can be described as a category or stage of mystical knowledge found in a heart that has been purified.

To follow this is a *beyt* (couplet) from a *ghazal* by the great Persian poet Hāfez of Shiraz, invoking the singing of a protective and celebratory support of the heart's knowledge:[4]

وان که این کار ندانست در انکار بماند   هر که شد محرم دل در حرم یار بماند

شکر ایزد که نه در پرده پندار بماند   اگر از پرده برون شد دل ما عیب مکن

ا

(ā.................)

Anyone who became an intimate of the heart, in the intimacy of the beloved
may remain
(*Har ke shod mahram-e del, dar haram-e yār bemānd*)
And anyone who knows not of this work, in denial may remain
(*Vān ke in kār nadānest, dar enkār bemānd*)
If through the membrane our heart emerges, do not find fault
(*Agar az pardeh borun shod del-e-mā, 'eib makon*)
Thank the Divine that nothing, in the partition of thought, may remain
(*Shokr-e Izad ke na dar pardeh-ye pendār bemānd*)

ا

(ā.................)

Wanbayaning

At this point I would like to introduce an original term constructed using Javanese words and concepts, *wanbayaning*, which represents the idea found in the title of this chapter, a type of feminist exegesis through vocalization. *Wanbayaning* is composed of three parts: *wan*, as in *wanita* or woman; *bayan*, or explanation; and *ning* as in clarity of sound.

Wan

We begin with the Javanese word *wanita*, and its first syllable, *wan*. Defining "woman" is generally better done in reverse through the unraveling of the inconsistencies of the social conditioning of gender, and the rebuilding of our understanding of gendered identities. Coming from yet another direction, one free of gender but substantiated by gender-fluid wombs, we conjure each of our earliest intrauterine experiences. Pursing our lips together to form the *w* of *wan* or womb, the image of the primordial mother coalesces. Tracing the embryonic core of an umbilical breath, we recognize that before we were one, we were two, ourself and our mother. This emphasizes the foundational paradox of the non-existence of a separate self. As Rumi said, referring to the definition of woman and/or the womb-holding ones:

خالقست آن گوییا مخلوق نیست   پرتو حقست آن معشوق نیست

Partov-e Haqq-ast, ān ma'ashugh nist, Khālegh-ast, ān guyyā makhlugh nist
Woman is the Light of Truth, not only Beloved, Creative, not only created[5]

In this context of *wanita*, as the ensoulment and creation of the body, the site and subject of our original "clot" of twoness, our sounding of *wan* becomes an active illumination of the body, an enactment of Rumi's truth or *haqq*. Another example of a similar process is found in "Kidung Rumeksa Ing Wengi" (A Song of Protection in the Night), a work of Javanese poetry in the *macapat* poetic form *dhandhanggula*, attributed to Sunan Kalijaga, one of the nine Sufi saints or *wali* who are credited with bringing Islam peacefully to Java from India and China in the fifteenth century CE/eighth century AH.

Sungsum ingsun Patimah linuwih	Make my marrow that of the noble Fatima
Siti Aminah bayuning anggå	Make my body's energy strong like Siti Aminah
Ayup ing ususku mangke	The spirit of Prophet Job, in my intestines
Nabi Nuh ing jejantung	of Prophet Noah inside my liver
Nabi Yunus ing otot mami	of Prophet Jonah in my brain
Netraku ya Muhammad	My eyes, Oh Prophet Muhammad!
Pamuluku Rasul	Beloved Messenger
Pinayungan Adam Kawa,	My dignity in the union of Adam and Eve
sampun pepak sakatahe para Nabi	As the entirety of the Prophets women and men
dadyå sarirå tunggal	become this one sacred body[6]

This is the fourth stanza of the longer poem, which throughout includes lists of prophets and their particular virtuous embodiments.[7] When it is sung, the meaning spirals in on itself: "Suwaraku Dawud" ("my voice is of David," from the previous stanza), then even more deeply reflective, "Sumsum ingsun Patima linuwih" (my veins are of Fatima), as our deepest voice is the sound of our blood pulsing through our veins. *Sumsum* is veins and *ingsun* is a complex concept of inclusive self-reference, referring to the union of devotee and divine, as well as the greater "we," and the higher self of the practitioner. It is no mistake that *ingsun* is used in regards to Fatima and the veins, which connects the idea of the sacred Mother and the blood or *rah* shared by her children and traced through the veins of her lineage, representing a cosmological matriarchy with culturally rich and specific interconnectedness.

Biosemiotics might be of interest for *wanbayaning*, a lens that draws on analysis of the language of signifiers as described by Saussure and Peirce (Brier 2006) but brings in elements of nonintentional biologically oriented signs such as heart and breathing rhythms, or quantifiable physical moods such as fight or flight states or the brain wave patterns of deep sleep as biological signifiers.[8] More tangibly, the intersection of biological body and the social constructs of gender and race in specific cultural contexts aurally intertwine in the way we use and perceive a "feminine" vocal sound.[9] Therefore, the *wan* of *wanbayaning* does not make assumptions about the essence of Javanese cultural conceptions of woman, nor does it impose an outside essentialization of a universal woman. *Wanbayaning* invites an experiential and shifting aestheticization through listening that requires a heightened sense of distinctions beyond binaries, while embracing this multiplicity of irreconcilable definitions of woman. Regardless, the obstacles that Javanese women may broadly face in regard to self-construction and articulation of knowledge are many. As Hortense Spillers says in her seminal Black feminist text "Mama's Baby, Papa's Maybe: An American Grammar Book":

> In order for me to speak a truer word concerning myself, I must strip down through layers of attenuated meanings, made an excess in time, over time, assigned by a particular historical order, and there await whatever marvels of my own inventiveness. (Spillers 1987, 65)[10]

I witness these historical legacies as well as the process in which women invent new realities, including my first teacher in *sindhenan*, Nyi Supadmi, famed for her work with the renowned *dhalang* Ki Nartosabdho.[11] When I first met her in 1997, Supadmi was newly back from the hajj, years after her time teaching in Berkeley and Seattle. She was continuously creating new *cengkok* or melodic patterns, and lessons with her focused on specific performance results in the context of *wayang kulit*.[12] Supadmi was controversial for her use of *hijab* in wayang performance, as well as wearing glasses, in assertion of her intellectual and spiritual status. She was also known for having started a union for *pesindhèn*. Witnessing Supadmi's creative genius and devotion to the literary and spiritual aspects of her vocal tradition, as well as her strong social awareness, offered a real-life image of one of many transcultural Islamic feminist *pesindhèn* engaged profoundly with the interpretation of sung text. One example of her transculturalism became apparent when, after listening to a recording of the great flamenco *cantaora* Pastora Pavon, "La Niña de los Peines," she proceeded to compose a new *cengkok*. In her later years she became an important vocal teacher at the Solo Kraton or palace, received the appellation Supadminingtyas, and wrote her memoir/autobiography in *macapat*—in metered, hence singable, verse. Shortly before she passed away in 2015, I visited her bedside with singer Heni Savitri and scholar Susan Walton, and read verses of her autobiography with her.

In the *Wedhatama*, attributed to Mangkunegara IV, in the Pangkur *macapat* form, it says:

Tan samar pamor ing suksmå	Without hesitation, the luminous grain of the soul
Sinuksmåyå winahyå ing asepi	Manifests in the atmosphere of solitude
Sinimpen telenging kalbu	Stored in the garden of the heart
Pambukaning warånå	Opening a secret threshold
Tarlen saking liyep lalaping aluyup	Not from a dream but subsumed, delirium
Pindhå pesating supenå	Piercing through like an arrow,
Sumusuping råså jati	Lightning sense of truth.[13]

"Tan samar pamoring suksma"—without obscuration, one perceives the inscription of the soul.[14] The *pamor*, or metallurgical pattern formed by the alchemical mixture of elements, represents clarity of being, once the layers of tarnish and char are removed. This stanza, which takes place in the context of a moment of meditation, is packed with alliterative wordplay, with the word *suksma* (soul) as well as the lovely "liyep lalaping aluyup" (literally "falling over in layers semiconscious"). Finally, in the last line, the subject of *rasa jati* appears, the "sense of truth," prompting us toward a kind of Sophianic knowing that our syllable *wan* could represent, where wisdom itself is regarded as a gendered attribute of the Divine. There is also the question of intention or intentionlessness, in this state between waking and dream, and the relinquishment of self that lies there. Singing or hearing this poem sung might invoke that same feeling. For in the speech act the voice may be a site of the subject, but in singing the voice is often a site of surrender. This multilayering of vocal function is a particularly Islamic aesthetic in terms of self-relinquishment to the Divine, while at the same time being particularly Javanese in the context of *karawitan* in terms of submission to the structure of the musical context, and the form of holistic listening that does not separate one's self from the whole, similar to the Javanese concept of *narima* (acceptance). Most literally the release of a large quantity of the air in the lungs is a kind of acquiescence, and in a more skilled manner, vocalization is not control of the voice, but the allowing of the vibration of the vocal folds to resonate one's body and a space, requiring the sensation of releasing, like a ball bouncing or a pendulum swinging, rather than pushing a heavy object or striking out with force.

Bayan

The next word we have in our composite term *wanbayaning* is *bayan*. *Bayan* is a transcultural Islamic term, originally referring to an aspect of rhetoric. Through cultural transmissions, it became used for a colloquial part of a sermon (*khotbeh*) where the mother tongue of the Islamic majority is not Arabic, or where the local Arabic dialect is used instead of the classical Arabic of the Qur'an. *Bayan* in this context means a pre-*khotbeh* talk that explains, translates, or prepares the listeners for the Arabic-language *khotbeh* in a variety of ways. A *bayan* can attempt to explain the sermon, but it does not replace it. In the same way that *wan* points to the deepest level of the embodiment of ideas in sound, *bayan* points to the benefits of translation itself in the decentering of epistemologies. The *bayan* is the linguistic space in a reverential context that designates and acknowledges cultural difference (conversation with Imam Yasin Dwyer, 2018). In Javanese mysticism (*kebatinan*), *batin*, meaning "inner," the focus of exegesis is on esoteric or inner meaning, which may or may not be in contradiction with the *lahir* or outer meaning. In this sense the *bayan* form, although it may appear as an introduction, can also hold the space for inner meaning, which is culturally or even situationally specific. The *bayan* can also create and preserve cultural responses in literary and artistic forms to religious material, such as nineteenth-century *suluk* literature and contemporary Islamic-influenced devotional songs. The *Batiniyyah* of early Islam, meaning those who preferred the esoteric meaning of the Qur'an, were perhaps also involved in the first translation of the Qur'an into another language, which was Persian. Perhaps their interest in the inner meaning was also a method of preserving elements of other cultures inside the religious community (*ummah*). For *wanbayaning*, *bayan* is the element that underlines the capacity for vocalization to translate cultural concepts, through multiple verbal and musical languages. This is a powerful model for transcultural singing, where multiple sources of knowledge and experiences do not cancel each other out in their multiple origins but rather are mutually and materially altered, resulting in surprising visions of the future. A mobile and adaptable *bayan* is also found in the title of one of the oldest works of classical Malay literature, the *Hikayat Bayan Budiman*, a collection of stories that finds its origins in the Sanskrit *Sukasaptati* and the Persian *Tutinameh*. In Persian, *bayan* means "explanation." In his *Masnavi-ye Ma'navi* (Spiritual Verses), Rumi says:

هر چه گویم عشق را شرح و بیان ....

Harche guyam eshgh rā sharh o bayān
Every time I speak of love, explaining and describing

چون به عشق آیم خجل باشم از آن

Chon be eshgh āmad khejel bāsham az ān
When I come to love I will be ashamed by that[15]

This *beyt* is from the story of the king and the enslaved young woman, a story that traveled through many eras, places, and languages, and enters at the moment in the story where the king can't understand why she is not responding to his gestures of love.[16] It is Rumi's voice speaking here, or perhaps the doctor whom the king has called to diagnosis the "heart" of the problem, which is another love, with someone else. As in this story, the *bayan* can try to explain connections or assert itself, but in the end it may inadvertently transform into something new or different. The *bayan* can take the pulse of a congregation, like the doctor does with this patient, discovering her illness through the way her pulse speeds up at the mention of the goldsmith's village, an example of the haptic information found in a heartbeat, a silence, a sacred text. This transmuting of revelation in everyday life is part of what renowned Islamic African American feminist scholar and religious leader amina wadud, who now lives in Malaysia, calls "exegesis of praxis" (Ali and wadud 2019, 72). This seems to me to be a particularly Indonesian/Malaysian ethos, built around the idea of learning through experiencing, which is described beautifully in this stanza, in the Pocung *macapat* form, from the "Wulangreh" of Pakubuwana IV:

Ngelmu iku	That knowledge
Kalakone kanthi laku	Is a way of being through doing
Lekase lawan kas tegese kas nyantosani	Sought diligently and peacefully
Setyå budyå pangekese durangkårå	Integrity conquers rage[17]

Ning

The *ning* of *wanbayaning* is the word component closest to describing the experience of sound itself. "Ning" can be tones, or the vocable for one of five tones, or notations, or a transliteration in reverse, where an object's sonic language becomes visible. The sound of *ning* in *wanbayaning* is helpful in invoking a particular aesthetic sonic space found in *karawitan*, where the sound of struck metal represents or embodies ideas of scholarliness, ethics, manners, mantra, meditation, sacredness, connection and communication with the natural world, and even spiritual realms, suggesting that these realms may have their own languages more akin to music. In his liner notes to his composition "Anané ånå," Rahayu Supanggah writes about the "origins of Javanese life" as expressed by the everyday musical syllables "nang nung nang ning," and the fact that babies hear music and sound before they recognize shapes (Supanggah 2012). This challenges us to listen more deeply but also to practice quotidian listening, which may lead to more than new meanings, but heightened sensibilities and perceptions. Although exegesis is often applied to concepts or texts, it can also as in this case be applied to sounds, and conversely, a sound may do an exegesis of us, in the sense of registering our capacities for particular resonances and our listening abilities. Another possibility is that *ning* can hold the space for a stillness, a potential sound, or a barely perceivable otoacoustic emission, when the memory of a sound is so clear that the cochlea itself becomes a tiny speaker for the mind.[18] Like a signature that can't be read yet designates the name of a person, *ning* can hold the vibrational or felt-sense haptic imprint of an experience. *Wening* means "clear" in Javanese, so I want to ask, what is more clear than when meaning is received as a heartfelt feeling? As Leonora Carrington once said, "Reason *must* know the heart's reason and all the other reasons" (1988, 28). *Ning* can also be a part of speech, an adaptable preposition, as in "of," "but," "with," or "from" her. The zone of inverted arborescent movement the preposition occupies is one of the exegetical windows through to a liberation of language, like a map of heavenly roots seeking sustenance and communication in the clouds. In names, *ning* can be *ningtyas*, meaning "clear heart," "peaceful heart," or "from the heart." This clarity of innerness or *ningtyas* is not just a separation from the external world or renunciation but a completeness invoked from beyond the self, shining new light on the struggles and injustices of our ancestral inheritances and transforming fragments of those burdens bit by bit into acts of compassion free of expectation. This form of *ning* shines back into our interlocking pasts through our *bayan* as translated specificities of utterances, and forward into our becoming as identifiable individuals creating our collective futures, with *wan*. With these words, as images, sounds, concepts, and evocations of love, I hope to *memayu hayuning bawana*, or "contribute to the beauty of this universe," to participate in the revolutions of this resonant dome.

Let us close this chapter by reciting, singing, mumbling, humming, another *beyt* from the same Hāfez *ghazal* quoted earlier in this writing:

از صدای سخن عشق ندیدم خوشتر

Az sedā-ye sokhan-e eshgh nadidam khoshtar
Than the echo of words of love I've never heard more beautiful

یادگاری که در این گنبد دوار بماند

Yādegāri ke dar in gonbad-e davvār bemānd
The memory of which in this revolving dome may remain

In closing with these utterances and resonances, and through these ideas that motivate and imprint themselves within sound, there is a sense that many great possibilities are present for transdisciplinary work inside and outside of academic and other collective environments, becoming immanently more free of the epistemological violence that threatens to reiterate itself, embedded in language patterns, social relations, and shared traumas passed down through generations. Our work in whatever realms we may focus on has an urgency based on the wish for the survival of this planet, as well as a surviving in the moment that allows for a miraculous specificity of selflessness in our various methods of communion. I hope and pray that the striving to learn will not compromise the striving for collective liberation and rebalancing of the scales. Thank you for participating in these efforts and for being willing to interpret these ideas from the point of view of your own stories and quests, and for your patience with ideas that I truly hope become a flood of sound, an unstoppable and clear resonance within which is a responsiveness to each cell's call. I look forward to further research on the tension between the construction and point of view of a subject and a sense of what is being surrendered to, without compromise to unjust powers and dynamics. The ability to decenter ourselves has become one of the most important tools, and our previous toolkits have become obsolete as we are required to live inside of our work, to truly embrace the processes and means by which we actualize our ideas and relationships.

There are many potential conclusions to this writing and this exegesis using the method now known to us as *Wanbayaning*; we may wish to listen differently, to trace the poetic and sacred texts in reverse, to disassemble the *ning* from the *bayan* from the *wan* and offer these terms back to their multiplicity of origins. At the point where our participation in sounding and interpreting the texts has been reversed and removed from our sense of connection, when we pare down to a feeling of isolation after this process, I wonder how we will be altered, and what road, an on-ramp or off-ramp, we might throw ourselves even more wholeheartedly upon. To value this inconclusiveness gives promise of another composition, another interpretation, another performance. This time we may have more patience to notice the surging responsiveness of our environments, bird songs sliding like a whistle from the nearby tree, or from a heated desire for connection churning in our hearts.

As a closing practice and prayer:

Take apart and return *wanbayaning* to its sources
Make an offering of equal or greater proportion
Find the gender beyond genders and use it to voice the unknown

Women of prophecy unravel the end of this chapter, separating the syllables and languages and making them unintelligible to human ears, knowable to spirit alone.

Make a space in our hearts for the relinquishment of knowing, and trace the path to that place through the movements of the ancestors flowing through our sacred resonant flesh.

Bismillah irrahman irrahim
O women of prophecy
you are no longer women as known
your vow is unknowable
your heart dissolves reconciled
your words disappear and are born in us
Amin

Dedicated to all those participating in the worldwide Black Lives Matter uprisings of the summer of 2020.

NOTES

Unless specified, or implied by context or source, all non-English terms are Javanese, which includes several transcultural Islamic terms originating in Arabic. All translations and transliterations are my own. The transliterations, drawing on the generous instruction of my teachers, are geared toward singing. In particular, ā for Persian *alef* sounds like "awe"; the Javanese vowel *å* is between a long *a* and *o*.

I am very grateful for these studies with Ostad Hossein Omoumi while he taught at the University of Washington in Seattle, as well as when he moved to southern California to teach at UC Irvine. It is an unbelievable blessing to have this opportunity and I am so grateful for his generosity and kindness. I also want to thank my teachers in the Persian language at the University of Washington in Seattle, Shahrzad Shams and Maryam Rahimian, and also give profound thanks to Sheida Besharat Omoumi for years of weekly language sessions. I also want to thank Dr. Fatemeh Keshavarz, for her profound and loving mentorship and our many inspiring collaborations.

1. I take this characterization of the English language from a conversation with a friend in Solo in 1997. See also Audre Lorde's canonical 1984 essay "The Master's Tools Will Not Dismantle the Master's House," in Lorde 2007, 110–14.

2. I studied in Cornish College of the Arts Jazz Department from 1994 to 1997, with jazz greats including Jay Clayton, Julian Priester, and Hadley Caliman. I was particularly inspired by Ornette Coleman and his Prime Time ensemble, whom I had the chance to hear at the King Cat Theater in Seattle.

3. I am grateful for the encouragement and support of the community formed around the Women's Mosque of America, directed and founded by M. Hasna Maznavi, held as a monthly women-led *jummah* or Friday prayer gathering in Los Angeles. As a volunteer *muazzanah* (female caller-to-prayer) and *khateebah* (female sermon-giver), and as a regular attendee of the mosque's services since 2016, I have been incredibly inspired by the diverse, holistic, and pluralistic Islamic scholarship of the *khateebahs*, including by the *khotbeh* of Nayawiyyah Muhammad, Hajjah Abrafi S. Sanyika, Sister Dalal Hassoun, covering a wide range of subjects, including the women of early Islam, the origin of

monotheism in ancient Egypt, and contemporary women's Islamic study organizations in Syria. I refer to Gail Kennard's *khotbeh* on evidence that the Qur'anic "Women of the Prophet" refers to the Prophet Muhammad's primary religious disciples, based on the fact that they were the first memorizers of the Qur'an (Kennard 2015). I have also been grateful for the model of intrafaith inclusivity provided for Shi'a sisters, as well as a three-part series with discussions on Black Lives Matter.

4. The original Persian of this and all other quotations of Hāfez is taken from Hāfez 1995.

5. The original Persian is taken from https://ganjoor.net/moulavi/masnavi/daftar1/sh119/.

6. The Javanese is taken from Purwadi et al. (2005, 261).

7. This "embodiment" section of the poem was featured in "Body of Gods," a video work by Indonesian artist Jompet Kuswidananto, in which a traditional Javanese dancer slowly put on and took off his ornate costume. The work was screened at the Johnson Museum of Art at Cornell University at the time of the SOSIM conference.

8. For example, the performance piece "If We Were XYZ," by Melati Suryodarmo, in collaboration with Antonius Oki Wiradjaja and the author, was based on dream stories and brain wave data. The piece was performed at Asia Society, New York, on October 17 and 18, 2019.

9. As a white woman, I interrogate my own biases, ignorance, privilege, and sense of entitlement with regard to the specificity of *wanita*, for example, in the case where trans men have wombs or in many cases where there are cultural designations for more than two genders.

10. See also Campt's commentary in her prescient and innovative 2017 book *Listening to Images*. Thanks to Nancy Marie Mithlo for drawing my attention to this source.

11. I would like to thank all the women who have shared their voices with me through performance, teaching, and collaboration in realms of all that Indonesian-ness overlaps, particularly my first Central Javanese *sindhenan* teacher, Hj Supadminingtyas. I would also like to thank the *pesindhèn* and teachers Ibu Cendhani Laras, who performed at the SOSIM conference, and Ibu Madu Laras, also of Baluwarti, Surakarta, who supported me in every way as a *pesindhèn* and friend in the beginning of my learning process. I would like to thank the late Ibu Euis Komariah, who was an incredible teacher of singing technique as well as Sundanese *tembang*. I thank Ibu Neneng Dinar for continuing Ibu Euis's work so beautifully. I would also like to thank Nancy Florida, Kitsie Emerson, and Joan Suyenaga, for English translations and works on *suluk* literature; Endang Tri Winarni for her Indonesian translations of particular *suluk* that are interesting to me; Anne Rasmussen, for bringing the work of the great Qur'an reciter Hajjah Mariah Ulfah to my attention; and Martini for her literary, spiritual, and artistic support. Lastly, in this very partial list of a web of gratefulness, I would like to thank some women singers of Indonesian musics who have personally inspired me and contributed to this work, including Muriah Budiarti, Anis Astuti, Peni Candra Rini, Heni Savitri, Denni Harjito, Emiko Saraswati Susilo, Nova Ruth, Anne Stebinger, Christina Sunardi, Jody Diamond, Kathy Foley, Sarah Weiss, Sean Williams, Anita Balasubramaniam, Holly Durahim, Laura Mccolm, Helen Pausacker, Dòra Györfi, and last but certainly not least Seattle-based Saraswati Sunindyo.

12. For an account and interpretation of Supadmi's creative work, see Walton 1998.

13. The Javanese is taken from Purwadi et al. 2005, 575.

14. I would like to thank Suprapto Suryodarmo, *almarhum*, for his elucidation of this text during his workshop at Earthdance in Massachusetts in 2010.

15. The original Persian is taken from https://ganjoor.net/moulavi/masnavi/daftar1/sh6/.

16. See Shigehisa Kuriyama 1999 for Greek and Chinese versions of this story.

17. The Javanese is taken from Purwadi et al. 2005, 299.

18. In their 2015 paper on "otoacoustic emissions," Bergevin et al. write, "Healthy ears not only detect sound but can emit it as well. These sounds can occur either spontaneously and continuously or in response to acoustic stimulation. Evoked emissions are increasingly used as clinical diagnostic tools. The mechanisms underlying their generation, however, are incompletely understood" (3362).

WORKS CITED

Ali, Kecia, and amina wadud. 2019. "The Making of the 'Lady Imam': An Interview with amina wadud." *Journal of Feminist Studies in Religion* 35 (1): 67–79.

Al-Qur'an Al Karim dan Terjemahnya, Dengan Transliterasi Arab-Latin. 1998. Semarang: PT Karya Toha Putra Semarang.

Bergevin, Christopher, Geoffrey A. Manley, and Christine Köppl. 2015. "Salient Features of Otoacoustic Emissions Are Common across Tetrapod Groups and Suggest Shared Properties of Generation Mechanisms." In *Proceedings of the National Academy of Sciences of the United States of America* 112 (11): 3362–67.

Brier, Søren. 2006. "Biosemiotics." In *International Encyclopedia of Language and Linguistics.* 2nd ed. Amsterdam: Elsevier.

Campt, Tina. 2017. *Listening to Images.* Durham, NC: Duke University Press.

Carrington, Leonora. 1988. *Down Below.* Chicago: Black Swan Editions.

Hāfez, Shams Uddin Muhammad. 1995. *Divan-e Hāfez.* Translated by Reza Saberi. Lanham, MD: University Press of America.

Kapadia, Ronak K. 2019. *Insurgent Aesthetics: Security and the Queer Life of the Forever War.* Durham, NC: Duke University Press.

Kennard, Gail. 2015. "The 12 Female Disciples of the Prophet." Sermon delivered to the Women's Mosque of America, Los Angeles, August 28. https://www.youtube.com/watch?v=47BtZqdix7E.

Keshavarz, Fatemeh. 1998. *Reading Mystical Lyric: The Case of Jalal al-Din Rumi.* Columbia: University of South Carolina Press.

Kuriyama, Shigehisa. 1999. *The Expressiveness of the Body and the Divergence of Greek and Chinese Medicine.* New York: Zone Books.

Lorde, Audre. 2007. *Sister Outsider: Essays and Speeches.* Berkeley, CA: Crossing Press.

Purwadi, Siti Maziyah, Mahmudi, Djoko Dwiyanto, Maharsi, and Megandaru W. Kawuryan. 2005. *Ensiklopedi Kebudayaan Jawa* (Encyclopedia of Javanese Culture). Yogyakarta: Bina Media.

Spillers, Hortense. 1987. "Mama's Baby, Papa's Maybe: An American Grammar Book." *Diacritics* 17 (2): 64–81.

Supanggah, Rahayu. 2012. *Anane ana = raison d'etre: Classical and New Music on Javanese Gamelan.* Music CD with liner notes. Karanganyar, Jawa Tengah, Indonesia: Benawa Arts Garage.

Walton, Susan Pratt. 1998. "Singing against the Grain: A Javanese Composer Challenges Gender Ideologies." *Women and Music* 2: 110–22.

Contributors

Participants and attendees at the Sounding Out the State of Indonesian Music confer-
ence, on a brisk March 31, 2018, in Ithaca, New York. Back (*left to right*): Danis Sugiyanto,
Andrew McGraw, Urip Sri Maeny, G. G. Weix, Tinuk Yampolsky, Philip Yampolsky, Ethan
Axlerod, Jessika Kenney, Kelly Miller Schreiner, Elizabeth A. Clendinning, Usman Haq, Jody
Diamond, Daniel Lesniak, Katie Weissman, I Nyoman Catra, Jeremy Wallach, Putu Tangkas
Adi Hiranmayena, Bethany J. Collier, Brian Arnold, Jennifer Fraser, Maho A. Ishiguro. Front:
Andrew Timar, Matt Dunning, Christina Sunardi, Rebekah E. Moore, Anne K. Rasmussen,
Sumarsam, Henry Spiller, Julia Byl, Dimitri della Faille, Darsono Hadiraharjo, Sri Mulyana,
Christopher J. Miller. Courtesy of the Cornell Southeast Asia Program.

Julia Byl is assistant professor in ethnomusicology at the University of Alberta, and has
published on music of Sumatra, the Malay world, and the broader Indian Ocean. Her
current project, Civic Modulations, explores public music, the individual, and the
transnational institution in East Timor.

I Nyoman Catra is faculty at the Indonesian Institute of the Arts in Denpasar, Bali. He has
taught several times as a visiting professor at the College of the Holy Cross in Worces-
ter, Massachusetts. In Bali he codirects Sanggar Seni Citta Usadhi.

Elizabeth A. Clendinning is associate professor of music at Wake Forest University and
director of the WFU Balinese gamelan, Gamelan Giri Murti. Her book *American
Gamelan and the Ethnomusicological Imagination* examines American collegiate world
music ensemble education through the lens of transnational gamelan communities.

Bethany J. Collier is associate professor of music and director of the gamelan at Bucknell University in Lewisburg, Pennsylvania. She studies and performs Balinese vocal music and gamelan with various groups in the United States and Bali.

Dimitri della Faille is a professor of international development at the Université du Québec en Outaouais, Canada. He specializes in discourse analysis and critical studies, and has an interest in postcolonial and gender studies. He has performed noise and ambient music in North America, Latin America, Europe, and throughout Asia since the 1990s. His coauthored book with Cedrik Fermont on noise music in Southeast Asia, *Not Your World Music*, received the prestigious Golden Nica award from Prix Ars Electronica in 2017.

Jody Diamond is a composer, performer, writer, publisher, editor, and educator. She has held posts at SUNY New Paltz, MIT, Bucknell University, Dartmouth University, and Harvard University, and is the editor of the journal *Balungan*.

Cedrik Fermont is a Berlin-based Belgian Congolese composer, musician, mastering engineer, author, radio host, concert organizer, independent researcher, and label manager, active in the field of noise, electronic, and experimental music since 1989. His compositions and installations vary from sound art and electroacoustic to noise to industrial to more conventional genres of electronic dance music. He has toured extensively in Asia, the Middle East, Africa, Europe, and North America, and his main research focuses on electronic, electroacoustic, experimental, and noise music from Asia and Africa.

Jennifer Fraser is an associate professor of ethnomusicology and anthropology at Oberlin College. She is project director and editor of *Song in the Sumatran Highlands*, a large-scale digital humanities project.

Darsono Hadiraharjo is a lecturer in the Department of Music at Yale University.

Putu Tangkas Adi Hiranmayena is an Indonesian artist-scholar focusing on contemporary and traditional arts of Bali through the lens of performance, indigeneity, and cosmology. Hiranmayena currently holds faculty positions at Metropolitan State University of Denver and the University of Colorado (Colorado Springs), and he is artistic director of Gamelan Tunas Mekar and director of Balinese Allstars Collective.

Maho A. Ishiguro is a visiting assistant professor in the Department of Music at Bates College and a visiting assistant professor in the Department of Dance at Wesleyan University.

Jessika Kenney is an independent scholar, a member of the Women's Mosque of America, and a music teacher at California Institute of the Arts. She is also a practitioner and teacher of the Pish Radif of Ostad Hossein Omoumi, and she was a *sindhenan* student of Ibu Hj Supadminingtyas, *almarhum*.

Andrew McGraw is an associate professor of music at the University of Richmond. He leads Gamelan Raga Kusuma and codirects Orkes Kroncong Rumput in Richmond.

Christopher J. Miller is a senior lecturer in music at Cornell University, where he directs the gamelan ensemble and steel band. Alongside his research on Indonesian *musik kontemporer*, he is active as a composer, performer, and improviser.

Rebekah E. Moore is assistant professor of music and faculty scholar for the Institute for Health Equity and Social Justice Research at Northeastern University.

Anne K. Rasmussen is professor of ethnomusicology and Bickers Professor of Middle Eastern Studies at the College of William and Mary. She is also director of the William and Mary Middle Eastern Music Ensemble and past president of the Society for Ethnomusicology. She is author of *Women, the Recited Qur'an, and Islamic Music in Indonesia* and editor (with Kip Lornell) of *The Music of Multicultural America: Performance, Identity, and Community in the United States* and (with David Harnish) of *Divine Inspiration: Music and Islam in Indonesia*.

Henry Spiller is an ethnomusicologist whose research focuses on both historical and ethnographic perspectives on Sundanese music and dance from West Java and Indonesia, and on gender and sexuality. He is professor in the Department of Music at the University of California, Davis, where he teaches world music classes and graduate seminars and directs the department's gamelan ensemble.

Danis Sugiyanto is faculty at the Indonesian Institute of the Arts in Surakarta, Indonesia. He has taught gamelan and *kroncong* in the United States as a Fulbright grantee and in several universities in Europe as a visiting artist.

Sumarsam is the Winslow-Kaplan Professor of Music at Wesleyan University, and author of *Gamelan: Cultural Interaction and Musical Development in Central Java* and *Javanese Gamelan and the West*.

Christina Sunardi is an associate professor of ethnomusicology and chair of the Department of Dance at the University of Washington.

Jeremy Wallach is professor of popular culture at Bowling Green State University and author of *Modern Noise, Fluid Genres: Popular Music in Indonesia, 1997–2001*, published in Indonesia as *Musik Indonesia 1997–2001: Kebisingan dan Keberagaman Aliran Lagu*. He also coedited (with Harris M. Berger and Paul D. Greene) *Metal Rules the Globe: Heavy Metal Music around the World* and (with Esther Clinton) a special issue of *Asian Music* on the history of Indonesian music genres.

Philip Yampolsky has been studying the music of Indonesia and its neighbors since 1971. He recorded, edited, and annotated the twenty-CD series Music of Indonesia for Smithsonian Folkways recordings; served as program officer for arts and culture in the Jakarta office of the Ford Foundation; and was the founding director of the Robert E. Brown Center for World Music at the University of Illinois (Urbana-Champaign). Since retiring in 2011 he has received grants from the Asian Cultural Council, Fulbright, and the NEH to research and document traditional music in rural areas of Timor.

Index

CPSIA information can be obtained
at www.ICGtesting.com
Printed in the USA
LVHW040158030922
727485LV00001B/93